Redressing the Balance

American Women's Literary Humor from Colonial Times to the 1980s

Redressing the Balance

American Women's Literary Humor
from Colonial Times to the 1980s

Edited by *Nancy Walker*
and *Zita Dresner*

UNIVERSITY PRESS OF MISSISSIPPI
JACKSON AND LONDON

The paper in this book meets the guidelines for permanence and
durability of the Committee on Production Guidelines for Book
Longevity of the Council on Library Resources.

Library of Congress Cataloging-in-Publication Data

Redressing the balance : American women's literary humor from Colonial
times to the 1980s / edited by Nancy Walker and Zita Dresner.
    p.   cm.
    Bibliography: p.
    ISBN 0-87805-363-8 (alk. paper).   ISBN 0-87805-364-6 (pbk. : alk.
paper)
    1. American wit and humor—Women authors.   2. Women—United
States—Humor.   I. Walker, Nancy.   II. Dresner, Zita.
PN6231.W6R43   1988
817'.008'09287—dc19   88-17536
                                                                CIP

Contents

Preface

This anthology has been a long time in the making, and we are delighted to finally see in print an idea that we first conceived more than six years ago. Since then we have spent many hours in used-book stores and libraries tracking down out-of-print books and information about their authors. It has been a fascinating, rewarding, and sometimes frustrating trip. Nancy remembers an animated discussion with Gerda Lerner in a Chinese restaurant in New York about the humor of minority women; Zita remembers (with considerably less joy) the squirrel whose antics on the power line feeding her computer sent an early draft of the Introduction into oblivion. And many stamps, and many telephone conferences.

Nevertheless, the result, we hope, will bring readers both pleasure and enlightenment. The humorous writing of American women reveals a great deal about their lives, their perceptions, and their roles in American culture, especially as these have changed over time. We have chosen a chronological order for the selections in this anthology to document those changes, but we are equally aware of what has *not* changed. From Anne Bradstreet, seventeenth-century mother of eight, using the metaphor of a child for her book of poetry to Gail Sausser in the 1980s tracing the history of the lesbian potluck dinner, these writers remind us that women are the care givers, the providers of food and nurturance, even when they have professional aspirations. The fundamental condition their humor addresses is women's subordinate status and treatment in American culture, even as their talent for satire, wit, and comedy reveals their important contribution to that culture.

A number of people have provided advice and assistance along the way, and we extend to them our thanks. M. Thomas Inge and Larry Mintz were indispensible supporters of the project; Joanna Todd, of the Stephens College library, accepted and fulfilled many interlibrary-loan challenges;

Jane Curry, Alice Sheppard, and John Lowe provided essential cheers from the sidelines; and Seetha Srinivasan, our editor at the University Press of Mississippi, gave committed support at every stage. Finally, we want to express our gratitude to all the friends, colleagues, and family who offered encouragement, advice, jokes, and leads throughout the years of our immersion in this enterprise.

Nancy Walker
Stephens College

Zita Dresner
University of the District of Columbia

Introduction

I

Until recently, women's literary humor, like other genres and subgenres of women's writing in America, was relatively unexplored by critics and scholars. Students of American literature and even those who study American humor have been largely unaware of the rich tradition of women's humor that has flourished ever since women began writing and publishing in the New World in the seventeenth century. Such a critical lapse might, on the surface, seem to stem partly from the fact that humor is an ephemeral art, often depending upon the fleeting interests and events of a particular time and place for its appeal to the reader, and partly from the notion that humor, in general, is less significant as a record of human aspirations and experience than is "serious" literature. As E. B. White wrote in 1941, "The world likes humor, but treats it patronizingly. It decorates its serious artists with laurel, and its wags with Brussels sprouts."[1] More recently, in his introduction to *American Humor,* editor Arthur P. Dudden again acknowledges this bias: "American humor, in spite of the genius of many of its practitioners, has received little serious attention from critics or historians."[2]

Yet, beginning in the 1930s, a series of studies of American humor have attempted to demonstrate how closely tied are humorous expression and cultural values, as the humorist exposes and mocks the absurdities and incongruities of society.[3] None of these studies, however, gives significant consideration to women's contributions to the humorous exploration of American values. Many reasons have been advanced to account for this omission, ranging from masculine attacks on the quality of women's humor to feminist assertions that women's humor threatens men and has therefore been derogated by them. Despite disagreement about causes, however, the uncontestable result is that women writers have been consistently underrepresented in or excluded from anthologies of humor and also underrated or relegated to the footnotes in scholarly studies of American humor.

Clearly, the subordinate position of women in American society—legally, economically, socially, politically, and culturally—from the Puritan era through the twentieth century, has been responsible in large part for women's secondary status as both writers and humorists.[4] In addition, the antifemale bias of humor written by men—for example, the assortment of stereotypical gossips, nags, gold diggers, and harridans that populate such humor—has helped to perpetuate the assumption that women are devoid of humor.[5] Perhaps more important, the established tendency of male critics to define American humor in terms of traditionally male (rather than female) concerns, language, and style has set a standard of humor based on what men have promoted as funny and, consequently, has demoted women's humorous writing to a lesser, minor class of literature when it has been considered at all. Finally, the social perception of humor as a masculine prerogative and as an aggressive, unfeminine mode not "proper" for women has further contributed to what Mahadev L. Apte calls the social unacceptability of women's humor, which he finds worldwide and which he attributes to two basic factors:

> First, women's humor reflects the existing inequality between the sexes, not so much in its substance as in the constraints imposed on its occurrence, on the techniques used, on the social settings in which it occurs, and on the kind of audience that appreciates it. Second, these constraints generally, but not necessarily universally, stem from the prevalent cultural values that emphasize male superiority and dominance together with female passivity and create role models for women in keeping with such values and attitudes. . . . men's capacity for humor is not superior to women's. Rather, both the prevalent cultural values and the resultant constraints prevent women from fully utilizing their talents.[6]

Apte's conclusions only echo those that have been advanced by American women in arguments about women's humor since the nineteenth century—arguments that inform the four anthologies of women's humor that have appeared in this country to date.

Inspired by a debate in two 1884 issues of the *Critic* concerning women's sense of humor, Kate Sanborn, in her 1885 anthology *The Wit of Women,* intended to prove that women did indeed possess a capacity for humor and wit. Including chiefly, though not exclusively, the humor of American women, Sanborn's anthology ranges widely over various forms of humor, from the dinner-party bon mot and children's stories to satire and literary parody. Although Sanborn's tendency to use brief quotations from individuals and works (rather than longer excerpts or entire selections) makes the collection more useful as a starting point for research than as a compendium of women's humor for the modern reader, she demonstrates that women writers in the nineteenth century were not merely the sentimentalists that critics have traditionally labeled them. In addition, the selections testify to women's active interest in political and social, as well as domestic, concerns.

In 1934 Martha Bensley Bruère and Mary Ritter Beard edited *Laughing Their Way: Women's Humor in America* with a motive somewhat different from Sanborn's. Citing *The Wit of Women* in their introduction, Bruère and Beard consider "a corrective for ill-conceived notions" about female humorlessness no longer necessary, but they do see a need to correct America's "partial view"—i.e., masculine view—of its tradition of humor. They declare their intent to provide that corrective by presenting women's works that had been ignored by those who equated "native" American humor with men's humor. At the same time, they take pains to show that women have created their own tradition in humor—a tradition, however, that the editors do not analyze other than to assert that it reflects the different world of women, "a world always a little apart."[7]

Despite Bruère and Beard's rather optimistic assessment of the acceptance of women as humorists in the 1930s, some forty years later Deanne Stillman and Anne Beatts, in apparent ignorance of Sanborn's and Bruère and Beard's collections, subtitled their own anthology *The First Collection of Humor by Women*. Stillman and Beatts's assumption that they were breaking new ground belies their predecessors' optimism about women's humor; because both earlier anthologies had long been out of print by the 1970s, the word *first* in their title is not surprising. Mark Twain and James Thurber had endured and were household names to many Americans, but the authors collected by Sanborn, Bruère, and Beard—Frances Whitcher, Josephine Daskam, Cornelia Otis Skinner, and many others—were by this time almost lost to history.

What *is* surprising is that, despite the success of female stand-up comedians and comedy writers in the 1960s and 1970s, Beatts and Stillman begin their introduction to *Titters* by stating: "Nobody will admit to not having a sense of humor. . . . Nobody, that is, except women. . . . Women aren't supposed to be funny, particularly. It's not part of the feminine role-model, the set of stereotypes that got dished out to us along with our pablum. . . . Just because women really *are* funny doesn't change the prevailing attitude. And the prevailing attitude has been, and to some extent continues to be, 'Chicks just aren't funny.' "[8] The editors' comments echo those of Sanborn almost a hundred years before, and the purpose of *Titters,* like that of *The Wit of Women,* was to demonstrate once again that women *are* funny—at least to other women. However, unlike their predecessors, who attempted to be comprehensive, Stillman and Beatts limited their selections to contributions from their contemporaries, friends, and colleagues. Similarly, Gloria Kaufman and Mary Kay Blakely, editors of *Pulling Our Own Strings: Feminist Humor and Satire* (1980), collected examples, almost exclusively from the 1970s, of what they define as "feminist" humor, including cartoons, jokes, verse, comic routines, articles, and excerpts from larger works. While the editors' primary motive seems to have been the preservation of humor that, because of its feminist orientation, they assumed would be ignored by male and nonfeminist female anthologists, the introductory segments of the book also suggest other intentions: to rebut the popular attacks on the women's movement and on feminists for being humorless and to scuttle the notion (an aim also of the editors of *Titters*) that women who purport to be humorists have to limit themselves to what have been considered "feminine" tools of expression: self-deprecation, ladylike language, and negative female stereotypes.

These earlier anthologies, though they have been important sources for this one, have certain limitations this anthology seeks to address. In Sanborn's and Bruère and Beard's work, for example, the selections are fragmentary (and in Sanborn's book sometimes even unidentified by author). The two later anthologies focus, by design, on a particular type of humor from a fairly narrow time period. Moreover, none of the previous collections provides the biographical, bibliographical, and critical source material so necessary to the scholar and so useful to the student or the general reader who wishes to find additional work by or about an author. The present anthology is intended in part to supply this information by providing reference material to document and selections to illustrate, comprehensively and over time, the varied threads that make up the tapestry of American women's literary humor.

Some of the authors who appear in this volume will be familiar to most readers. For example, Erma Bombeck is a household word today, even more so than was Dorothy Parker in the 1920s; Jean Kerr's *Please Don't Eat the Daisies* (1957) inspired a movie and a television series, and Anita Loos's *Gentlemen Prefer Blondes* (1925) inspired film and stage versions spanning five decades; Judith Viorst's verse appeared first in *New York* magazine; Ellen Goodman's column appears in newspapers nationwide. Other authors, now unfamiliar but often as well known in their own time as these are today, have been retrieved from out-of-print sources to be restored to their rightful place in the history of American women's humor. Frances Whitcher's mid-nineteenth-century dialect sketches, Caroline Kirkland's depictions of frontier characters and ways of life, Florence Guy Seabury's comments on the difficulties of dual-career marriage, and Helen Rowland's delightful satires on male-female relationships are just some of the many works that retain a sparkle and freshness while evoking the particular circumstances of women's lives in different periods of our history.

Not all the authors represented here are primarily humorists. For example, Anne Bradstreet, the first published poet in America, was a serious writer of meditative poetry, and "Fanny Fern" was known in the nineteenth century and again today for her sentimental prose as well as her realistic 1855 novel *Ruth Hall*. Judith Sargent Murray, Charlotte Perkins Gilman, and Gloria Steinem are thought of as social critics; "Gail Hamilton" and Nora Ephron, as columnists. Mary Roberts Rinehart achieved fame as a mystery writer, and Edna St. Vincent Millay and Paula Gunn Allen as serious poets. However, all the pieces in this collection display the sense of irony and awareness of absurdity that underlie humorous expression. Further, they all reflect perhaps the major function of humor: redressing the balance. Our hope is that the selections in this volume not only entertain and enlighten the reader but also stimulate further study of women's humor, a task that has begun only within the past ten years.

II

Despite the relative recency of American humor studies, a considerable body of literature has accumulated over the past century concerning the nature and functions of humor. Within the past two decades in particular, psychologists, sociologists, and cultural anthropologists have conducted research into humor motivations and responses and, emphasizing the social uses of humor, have analyzed the roles of the humorist and the humor preferences of different groups within cultures. Looking at the samples of women's humor presented in this volume in light of humor research and theory, as well as in relation to the critical studies of literary humor and feminist analyses of women's literature that have appeared in recent decades, we can draw some preliminary conclusions about the themes, techniques, and purposes that distinguish American women's literary humor.

First, while America's female humorists have often written in the same modes as their male counterparts, used many of the same devices, and followed similar trends in humor, their work has been neither imitative nor derivative. As a popular art that must appeal to large numbers of readers, humorous writing by both genders is as subject to changes in fashion as are clothing styles and television programming. Public taste and current fads are in part responsible for the subject matter and style of the newspaper column, the book of light verse, and the humorous sketch or novel. But while responding to the pressure to conform to the expectations of the marketplace, American female writers have created a distinctive body of humor with common subjects and themes that set it apart from the male tradition of American humor. Reflecting, by necessity, their roles and positions as women in the culture, female writers have focused largely on the domestic sphere of wife and mother and on the social sphere that, differently in different eras, has been defined as women's work and activities. In short, they have written about "things which women in general find interesting," as Stillman and Beatts note in explaining why their collection, *Titters*, does not contain jokes about "jock straps, beer, trains, mothers-in-law, dumb blondes, cars, boxing, the Navy, chemistry, physics, stamp catalogues, spelunking, pud-pulling or poker" (4).

Second, as Mahadev Apte argues convincingly, because of "the behavioral, expressive, and other sociocultural constraints imposed on women . . . many common attributes of men's humor seem to be much less evident or even absent in women's humor" (69). In particular, Apte notes, cross-cultural research has shown that "women's humor generally lacks the aggressive and hostile quality of men's humor. The use of humor to compete with or to belittle others, thereby enhancing a person's own status, or to humiliate others either psychologically or physically, seems generally absent among women. Thus the most commonly institutionalized ways of engaging in such humor, namely, verbal duels, ritual insults, and practical jokes and pranks, are rarely reported for women" (70). Consequently, the degree to which aggression and hostility are overt in a particular woman's humorous expression depends on the degree of gender equality permitted in her society, as well as on her audience and on those who control the dissemination of her humor. For example, as Apte's research confirms, women are generally more free to ridicule men and make sexual jokes when the audience is exclusively female than they are when it is mixed.

Because of the constraints on women's expression, which in most cultures have included taboos against women's appropriation of sexual subject matter and language, women's humor has been described as more gentle and genteel than men's, more concerned with wit than derision, more interested in sympathy than ridicule, more focused on private than on public issues. These attributes, along with women's greater reliance on verbal devices of understatement, irony, and self-deprecation, have enabled women to mask or defuse the aggressive component of humor making, thereby minimizing the risks involved in challenging the status quo.

Third, because of women's unequal social, political, and economic status in most cultures, and the fact that they are regarded by men as "other" (factors compounded for women belonging to racial or ethnic minorities), women's and men's humor have been directed to different ends and/or realized in different ways. For example, most humor theorists consider the venting of aggression to be a major function of humor.[9] Freud was the first to suggest that humor is a socially acceptable way of releasing repressed antisocial or hostile impulses, and recent proponents of the aggression theory maintain that humorous pleasure drives from the derision, ridicule, deprecation, deflation, degradation, humiliation, and general mockery of individuals, groups, institutions, values, or ideas that threaten one's sense of security or well-being. As has already been suggested, however, most cultures harbor prohibitions against women's expression of aggression and hostility, especially in public and in mixed audiences. Moreover, women have been traditionally conditioned to assume passive, subordinate roles, and as Naomi Weisstein asserts in "Why We Aren't Laughing . . . Anymore," the role of "a funny, nasty clown doesn't go along with the definition of WOMAN that gets us our provider."[10] These factors have not eliminated aggression as a motivation of women's humor, but they have compelled women to exercise it in more covert and indirect ways than men do.

In addition to the release of aggression or hostility, the exposure of incongruity is generally accepted by theorists as a major, universal function of humor. Proponents of the incongruity theory believe that humor operates primarily through surprise, shock, dislocation, or sudden reversal of expectations. However, because the perception of incongruity is based on shared values, beliefs, customs, habits, and experiences, the degree to which the genders (and races or ethnic groups) are differentiated by their cultures into separate classes of people will determine the degree to which they can share and enjoy each other's perceptions of the incongruities that make up their humorous visions. At the same time, whereas all groups in a society are aware of the values, beliefs, and behaviors that are promoted by the dominant culture, those belonging to the dominant culture do not generally have the same awareness of the attitudes, habits, and experiences of those excluded from or oppressed by it. Thus, as Bruère and Beard contend, "the angle of vision from which women see a lack of balance, wrong proportions, disharmonies, and incongruities in life is a thing of their world as it must be—a world always a little apart" (viii).

To the extent that woman's world is differentiated from man's, the incongruities revealed in women's humor reflect a world at odds with, and potentially threatening to, that of men. Because in women's humor, frustration and anger at gender-based inequities have had to be expressed obliquely, incongruity has been a major device for decoding the myths of the patriarchy. By exposing the discrepancies between the realities of women's lives and the images of women promoted by the culture, between the inequities to which women have been subjected and the egalitarian ideals upon which the nation was founded, American women humorists have targeted the patriarchal social system. For women of racial or ethnic minorities, of course, the conditions to be attacked and discrepanices to be exposed have been at least doubled.

Finally, the aggression and incongruity theories of humor have been further refined by social theorists who agree with Henri Bergson's position in *Laughter* that humor, in all of its manifestations, has primary social functions; they have argued that both the expression of hostility and the disclosure of discordance through humor depend upon social factors. Analysts have proposed, for example, that humor works in a number of ways as an agent of group enhancement and social control.[11] If the humor expressed in one group (the ingroup) disparages another group (the outgroup), it boosts the morale of and solidifies the ingroup as well as promoting hostility against the outgroup. If the ingroup is culturally dominant (in America, white middle-class men), the humor not only reinforces its sense of superiority but, at the same time, controls the behavior of the disparaged group (e.g., women, minorities) by creating or fostering conflict in or the demoralization of the disparaged group. In other words, humor is used by those in power, whether consciously or not, to preserve the status quo.

On the other hand, humor initiated in a group lacking status in the culture may bolster the members' self-esteem by disparaging the bases of the dominant group's claim to superiority. However, researchers have found that individuals and groups at the top of a social heirarchy use humor more often than those at the bottom, and generally direct it downward, while those at the lower level (e.g., women, minorities), when they use humor, direct it more frequently at themselves or at those below them than at those above them.

The use of self-deprecating humor by women could be a defensive reaction of those who feel themselves too weak or vulnerable to attack with impunity the forces that oppress them, but the seemingly defensive weapons of humor can also become offensive in the hands of women and other outgroups. For example, as psychologists have observed, laughing at one's shortcomings is not only a way of diminishing their importance and potentially overcoming them but is also a technique for cleansing them of pejorative connotations imposed by the dominant culture and, thereby, turning them into strengths. Similarly, the use of incongruity in humor by women as a means of targeting attributes and behaviors prescribed for them by the dominant culture is an act of rebellion. Finally, the use of humor by women against women, when it is used to advance ideas that might conflict with those of the male establishment about women's roles and prerogatives, represents a step toward empowerment rather than capitulation.

III

These various ideas about the nature, functions, and concerns of women's humor, which account for the different "angle of vision," the "world always a little apart," of American women's literary humor, can be seen in women's writing from the colonial era to the contemporary period. Two types of early American humor, usually identified with male writers, have been described by literary critics and historians: the formal, or "high," literary style of the British satirical mode and the informal, seemingly unconscious ironic style of such personal literary forms as diaries, journals, and travel books. The poetry of Anne Bradstreet (1612–1672), for example, uses devices of wit associated with male Elizabethan and Metaphysical poets, but Bradstreet uses these devices to express a woman's thoughts on marriage, motherhood, creativity, and religion at a time and in a place, Puritan New England, especially hostile to any public role or voice for women. In a poem such as "The Author to Her Book," therefore, Bradstreet adopts an overtly deferential tone about her work to appease her potential critics, but at the same time, the irony with which she presents her anomalous position as a woman poet serves to undermine both the seriousness of her apology and the logic of the patriarchal attitudes that would deny women minds, voices, and talents in anything other than domestic work. Similar uses of such double-edged irony can be found in the "apologies" of succeeding humorists, from Judith Sargent Murray in the eighteenth century to Jean Kerr in the twentieth, especially in what has been called "domestic" or "housewife" humor. As Neil Schmitz writes in reference to Gertrude Stein's work, "What aggression lurks in the deferential tone of the humorous woman, the ironist knows."[12]

The second strain of early American humor appears in Sarah Kemble Knight's diary, which records her five-month journey in 1704 from Boston to New York City and back. While the journal contains many of the elements of humor found in the travel accounts of such early American male writers as William Byrd II, its satiric treatment of regional manners, customs, and dialects reflects Knight's particular concern, as a Puritan woman, with ideas of proper "housewifery." This emphasis on women's roles, as well as the realistic details that make up her humorous depictions of people and places, continues to inform the humor of regional writers, from Caroline Kirkland in the nineteenth century to Betty MacDonald and Cyra McFadden in the twentieth.

During the Revolutionary era, both Mercy Otis Warren and Judith Sargent Murray, like their male contemporaries, used satire to promote the cause of the American patriots, but unlike the men, Warren and Murray were also concerned with women's rights and status in the new republic. Warren's patriotic play *The Group,* for example, closes with a female Patriot speaking about the connections between the Patriots' fight for freedom, women's desire for equality, and nature's revolt against the corruptions of Britain's tyranny. Similarly, while her political poetry has been compared to that of the "Connecticut Wits," other poems reveal that Warren's irony and wit, like Bradstreet's, served to present views that opposed the prevailing masculine views of religion, rationality, and relationship between the sexes.

While Warren's interest in women's rights tended to be voiced covertly in her poetry and plays, Judith Sargent Murray addressed questions of women's place in the new nation more openly. In essays, articles, comedies, and fiction, she directed her wit against those male assumptions about woman's physical, mental, and moral weakness that were used to preclude women's political participation in the Republic. Following Mary Wollstonecraft's position in *A Vindication of the Rights of Women* (1792), Murray protested restrictions on women's training, education, and political activity. In addition, in connecting women's moral behavior with civic virtue and in positing a social order based on marital equity and a balance between domestic and political activity, she not only represented what Nancy Cott calls "the equalitarian feminist view" of the late eighteenth century[13] but also anticipated the position of subsequent women writers who employed the devices of humor to deal with similar issues of women's rights in the nineteenth and twentieth centuries.

By advocating education and training for women that would promote their self-sufficiency and informed civic involvement, Murray sought, at least in part, to counter the prevailing sentimentalism of late-eighteenth-century popular literature. As the sentimental novel proliferated in the nineteenth century, later humorists attempted to do the same by painting satirical portraits of women suffering from the disease of sentimentality. The earliest of these, Tabitha Tenney's satirical novel, *Female Quixotism* (1801), recounts the lifelong romantic delusions that leave the heroine, Dorcasina Sheldon, in old age, with a wasted life, for which she blames her addiction to sentimental novels. Similarly, Caroline Kirkland's depiction of the "poet" Miss Eloise Fidler, in *A New Home—Who'll Follow?* (1839), ridicules both the claptrap of sentimental poetry and the pretensions of Miss Fidler herself, whose behavior and dress, modeled on sentimental literature, are particularly absurd in the backwoods Michigan environment that Kirkland describes. Continued satirical treatment of sentimental women in the work of Frances Whitcher and Marietta Holley prefigure the portraits in twentieth-century humor, from Betty MacDonald in the 1940s to Erma Bombeck in the 1970s, of women who accept and promote romanticized fantasies of female attributes and roles.

In Kirkland's work, the portrait of Miss Fidler is just one example of the "strong antiromance sentiment"[14] that, as in the work of later male frontier humorists, served to counterbalance increasingly romanticized accounts of life in the American West. But what differentiates Kirkland's work from that of the male humorists/realists is her emphasis on the problems and hardships faced by women living on the fringes of civilization. In addition, Kirkland's antiromanticism; descriptions of regional characteristics, language, and customs; and emphasis on depicting the realities of women's lives place her work in a line of women's humorous writing that began with Sarah Kemble Knight and extends to the work of journalist Mary Abigail Dodge (pseud. Gail Hamilton) and the local color realists of the latter part of the nineteenth century, as well as to twentieth-century writers who have used irony and satire to challenge prevailing myths about women's roles and about the communities in which they live.

As the cult of domesticity and the notion of separate spheres for men and women gained adherents in the nineteenth century, the contrasts between Kirkland's perspective and that of male humorists expanded to include other differences in men's and women's humorous literature. While men were developing a brand of American humor that began, as Bruère and Beard wrote, "in the robust expression of frontiersmen and [remained] in that gusto and temper while a new world was subdued to the plow, while an agricultural civilization swung toward an industrial one, while the nation was hammered into form by war and peace, prosperity and depression" (v), women were increasingly restricted to roles and admonished to cultivate qualities that were at odds with these changes and developments. Consequently, in the work of nineteenth-century female humorists, from Caroline Kirkland to Marietta Holley, there is a concern with the discrepancies between the opportunities opening up for men and the constraints closing in on women.

This concern appears most obviously in the locale of women's humorous stories: the kitchen or the sewing circle, the parlor or the dress shop, rather than the mining camp, the riverboat, the business or political office, or the saloon. The world perceived to be comically askew is the world of children and neighbors and teakettles, of relationships between men and women in the family and in society, of all that constituted what has traditionally been designated women's "proper sphere." Throughout the nineteenth century, most female humorists took as their subjects the domestic environment that formed a large part of their acquaintance with the world: the home, courtship and marriage, and those community activities assumed to be the special province of women—shopping, volunteer work, church and school groups. Ann Warner's "Susan Clegg" stories, for example, published at the turn of the twentieth century, show the garrulous and unconsciously funny Susan enmeshed in housework and the care of her invalid father, having postponed thoughts of marriage in order to fill the role of housekeeper and nurse. Even Emily Dickinson, who did not participate directly in most community activities, comments ironically on woman's "sphere" and the social perception of her role, and the imagery of domestic life permeates both her comic and serious poetry.

Along with this common subject matter, women who have written humor have pursued several common themes. The most pervasive of these has been a concern with the incongruities between the realities of women's lives and the sentimental or idealized images fostered by the culture; between women's awareness of their abilities and ambitions, and their perception of the laws and conventions that have restricted them to a limited sphere of activity. In pointing out these incongruities, female humorists have encouraged an enlargement of woman's sphere and protested the restrictions that, in barring women from utilizing their talents and abilities in the public arena, have countenanced their dissipating their energies in the pursuit of husbands, social status, fashion, spotless floors, perfect bodies, and super momism. Their techniques have included realistic portrayals of women's lives; contrasts between what the authors believe to be strong, positive images of women and weak, negative stereotypes; and deflation of masculine notions of male superiority.

These themes and techniques were first evident in nineteenth-century works, from Anna Cora Mowatt's popular comedy *Fashion* (1850) to Marietta Holley's "Samantha Allen" series, published between 1873 and 1914. While Mowatt satirizes the genteel pretensions and frivolous behavior of middle-class urban women through the characters of Mrs. Tiffany and her daughter, she also shows, through the contrasting character of Gertrude Truelove, that women become virtuous and self-reliant when they are raised with traditional rural values and taught the skills with which to support themselves. Frances Whitcher's work also ridicules the excesses of gentility by using women as both subjects and objects of her humor. The Widow Bedott, the narrator of her most popular work, is a garrulous, middle-aged widow obsessed with finding a second husband. In lampooning Bedott and her circle for self-righteousness and malicious gossiping, however, Whitcher did not intend, as did her male counterparts, merely to perpetuate negative stereotypes of women. Rather, as her "Aunt Maguire" letters and her novel *Mary Elmer* illustrate, she hoped to motivate change by depicting the ways in which women betray their nature, themselves, and each other by adopting the cold, commercial values of the male world. Marietta Holley, whose books rivaled Mark Twain's in sales at the turn of the twentieth century, followed Whitcher's Aunt Maguire in creating as her spokesperson Samantha

Allen, an unsophisticated farm wife who combines commonsense prac-
ticality with the simple logic born of experience. Through Samantha's
discussions of her domestic responsibilities with Betsey Bobbet—another
caricature of a sentimental spinster given to perorations about women as
ivy needing man as oak to cling to—Holley exposes the contradictions
between the illusions and the realities of married life. In the twentieth
century, the tradition of using contrasting characters to explore the conflict between the real and ideal is continued in the juxtaposition of the
compulsive Mrs. Hicks to the slovenly Mrs. Kettle in Betty MacDonald's
Egg and I, and of black domestic servant and white employer in Alice
Childress's *Like One of the Family.*

This conflict between real and ideal serves to point up another theme in
women's humor: the need to be taken seriously. Sara Willis Parton, for
example, a newspaper columnist who published two volumes of articles
titled *Fern Leaves from Fanny's Port-Folio* (1853 and 1854) using the
pseudonym Fanny Fern, is in the tradition of those, from Bradstreet to
Beatts, who have attacked male attitudes toward women writers, as well as
exposed the difficulties of trying to combine a literary career with housework and child rearing. As a social commentator, she used satire to
expose, in particular, the ways in which an obsession with power and
money corrupts. As an advocate of education and independence for
women, she challenged the idea that married women were happy, or at
least happier than single women, echoing Judith Sargent Murray in
attributing much of the unhappiness in marriage to imbalances of power
and calling for greater equality for women. Harriet Beecher Stowe's "The
Minister's Housekeeper" similarly urges a re-vision of women's talent and
worth, as represented by the efficiency and common sense of Huldy. And
Marietta Holley, in her twenty-one humorous books, used Samantha
Allen in part to illustrate that although "women's work" has been presumed to be trivial, it is, in fact, important and should be taken seriously.
As Samantha avows in Holley's first book, *My Opinions and Betsey
Bobbet's* (1873), "Why jest the idee of paradin' out the table and teakettle
3 times 3 hundred and 65 times every year is enough to make a woman
sweat."[15] Women's work was also vehemently defended by Phyllis
McGinley for several decades of the twentieth century and, slyly, by
Shirley Jackson, who remarks in *Life among the Savages* (1953) after a
flurry of housework and child care, "I don't care what *any*one says, that's
a morning's work."[16]

Taking women seriously, for Marietta Holley, also meant granting them equal rights, and by focusing on the issues that most concerned women's rights proponents of the late nineteenth century—suffrage, temperance, entry into the professions, equal pay for equal work—Holley introduced a feminist theme that sharply distinguishes women's humor from men's. As Jane Curry notes in her introduction to *Samantha Rastles the Woman Question,* a selection of excerpts from Holley's books, "When one reads the Samantha books, she begins to view the 19th century not as 'then' so much as it was the beginning of 'now.' "[17] Like Jonathan Slick, the "wise fool" figure of Ann Stephens's work, and the popular personae of early nineteenth-century "Down East" humor, Samantha exposes pretentiousness and hypocrisy through her ability to see and call a spade a spade. Throughout the many Samantha books, Holley's implacable logic contrasts with other people's illogicality of sentiment or prejudice. In her first book, for example, Holley reverses the traditional images of the genders, depicting Josiah, Samantha's husband, as physically smaller and weaker than she, less rational, more susceptible to fads and fashions, and more dependent. Consequently, the arguments advanced by Josiah against women's rights—based on popular notions of woman's weakness, flickleness, and irrationality—are reduced to absurdity. Holley's use of ironic role reversal and her concern with social issues, particularly political equality for women, anticipate the suffrage work of Alice Duer Miller and Josephine Daskam in the early twentieth century, as well as the more recent feminist humor of the 1970s and 1980s. Similar techniques have been used by ethnic humorists to undermine the cultural assumptions of inferiority that have been used to deny them equal rights.

By the turn of the century, some of the characteristics that had distinguished women's humor through the nineteenth century began to change as American humor in general began to reflect the shift in population from rural areas to the cities and as new magazines emerged to appeal to the values and tastes of an increasingly urbane, cosmopolitan audience for humor. Providing outlets for cartoons, light verse, and humorous sketches that emphasized sophisticated wordplay rather than dialect humor, these new publications also reflected the new interest of an urban cultural elite in technological advances, in the social sciences and psychology, and in the images of the "new woman" and "little man" that were transforming American life.

The increased freedom that women achieved in the decades just before and after the passage of the suffrage amendment in 1920, at the same time that men were experiencing what Norris Yates describes as a diminution of their status and influence,[18] contributed to the "war between the sexes" that American humorists of both genders waged in their work during the first three decades of the twentieth century. At the same time, the new freedoms for women increased the opportunities for social mingling of men and women, while the growth of the media promoted a popular culture of interests and activities, fads and fashions that cut across gender and even class lines. In Bruère and Beard's selection of humor by women after 1900, these shifts are apparent both in the subject matter and in the publications in which the humor originally appeared. Working as journalists, columnists, and cartoonists for major newspapers in New York and Chicago and for magazines such as *Harper's,* the *New Yorker, Vanity Fair,* the *Saturday Evening Post,* and even political organs such as the *New Leader,* these early twentieth-century female humorists had a less restricted audience than did many of their nineteenth-century counterparts. Consequently, their humor reflects greater diversity of subject matter, as well as concern with gender roles and relationships in a rapidly changing society.

One indication of these changes is that the prevalent nineteenth-century notions of separate spheres for men and women and of distinct masculine and feminine natures and functions do not serve as a basic premise for this later humor. For example, in the political satire of Alice Duer Miller and Charlotte Perkins Gilman, it is not women's special, feminine contributions that are emphasized to justify their gaining the vote so much as their simple right as human beings in a democratic society to legal and political equality with men. Similarly, tacit assumptions about woman's moral superiority, nurturing qualities, and instinctive sensitivity to others are challenged by writers such as Josephine Daskam, Helen Rowland, and Florence Guy Seabury, who work both with and against established stereotypes of men and women to give the genders "realistic" advice about, and images of, each other. Moreover, in the work of such writers as Dorothy Parker and Anita Loos, who deal with the "war between the sexes," women characters are portrayed as being just as morally and psychologically confused, self-absorbed, and manipulative as their male counterparts. Finally, the expansion of women's options is reflected in Mary Roberts Rinehart's "Tish" stories, published betwen 1910 and 1937, which present an embodiment of the "new woman" in the attitudes and behavior of Letitia "Tish" Carberry, an independent spinster who, content with her single status, engages herself and two spinster friends in a variety of activities and adventures, from automobile racing, flying, and camping to catching crooks and even liberating a town from the Germans in World War I.

Despite the proliferation in the early decades of the twentieth century of female humorists exhibiting a wide diversity in style, form, and subject matter, the main thread that continued to run through women's humor of the 1930s and 1940s was the "little woman," the counterpart of the "little man" of male humorists such as Thurber and Benchley. Whether urban, suburban, or rural, the young housewives and new mothers depicted first by Parker and later by Cornelia Otis Skinner and Betty MacDonald are as bewildered by the conflicting demands of other people, as controlled by the technology and bureaucracy of modern life, and as intimidated by their own fear of failure as the "little men."

By the fifties and sixties, the "little woman" had become the housewife heroine of the "domestic" humor that dominated the period. Inspired by the post–World War II campaign to return the American woman to the home, this humor concerns the trials and tribulations of middle-class housewives who, in increasing numbers, inhabited suburban communities featuring commuting husbands, children, and other frantic women. Disseminated primarily in magazines and sections of newspapers addressed to women, this humor spoke to an audience that could be characterized by the title of Phyllis McGinley's poem "Occupation: Housewife." Like their nineteenth-century forebears, these women were cut off from the public world of business and enterprise that their husbands inhabited and restricted to a routine of domestic chores and child rearing. Domestic humor provided a way for both writer and audience to minimize through laughter and, thereby, better cope with the frustrations and demands of their lives.

Betty Friedan's 1963 analysis of the housewife's discontent, *The Feminine Mystique*, not only helped to spark the rebirth of a movement for female equality but also abetted the emergence in the late sixties and early seventies of a feminist humor more overt and aggressive than the political humor of the suffrage era. The women who created this humor were influenced by the iconoclastic style and irreverent tone of a new generation of black and white male comics, beginning with Lenny Bruce, whose political and social satire appealed to increasing numbers of college students and young adults who were in rebellion against the competitive and conformist values of the fifties and inspired by the civil rights and peace movements of the sixties.

Selecting specific agents of oppression as targets, women humorists of the seventies and eighties have attacked the greater privilege and freedom of men, derided patriarchal institutions, and ridiculed social, sexual, and racial stereotyping. Influenced by the new wave of male comics, women humorists have appropriated subject matter once considered taboo for women, accepting the totality of female experience—including sexual relationships, menstruation, lesbianism, anxieties about one's attractiveness, and the ineptitude of men—as material for humor. Moreover, humorists such as Erica Jong have addressed these topics with a bawdy tone and in graphic sexual and scatological terms that, because they come from a woman, still shock or offend segments of the population. Although domestic humor has maintained its popularity alongside feminist and new wave humor, women's humor of the past two decades has generally become more confrontational on social and political issues, rather than sly or cute.

IV

A careful reading of the humor of American women from the seventeenth century to the 1980s, then, makes it clear that we must revise our notions of "traditional" American humor. Most twentieth-century analysts have assumed that the large subjects of this nation's humor have been the frontier experience, democracy, and the growth of bureaucracy and technology. They have seen humor as an index to national identity, a guide to changes in values. There is no doubt that its humor provides important clues about the character of the nation, but considering as relevant the humor of only half the population, as most scholars have done, leads to a partial and distorted picture. The humor of the American male has posited a world of energy, mobility, and privilege—a world from which women have been systematically excluded.

The humor in this anthology shows us a different world, one in which the minutiae of the private, daily existence loom larger than the political misdeed or the corporate maneuver, but one which can have an impact, for good or ill, on the public sphere. The important developments of American society, according to this separate tradition, have been those that have affected woman's place in the culture: changes in clothing styles and etiquette manuals; successive child-raising theories; moves to the frontier or to the city; industrial and technical advancements that have changed women's work; social movements that have influenced society's conceptions of women's nature and roles; cultural theories that have altered women's images of themselves and relationships to others; and periods of political or economic agitation, especially about women's rights, that have enlarged women's options for participation in the world.

Consequently, an anthology of women's humor is an important and necessary first step in demonstrating the range and complexity of the "other half" of America's humorous tradition. A second, equally important reason for such a collection is to make available some nearly forgotten, out-of-print examples of women's humor from various periods in American literary history. At the end of each headnote is a list of sources consulted and a selected list of humorous works by the author.

The choice of selections, as in all such anthologies, is limited to some extent by space and reprint restrictions, as well as by the fact that humor is a matter of taste as much as of aesthetic judgment. Nonetheless, we have attempted to present a fair representation of authors, eras, genres, and styles, in choosing pieces that seek, through the devices of humor, to mirror and to motivate changes in the experiences, character, and aspirations of American women.

NOTES

1. E. B. White and Katharine S. White, eds., *A Subtreasury of American Humor* (New York: Modern Library, 1948), xviii.

2. Arthur Power Dudden, ed., *American Humor* (New York: Oxford Univ. Press, 1987), xi–xii.

3. This series includes Constance Rourke, *American Humor: A Study of the National Character* (New York: Harcourt, 1931); Walter Blair, *Native American Humor* (1800–1900) (Hartford: American Book, 1937); Norris Yates, *The American Humorist: Conscience of the Twentieth Century* (Ames: Iowa State Univ. Press, 1964); Jesse Bier, *The Rise and Fall of American Humor* (New York: Holt, 1968); Louis D. Rubin, Jr., *The Comic Imagination in American Literature* (New Brunswick, N.J.: Rutgers Univ. Press, 1973); Walter Blair and Hamlin Hill, *America's Humor: From Poor Richard to Doonesbury* (New York: Oxford Univ. Press, 1978); Neil Schmitz, *Of Huck and Alice: Humorous Writing in American Literature* (Minneapolis: Univ. of Minnesota Press, 1983).

4. See Judith Fetterly's discussion of the treatment of nineteenth-century women writers in her introduction to *Provisions: A Reader from 19th Century American Women* (Bloomington: Indiana Univ. Press, 1985), 16–31.

5. See Jesse Bier's discussion of misogyny in *The Rise and Fall of American Humor*, 22.

6. Mahadev L. Apte, *Humor and Laughter: An Anthropological Approach* (Ithaca, N.Y.: Cornell Univ. Press, 1985), 69.

7. Martha Bensley Bruère and Mary Ritter Beard, eds., *Laughing Their Way: Women's Humor in America* (New York: Macmillan, 1934), v–viii.

8. Deanne Stillman and Anne Beatts, eds., *Titters: The First Collection of Humor by Women* (New York: Collier, 1976), 3.

9. This discussion of the aggression theory and the following discussion of the incongruity theory of humor is based on papers in Antony J. Chapman and Hugh C. Foot, eds., *Humor and Laughter: Theory, Research, and Applications* (New York: Wiley, 1976),

and *It's A Funny Thing, Humour.* (New York: Pergamon, 1977); Jeffrey H. Goldstein and Paul E. McGhee, eds., *The Psychology of Humor* (New York: Academic Press, 1972).

10. Naomi Weisstein, "Why we Aren't Laughing . . . Anymore," *Ms.* (November 1973): 89.

11. See, for example, William H. Martineau, "A Model of the Social Functions of Humour," in *The Psychology of Humor;* Charles Winick, "The Social Contexts of Humour," *Journal of Communication* 26 (Summer 1976): 124–28; Joseph Boskin, *Humor and Social Change in Twentieth–Century America,* Lectures delivered for the NEH Boston Public Library Learning Library Program (Boston: Trustees of the Public Library of the City of Boston, 1979).

12. *Of Huck and Alice,* 210.

13. Nancy Cott, *The Bonds of Womanhood: "Woman's Sphere" in New England, 1780–1875* (New Haven: Yale Univ. Press, 1977), 202.

14. Josephine Donovan, *New England Local Color Literature* (New York: Frederick Ungar, 1982), 26.

15. Marietta Holley, *My Opinions and Betsey Bobbet's* (Hartford: American Publishing Co., 1873), 59.

16. Shirley Jackson, *Life among the Savages* (New York: Farrar, Straus and Young, 1953), 2.

17. Jane Curry, Introduction to *Samantha Rastles the Women Question* (Urbana: Univ. of Illinois Press, 1983), 1.

18. Yates, *The American Humorist,* 38.

PART I
Early Voices

Anne Bradstreet
(1612–1672)

As America's first published poet, Anne Bradstreet was also one of the country's first witty women. The prologues with which she introduced both the first and the second editions (1650 and 1678) by a London publisher, of her collection of poems, titled *The Tenth Muse Lately Sprung Up in America,* display Bradstreet's consciousness that as a female poet she was an anomaly in the Puritan colonies. In the prologue to the first edition, she anticipates the accusation that she should be wielding a needle rather than a pen; and in "The Author to Her Book," which prefaces the second edition, she refers to the collection as a poorly-dressed child "snatched" from her before she has been able to clothe it properly—a reference to the fact that the poems comprising *The Tenth Muse* were taken to London without her knowledge. Bradstreet thus subtly pokes fun at those who would misunderstand or disapprove of her work. Yet in most ways, Bradstreet complied with the expectations for women of her day. By the age of sixteen, when she emigrated to the New World, she had been married for almost two years. In Salem and then Ipswich, Massachusetts, she bore eight children and coped with the illness and other physical dangers of wilderness life, complicated by the frequent absences of her husband, Simon, who ultimately became Governor of the Massachusetts Bay Colony. While in the seventeenth-century Bradstreet was admired primarily for her monumental, conventional poems about the ages of man and the succession of British monarchies, contemporary readers prefer her personal poetry, which expresses her love for her husband, her grief at the death of a grandchild, and her perception of the incongruity of being a poet and a woman in colonial America.

SOURCES   Hutchinson, Robert. Introduction. *Poems of Anne Bradstreet.* New York: Dover, 1969; Martin, Wendy. *An American Triptych: Anne Bradstreet, Emily Dickinson, and Adrienne Rich.* Chapel Hill: University of North Carolina Press, 1984; Stanford, Ann. *Anne Bradstreet: The Worldly Puritan.* New York: B. Franklin, 1974.

WORKS   *The Tenth Muse Lately Sprung Up in America* (1650) and *the Tenth Muse*, 2nd ed. (1678)

from *The Tenth Muse Lately Sprung Up in America*

The Author to Her Book

Thou ill-form'd offspring of my feeble brain,
Who after birth did'st by my side remain,
Till snatcht from thence by friends, less wise than true
Who thee abroad, expos'd to publick view;
Made thee in raggs, halting to th' press to trudg,
Where errors were not lessened (all may judg)
At thy return my blushing was not small,
My rambling brat (in print) should mother call,
I cast thee by as one unfit for light,
Thy Visage was so irksome in my sight;
Yet being mine own, at length affection would
Thy blemishes amend, if so I could:
I wash'd thy face, but more defects I saw,
And rubbing off a spot, still made a flaw.
I stretcht thy joynts to make thee even feet,
Yet still thou run'st more hobling than is meet;
In better dress to trim thee was my mind,
But nought save home-spun Cloth, i'th' house I find.
In this array, 'mongst Vulgars mayst thou roam
In Criticks hands, beware thou dost not come;
And take thy way where yet thou art not known,
If for thy Father askt, say, thou hadst none:
And for thy Mother, she alas is poor,
Which caus'd her thus to send thee out of door.

Sarah Kemble Knight

(1666–1727)

Like her countrywoman Caroline Kirkland would do more than 100 years later, Sarah Kemble Knight found the behavior of her less sophisticated frontier neighbors amusing and sometimes alarming, and wrote about them with candor and wit. *The Journal of Madam Knight,* written in 1704–05 and first published in 1825, is the account in diary form of a journey from Boston to New York and back that Madam Knight made without escort, depending on various guides to make her way. Like many other women writers, Madam Knight was more concerned with her immediate surroundings and circumstances than with issues of politics and religion, and her journal features sharp observations of the manners (or lack of them), dialects, dress, and modes of life of people she encountered on her five-month journey. Enduring bad food, poor lodgings, and sometimes rude treatment on her trip through this barely-settled country, Madam Knight notes that a dish of pork and cabbage has a purple sauce, so that it seems to have been boiled in the cook's dye kettle; and she comments on the boisterous behavior of fellow guests at an inn that inspired her to write a poem which begins, "I ask thy Aid, O Potent Rum!/To Charm these wrangling Topers Dum," as a means of dealing with her frustration. Although details of Sarah Kemble Knight's life are sketchy, she seems to have been a businesswoman—a shopkeeper and innkeeper—who might well have surveyed the lodging places of her journey with a professional eye. She was born in Charlestown, Massachusetts, into a middle-class, shop-keeping family, and married Richard Knight, whose business caused him to travel extensively, so it is not surprising that at the age of 38 she undertook a trip to New York to settle her cousin's estate. Her skill as a writer was frequently sought by those having letters or legal documents to transcribe, and she taught reading and writing to neighborhood children, one of whom is said to have been Benjamin Franklin. Madam Knight's *Journal* has been reprinted several times since 1825 and provides a fascinating insight into the experience of a colonial woman who used humor as a means of survival.

SOURCES   Kenney, W. Howland. Ed. *Laughter in the Wilderness: Early American Humor to 1783.* Kent, OH: Kent State University Press, 1976; Stanford, Ann. "Three Puritan Women: Anne Bradstreet, Mary Rowlandson, and Sarah Kemble Knight." *American Women Writers: Bibliographical Essays.* Eds. Maurice Duke, Jackson R. Bryer, and M. Thomas Inge. Westport, CT: Greenwood, 1983; Winship, George Parker. Introductory Note. *The Journal of Madame Knight.* 1935; rpt. St. Clair Shores, MI: Scholarly Press, 1970.

WORKS   *The Journal of Madam Knight* (1825)

from *The Journal of Madam Knight*

Monday, Octb'r Ye Second, 1704.—About three o'clock afternoon, I began my Journey from Boston to New-Haven; being about two Hundred Mile. My Kinsman, Capt. Robert Luist, waited on me as farr as Dedham, where I was to meet ye Western post.

I vissitted the Reverd. Mr. Belcher, ye Minister of ye town, and tarried there till evening, in hopes ye post would come along. But he not coming, I resolved to go to Billingses where he used to lodg, being 12 miles further. But being ignorant of the way, Madm Billings, seing no persuasions of her good spouses or hers could prevail with me to Lodg there that night, Very kindly went wyth me to ye Tavern, where I hoped to get my guide, And desired the Hostess to inquire of her guests whether any of them would go with mee. But they being tyed by the Lipps to a pewter engine, scarcely allowed themselves time to say what clownish . . . *(manuscript torn at this point)* . . . Pieces of eight, I told her no, I would not be accessary to such extortion.

Then John shan't go, sais shee. No, indeed, shan't hee; And held forth at that rate a long time, that I began to fear I was got among the Quaking tribe, beleeving not a Limbertong'd sister among them could out do Madm. Hostes.

Upon this, to my no small surprise, son John arrose, and gravely demanded what I would give him to go with me? Give you, sais I, are you John? Yes, says he, for want of a Better [name]; and behold! this John look't as old as my Host, and perhaps had bin a man in this last Century. Well, Mr. John, sais I, make your demands. Why, half a pss. of eight and a dram, sais John. I agreed, and gave him a Dram (now) in hand to bind the bargain,

My hostess catechis'd John for going so cheep, saying his poor wife would break her heart. . . . His shade of his Hors resembled a Globe on a Gate post. His habitt, Hors and furniture, its looks and goings Incomparably answered the rest.

Thus Jogging on with an easy pace, my Guide telling mee it was dangero's to Ride hard in the Night, (which his horse had the sence to avoid,) Hee entertained me with the Adventurs he had passed by late Rideing, and eminent Dangers he had escaped, so that, Remembering the Hero's in Parismus and the Knight of the Oracle, I didn't know but I had mett with a Prince disguis'd.

When we had Ridd an how'r, wee come into a thick swamp, wch. by Reason of a great fogg, very much startled mee, it being now very Dark. But nothing dismay'd John: Hee had encountered a thousand and a thousand such Swamps, having a Universall Knowledge in the woods; and readily Answered all my inquiries wch. were not a few.

In about an how'r, or something more, after we left the Swamp, we come to Billinges, where I was to Lodg. My Guide dismounted and very Complasantly help't me down and shewd the door, signing to me wth his hand to Go in; wch I Gladly did—But had not gone many steps into the Room, ere I was Interogated by a young Lady I understood afterwards was the Eldest daughter of the family, with these, or words to this purpose, (viz.) Law for mee—what in the world brings You here at this time a night?—I never see a woman on the Rode so Dreadfull late, in all the days of my versall [whole] life. Who are you? Where are You going? I'me scar'd out of my wits—with much now of the same Kind. I stood aghast, Prepareing to reply, when in comes my Guide—to him, Madam turn'd, Roreing out: Lawfull heart, John, is it You?—how de do! Where in the world are you going with this woman? Who is she? John made to Ansr. but sat down in the corner, fumbled out his black Junk [pipe], and saluted that instead of Debb; she then turned agen to mee and fell anew into her silly questions, without asking me to sitt down.

I told her shee treated me very Rudely, and I did not think it my duty to answer her unmannerly Questions. But to get ridd of them, I told her I come there to have the post's company with me tomorrow on my Journey, &c. Miss star'd awhile, drew a chair, bid me sitt, And then run up stairs and putts on two or three Rings, (or else I had not seen them before,) and returning, sett herself just before me, showing the way to Reding, that I might see her Ornaments, perhaps to gain the more respect. But her Granam's new Rung sow, had it appeared would affected me as much. I paid honest John wth money and dram according to contract, and Dismist him, and pray'd Miss to shew me where I must Lodg. Shee conducted me to a parlour in a little back Lento [lean-to], wch was almost fill'd with the bedsted, wch was so high I was forced to climb on a chair to gitt up to ye wretched bed that lay on it; on wch having Stretcht my tired Limbs, and lay'd my head on a Sadcolourd pillow, I began to think on the transactions of ye past day.

TUESDAY, OCTOBER YE THIRD . . . about two, afternoon. Arrived at the Post's second stage . . . Here, having called for something to eat, ye woman bro't in a Twisted thing like a cable, but something whiter; and laying it on the bord, tugg'd for life to bring it into a capacity to spread; wch having wth great pains accomplished, shee serv'd in a dish of Pork and Cabage, I suppose the remains of Dinner. The sause was of a deep Purple, wch I tho't was boil'd in her dye Kettle; the bread was Indian, and every thing on the Table service Agreeable to these. I, being hungry, gott a little down; but my stomach was soon cloy'd, and what cabbage I swallowed serv'd me for a Cudd the whole day after.

. . . About Three afternoon went on with my Third Guide, who Rode very hard; and having crossed Providence Ferry, we come to a River wch they Generally Ride thro'. But I dare not venture; so the Post got a Ladd and Cannoo to carry me to tother side, and hee rid thro' and Led my hors. The Cannoo was very small and shallow, so that when we were in she seem'd redy to take in water, which greatly terrified mee, and caused me to be very circumspect, sitting with my hands fast on each side, my eyes stedy, not daring so much as to lodg my tongue a hair's breadth more on one side of my mouth then tother, nor so much as think on Lott's wife, [Genesis 19:26] for a wry thought would have oversett our wherey: But was soon put out of this pain, by feeling the Cannoo on shore, wch I as soon almost saluted with my feet; and Rewarding my sculler, again mounted and made the best of our way forwards. . . . the Post told mee we had neer 14 miles to Ride to the next Stage, (where we were to Lodg.) I askt him of the rest of the Rode, foreseeing wee must travail in the night. Hee told mee there was a bad River we were to Ride thro', wch was so very firce a hors could sometimes hardly stem it: But it was narrow, and wee should soon be over. I cannot express The concern of mind this relation sett me in: no thoughts but those of the dang'ros River could entertain my Imagination, and they were as formidable as varios, still Tormenting me with blackest Ideas of my Approaching fate—Sometimes seing my self drowning, otherwhiles drowned, and at the best like a holy Sister Just come out of a Spiritual Bath in dripping Garments.

. . .

I gave Reins to my Nagg; and sitting as Stedy as Just before in the Cannoo, in a few minutes got safe to the other side, which hee told mee was the Narragansett country.

. . .

From hence wee kept on, with more ease yn before: the way being smooth and even, the night warm and serene. . . .

. . . Being come to mr. Havens', I was very civilly Received, and courteously entertained, in a clean comfortable House; and the Good woman was very active in helping off my Riding clothes, and then ask't what I would eat. I told her I had some Chocolett, if shee would prepare it, which with the help of some Milk, and a little clean brass Kettle, she soon effected to my satisfaction. I then betook me to my Apartment, wch was a little Room parted from the Kitchen by a single bord partition; where, after I had noted the Occurances of the past day, I went to bed, which, tho' pretty hard, Yet neet and handsome. But I could get no sleep, because of the Clamor of some of the Town tope-ers in next Room, Who were entred into a strong debate concerning ye Signifycation of the name of their Country, (viz.) *Narraganset.* One said it was named so by ye Indians, because there grew a Brier there, of a prodigious Highth and bigness, the like hardly ever known, called by the Indians Narrangansett; And quotes an Indian of so Barberous a name for his Author, that I could not write it. His Antagonist Replyed no—It was from a Spring it had its name, wch hee well knew where it was, which was extreem cold in summer, and as Hott as could be imagined in the winter, which was much resorted too by the natives, and by them called Narragansett, (Hott and Cold,) and that was the originall of their places name—with a thousand Impertinances not worth notice, wch He utter'd with such a Roreing voice and Thundering blows with the fist of wickedness on the Table, that it peirced my very head. I heartily fretted, and wish't t'um tongue tyed; but wth as little succes as a friend of mine once, who was (as shee said) kept a whole night awake, on a Jorny, by a country Left. and a Sergent, Insigne and a Deacon, contriving how to bring a triangle into a Square. They kept calling for tother Gill, wch while they were swallowing, was some Intermission; But presently, like Oyle to fire, encreased the flame. I set my Candle on a Chest by the bed side, an setting up, fell to my old way of composing my Resentments, in the following manner:

> I ask thy Aid, O Potent-Rum!
> To Charm these wrangling Topers Dum.
> Thou hast their Giddy Brains possest-
> The man confounded with the Beast-
> And I, poor I, can get no rest.
> Intoxicate them with thy fumes:
> O still their Tongues till morning comes!

And I know not but my wishes took effect; for the dispute soon ended wth' tother Dram; and so Good night!

Mercy Otis Warren
(1728–1814)

The sole woman traditionally cited in studies of Revolutionary War-era drama and satire, Mercy Otis Warren was a poet and historian, as well as a writer of patriotic pamphlet plays. The sister of James Otis, an early anti-British activist, and wife of James Warren, a Massachusetts political leader, Warren knew personally most of the leaders of the American Revolution and sought in her writing to make a contribution to the patriot cause. She wrote five anonymous propaganda plays during the 1770s that attacked the Tories and denounced the British: *The Adulateur* (1772), *The Defeat* (1773), *The Group* (1775), *The Blockheads* (1776), and *The Motley Assembly* (1779). In the mid-1780s she composed two five-act tragedies—*The Sack of Rome* and *The Ladies of Castile*—which were published, along with her poetry, in 1790. She then turned her energies to a three-volume *History of the Rise, Progress and Termination of the American Revolution,* published in 1805, which reflected the strong opposition to Federalism that she had first expressed in 1788 in *Observations on the New Constitution,* whose ratification she opposed. Her concern with political freedom and civil rights made her an advocate of women's participation in the political process, but she expressed her views of women's rights and responsibilities more directly in her correspondence, particularly with Abigail Adams, a close friend, than in her poetry and plays. Nevertheless, the fact that she took politics, philosophy, and religion as appropriate topics for her own writing supports her view that women had not only the right but also the duty to involve themselves in and speak freely on such "masculine" concerns; and she satirizes masculine positions on these topics as well as on women's role. Moreover, her plays, particularly her tragedies, contain strong and sympathetic female characters and depict despotic

11

male characters who abuse women and destroy freedom. The first recognized female political satirist in America, Warren preceded later feminists who have used humor and satire to effect political change.

SOURCES   Anthony, Katharine. *First Lady of the Revolution: The Life of Mercy Otis Warren.* Garden City, NY: Doubleday, 1958; Feen, Robert A. "Mercy Otis Warren." *Notable American Women 1603–1930, Vol. 3: 545–46;* Franklin, Benjamin V. Introduction. *The Plays and Poems of Mercy Otis Warren,* Delmar, NY: Scholars' Facsimiles and Reprints, 1980; Granger, Bruce I. *Political Satire in the American Revolution, 1763–1783.* Cornell University Press, 1960; Kerber, Linda K. *Women of the Republic.* University of North Carolina Press, 1980; Meserve, Walter J. *An Emerging Entertainment: The Drama of the American People to 1828.* Bloomington: Indiana University Press, 1977.

WORKS   *Poems Dramatic and Miscellaneous* (1790)

from *Poems Dramatic and Miscellaneous*

To a Young Lady,
On observing an excellent Piece of Painting, much faded.

Come, and attend, my charming maid;
See how the gayest colours fade;
As beauteous paintings lose their dye,
Age sinks the lustre of your eye.

Then seize the minutes as they pass;
Behold! how swift runs down the glass;
The hasty sands that measure time,
Point you to pleasures more sublime;
And bid you shun the flow'ry path,
That cheats the millions into death.

Snatch every moment time shall give,
And uniformly virtuous live;
Let no vain cares retard they soul,
But strive to reach the happy goal;
When pale, when unrelenting Death,

Shall say, resign life's vital breath!
May you, swift as the morning lark
That stems her course to heav'n's high arch,
Leave every earthly care, and soar,
Where numerous seraphims adore;
Thy pinions spread and wafted high,
Beyond the blue etherial sky,
May you there chant the glorious lays,
The carols of eternal praise,
To that exhaustless source of light,
Who rules the shadows of the night,
Who lends each orb its splendid ray,
And points the glorious beams of day.

Time and eternity he holds;
Nor all eternity unfolds,
The glories of Jehovah's name;
Nor highest angels can proclaim,
The wonders of his boundless grace,
They bow, and veil before his face.

What then shall mortals of an hour
But bend submissive to his power;
And learn as wisdom's happy lore,
Nature's great author to adore.

To the Hon. J. Winthrop, Esq.

Who, on the American Determination, in 1774, to suspend all Commerce with
Britain (except for the real Necessaries of life) requested a poetical List of the
Articles the Ladies might comprise under that Head.

Freedom may weep, and tyranny prevail,
And stubborn patriots either frown, or rail;
Let them of grave economy talk loud,
Prate prudent measures to the list'ning crowd;
With all the rhetoric of ancient schools,

Despise the mode, and fashion's modish fools;
Or shew fair liberty, who us'd to smile,
The guardian godess of Britannia's isle,
In sable weeds, anticipate the blow,
Aim'd at Columbia by her royal foe;
And mark the period when inglorious kings
Deal round the curses that a Churchill sings.

But what's the anguish of whole towns in tears,
Or trembling cities groaning out their fears?
The state may totter on proud ruin's brink,
The sword be brandished, or the bark may sink;
Yet shall Clarissa check her wanton pride,
And lay her female ornaments aside?
Quit all the shining pomp, the gay parade,
The costly trappings that adorn the maid?
What! all the aid of foreign looms refuse!
(As beds of tulips strip'd of richest hues,
Or the sweet bloom that's nip'd by sudden frost)
Clarissa reigns no more a favorite toast.
For what is virtue, or the winning grace,
Of soft good humour, playing round the face;
Or what those modest antiquated charms
That lur'd a Brutus to a Portia's arms;
Or all the hidden beauties of the mind,
Compar'd with gauze, and tassels well combined?

This mighty theme produc'd a long debate,
On the best plan to save a sinking state;
The oratorial fair, as they inclin'd,
Freely discuss'd, and frankly spake their mind.

Lamira wish'd that freedom might succeed,
But to such terms what female ere agreed?
To British marts forbidden to repair,
(Where ev'ry lux'ry tempts the blooming fair,)
Equals the rigour of those ancient times
When Pharoah, harden'd as a G------ in crimes,
Plagu'd Israel's race, and tax'd them by a law,
Demanding brick, when destitute of straw;

Miraculously led from Egypt's port,
They lov'd the fashions of the tyrant's court;
Sigh'd for the leeks, and waters of the Nile,
As we for gewgaws from Britannia's isle;
That haughty isle, whose mercenary hand
Spreads wide confusion round this fertile land,
Destroys the concord, and breaks down the shrine,
By virtue rear'd, to harmony divine.

Prudentia sigh'd—shall all our country mourn,
A powerful despot's low'ring, haughty frown,
Whose hostile mandates, sent from venal courts,
Rob the fair vintage, and blockade our ports;
While troops of guards are planted on each plain,
Whose crimes contagious, youth and beauty slain?
Fierce rancour blazen'd on each breast's display'd,
And for a crest, a gorgon's snaky head.

The good, the wise, the prudent, and the gay,
Mingle their tears, and sighs for sighs repay;
Deep anxious thought each gen'rous bosom fills,
How to avert the dread approaching ills;
Let us resolve on a small sacrifice,
And in the pride of Roman matrons rise;
Good as Cornelia, or a Pompey's wife,
We'll quit the useless vanities of life.
Amidst loud discord, sadness, and dismay,
Hope spread her wing, and flit across the way:
Thanks to the sex, by heavenly hand design'd,
Either to bless, or ruin all mankind.

A sharp debate ensu'd on wrong and right,
A little warm, 'tis true, yet all unite,
At once to end the great politic strife,
And yield up all but real wants of life.

But does Helvidius, vigilant and wise,
Call for a schedule, that may all comprise?
'Tis so contracted, that a Spartan sage,
Will sure applaud th' economizing age.

But if ye doubt, an inventory clear,
Of all the needs, Lamira offers here;
Nor does she fear a rigid Cato's frown,
When she lays by the rich embroider'd gown,
And modestly compounds for just enough—
Perhaps, some dozens of more flightly stuff;
With lawns and lustrings—blond, and mecklin laces,
Fringes and jewels, fans and tweezer cases;
Gay cloaks and hats, of every shape and size,
Scarfs, cardinals, and ribbons of all dyes;
With ruffles stamp'd, and aprons of tambour,
Tippets and handkerchiefs, as least, three score;
With finest muslins that fair India boasts,
And the choice herbage from Chinesan coasts;
(But while the fragrant hyson leaf regales,
Who'll wear the homespun produce of the vales?
For if 'twould save the nation from the curse
Of standing troops; or, name a plague still worse,
Few can this choice delicious draught give up,
Though all Medea's poisons fill the cup.)
Add feathers, furs, rich sattins, and ducapes,
And head dresses in pyramidial shapes;
Side boards of plate, and porcelain profuse,
With fifty ditto's that the ladies use;
If my poor treach'rous memory has miss'd,
Ingenious T------l shall complete the list.
So weak Lamira, and her wants so few,
Who can refuse?—They're but the sex's due.

In youth, indeed, an antiquated page,
Taught us the threatenings of an Hebrew sage
'Gainst wimples, mantles, curls, and crisping pins,
But rank not these among our modern sins:
For when our manners are well understood,
What in the scale is stomacher or hood?

'Tis true, we love the courtly mein and air,
The pride of dress, and all the debonair,
Yet Clara quits the more dress'd negligee,
And substitutes the careless polanee;
Until some fair one from Britannia's court,

Some jaunty dress, or newer tasle import;
This sweet temptation could not be withstood,
Though for the purchase's paid her father's blood;
Though loss of freedom were the costly price,
Or flaming comets sweep the angry skies;
Or earthquakes rattle, or volcanoes roar;
Indulge this trifle, and she asks no more.
Can the stern patriot Clara's suit deny?
'Tis beauty asks, and reason must comply.

But while the sex round folly's vortex play,
Say, if their lords are wiser far than they;
Few manly bosoms feel a nobler flame,
Some cog the dye, and others win the game;
Trace their meanders to their tainted source,
What's the grand pole star that directs their course?
Perhaps revenge, or some less glaring vice,
Their bold ambition, or their avarice,
Or vanity unmeaning, throw the bowl;
'Till pride and passion urge the narrow foul,
To claim the honours of that heavenly flame,
That warms the breast, and crowns the patriot's name.

But though your wives in fripperies are dress'd,
And public virtue is the minion's jest,
America has many a worthy name,
Who shall, hereafter, grace the rolls of fame.
Her good Cornelias, and her Arrias fair,
Who, death, in its most hideous forms, can dare,
Rather than live vain fickle fortune's sport,
Amidst the panders of a tyrant's court;
With a long list of gen'rous, worthy men,
Who spurn the yoke, and servitude disdain;
Who nobly struggle in a vicious age,
To stem the torrent of despotic rage;
Who leagu'd, in solemn covenant unite,
And by the manes of good Hampden plight,
That while the surges lash Britannia's shore,
Or wild Ni'gara's cataracts shall roar,
And Heaven looks down, and sanctifies the deed,
They'll fight for freedom, and for virtue bleed.

Judith Sargent Murray
(1751–1820)

Representing what Nancy Cott, in *The Bonds of Woman-hood* (1977) calls the "equalitarian feminist view" of the late eighteenth century, Judith Sargent Murray's work attacked the idea that women were inferior to men and protested the restrictions women faced in training, education, and political activity in the new Republic. Similar in thought to Mercy Otis Warren, whose work she praised, and influenced by Mary Wollstonecraft's *Vindication of the Rights of Women*, Murray's writings, collected in three volumes titled *The Gleaner* (1798), stressed women's and men's equal capacity for moral and intellectual development, argued in favor of women's education and training for independent living, and defended women's right to pursue any career that attracted them. In addition to her 1779 essay "On the Equality of the Sexes," which made a public declaration of women's equality with men, Murray also set a precedent, as Alice Rossi emphasizes in *The Feminist Papers* (1973), by defending this view on religious grounds. Under the pseudonym of "Constantia," she began publishing essays and poems, first in the *Gentlemen and Lady's Town and Country Magazine* and latter in the *Massachusetts Magazine*. The first of these, "Desultory Thought Upon the Utility of Encouraging a Degree of Self-Complacency, Especially in Female Bosoms," may have been inspired by reflections on her marriage, at the age of eighteen, to sea captain John Stevens, who left Gloucester in 1786 to avoid debtors' prison and died in the West Indies shortly thereafter. Her subsequent marriage to John Murray, founder of the Universalist Church in America, is apparently reflected in the positive marriages offered in her work as models of egalitarianism. Throughout her essays, her serialized novel about the upbringing of a young girl, Margaretta Mellworth, and her two comedies of manners, *The*

Medium; or Virtue Triumphant and *The Traveller Returned*,
Murray focused on the importance of training women to be
independent and self-sufficient, of nurturing virtue and intellect rather than flirtatiousness and frivolity in young women,
and of basing marriage on the mutual respect, interests, and
values of husband and wife. Her wit and satire are used to
target the private and public vices and deceptions that lead to
personal and civic corruption and disharmony.

SOURCES   Cederstrom, Eleanor R. "Remember the Ladies." Gloucester, MA:
Sargent-Murray-Gilman-Hough House Association, Publication No. 2, 1983;
Cott, Nancy F. *The Bonds of Womanhood: "Woman's Sphere" in New England,
1780–1835*. New Haven, CT: Yale University Press, 1977; Field, Vena Bernadette.
"Constantia. A Study of the Life and Works of Judith Sargent Murray, 1751–
1820." *Maine Bulletin, University of Maine Studies* 33:7 (February 1931);
Norton, Mary Beth. *Liberty's Daughters*. Boston: Little, Brown, 1980; Rossi,
Alice S., ed. *The Feminist Papers: From Adams to de Beauvoir*. New York:
Columbia University Press, 1973.

WORKS   *The Gleaner* (3 vols.) (1798)

selected letters from *The Gleaner*

The essays in volume one were written for and first appeared in the "Monthly
Museum," a column of the *Massachusetts Magazine*. These essays, written under
the *persona* of a plain family man who signs himself "Gleaner," include what may
loosely be called a novel: the story of the adoption and rearing of Margaretta
Melworth by the Gleaner and his wife. The chapters of the story (which extend
into volume two) are interrupted by meditative essays on a variety of social,
political, and moral questions, as well as by letters supposedly received by the
Gleaner in response to the publication of his column.

August 13, 1792

Good Man Gleaner,

I am, d'ye see, an old sea commander, and many a tough bout have I
had on it in my day; with the wind in my teeth, I have been blown hither
and thither, coast wise, and every wise; but what of that? With a pretty
breeze, mayhap, I can carry as much sail, and steer as strait forward as
another man. Now I have been plaguily puzzled to know at what you were
driving; I never, in the whole course of my life, was fond of an uncertain
navigation, because, d'ye see, there is no knowing what rocks and quick-

sands may take one up. For my part, I never wasted many glasses in poring over your books, and your histories, and all that—not I—it was my business to mind how the ship worked, to see if she made good way, and sailed as many knots in an hour as the charming Sall, or Bet . . . But what is all this to the purpose? Avast a moment, and you shall hear. Being pretty much weather beaten, I thought best, sometime since, to make the safe and convenient harbor of matrimony, and my daughter Molly, for that was the sober name we gave her at the fount, though, by the bye, my wife very soon tacking about, chose to call her Maria, till returning from a trip she hath made to a neighbouring town, the wind again shifting, there is nothing so proper, so sedate, and which, she says, squares so well with her ideas, as Mary; thus reducing us to the necessity of beginning our traverse anew; well, but my said daughter Molly, Maria, or Mary, being born just a year after our marriage, and very soon becoming a fine rosy cheeked girl, I have ever since been examining every point of direction, so belaying the lifts and the braces, the clewlines and the buntlines, that she may be as good a sail, make as good way, and procure as good a berth, as any little tight sea boat of them all. Her mother was for putting her adrift at a boarding school, but by virtue of my authority, I have hitherto kept her in her old moorings, being hugely afraid of the breakers, which she may encounter upon the ocean of inexperience; but . . . being embarked in so difficult a navigation, I am, for the first time since I took command of a ship, rather doubtful of my course . . . upon the first of last April, my wife and I being safely hauled up along side of a good fire, were mightily taken with your Margaretta, and . . . we lovingly agreed to dispose of our Molly, precisely as you should inform us you had done of the little yawl belayed along side your anchorage by Dame Arbuthnot; but now, Mr. Gleaner, I am coming to the point; though we have ever since kept watch and watch, placing upon the mast-head of scrutiny the careful eye of intelligence, yet we cannot espy the smallest appearance of the little skiff for which we are looking out; on the contrary, you seem to have hoisted every sail, bearing directly from the port to which we supposed you were bound! And pray now what have you got by all this? I doubt your voyage will prove rather unprofitable; for, say what you will, people will turn in when they please, and though your mornings should break ten times handsomer, they will not quit their cabins a single glass the sooner. It is true, you have taken us a round about course to Athens, and the Lord knows where, paragraphing upon the times, and the times, though do not make them a rope's end the better; and I know, in the very teeth of all you say, that I have never had more taxes, or more duties to pay, since I first stepped on board a ship; . . . and I now declare to you, Sir, that if you do not resume your plain sailing, you shall no more be read by

GEORGE AND DEBORAH SEAFORT

Dear Good Mr. Gleaner,

You can have no notion how vastly we are all disappointed; I does not date my letters, because, as how, I would not for the whole world that you should find me out; but I am one of a great many ladies, which is absolutely dying to see something more about Margaretta. My papa hath given his *hibitation* against my reading your novels, and your *theatricks*, and all that; but he is a subscriber to the magazines, and says how I may read in them from morning till night; and we are mightily delighted when we find such pretty *historiettes* as we sometimes does; but we would not give a fig for any thing else, and indeed we could not get through your two last Gleaners, though we read *alternately*, as the folks say, that is, first Miss Primrose, and then I, till we went down two columns, on purpose to see if we could find as much as the name of dear Margaretta. Do pray, Sir, oblige us, and let us know something of her dress, and if she wears a head as high as Miss Sycamore, which my papa says is quite *metreposterous*; I don't know if I spell these ere hard words right, for my brother Valentine has stole my dictionary; but I assure you, Sir, you cannot do better, for so Miss Sabina says. I sometimes visits Miss Sabina with my papa, for my mamma is dead, and she is a vast cute lady, and she writes *poetics* like any thing, and her mamma says that she writes um very near as glibly and as handsomely as Madam Philenia. And Miss Sabina says, that supposing Miss Margaretta is a *visual* being, and not a *real*, and a *deeden* lady, that you might make her the *vetrick* of a *serus* of *epics*, and so teach *demeanours* and *proprieties*, and all that, to the *varsal world*; and so I knows that you will mind her, for every body says how that Miss Sabina is a very learned lady; and besides all that, I will love you dearly, and will remain until death your ever dutiful—I must subscribe a *fiction* name— and to tell you the truth my brother Valentine is not my brother's *true* and *deeden* name; but I am—that is, if you tell us some more of Margaretta, your ever loving

MONIMIA CASTALIO

P.S. I got my name from a play book, which Miss Primrose lent me. My papa does not know it but the Gleaner must not tell secrets.

Dissipation Hall, July 18th, 1792

Old Square Toes,

To tell you the truth, I think you have conducted your matters devilishly oddly, and the whole town are of my opinion. What, to raise our curiosity, leading us to expect the history of a fine girl, and then to fob us off with your *musty morals*, which are to the full as old as your grandfather Adam—*fore gad* 'tis not be be borne, but nevertheless I will play a fair game with you; and I know you are too *conscientious a prig* to keep from your ward any thing which will redound so immensely to her advantage. Know then, that I inherited from my father a clear estate, the income of which, would have supported me in tolerable style; but not choosing to encumber myself with business, and living rather beyond the line, I have got, as the saying is, *a little out at the elbows*; however a few of your acres (and I am confident that you are either a *Connecticut* landholder, or a *Pennsylvania* Quaker) serving as decent patches, will set all right again; and you may depend upon it, that I will *reform, live within bounds*, and if I like your girl, make her a very good sort of husband. One thing let me tell you, old fellow, she will be the envy of all the ladies in _____ , married and single—dear tender creatures, there is not one of them, *who hath not made the kindest advances*; but I like to do things out of the common course; and so, if you will, let me hear from you, and tell me how you go on; if you will order matters properly; and if your Margaretta answers my expectations—why then—what then—hang it—I must come to it at last—why then—offer her my devoirs, and inform her, that she may assure herself of the hand of the gay, and hitherto inconstant

BELLAMOUR

From my Estate in the Country
July 21st 1792

Worthy Sir,

As I suppose it will be your care to dispose of Miss Melworth to the best advantage; as I think that she must now be marriageable, and as I have been for some time looking out for a wife, I have thought best to address you on the subject. Indeed, I should have wrote you before; but expecting every number, to hear something further of the girl, I postponed my intention, until by your long-winded remarks, my patience is exhausted. In truth, as I am turned of fifty, I have no time to spare; and having a handsome and unencumbered estate, it is fit that I procure lineal descendants who, in case of my decease, may become legal possessors. From applying to the girls of our day, whom I have seen, notwithstanding your opinion of *"present times,"* I am deterred by the little chance which a man hath of obtaining a woman possessed of that discretion which is so requisite in a wife; for, what with *morning visits, family and public dinings, riding, mall strolling, evening tea parties, midnight balls*, and the time which is necessarily devoted to sleep and dressing, the four and twenty hours are completely filled up! Now, as I look upon you, Mr. Gleaner, to be a very wise man, I take it that your Margaretta must be a girl of a different sort; and, as I suppose that she has been educated in the country, I take it for certain, that she is a complete house-wife; that she can superintend in a dairy; take care of her children, when she has any; see that I have my meals in due season; and that my clothes are brushed and laid in good order. Moreover, as from a hint in one of your papers, I imagine that you have a proper idea of the subordination which is so essential to the character of a woman; I presume that you have not failed to document your pupil, with sufficient gravity, upon the article of *subjection* and, I assure you, that I shall expect *obedience from my wife*; that she must not only be very well taught, *industrious*, and *uniformly economical*, but also extremely *docile*. These things premised, if you will introduce me to Miss Melworth, and we should happen to fancy each other, I will, if you please, order the banns to be published, and very speedily invest her with all the *privileges and immunities* of a wife. I am, worthy Sir, your very humble servant to command,

TIMOTHY PLODDER

PART II
The Nineteenth Century:
Pioneers and Wits

Tabitha Gilman Tenney

(1762–1837)

Tabitha Tenney's *Female Quixotism, Exhibited in the Romantic Opinions and Extravagant Adventures of Dorcasina Sheldon,* published in 1801, marks the beginning of a tradition of satiric "advice" literature by women for women, a tradition that includes Fanny Fern's *Fern Leaves* (1853) and Josephine Daskam's *Fables for the Fair* (1901). Tenney's two-volume novel is a cautionary tale for women who were tempted to believe the romantic blandishments of men, and its popularity into the 1840s speaks to the concern in the nineteenth century that reading romantic novels would cause women to be foolish and sentimental. The novel's main character, Dorcasina Sheldon, is similar to Marietta Holley's character Betsey Bobbet much later in the century in her susceptibility to flattery and her romantic visions of herself. Tenney was born in Exeter, New Hampshire, and was descended from early colonists. She was married in 1788 to Dr. Samuel Tenney, who had been a surgeon during the Revolutionary War and who subsequently had a career in politics, serving three terms in Congress beginning in 1800. Tabitha Tenney's first publication was a conventional one for the day: titled *The New Pleasing Instructor,* it was an anthology of selections from classical poetry intended for young women. Little is known of Tenney's formal education, but her ability to make fun of the conventions of the sentimental novel suggests wide reading, as does the fact that an obvious literary precedent for *Female Quixotism* is Cervantes' *Don Quixote,* whose title character also suffers from romantic delusions. A more immediate predecessor of Tenney's novel was Charlotte Lennox's *The Female Quixote; or, The Adventures of Arabella* (1752), an English novel that similarly addressed female foolishness and romanticism. *Female Quixotism* was apparently both the peak and the conclusion of

Tenney's career as a writer; following her husband's death in 1816 she moved from Washington back to her native New Hampshire, where she died at the age of seventy-five.

SOURCES   Brown, Herbert Ross. *The Sentimental Novel in America.* Durham: Duke University Press, 1940; Hoople, Sally C. "Tabitha Tenney." *Encyclopedia of American Humorists.* Ed. Steven H. Gale. New York: Garland, 1988. 430–434; *Notable American Women, 1607–1950;* Petter, Henri. *The Early American Novel.* Columbus: Ohio State University Press, 1971.

WORKS   *Female Quixotism* (1801)

from *Female Quixotism*

To all Columbian Young Ladies, who read Novels and Romances

Dear Girls,

During half a year's residence at Philadelphia, I was frequently diverted with a recital of some particulars of the life of Miss Dorcas Sheldon. These appeared so whimsical and outré that I had a strong inclination to acquire a knowledge of her whole history. With this view, I got introduced to her, at the house of her friend, Mrs. Barry; and after a few weeks acquaintance, prevailed on her to favor me with a minute account of her adventures, with a generous permission to publish them, if I thought proper, for the advantage of the younger part of her sex.

The work, ladies, now courts your attention; and I hope you will be induced to read it, as well for my sake, who have spent much time in compiling, and cash in publishing it, as for your own, for whose particular use it is designed, and to whom it is most respectfully dedicated.

I am sensible you will find it a very singular and extraordinary piece of biography, and that you may suspect it to be a mere romance, and Hogarthian caricatura, instead of a true picture of real life. But when you compare it with the most extravagant parts of the authentic history of the celebrated hero of La Mancha, the renowned Don Quixote, I presume you will no longer doubt its being a true uncolored history of a romantic country girl, whose head had been turned by the unrestrained perusal of Novels and Romances. That by observing their baneful effects on Miss Sheldon, who was in every respect a sensible, judicious, and amiable girl, you may avoid the disgraces and disasters that so long rendered her despicable and miserable, is the sincere wish,

My dear young Ladies,
Of your Friend and Admirer,

THE COMPILER

CHAPTER 1

On the beautiful banks of the Delaware, about thirty miles from Philadelphia, dwelt a worthy and venerable man, by the name of Sheldon. In
his younger days, he had been a considerable traveller, and had consequently seen much of the world. Some disappointments and mortifica-
tions, to which a turn of mind somewhat singular had subjected him, in
some European city, had inspired him with a total dislike of all populous
places. On his return, therefore, from his last foreign tour, he could not be
persuaded to fix his residence in Philadelphia, the place of his nativity; but
having married a wife, a necessary ingredient in man's domestic happiness, he purchased an estate near enough to this capital of North
America, to enjoy its conveniences and the society of a few of its inhabitants, for whom he had a particular friendship; and devoted himself to
agriculture. One daughter was the only fruit of this connexion. Her
history, being filled with incidents of a singular nature, we are now about
to give to the public.

At the age of three years, this child had the misfortune to lose an
excellent mother, whose advice would have pointed out to her the plain
rational path of life, and prevented her imagination from being filled with
the airy delusions and visionary dreams of love and raptures, darts, fire
and flames, with which the indiscreet writers of that fascinating kind of
books, denominated novels, fill the heads of artless young girls, to their
great injury, and sometimes to their utter ruin.

Little Dorcas, for so was our heroine called after her paternal grandmother, was too young to be sensible of the loss she had sustained; but her
father lamented their common bereavement with keen and unutterable
anguish. It is wisely ordered, by a kind providence, that time should blunt
the edge of the sharpest sorrows. Were it otherwise, and were our grief for
the death of a dear friend to be always as lively and keen as in its first days,
life would be a burden too heavy to be borne. But, thanks to that benign
power, who kindly "tempers the wind to the shorn lamb," every day
usually lessens its poignancy. Thus it was with Mr. Sheldon. By degrees
his grief subsided, and his affection for his infant daughter increased, till it

engrossed almost every thought of his mind; and his very existence seemed to be bound up in her's. He attended to her education with the utmost care and assiduity; procuring her suitable instructors of every kind, and frequently executing the pleasing office himself, for which his native good sense and various acquirement eminently fitted him. In every branch of her education, Miss Sheldon made great proficiency. She had received from nature a good understanding, a lively fancy, an amiable cheerful temper, and a kind and affectionate heart. What a number of valuable qualities were here blended. But it is a mortifying truth that perfection is not to be found in human nature. With all these engaging endowments, she was unfortunately of a very romantic turn, had a small degree of obstinacy, and a spice too much of vanity.

Now I suppose it will be expected that, in imitation of sister novel writers, (for the ladies of late seem to have almost appropriated this department of writing,) I should describe her as distinguished by the elegant form, delicately turned limbs, auburn hair, alabaster skin, heavenly languishing eyes, silken eyelashes, rosy cheeks, aquiline nose, ruby lips, dimpled chin, and azure veins, with which almost all our heroines of romance are indiscriminately decorated. In truth she possessed few of those beauties in any great degree. She was of a middling stature, a little enbonpoint, but neither elegant nor clumsy. Her complexion was rather dark; her skin somewhat rough; and features remarkable neither for beauty nor deformity. Her eyes were grey and full of expression, and her whole countenance rather pleasing than otherwise. In short, she was a middling kind of person, like the greater part of her country women; such as no man would be smitten with at first sight, but such as any man might love upon intimate acquaintance.

Mr. Sheldon, as was before observed, had conceived an extreme aversion to cities. He therefore, after the death of his wife, visited Philadelphia but rarely; and still more rarely took his daughter thither. In his neighborhood were a few genteel families, with whom he associated occasionally, but with one only intimately. He had a fondness for books which he indulged to the utmost extent. History was his favorite reading; and next to that, (a singular taste for a man) he delighted in novels. Consequently his library was furnished with the best histories, ancient and modern; and every novel, good, bad and indifferent, which the bookstores of Philadelphia afforded.

Miss Dorcas Sheldon, either from nature or education, possessed nearly the same taste in books as her father, with this difference only, that novels were her study, and history only her amusement. Mr. Sheldon, who himself had experienced nothing but pleasure in the time spent in reading the former, unfortunately indulged his daughter in the full latitude of her inclination; never considering their dangerous tendency to a young inexperienced female mind; nor the false ideas of life and manners, with which they would inspire a fanciful girl, educated in retirement and totally unacquainted with the ways of the world.

One year after another passed away in great harmony and domestic happiness, Dorcas dividing her time between her father, (of whom she was extremely fond,) the superintendance of his domestic concerns, and her favorite occupation of reading, till she had reached her eighteenth year. At this time Miss Dorcas became extremely dissatisfied with her unfashionable and unromantic name; but as she could not easily change it, she was determined to alter and give it a romantic termination. She therefore one day, after expressing great dislike to it, begged her father, in future, to call her Dorcasina. Mr. Sheldon laughed at first, at the whim she had conceived, and endeavored to rally her out of it; but finding that it was to her a matter of serious importance, and thinking there could be neither harm nor impropriety in granting her request, he acceded to her wishes, and she was ever after called Dorcasina.

About two years after this, a circumstance happened which formed an important era in the life of Miss Dorcasina. Mr. Sheldon one day received a letter from an old esteemed friend in Virginia, whom he had not seen for fifteen years, informing him of his intention of making him a visit; adding that he should bring with him his only son, the stay and prop of his declining age, and the darling of his fondest affections. Lysander, (by which name we shall call the younger gentleman,) was about twenty-five. His person was noble and commanding; his countenance open and liberal; and his address manly and pleasing. His understanding was rather solid than brilliant, and much improved by education and travel. His ideas of domestic happiness were just and rational; and he judged from what he had observed, that an agreeable matrimonial connexion was much the happiest state in life. He, therefore, wished to marry; but there happened to be no lady in the circle of his acquaintance, who perfectly both satisfied his judgment and pleased his fancy.

Miss Dorcasina, on perusing the letter handed by her father, thought the time was now come, when she should experience the sweet satisfaction of loving and being loved. The similarity of their circumstances; Lysander an only son and she an only daughter; the old gentleman coming so far to see her father; his never having done it before; and his bringing his son with him, all served to confirm her in the opinion, that he was the person decreed by the stars to become her husband. She would, to be sure, have been better pleased, had their acquaintance commenced in a more romantic manner. She wished that in passing by, his carriage had broken down, and he had been brought in wounded; or that he had accidentally met her scouring the woods on horseback, (an amusement in which she took great delight,) and that her horse being unruly, he had arrived just in time to save her from falling; or, which would have been still more to her taste, that some resolute fellow, in love with her to distraction, but who had made no impression on her heart, had carried her off by force to marry her, and that Lysander had rescued her by his gallantry, and conveyed her back in safety to the arms of her distracted parent. But as none of these romantic adventures, with which she had been so delighted in novels, had ever happened to her, she thought she must be satisfied, if at their first interview, he beheld her with raptures of delight; and of this she entertained not a shadow of doubt.

The night previous to the day on which, with alternate emotions of hope, fear and pleasure, she expected the arrival of Lysander, she retired at her usual hour to her chamber, attended by a female domestic, who having been brought up in the family from seven years old, had become her confidante and favorite. This she considered indispensible; for it would have been entirely out of character, and setting aside a most essential circumstance in the life of a heroine, not to have had either a friend, to whom she could confide the secret of her love, or a maid who could be bribed by an enamorato to place a letter in her way, and then confidentially assert that she knew not from whence it came. Both these characters are frequently united in the same person, as was the case in the present instance; for there being no female among her acquaintance in the neighborhood, whose notions of love were so refined, or if you please so romantic, as were those of Miss Dorcasina, she declined all intimacy with them, and preferred Betty to the double capacity of servant and confidante. Betty was a few years older than her mistress; she was a good hearted, honest creature, possessed of a tolerable good natural understanding; but very ignorant and extremely superstitious.

After Dorcasina had disposed herself in bed, she requested Betty to sit down by her bed-side, saying she had something of consequence to communicate. Betty having seated herself in an attentive posture, Dorcasina began by informing her that it was impressed on her mind, that she and the young gentleman, who was next day expected, should, at first sight, fall violently in love with each other; and that she had not the least doubt but he was the person destined by Heaven to become her husband. Betty remained silent, (for indeed she was at a loss for a reply,) Dorcasina thus continued: "Though I know that love is stronger than death, and that with a beloved object a person may be happy on the top of the Alleghanies, or among the snows of Greenland; yet I must confess I shall feel a sensible pain at quitting my dear and affectionate father, and this delightful spot where I have passed all my life, and to which I feel the strongest attachment. But what gives me the greatest pain, is that I shall be obliged to live in Virginia, be served by slaves, and be supported by the sweat, toil and blood of that unfortunate and miserable part of mankind." "Perhaps, ma'am," said Betty, "Lysander and his father treat their slaves well, and they live comfortable and happy." "Comfortable they may be," replied Dorcasina, "but slavery and happiness are in my opinion totally incompatible; 'disguise thyself as thou wilt, still, slavery, thou art a bitter pill.' They complain of the idle, thievish, unfaithful disposition of their slaves; but let the proprietors in their turn, be degraded to servitude, let them be made prisoners by the Algerines, let them have task-masters set over them to drive them out to labor in herds, like the beasts of the field; then should we see whether they would be more faithful or more industrious than the wretched Africans: then should we see whether, after a number of years had elapsed, and they knew their servitude would terminate but with life, their minds would not become degraded and vicious with their situation." "I heard your father and another gentleman arguing upon this very point, ma'am, t'other day; and says your father, says he, for I remember his very words, 'the most judicious among the proprietors of slaves think it is a great evil transmitted them by their forefathers; but an evil they know not how to remedy." "Yes, but there is a remedy," replied Dorcasina, with quickness, (who by this time was warmed by the subject, it being one upon which she never could with patience reflect,) "it is said, that some whole districts in one of the Southern States, have emancipated their slaves, and pay them wages for their labor; and that they find their account in it; the negroes with a spirit of emulation and gratitude, performed much more service than while held in bondage." "Well ma'am, said Betty, ' 'tis pity you should make yourself so uneasy beforehand; perhaps you and the young gentleman wont fall so violently in love with each other as you imagine; and perhaps you never will become his wife." "Oh! I have so strong a presentiment, that I am as sure of it as if we were actually married." "If that is the case," said Betty, (who seeing the young lady so fixed in her expectations, declined disputing farther about it,) "may be you will prove a blessing to the poor blacks. If you marry Lysander, perhaps you can coax him to set them at liberty, and hire them as you hire white servants." "Who knows but I shall," exclaimed Dorcasina, quite transported with the idea, "and I assure you Betty, my influence shall be exerted to the utmost in their favour, when I become their mistress." Having no farther occasion for Betty, she dismissed her. She then indulged herself in the agreeable, humane, but romantic idea, that being the wife of Lysander, she should become the benefactress of his slaves. She even extended her benevolent reveries beyond the plantation of her future husband, and wrapt in the glow of enthusiasm, saw his neighbors imitating his example, and others imitating them, till the spirit of justice and humanity should extend to the utmost limits of the United States, and all the blacks be emancipated from bondage, from New Hampshire, even to Georgia. By these pleasing illusions her mind was so soothed and composed, that she soon become a fit companion for the drowsy god, who held her fast locked in his embraces till late the next morning.

CHAPTER 2

When Dorcasina arose, her features were lighted up with an unusual glow; and an uncommon degree of expression sparkling in her eyes. Her father observing it, as they sat at breakfast, told her that by the pleasure which appeared in her countenance, he fancied her dreams had been agreeable. She blushed extremely at a consciousness of the cause, but made no reply. The whole of that day she amused herself by forming ideas of the person of Lysander, and his first address when he should be introduced to her.

The long expected hour at length arrived. Just as they were sitting down to tea a carriage drove up to the gate, and Lysander and his father were announced. The two old gentlemen were extremely pleased at meeting again, after so long an absence. They had travelled together upon an intimate footing, in their youth; and had never met but once since, which was in Philadelphia, fifteen years before. Mr. Sheldon received the son of his friend with the greatest satisfaction; who on his part, was equally pleased with a person whom he had so often heard his father mention in terms of the warmest friendship. Mr. Sheldon then introducing his daughter to the father and son, the latter complimented her in the same style of easy politeness in which he had done her father; no trembling, no emotion, no hesitation in speaking to her. What a thunder-stroke for poor Dorcasina, who had calculated upon piercing him through and through at the very first glance. So great was her chagrin and disappointment, that she appeared to great disadvantage, sitting silent and thoughtful, through the tedious hours of the evening, which to her had never before appeared so long. Lysander several times politely endeavored to engage her in conversation; but all his attempts proving fruitless, he listened the remainder of the evening to the two old gentlemen, who were talking over the adventures of their youth.

As soon as supper was over and the gentlemen retired, Dorcasina retreated to her chamber, in a far different state of mind from that in which she had entered it the evening preceding. Disappointed in her sanguine expectations of making an immediate conquest of the heart of Lysander, she felt the same indifference towards him that he had manifested towards her. Her mind being so warped by the false and romantic ideas of love, which she had imbibed from her favorite authors, she never considered that the purest and most lasting affection is founded upon esteem and the amiable qualities of the mind, rather than upon transitory personal attractions. Her understanding was not, however, so entirely perverted as to prevent her seeing that she had, by her coolness and reserve, treated Lysander in a very improper manner. She, therefore, though baulked in her dearest hopes, determined to repair the fault, and to treat him with the same polite attention with which her conduct was marked towards every other person. With this determination she composed herself to rest; not, however, without a sigh at the sudden downfall of the pleasing fabric she had the night before raised.

Lysander, on his part, was much disappointed in Dorcasina, having heard that she was a sensible, agreeable, and amiable girl. Amiable he knew not but she might be; but she appeared far from agreeable; nor did she discover any striking marks of understanding, either in her looks or conversation.

Dorcasina the next morning arose with more composure than she had experienced for some days before. She frequently addressed her discourse to Lysander, resolved to make amends for her last night's deficiency. Her usual intelligence sparkled in her countenance; affability and attention to her guests, and duty and affection to her father, were so eminently conspicuous, that Lysander could hardly persuade himself to believe that she was the same cold, inanimate piece of clay, he had attempted to converse with the preceding evening.

The two gentlemen were so well pleased with their visit, that they lengthened it out to almost a month; during which time Lysander became insensibly fond of the company of Dorcasina; he discovered new beauties in her every day; and saw so many proofs of her sweetness of temper, condescension to the servants, and duty and affection to her father, that he thought he never had seen a lady so well calculated to render a man happy; and although at first, he thought her ordinary in person, she now, by the force of her many engaging qualities, appeared to his admiring eyes to be almost a beauty. But he was not sensible of the strength of his attachment, till the time arrived to bid her adieu. The reluctance with which he performed it, and the pain he felt at parting, fully convinced him that he had left his heart at L——.

As soon, therefore, as he reached home, he formed a design to address her by letter, on the subject of a connexion. The only reason for not putting it in immediate execution, was the uncertainty of its success. He did not relish the idea of a refusal. She being the only lady to whom he ever thought of making an offer of his hand, he wished at least to be sensible that he was not wholly indifferent to her. He ran over in his mind every circumstance of her conduct towards him, and recognized in it a great deal of sweetness and politeness; but nothing that indicated any partiality or preference of him to any other gentleman who was a guest of the house, even for a few hours. After having deliberated for several days and nights (for so much was his mind engaged in this affair, that it deprived him of a good part of his sleep) he determined to communicate to her the sentiments with which she had inspired him, in the manner before mentioned; wisely considering that such a prize was worth endeavoring to obtain, though he should fail in the attempt. He, therefore, by the next post sent her the following letter:

"Will the amiable Miss Sheldon be offended at my consulting her on a subject, in which my heart is deeply interested? Before my late visit at L——, I had never seen the woman whom I wished to make my wife; but it was impossible to live under the same roof with you a month, to have daily opportunities of observing your numerous virtues and amiable qualities, and to remain indifferent to you. I knew not how deeply my heart was engaged, until I had quitted your hospitable mansion. I then felt in it a void, which I am confident nothing but your presence can ever fill.

We are now no strangers to each other's person, character or situation. I flatter myself, therefore, that you will not judge this an abrupt declaration, or think me presuming when I solicit the happiness of being considered as your lover. From the opinion I have of your goodness, I imagine that you will not take pleasure in inflicting pain, or keeping in suspence an honest heart, entirely devoted to you. I, therefore, beg the favour of you to grant me a speedy answer. If I find I am not agreeable to you, it will render me extremely unhappy; but if my passion meet your approbation, I shall esteem myself the most fortunate of mankind.

LYSANDER."

Upon the perusal of this letter, Dorcasina experienced but one sentiment, and that was mortification. She read it over and over again; and was, to the last degree, chagrined at his coldness. She compared it with various letters in her favorite authors, and found it so widely different in style and sentiment, that she abhorred the idea of a connexion with a person who could be the author of it. What added greatly to her disgust was that he said not a word of her personal charms, upon which she so much valued herself. Not even the slightest compliment to her person; nothing of angel or goddess, raptures or flames, in the whole letter. She determined, therefore, without much deliberation, to answer it in plain terms, and to give him a flat refusal; and accordingly wrote as follows:

"Sir—I received your letter safe by post, and will answer you with the same sincerity by which it appears to have been dictated. I know not the man who possesses a larger share of my esteem. I have noticed your good qualities, and acknowledge your merit; and your friendship I should think it an honor to deserve. But my heart is untouched; and I experienced not that violent emotion, at first sight of you, which always accompanies genuine love; nor do I think the passion with which I have inspired you, sufficiently ardent to insure my happiness; as your letter was such as I suppose your grandfather might write, were he, at the age of eighty, to take it into his head to marry. I hope you will not take amiss the freedom with which I speak my sentiments, or suppose it the effect of levity; but be assured that it is from a firm conviction, that we are not destined by Heaven to make each other happy.

With sentiments of the highest esteem,

I wish to remain your friend,

DORCASINA SHELDON."

Upon the receipt of this curious epistle, Lysander was lost in astonishment. He could hardly credit the evidence of his own senses, or believe that the agreeable Miss Sheldon could think and write in so whimsical and romantic a manner, when upon every other subject she conversed with the greatest good sense and propriety. He at length concluded that to be her weak side; and endeavored to console himself by reflecting that he was fortunate in escaping a connexion with a woman whose ideas of matrimonial happiness were too exalted ever to be realized; convinced that violent raptures are never lasting, and that the greatest connubial happiness is enjoyed, where the passion on both sides is founded on the solid basis of esteem, and heightened by a knowledge of the good qualities of the beloved object.

Mrs. Mary Clavers

Caroline Matilda Stansbury Kirkland
(1801–1864)

Caroline Kirkland, like her contemporary Sara Willis Parton
("Fanny Fern"), was one of several women writers who are
beginning to be credited—belatedly—with the origins of
realism in American literature. By countering sentimentality
and romanticism with commonsense satire, Kirkland, like
Parton, encouraged readers to take a clear-eyed view of topics
as disparate as fashions and the frontier long before the more
widely-acknowledged realistic works of Hamlin Garland and
Joseph Kirkland in the second half of the nineteenth century.
Whether or not Joseph Kirkland's realism was influenced by
his mother Caroline's work, her 1839 account of frontier life
in Michigan, *A New Home—Who'll Follow?*, presented a
view of the actualities of such life that stood in direct
opposition to the idealized images created by James Fenimore
Cooper and others. Born in New York into a literary family
(her grandfather had been a satirist during the Revolutionary
period), Caroline Stansbury married William Kirkland in
1828, and in 1836 the couple moved to the tiny settlement of
Pinckney, Michigan, in the midst of more than a thousand
acres of land that William Kirkland had purchased. For
nearly six years the Kirklands endured the deprivations of
frontier life that Kirkland describes in *A New Home* and the
subsequent *Forest Life* (1842) before returning to New York,
where Kirkland's writing and editing supported her family
following her husband's death in 1846. Kirkland's method in
A New Home is to make fun of pretentiousness, such as that
of Miss Fidler; the gossipy habits of people in a remote area;
and the lack of manners and polish of her Michigan neighbors. This last did not make her popular with her fellow
settlers; like Frances Whitcher, her contemporary, she was
resented for her satiric portrayals of silly or crude behavior,

but those who felt unfairly satirized failed to recognize that Kirkland also makes fun of her own unrealistic notions of the frontier: she comes to understand, for example, that her china soup tureen will do better service as a chamber pot, and that the mahogany cabinet that will not fit into the tiny log cabin makes a fine corn crib. In addition to its satiric realism, *A New Home* is distinctive also as a view of the woman's rather than the man's experience of the frontier, having more to do with raising children on dirt floors than with land speculation and town boosterism.

SOURCES   Keyes, Langley Carleton. "Caroline M. Kirkland: A Pioneer in American Realism." Diss. Harvard University, 1935; *Notable American Women, 1607–1950*. Cambridge: Belknap, 1971. 337–339; Osborne, William S. Introduction. *A New Home—Who'll Follow?* Rpt. New Haven, CT: Yale University Press, 1965.

WORKS   *A New Home—Who'll Follow?* (1839) and *Forest Life* (1842)

from *A New Home—Who'll Follow?*
   or *Glimpses of Western Life* (1839)

Chapter 18

Lend me your *ears*. —SHAKSPEARE.
Grant graciously what you cannot refuse safely. —LACON.

'Mother wants your sifter,' said Miss Ianthe Howard, a young lady of six years' standing, attired in a tattered calico, thickened with dirt; her unkempt locks straggling from under that hideous substitute for a bonnet, so universal in the western country, a dirty cotton handkerchief, which is used, *ad nauseam*, for all sorts of purposes.

'Mother wants your sifter, and she says she guesses you can let her have some sugar and tea, 'cause you've got plenty.

This excellent reason, 'cause you've got plenty,' is conclusive as to sharing with your neighbors. Whoever comes into Michigan with nothing, will be sure to better his condition; but wo to him that brings with him any thing like an appearance of abundance, whether of money or mere household conveniences. To have them, and not be willing to share them in some sort with the whole community, is an unpardonable crime. You must lend your best horse to *qui que ce soit* to go ten miles over hill and marsh, in the darkest night, for a doctor; or your team to travel twenty after a 'gal;' your wheel-barrows, your shovels, your utensils of all sorts, belong, not to yourself, but to the public, who do not think it necessary even to *ask* to loan, but take it for granted. The two saddles and bridles of Montacute spend most of their time travelling from house to house a-man-back; and I have actually known a stray martingale to be traced to four dwellings two miles apart, having been lent from one to another, without a word to the original proprietor, who sat waiting, not very patiently, to commence a journey.

Then within doors, an inventory of your plenishing of all sorts, would scarcely more than include the articles which you are solicited to lend. Not only are all kitchen utensils as much your neighbor's as your own, but bedsteads, beds, blankets, sheets, travel from house to house, a pleasant and effectual mode of securing the perpetuity of certain efflorescent peculiarities of the skin, for which Michigan is becoming almost as famous as the land ''twixt Maidenkirk and John o' Groat's.' Sieves, smoothing irons, and churns, run about as if they had legs; one brass kettle is enough for a whole neighborhood; and I could point to a cradle which has rocked half the babies in Montacute. For my own part, I have lent my broom, my thread, my tape, my spoons, my cat, my thimble, my scissors, my shawl, my shoes; and have been asked for my combs and brushes: and my husband, for his shaving apparatus and his pantaloons.

But the cream of the joke lies in the manner of the thing. It is so straight-forward and honest, none of your hypocritical civility and servile gratitude! Your true republican, when he finds that you possess any thing which would contribute to his convenience, walks in with, 'Are you going to use your horses *to-day?*' if horses happen to be the thing he needs.

'Yes, I shall probably want them.'

"O, well; if you want them————I was thinking to get 'em to go up north a piece.'

Or perhaps the desired article comes within the female department.

'Mother wants to get some butter: that 'ere butter you bought of Miss Barton this mornin.'

And away goes your golden store, to be repaid perhaps with some cheesy, greasy stuff, brought in a dirty pail, with, 'Here's your butter!'

A girl came in to borrow a 'wash-dish,' 'because we've got company.' Presently she came back: 'Mother says you've forgot to send a towel.'

'The pen and ink, and a sheet o' paper and a wafer,' is no unusual request; and when the pen is returned, you are generally informed that you sent 'an awful bad pen.'

I have been frequently reminded of one of Johnson's humorous sketches. A man returning a broken wheel-barrow to a Quaker, with, 'Here, I've broke your rotten wheel-barrow usin' on't. I wish you'd get it mended right off, 'cause I want to borrow it again this afternoon.' The Quaker is made to reply, 'Friend, it shall be done:' and I wish I possessed more of his spirit.

But I did not intend to write a chapter on involuntary loans; I have a story to tell.

One of my best neighbors is Mr Philo Doubleday, a long, awkward, honest, hard-working Maine-man, or Mainote I suppose one might say; so good-natured, that he might be mistaken for a simpleton; but that must be by those that do not know him. He is quite an old settler, came in four years ago, bringing with him a wife who is to him as vinegar-bottle to oil-cruit, or as mustard to the sugar which is used to soften its biting qualities. Mrs Doubleday has the sharpest eyes, the sharpest nose, the sharpest tongue, the sharpest elbows, and above all, the sharpest voice that ever 'penetrated the interior' of Michigan. She has a tall, straight, bony figure, in contour somewhat resembling two hard-oak planks fastened together and stood on end; and, strange to say! she was full five-and-thirty when her mature graces attracted the eye and won the affections of the worthy Philo. What eclipse had come over Mr Doubleday's usual sagacity when he made choice of his Polly, I am sure I never could guess; but he is certainly the only man in the wide world who could possibly have lived with her; and he makes her a most excellent husband.

She is possessed with a neat devil; I have known many such cases; her floor is scoured every night, after all are in bed but the unlucky scrubber, Betsey, the maid of all work; and wo to the unfortunate 'indifiddle,' as neighbor Jenkins says, who first sets dirty boot on it in the morning. If men come in to talk over road business, for Philo is much sought when 'the public' has any work to do, or school-business, for that being very troublesome, and quite devoid of profit, is often conferred upon Philo, Mrs Doubleday makes twenty errands into the room, expressing in her visage all the force of Mrs Raddle's inquiry, "*Is* them wretches going?" And when at length their backs are turned, out comes the bottled vengeance. The sharp eyes, tongue, elbow, and voice, are all in instant requisition.

'Fetch the broom, Betsey; and the scrub broom, Betsey! and the mop, and that 'ere dish of soap, Betsey; and why on earth didn't you bring some ashes? You didn't expect to clean such a floor as this without ashes, did you?'—'What time are you going to have dinner, my dear?' says the imperturbable Philo, who is getting ready to go out.

'Dinner! I'm sure I don't know! there's no time to cook dinner in this house! nothing but slave, slave, slave, from morning till night, cleaning up after a set of nasty, dirty,' &c. &c. 'Phew!' says Mr Doubleday, looking at his fuming helpmate with a calm smile, 'It'll all rub out when it's dry, if you'll only let it alone.'

'Yes, yes; and it would be plenty clean enough for you if there had been forty horses in here.'

Philo on some such occasion waited till his Polly had stepped out of the room, and then with a bit of chalk wrote on the broad black-walnut mantel-piece:—

> Bolt and bar hold gate of wood,
> Gate of iron springs make good,
> Bolt nor spring can bind the flame,
> Woman's tongue can no man tame.

and then took his hat and walked off.

This is the favorite mode of vengeance—'poetical justice' he calls it; and as he is never at a loss for a rhyme of his own or other people's, Mrs Doubleday stands in no small dread of these efforts of genius. Once, when Philo's crony, James Porter, the blacksmith, had left the print of his blackened knuckles on the outside of the oft-scrubbed door, and was the subject of some rather severe remarks from the gentle Polly, Philo, as he left the house with his friend, turned and wrote over the offended spot:—

> Knock not here!
> Or dread my dear.
> P.D.

and the very next person that came was Mrs Skinner, the merchant's wife, all dressed in her red merino, to make a visit. Mrs Skinner, who did not possess an unusual share of tact, walked gravely round to the back-door, and there was Mrs Doubleday up to the eyes in soap-making. Dire was the mortification, and point-blank were the questions as to how the visiter came to go round that way; and when the warning couplet was produced in justification, we must draw a veil over what followed—as the novelists say.

Sometimes these poeticals came in aid of poor Betsey; as once, when on hearing a crash in the little shanty-kitchen, Mrs Doubleday called in her shrillest tones, 'Betsey! what on earth's the matter?' Poor Betsey, knowing what was coming, answered in a deprecatory whine, 'The cow's kicked over the buckwheat batter!'

When the clear, hilarious voice of Philo from the yard, where he was chopping, instantly completed the triplet—

'Take up the pieces and throw 'em at her!' for once the grim features of his spouse relaxed into a smile, and Betsey escaped her scolding.

Yet, Mrs Doubleday is not without her excellent qualities as a wife, a friend, and a neighbor. She keeps her husband's house and stockings in unexceptionable trim. Her *emptins* are the envy of the neighborhood. Her vinegar is—as how should it fail?—the *ne plus ultra* of sharpness; and her pickles are greener than the grass of the field. She will watch night after night with the sick, perform the last sad offices for the dead, or take to her home and heart the little ones whose mother is removed forever from her place at the fireside. All this she can do cheerfully, and she will not repay herself as many good people do by recounting every word of the querulous, sick man, or the desolate mourner, with added hints of tumbled drawers, closets all in heaps, or *awful* dirty kitchens.

I was sitting one morning with my neighbor, Mrs Jenkins, who is a sister of Mr Doubleday, when Betsey, Mrs Doubleday's 'hired girl,' came in with one of the shingles of Philo's handiwork in her hand, which bore in Mr Doubleday's well-known chalk marks—

> Come quick, Fanny!
> And bring the granny,
> For Mrs Double-
> day's in trouble.

And the next intelligence was of a fine new pair of lungs at that hitherto silent mansion. I called very soon after to take a peep at the 'latest found;' and if the suppressed delight of the new papa was a treat, how much more was the softened aspect, the womanized tone of the proud and happy mother. I never saw a being so completely transformed. She would almost forget to answer me, in her absorbed watching of the breath of the little sleeper. Even when trying to be polite, and to say what the occasion demanded, her eyes would *not* be withdrawn from the tiny face. Conversation on any subject but the ever-new theme of 'babies' was out of the question. Whatever we began upon whirled round sooner or later to the one point. The needle may tremble, but it turns not with the less constancy to the pole.

As I pass for an oracle in the matter of paps and possets, I had frequent communication with my now happy neighbor, who had forgotten to scold her husband, learned to let Betsey have time to eat, and omitted the nightly scouring of the floor, lest so much dampness might be bad for the baby. We were in deep consultation one morning on some important point touching the well-being of this sole object of Mrs Doubleday's thoughts and dreams, when the very same little Ianthe Howard, dirty as ever, presented herself. She sat down and stared, awhile without speaking, *à l' ordinaire;* and then informed us that her mother 'wanted Miss Doubleday to let her have her baby for a little while, 'cause Benny's mouth's so sore that'————but she had no time to finish the sentence.

"Lend my baby!!!'—and her utterance failed. The new mother's feelings were fortunately too big for speech, and Ianthe wisely disappeared before Mrs Doubleday found her tongue. Philo, who entered on the instant, burst into one of his electrifying laughs, with,—

> 'Ask my Polly,
> To lend her dolly!'

—and I could not help thinking that one must come 'west' in order to learn a little of every thing.

The identical glass tube which I offered Mrs Howard, as a substitute for Mrs Doubleday's baby, and which had already, frail as it is, threaded the country for miles in all directions, is, even as I write, in demand; a man on horseback comes from somewhere near Danforth's, and asks in mysterious whispers for ——— but I shall not tell what he calls it. The reader must come to Michigan.

Fanny Fern

Sara Willis Parton (1811–1872)

The alliterative pseudonym which Sara Willis used for many years (Parton was the name of her third husband), coupled with her ability to write truly lachrymose prose at times, has caused some critics to classify her with the moralistic, sentimental school of female writing in the mid-nineteenth century. Yet the majority of her "Fern Leaves"—columns written for *The Boston True Flag* and *The New York Ledger*—are witty, sharp commentaries on manners, literature, and the sexes that were enormously popular in the 1850s. Though she was not, as some have claimed, the first woman to write a regular newspaper column (Frances Whitcher, at least, preceded her), she was certainly one of the most productive and successful, writing a weekly column for more than twenty years, beginning in 1851. Several collections of her columns, including the first and second series of *Fern Leaves from Fanny's Port-Folio* (1853 and 1854), sold very well, and her first novel, *Ruth Hall* (1854), provoked Hawthorne to say admiringly that she wrote "as if the Devil were in her." The novel, recently reissued by Rutgers University Press, details Willis's struggle to earn a living with her writing without the help (and at times with the active interference) of her family. Fanny Fern's columns are often responses to public statements that she finds absurd or plain wrong. Sometimes she writes monologues, sometimes conversations; her tone varies with the subject addressed, and ranges from mildly amused to sharply satiric. "Aunt Hetty on Matrimony" is an admonition to young women concerning the evils of marriage. "Women and Money" and "Mrs. Adolphus Smith" address issues of independence for women that are as important now as they were in the mid-nineteenth century.

SOURCES   Adams, Florence Bannard. *Fanny Fern; or, A Pair of Flaming Shoes*. West Trenton, NJ: Hermitage Press, 1966; Warren, Joyce W. "Legacy Profile: Fanny Fern." *Legacy: A Journal of Nineteenth-Century American Women Writers*. 2:2 (Fall 1985): 54–60; Wood, Ann D. "The 'Scribbling Women' and Fanny Fern: Why Women Wrote." *American Quarterly* 23 (1971): 3–24.

WORKS   *Fern Leaves from Fanny's Port-Folio* (1853); *Fern Leaves*, Second Series (1854) and *Ruth Hall* (1854)

from *Fern Leaves from Fanny's Port-Folio*, First Series

Aunt Hetty on Matrimony

"Now girls," said Aunt Hetty, "put down your embroidery and worsted work; do something sensible, and stop building air-castles, and talking of lovers and honey-moons. It makes me sick; it is perfectly antimonial. Love is a farce; matrimony is a humbug; husbands are domestic Napoleons, Neroes, Alexanders,—sighing for other hearts to conquer, after they are sure of yours. The honey-moon is as short-lived as a lucifer-match; after that you may wear your wedding-dress at breakfast, and your night-cap to meeting, and your husband wouldn't know it. You may pick up your own pocket-handkerchief, help yourself to a chair, and split your gown across the back reaching over the table to get a piece of butter, while he is laying in his breakfast as if it was the last meal he should eat in this world. When he gets through he will aid your digestion,—while you are sipping your first cup of coffee,—by inquiring what you'll have for dinner; whether the cold lamb was all ate yesterday; if the charcoal is all out, and what you gave for the last green tea you bought. Then he gets up from the table, lights his cigar with the last evening's paper, that you have not had a chance to read; gives two or three whiffs of smoke,—which are sure to give you a headache for the afternoon,—and, just as his coattail is vanishing through the door, apologizes for not doing 'that errand' for you yesterday,—thinks it doubtful if he can to-day,—'so pressed with business.' Hear of him at eleven o'clock, taking an ice-cream with some ladies at a confectioner's, while you are at home new-lining his coat-sleeves. Children by the ears all day; can't get out to take the air; feel as crazy as a fly in a drum. Husband comes home at night; nods a 'How d'ye do, Fan?'

boxes Charley's ears; stands little Fanny in the corner; sits down in the easiest chair in the warmest nook; puts his feet up over the grate, shutting out all the fire, while the baby's little pug nose grows blue with the cold; reads the newspaper all to himself; solaces his inner man with a cup of tea, and, just as you are laboring under the hallucination that he will ask you to take a mouthful of fresh air with him, he puts on his dressing-gown and slippers, and begins to reckon up the family expenses; after which he lies down on the sofa, and you keep time with your needle, while he sleeps till nine o'clock. Next morning, ask him to leave you a 'little money,' he looks at you as if to be sure that you are in your right mind, draws a sigh long enough and strong enough to inflate a pair of bellows, and asks you 'what you want with it, and if a half-a-dollar won't do?' Gracious king! as if those little shoes, and stockings, and petticoats could be had for half-a-dollar! O, girls! set your affections on cats, poodles, parrots or lap-dogs; but let matrimony alone. It's the hardest way on earth of getting a living. You never know when your work is done. Think of carrying eight or nine children through the measles, chicken-pox, rash, mumps, and scarlet fever,—some of them twice over. It makes my head ache to think of it. O, you may scrimp and save, and twist and turn, and dig and delve, and economize and die; and your husband will marry again, and take what you have saved to dress his second wife with; and she'll take your portrait for a fire-board!

"But, what's the use of talking? I'll warrant every one of you'll try it the first chance you get; for, somehow, there's a sort of bewitchment about it. I wish one half the world were not fools, and the other half idiots."

from *Fern Leaves,* Second Series

Women and Money

"A wife shouldn't ask her husband for money at meal-times."—EXCHANGE.

By no manners of means; *nor at any other time*; because, it is to be hoped, he will be gentlemanly enough to spare her that humiliating necessity. Let him hand her his porte-monnaie every morning, with *carte-blanche* to help herself. The consequence would be, she would lose all desire for the contents, and hand it back, half the time without abstracting a single *sou*.

It's astonishing men have no more diplomacy about such matters. *I* should like to be a husband! There *are* wives whom I verily believe might be trusted to make way with a ten dollar bill without risk to the connubial donor! I'm not speaking of those doll-baby libels upon womanhood, whose chief ambition is to be walking advertisements for the dressmaker; but a rational, refined, sensible woman, who knows how to look like a lady upon small means; who would both love and respect a man less for requiring an account of every copper; but who, at the same time, would willingly wear a hat or garment that is "out of date," rather than involve a noble, generous-hearted husband in unneccessary expenditures.

I repeat it—"It *isn't every man who has a call to be a husband*." Half the married men should have their "licenses" taken away, and the same number of judicious bachelors put in their places. I think the attention of the representatives should be called to this. They can't expect to come down to town and peep under all the ladies' bonnets the way they do, and have all the newspapers free gratis, and two dollars a day besides, without "paying their way"!

It's none of *my* business, but I question whether their wives, whom they left at home, stringing dried apples, know how spruce they look in their new hats and coats, or how facetious they grow with their landlady's daughter; or how many of them pass themselves off for bachelors, to verdant spinsters. Nothing truer than that little couplet of *Shakspeare's*—

> "When the cat's away
> The mice *will* play."

Mrs. Adolphus Smith
Sporting the "Blue Stocking"

Well, I think I'll finish that story for the editor of the "Dutchman." Let me see; where did I leave off? The setting sun was just gilding with his last ray—"Ma, I want some bread and molassess"—(yes, dear,) gilding with his last ray the church spire—"Wife, where's my Sunday pants?" (*Under the bed, dear,*) the church spire of Inverness, when a—"There's nothing under the bed, dear, but your lace cap"—(Perhaps they are in the coal hod in the closet,) when a horseman was seen approaching—"Ma'am, the *pertators* is out; not one for dinner"—(Take some turnips,) approaching, covered with dust, and—"Wife! the baby has swallowed a button"—(*Reverse him*, dear—take him by the heels,) and waving in his hand a banner, on which was written—"Ma! I've torn my pantaloons"—liberty or death! The inhabitants rushed *en masse*—"Wife? WILL you leave off scribbling? (Don't be disagreeable, Smith, I'm just getting inspired,) to the public square, where DeBegnis, who had been secretly—"Butcher wants to see you, ma'am"—secretly informed of the traitors'—"forgot *which* you said, ma'am, sausages or mutton chop"—movements, gave orders to fire; not less than twenty——"My gracious! Smith, you haven't been *reversing* that child all this time; he's as black as your coat; and that boy of YOURS has torn up the first sheet of my manuscript. There! it's no use for a married woman to cultivate her intellect.——Smith, hand me those twins.

Ann Stephens
(1810–1886)

A prolific fiction writer and editor, Ann Stephens is remembered today primarily for her contributions to the Beadle Dime Novel Series in the 1860s and for her lengthy editorship of *Peterson's Magazine*, a competitor to *Godey's Lady's Book*. Like many female authors of her day, Stephens was a major contributor to the family income and produced more than twenty-five domestic/sentimental novels, many of which were originally published in serial form in *Peterson's*. Though raised in Connecticut, Stephens lived most of her adult life in New York, where from the 1840s to the 1870s she was a popular figure on the literary scene. Stephens' own transition from rural to urban life provided background for *High Life in New York by Jonathan, Slick, Esq.* (1843), her only major foray into humorous writing; but the work also had literary progenitors, beginning with the figure of Jonathan in Royall Tyler's play *The Contrast* (1787), and including Seba Smith's "Jack Downing" letters, which began in the 1830s. Stephens adopted Smith's letter format and the device of the uneducated but sensible and moral rural fellow who comments to the folks back home on the strange customs of city-dwellers. The humor in *High Life* arises from the contrast between Jonathan's perceptions of reality and the reader's greater understanding of that reality. Yet Jonathan is not merely a figure of fun: Stephens also satirizes through him the pretense and shallowness of urban high society.

SOURCES   Morris, Linda Ann Finton. "Women Vernacular Humorists in Nineteenth-Century America: Ann Stephens, Frances Whicher, and Marietta Holley." Diss. Univ. of California, Berkeley, 1978.

WORKS   *High Life in New York by Jonathan Slick, Esq.* (1843)

from *High Life in New York by Jonathan Slick, Esq.*

Letter 14

Advice to Jonathan from the Humstead—Jonathan's criticism on his Brother
Sam's book—The ennui of Jonathan in good society—Jonathan's entre in a
Milliner's Establishment, and sad mistake about a Side-saddle

Dear Par:

It raly makes me feel bad to have you keep a writin so much advice to
me. I du want to please you; and I don't think there ever is a time in the
world when a chap can know enough to turn up his nose at his father's
advice; but it's my ginuine opinion, that when you let a feller go away
from hum, it's best to let him cut his own fodder.

You've gin me a first rate edecation for your parts, and you've also told
me to be honest and industrious, but sharp as a razor. The truth is, you've
sort of cultivated me, as you du our onion patches, but arter you've dug
them up and put the seed in, and kept the weeds out till the ginuine roots
get stuck purty deep and the tops shoot up kinder thrifty, haint you also
found it to du best to leave 'em grow accordin to natur, with nothing but
the night dew and rich arth and the warm sunshine to help 'em along; and
don't they git ripe and run up to seed and down to root, and bring in the
hard chink jest as well as if you kept diggin about 'em and trimmin 'em up
from morning till night? If you keep the weeds out when they're young,
and manure the arth well in the spring, there haint so much danger that
the soil will grow barren all tu once, or that the weeds can spring up so
quick as to choke a good tough onion. It ain't in natur, ask our minister if
it is.

Now don't you be scared about me, if I du go to the theatre once in a
while, or dress up like a darned coot of an Injun jest to see what etarnal
ninny-hammers kings and queens and quality can make of themselves. I
ain't in no danger, I can tell you. A feller that's got his eye teeth in his head
can al'ers see enough to larf at in his sleeve, and to make him pity human
natur without forgitting that he's a man, and that he was born to du good,
and not spend his hull life in trying to cut a dash. Don't you nor marm
worry about me—I may be a leetle green at fust, but I shall come out right
side up with care, yit, you may be sartin on it.

I feel sort of wamblecropped to day, par, for I've jest been a reading our
Sam's new book about the Great Western. I was up to cousin Beebe's
when he brought it hum, and begun to read it to Mary. He hadn't read

more than twenty pages afore cousin Mary made believe a headache, as women always du when they feel oneasy about anything, and she cut and run with about the reddest face I ever did see. I felt as streaked as a winter apple, and cousin John, sez he—

"Jonathan, if the folks off in Canada hadn't made Sam a judge, I'd stick to it that he wasn't a relation of mine; his book raly ain't fit to read afore the wimmen folks."

I wanted to stick up for Sam, but I'll be darn'd if I could see how to du it, for the book's an allfired smutty thing, and that's the fact; but I thought what consarned rough words the printers sometimes put in my letters to you, when I've writ something very different,—and so, think sez I, I'll put it off onto the printers and publishers; for I'll be choked if I don't believe they've made as much of a mistake in publishing the book as Sam did in writing it. So sez I,

"Sam's fust book was a peeler, and a credit to the family; and I hain't the least doubt that this one would been jest as good, if Sam hadn't strained to beat t'other, and so broke his bridle. The ginuine grit aint all sifted out on 'm, I'll bet a cookey; and I haint the least doubt that the printers spiled this one. They're etarnally twistifying my words into some darn'd thing or other that would make a minister swear. Sometimes they transmogrify what I write till I shouldn't know as it was mine; but then you know, cousin John, it aint everybody that knows how tu spell out the ginuine English as we du in Weathersfield," Cousin John he smiled, and then I kept on, and sez I,

"It raly made me grit my teeth to read sich things, and think the purty gals would believe that I writ them. I didn't blame my par," sez I, "for writing me a great long letter of admonition about sich words; but he ought to have known better than to believe I put them there. It aint in my natur to write anything than the most mealy-mouthed gal on arth mightn't read out loud afore all the chaps in creation; and if any on 'em see anything that don't come right up to the chalk, in the way of gentility, they may be sartin it aint *mine*."

My dear par, jest you keep easy about me,—and if you and marm want to jaw my body, haul our Sam over the coals and sarmonize him; you'll find fust rate picking on that goose,—but I haint but jest begun to put out my pin feathers yit.

Wal now, I may as well give you a leetle notion of my goings-on here, since I went to that smashing ball, and eat presarves with a rale queen. Somehow I've begun to git sort of tired of the big bugs and the tippies, they're all too much alike, and arter a chap's been to a few of their parties, and balls, and so on, he kinder loathes their darned soft finefied nonsense, as well as the cider and sweet sarse that they stuff a feller with.

Going among quality is like boarding at a fust rate tavern. At fust a critter don't know what to du with himself he's so tickled with the nice things on the table, but by-and-by his stomach begins to turn agin the chickens, and turkeys, and young pigs, and takes tu a hankering arter pot-luck and plain pork and beans.

This sort of feeling kinder settled on me arter the ball. I raly was eenamost sot agin the harnsome critters that sidle up and down Broadway, with leetle round things, made out of silk, about as big as a good sized toad-stool, stuck up before their faces, to keep the sun off; so I eenamost made up my mind to put on the old pepper and salts agin, see a leetle of human natur among the gals that git their own living, and work themselves to death to make them stuck up critters in Broadway look as harnsome as they du.

I'd heard say that there were lots of purty gals to work in the milliners' stores up in Division street, and in the Bowery, but somehow I didn't exactly know how to git acquainted with any on 'em. I never felt a mite bashful about scraping acquaintance with stuck up critters, like my pussey cousin's wife and Miss Miles; but when I see a harnsome innocent young gal a going out arly in the morning and a coming home late at night, and working like a dog to arn a decent living, somehow my heart rises up in my throat, and insted of shinning up to 'em, and talking soft sodder, as I du to the tippies, I feel sort of dashed, and as if a chap ought to take off his hat, and let them see that honest men respect them the more because they are alone, with nobody to take care of them.

I never see one of hem harnsome young critters going along hum, arter working hard all day, to arn something to live on, and mebby to feed their pars and mars with, but I git to thinkin how much a ginuine chap ought to prize them for keeping honest, and industrious, and vartuous, when they haint much to encourage them to du right, and generally have a good deal to tempt them to du wrong, insted of turning up their noses at 'em afore folks, or a trying to tempt them into sin and wickedness behind people's backs. It has raly made my blood bile more than ever to see foreign and dandefied chaps, like that hairy lipped Count, go by them gals in the day time, with their noses up in the air, and a looking as if the purty critters warn't good enough to go along the same stun walk with them, and the stuck up quality ladies; when any body that took pains to watch the eternal varments arter dark, might ketch them a hanging round the dark corners of the streets, and a chasing arter them same working gals like so many darn'd yaller foxes scouting round a hen coop, arter the geese and turkeys; chaps that would run a man through with a sword-cane or a bagonet if he dared to look sideways at his wife or sister, will impose on an honest gal if they can git a chance, and think it's allfired good fun tu. Darn such fellers! hangin's too good for 'em! I tell you what, par, you may talk about people's being born free and equal, and about liberty, and independence, and all that, but it's my opinion that there aint a place on arth, where the people try to stomp each down down to the dirt more than they du here in York.

Wal, I wont finish off this ere sarmon, so your minister needn't get wamblecropped, for fear I'll cut him out. But I'll jest tell you what put all these sober notions into my head.

You haint forgot that Judy White had a cousin that come here to York to larn a trade. She was a tarnal sweet purty critter when she come away from Weathersfield, as plump as a partridge, and with cheeks as red as a rosy. Judy made me promise a good while ago that if ever I come down to York I'd go and see her cousin; but somehow it does make a feller forget old friends to be always going to parties and dinners with these big bugs, and it warn't till t'other day that I thought anything about Susan Reed.

The fust minit she come into my head I up and went straight along the Bowery, detarmined to find the place that she worked at, and see how she was getting along. I had forgot the number, but when I came to a store that was all windows in front, and that had a smasher of a bonnet hung agin every square of glass, besides beautiful caps and ribbons and posies as nat'ral as life, hung up between, I made up my mind that I'd hit the right nail on the head, and so in I went as independent as a wood-sawyer's clerk.

A leetle bit of a stuck up old maid stood back of a counter, all sot off with bonnets and feathers that looked tempting enough to make a feller's purse jump right out of his trousers' pocket. She had on a cap all bowed off with pink ribbons, that looked queer enough round her leetle wizzled up face, and a calico frock, figgered out with great bright posies, besides one of them ere sort of collars round her neck, all sprigged and ruffled off as slick as a new pin. Her waist warn't bigger round than a quart cup, and she stuck her hands down in the pockets of her dashy silk apron, as nat'ral as I could a done it myself. I was jest a going to ask if Susan Reed worked there, when a lady come in and wanted to buy a bonnet. At it they went, hand over first, a bargainin and a tryin on red and yaller and pink and blue bonnets.

The milliner she put one sort on, and then another, and went on pouring out a stream of soft sodder, while the lady peaked at herself in a looking-glass, and twistified her head about like a bird on a bramble bush, and at last said, she didn't know, she'd look a leetle further, mebby she'd call agin, if she didn't suit herself, and a heap more palaver, that made the leetle woman look as if she'd been drinking a mug of hard cider.

While the lady was trying to edge off to the door, and the milliner was a follering her with a blue bonnet, and a great long white feather a streaming in her hand, I jest took a slantindicular squint at the glass boxes that stood about chuck full of jimcracks and furbelows, for there was something in one of 'em that raly looked curious. It was a sort of a thing stuffed out and quilted over till it stood up in the glass box as stiff and parpendicular as a baby's go-cart.

I jest put my hands down in my pockets sort of puzzled, and stood a looking at the critter to see what I could make on it. Arter I'd took a good squint at the consarn, up one side, down t'other, and down the middle, right and left, I purty much made up my mind that it was one of them new-fashioned side-saddles, that I'd heard tell on, and I took a notion into my head that I'd buy one and send it to marm. So when the leetle old maid cum back from the door, I jest pinted at the saddle, and sez I,

"What's the charge for that are thing?"

"Why, that pair," sez she, a sticking her head on one side, and a burying her hands, that looked like a hawk's claws, down in the pocket of her cunning short apron, "I'll put them to you at twelve dollars; they're French-made, 'lastic shoulder straps, stitched beautifully in the front, chuck fall of whalebone—and they set to the shape like the skin to a bird."

Lord a massey, how the little stuck up critter did set off the talk! I couldn't shove in a word edgeways, till she stopped to git breath, and then sez I,

"I s'pose you throw in the martingales, sirsingle, and so on, don't you?"

"The what," says she, a stepping back, and squinting up in my face sort of cross, as if she didn't like to throw in the whole harnessing at that price.

"The martingale," sez I, "and the sirsingle; but mebby you have some other name for 'em down here in York. I mean the straps that come down in front to throw the chest out, and give the neck a harnsome bend, and the thing to girt up in the middle with. Marm wont know how to use this new-fashioned thing if I don't send all the tackle with it."

"Oh," sez the milliner, "I didn't understand; you want the laces and the steel in front; sartinly we give them in. The steel is kivered with kid, and the laces are of the strongest silk."

"Wal," sez I, "I never heard of a steel martingale, and I should be afeard they wouldn't be over pliable."

"Oh," sez she, "You can bend 'em double, they give so."

"How you talk," says I, "it raly is curious what new inventions people du have, but somehow it sort of seems to me that a silk girt might be a leetle too slimpsey, don't you think so marm?"

"Lor, no sir," sez she, "they are strong enough, I can tell you; jes take a look at the Broadway ladies, they never use anything else, and they girt tight enough, I'm sure."

I hadn't the least idea what the critter was a diving at; she see that I looked sort of puzzled, and I s'pose she begun to think that I shouldn't buy the saddle.

"Look a here," sez she, a putting her hands on both sides of her leetle stuck up waist; "I've got 'em on myself, so you can judge how tight they can be fitted."

"Gaully offalus!" sez I, a snorting out a larfing, and a eyeing the leetle finefied old maid; but I didn't think it was very good manners to burst right out so, and I tried all I could to choke in. Gracious me! I think sez I, no wonder the York gals have such humps on their backs, since they've got to wear saddles like horses.

By-am-by, arter I'd eenamost bust myself a trying to stop larfing, it come into my head that the critter of a milliner was a trying to poke fun at me, cause I wanted to beat her down; for I couldn't believe the tippies quite so bad as to girt up and strap down like a four year old colt. Wal, think sez I, I'll be up to her anyhow; so I looked jest as mealy-mouthed as if I believed her, and sez I, as innocent as a rabbit in a box trap, sez I,

"If the wimmen folks have took to wearing saddles, I s'pose they haint forgot the bridles tu; so I dont care if I take this ere pair for some old maids we've got in our parts. If I had my way, they'd all be bitted the minit they turned the fust corner. Darn'd talking critters them old maids are, marm," sez I, a looking at her sort of slanting, jest to let her see she hadn't got hold of quite so great a greenhorn as she seemed to think.

Lord a Massey, how she did look! Her leetle wizzled up face begun to twist itself up till it looked like a red winter apple puckered up by the frost. I didn't seem to mind it, but put my hand down in my pocket sort of easy, and begun to whistle Yankee Doodle.

"You haint got no bridle's then?" sez I, after a minut; for she looked wrathy enough to spit fire, and sot up sich an opposition in the pocket line, that I was raly afeard her leetle hands would bust through the silk or break her apron springs, she dug down so.

"Bridles! No!" sez she, as spiteful as a meat-axe jest ground, "but I'll send out and git a halter for you, with all my heart."

"Gaully!" sez I, "but you're clear grit—smart as a steel trap, aint you?"

"Yes," sez she, more spiteful yet, "when it snaps at some animal like you, that don't know enough to keep out of its teeth?"

Think sez I, Mr. Jonathan Slick, Esq., it's about time for you to haul in those horns of your'n. You aint no match for a woman, anyhow; there never was a critter of the feminine gender, that couldn't talk a chap out of his seven senses in less than no time.

"Gaully," sez I, "you've about used me up—I begin to feel streaked as lean pork in the bottom of a barrel. I guess I shan't tackle in with a smart critter like you agin in a hurry! but don't git too mad; it'll spile that harnsome face of your'n. I swan! but I should think you was eenamost thirty this minit, if I hadn't seen the difference before you begun to rile up."

Didn't the puckers go out of her face when I said this! She was mollified down in a minit. I don't s'pose she ever had twenty years took off her good fifty so slick afore in her hull life; but it ain't human natur to come out all to once,—at any rate, it ain't an old maid's natur, when her back once gits up. So when I see her darned thin lips begin to pucker and twist into sort of a smile, I let a leetle more soft sodder, that wilted her down like a cabbage-leaf in the sun; and then sez I, a pinting to the glass-box—

"Come, now, s'posing we strike up a trade. I've took a sort of a sneaking notion to that ere new-fashioned side-saddle. So if you'll throw in the tackling, I'll give you ten dollars for it, cash on the nail."

"That what?" said she, a looking fust at me and then at the saddle, with her mouth a leetle open and her eyes sticking out like peeled onions. "That what?"

"Why, that are saddle," sez I, beginning to feel my dander rise.

"That saddle," sez she, "that saddle; why, sir, did you take that pair of French corsets for a saddle?"

With that she slumped down into a chair, and kivered her face with both hands, and larfed till I raly thought the critter would a split her sides. The way she wriggled back'rd and fored, tee-heeing and haw-hawing, was enough to make a Presbyterian Missionary swear like a sea captain.

"That saddle!" sez she, a looking up from between her hands, and then letting off the fun again as bad as ever. "That saddle! *Oh, dear, I shall die.* Did you really take that pair of *French corsets* for a side-saddle, sir? Oh, dear, I shall die a larfin!"

Didn't I feel streaked though! Only think what an etarnal coot I had made of myself, to take a pair of gal's corsets for a side-saddle. "Darn the things," sez I, and it was as much as I could du to keep from putting foot to the glass case, and kicking it into the street. I felt the blood bile up into my face, and when the old maid bust out agin, and I see a hull grist of purty faces come a swarming to a glass door, that they'd hauled back a curtain from, I could have skulked through a knot hole, I felt so dreadful mean. But by-am-by I begun to think they had more cause to be ashamed than I had. Who on arth would ever have thought them stiff indecent looking things were made for a delicate gal to wear? I felt dreadfully though, to think that I'd been a talking about a gal's under-riggin, to a woman so long, but after a few minits I begun to think that I needn't fret myself much about that. The woman that stuck them things out in the street for young fellers to look at, needn't go off in a fit of "the dreadful suz," because a chap asks the price of them. "So, who cares!" sez I.

The old maid jumped up, arter she'd larfed herself into a caniption fit, and out on it agin—and she run into the back room where the gals were. It warn't more than a minit before there was in there sich a pow-wow and rumpus kicked up,—the gals begun to hop about like parched corn on a hot shovel. They sot up such a giggle and tee-heeing, that I couldn't a stood it one minit longer. But all tu once I heard somebody say,

"My gracious, it's Mr. Jonathan Slick, from our parts!"

At that they all choked in, and were as still as mice in a flour bin. I looked to the glass door, and there stood Susan Reed, a holding the curtain with one hand and peaking through a square of glass to be sartin it was me. I tell you what, but the gal looked like a picter, and a darned purty picter tu, as she stood a holding back the heap of red cloth in her dark colored calico dress, and black silk apron that made her neck and face look as white as a lily. The rosy cheeks that she used to have in Weathersfield were all gone, and her eyes seemed as if they'd grown larger than they ever were before. I don't know when I've seen a gal that has took my notion as she did while she was a standing in that door. Arter a minit I see her fling her head back till the long shiney curls streamed in heaps over her shoulder, and I heard her say,—

"Oh, let me go out!—I'm sure it's him."

"What of that?" I heard the old maid squeak out, as sour as vinegar; "he ain't no relation, is he?"

"No, no," sez Susan, a droppin the curtain, and a speaking as if her heart was brim full and a running over; "but he come from Weathersfield,—we went to school together; he come from *home*,—I must speak to him!"

With that she opened the door and come towards me, a holding out her hand and a trying to smile; but the tears were a standing in her great blue eyes, and I raly thought she was a going to bus right out a crying. I knew she was a thinking about the old humstead, and when I remembered how them darned lawyers cheated her old mother out of house and hum, I felt so bad I could a cried tu, jest as well as not.

I went right up and shook hands, and sez I—

"How do you du, Susan? I swanny! but the sight of you is good for sore eyes; it raly seems like old times, only jest to look at you."

She kinder smiled a leetle, and sez she "How are all the folks in Weathersfield?"

"Oh, they were all so as to be drawling about when I come away," sez I. "Sally Sikes has got married, I s'pose you know."

"And how is cousin Judy?" sez she.

"Purty well, considerin," sez I; and you can't think how all-overish I felt to hear any body speak of Judy so fur from hum. I was jest a going to say something to keep her from asking anything more about the gal, when the old maid she come out, and sez she—

"Miss Reed, I don't hire you to talk with young fellers in the front shop."

Gaully! didn't my blood bile, I could a knocked the stuck up leetle varmint into a cocked hat, but Susan she looked sort of scared, and, sez she,

"Call and see me, Mr. Slick, at my boarding-house: I shall be *so* glad to talk over old times." The tears bust right into her blue eyes as she spoke, and she looked so humsick I raly felt for her.

"What time shall I call?" sez I, a follering her to the glass door.

"I haint a minit that I can call my own till arter eight o'clock at night," sez she; "but if you'll call some evening I shall be glad to see you."

"I shall sartinly come," sez I, and arter shaking hands with her agin I went out of the store and hum to my office, a feeling purty considerably humsick and with more ginuine human natur bilin up in my heart than I'd felt since I cum to York.

Your loving son,
JONATHAN SLICK

Phoebe Cary

(1824-1871)

Although overshadowed during her lifetime by her sister
Alice's literary reputation, Phoebe Cary was considered by
her biographer, Mary Clemmer Ames, to be "the wittiest
woman in America." Kate Sanborn, in *the Wit of Women*
(1885), quotes Ames as suggesting that Cary, like Dorothy
Parker in the 1920s, was known as a clever conversationalist
whose "most brilliant sallies . . . came like flashes of heat
lightning, like a rush of meteors, so suddenly and constantly
you were dazzled while you were delighted" (100). Born near
Cincinnati four years after Alice, Phoebe was encouraged in
her writing by her sister and at fourteen published her first
poem in a Boston newspaper, about the same time that Alice
published a poem in the Cincinnati *Sentinel*. Both sisters
continued to contribute poetry to journals and newspapers,
and eventually their work was published in the Boston
Ladies' Repository and *Graham's Magazine*, where it came
to the attention of Horace Greeley and Rufus W. Griswold.
After including them in his *Female Poets of America* (1849),
Griswold helped them find a publisher for their first volume,
The Poems of Alice and Phoebe Cary (1849). Encouraged by
the book's reception, Alice moved to New York, where she
was soon joined by Phoebe and where they became known
for their popular Sunday evening salons, which were attended
by leading New York literary personalities of the time. The
sisters remained in the same house, living and working
together until their deaths in 1871. Although Phoebe published only two volumes of her own work—*Poems and
Parodies* (1854) and *Poems of Faith, Hope and Love* (1868),
she was praised for her polished verse and sophisticated style.
The humor of *Poems and Parodies* derives from the cleverness with which she treats the ways in which women were
socialized to conform to prescribed roles and images. A

strong supporter of the women's rights movement, Phoebe served briefly as an assistant editor of Susan B. Anthony's paper *Revolution*, and Kate Sanborn declared "her verses on the subject of Women's Rights" to be "capital!"

SOURCES   Ames, Mary Clemmer. *A Memorial of Alice and Phoebe Cary, With Some of Their Later Poems*. Boston: Houghton Mifflin, 1882; Kolodny, Annette. *The Land Before Her: Fantasy and Experience on the American Frontiers, 1630–1860*. Chapel Hill: University of North Carolina Press, 1984; Langworthy, Margaret Wyman. "Alice and Phoebe Cary." *Notable American Women*. Vol. 1: 195–97; Sanborn, Kate. *The Wit of Women*. New York: Funk & Wagnalls, 1885.

WORKS   *Poems and Parodies* (1854)

from *Poems and Parodies*

Girls Were Made to Mourn

When chill November's surly blast
   Made everybody shiver,
One evening as I wandered forth,
   Along the Wabash River;
I spied a woman past her prime,
   Yet with a youthful air,
Her face was covered o'er with curls
   Of *well-selected* hair!

Young woman, whither wanderest thou?
   Began the prim old maid;
Are visions of a home to be,
   In all thy dreams displayed?
Or haply wanting but a mate,
   Too soon thou hast began
To wander forth with me to mourn
   The indifference of man!

The sun that overhangs yon fields,
   Outspreading far and wide,

Where thousands by their own hearth sit,
  Or in their carriage ride,—
I've seen yon weary winter sun
  Just forty times return;
And every time has added proofs,
  That girls were made to mourn!

O girls! when in your early years,
  How prodigal of time!
Misspending all your precious hours,
  Your glorious youthful prime!
Thinking to wed just when you please,
  From beau to beau you turn,
Which tenfold force gives nature's law,
  That girls were made to mourn!

Look not on them in youthful prime,
  Ere life's best years are spent!
Man will be gallant to them then,
  And give encouragement!
But see them when they cease to speak
  Of each birthday's return;
Then want and single-blessedness
  Show girls were made to mourn!

A few seem favorites of fate,
  By husband's hands caressed,
But think not all the married folks
  Are likewise truly blest.
For, oh! what crowds, whose lords are out,
  That stay to patch and darn,
Through weary life this lesson learn,
  That girls were made to mourn!

Many and sharp and numerous ills,
  Inwoven with our frame!
More pointed still we make ourselves,
  Regret, remorse, and shame!
And man, whose heaven-erected face

The smiles of love adorn,—
Man's cold indifference to us
    Makes countless thousands mourn!

If I'm designed to live alone,—
    By nature's law designed,—
Why was this constant wish to wed
    E'er planted in my mind?
If not, why am I subject to
    Man's cruelty or scorn?
Or why has he the will and power
    To make me for him mourn?

See yonder young, accomplished girl,
    Whose words are smooth as oil,
Who'd marry almost any one
    To keep her hands from toil;
But see, the lordly gentleman
    Her favors don't return,
Unmindful though a weeping ma
    And bankrupt father mourn!

Yet let not this, my hopeful girl,
    Disturb thy youthful breast;
This awful view of woman's fate
    Is surely not the best!
The poor, despised, plain old maid
    Had never sure been born,
Had there not been some recompense
    To comfort those who mourn!

O death! the poor girl's dearest friend,
    The kindest and the best!
Welcome the hour my weary limbs
    Are laid with thee to rest!
The young, the married, fear thy blow
    From hope or husbands torn;
But oh! a blest relief to those
    In single life who mourn!

The Wife

Her washing ended with the day,
    Yet lives she at its close,
And passed the long, long night away,
    In darning ragged hose.

But when the sun in all his state
    Illumed the eastern skies,
She passed about the kitchen grate,
    And went to making pies.

A Psalm of Life

What The Heart of The Young Woman Said to The Old Maid.

Tell me not, in idle jingle,
    Marriage is an empty dream,
For the girl is dead that's single,
    And things are not what they seem.

Married life is real, earnest;
    Single blessedness a fib;
Taken from man, to man returnest,
    Has been spoken of the rib.

Not enjoyment, and not sorrow,
    Is our destined end or way;
But to act, that each to-morrow
    Nearer brings the wedding day.

Life is long, and youth is fleeting,
    And our hearts, if there we search,
Still like steady drums are beating
    Anxious marches to the church.

In the world's broad field of battle,
    In the bivouac of life,

Be not like dumb, driven cattle!
    Be a woman, be a wife!

Trust no Future, howe'er pleasant!
    Let the dead Past bury its dead!
Act,—act in the living Present:
    Heart within, and Man ahead!

Lives of married folks remind us
    We can live our lives as well,
And, departing, leave behind us
    Such examples as will tell;—

Such examples, that another,
    Sailing far from Hymen's port,
A forlorn, unmarried brother,
    Seeing, shall take heart, and court.

Let us then be up and doing,
    With the heart and head begin;
Still achieving, still pursuing,
    Learn to labor, and to win!

When Lovely Woman

When lovely woman wants a favor,
    And finds, too late, that man wont bend,
What earthly circumstance can save her
    From disappointment in the end?

The only way to bring him over,
    The last experiment to try,
Whether a husband or a lover,
    If he have feeling, is, to cry!

Frances Miriam Berry Whitcher

(1814–1852)

In a short career (she died of tuberculosis before she was forty), Frances Whitcher helped to establish several significant characteristics of the female humorist in America. As would later writers, she concentrated on a women's culture: in Whitcher's case, the sewing circles of small-town New York State. Women were the chief targets of her humor, but what she satirized were characteristics such as frivolity and sentimentality that detracted from women's potential to be viewed as rational, capable people. In doing so, she implicitly indicted a culture that made women economically and politically dependent upon men and therefore competitive with each other. Whitcher thus anticipated the more overt social criticism of Marietta Holley as well as the subtle critiques of the mid-twentieth-century domestic humorists. As a child in Whitesboro, New York, Frances Miriam Berry showed a talent for visual and verbal caricature that was not appreciated by those around her; as she later wrote to a friend, "I received, at my birth, the undesirable gift of a remarkably strong sense of the ridiculous." Whitcher went on to use her "undesirable gift" in sketches that were published in *Neal's Saturday Gazette* and *Godey's Lady's Book* in the 1840s, and subsequently collected in *The Widow Bedott Papers* (1856) and *Widow Spriggins, Mary Elmer, and Other Sketches* (1867). *The Widow Bedott Papers* was, for its time, a best seller, with 100,000 copies sold within a decade. The garrulous, husband-hunting Widow Bedott was further popularized by the actor Neil Burgess in a dramatized version. Whitcher used the vernacular style popular in the early nineteenth century; her three principal narrators—the Widow

Spriggins, the Widow Bedott, and Bedott's sister Aunt Maguire—speak in the dialect of rural New York, represented by spellings such as "sich" for "such" and "shet" for "shut." Yet for all their rural ties, Whitcher's women are affected by the pretensions and pseudo-sophistication of the "cult of domesticity" that accompanied the rise of a large middle class in the 1830s and 1840s and affected behavior, taste, and fashions. Whitcher's rejection of gentility is evident throughout her work, and her use of her minister husband's parishioners as models for her characters was all too evident to them, and was a factor in the couple's move from Elmira to Whitesboro, where Whitcher died three years after the birth of her only child.

SOURCES   Morris, Linda Ann Finton. "Women Vernacular Humorists in Nineteenth Century America: Ann Stephens, Frances Whitcher, and Marietta Holley." Diss. University of California, Berkeley, 1978; *Notable American Women: 1607–1950*. Cambridge: Belknap Press, 1971. 580–81; Walker, Nancy. "Wit, Sentimentality, and the Image of Women in the Nineteenth Century." *American Studies* 22:2 (1981): 5–22; Whitcher, Mrs. M. L. Ward. "Biographical Introduction." *Widow Springgins, Mary Elmer, and Other Sketches*. New York: Carleton, 1867. 11–35.

WORKS   *The Widow Bedott Papers* (1856) and *Widow Springgins, Mary Elmer, and Other Sketches* (1867)

from *The Widow Bedott Papers*

Hezekiah Bedott

He was a wonderful hand to moralize, husband was, 'specially after he begun to enjoy poor health. He made an observation once when he was in one of his poor turns, that I never shall forget the longest day I live. He says to me one winter evenin' as we was a settin' by the fire, I was a knittin' (I was always a wonderful great knitter) and he was a smokin' (he was a master hand to smoke, though the doctor used to tell him he'd be better off to let tobacker alone; when he was well, used to take his pipe and smoke a spell after he'd got the chores done up, and when he wa'n't well, used to smoke the biggest part o' the time). Well, he took his pipe out of his mouth and turned toward me, and I knowed something was comin', for he had a pertikkeler way of lookin' round when he was gwine to say any thing oncommon. Well, he says to me, says he, "Silly," (my name was Prissilly naterally, but he ginerally called me "Silly," cause 'twas handier, you know.) Well, he says to me, says he, "Silly," and he looked pretty sollem, I tell you, he had a sollem countenance naterally—and after he got to be deacon 'twas more so, but since he'd lost his health he looked sollemer than ever, and certingly you wouldent wonder at it if you knowed how much he underwent. He was troubled with a wonderful pain in his chest, and amazin' weakness in the spine of his back, besides the pleurissy in the side, and having the ager a considerable part of the time, and bein' broke of his rest o' nights 'cause he was so put to 't for breath when he laid down. Why its an onaccountable fact that when that man died he hadent seen a well day in fifteen year, though when he was married and for five or six year after I shouldent desire to see a ruggeder man than what he was. But the time I'm speakin' of he'd been out o' health nigh upon ten year, and O dear sakes! how he had altered since the first time I ever see him! That was to a quiltin' to Squire Smith's a spell afore Sally was married. I'd no idee then that Sal Smith was a gwine to be married to Sam Pendergrass. She'd ben keepin' company with Mose Hewlitt, for better'n a year, and every body said *that* was a settled thing, and lo and behold! all of a sudding she up and took Sam Pendergrass. Well, that was the first time I ever see my husband, and if any body'd a told me then that I should ever marry him, I should a said—but lawful sakes! I most forgot, I was gwine to tell you what he said to me that evenin', and when a body begins to tell a thing I believe in finishin' on't some time or other. Some folks have a way of talkin' round and round and round for evermore, and never comin' to the pint. Now there's Miss Jinkins, she that was Poll Bingham afore she was married, she is the tejusest individooal to tell a story that ever I see in all my born days. But I was a gwine to tell you what husband said. He says to me says he, "Silly," says I, "What?" I dident say "What, Hezekier?" for I dident like his name. The first time I ever heard it I near killed myself a laffin. "Hezekier Bedott," says I, "well, I would give up if I had sich a name," but then you know I had no more idee o' marryin' the feller than you have this minnit o' marryin' the governor. I s'pose you think it's curus we should a named our oldest son Hezekier. Well, we done it to please father and mother Bedott, it's father Bedott's name, and he and mother Bedott both used to think that names had ought to go down from gineration to gineration. But we always called him Kier, you know. Speakin' o' Kier, he *is* a blessin', ain't he? and I ain't the only one that thinks so, I guess. Now don't you never tell nobody that I said so, but between you and me I rather guess that if Kezier Winkle thinks she is a gwine to ketch Kier Bedott she is a *leetle* out of her reckonin'. But I was going to tell what husband said. He says to me, says he, "Silly," I says, say I, "What?" If I dident say "what" when he said "Silly," he'd a kept on saying "Silly," from time to eternity. He always did, because, you know, he wanted me to pay pertikkeler attention, and I ginerally did; no woman was ever more attentive to her husband than what I was. Well, he says to me, says he, "Silly." Says I, "What?" though I'd no idee what he was gwine to say, dident know but what 'twas something about his sufferings, though he wa'n't apt to complain, but he frequently used to remark that he wouldent wish his worst enemy to suffer one minnit as he did all the time, but that can't be called grumblin'—think it can?

Why, I've seen him in sitivations when you'd a thought no mortal could a helped grumblin', but *he* dident. He and me went once in the dead o' winter in a one hoss slay out to Boonville to see a sister o' hisen. You know the snow is amazin' deep in that section o' the kentry. Well, the hoss got stuck in one o' them are flambergasted snow-banks, and there we sot, onable to stir, and to cap all, while we was a sittin' there, husband was took with a dretful crick in his back. Now *that* was what I call a *perdickerment*, don't you? Most men would a swore, but husband dident. He only said, says he, "Consarn it." How did we get out, did you ask? Why we might a been sittin' there to this day fur as *I* know, if there hadent a happened to come along a mess o' men in a double team and they hysted us out. But I was gwine to tell you that observation o' hisen. Says he to me, says he, "Silly," (I could see by the light o' the fire, there dident happen to be no candle burnin', if I don't disremember, though my-memory is sometimes ruther forgitful, but I know we wa'n't apt to burn candles exceptin' when we had company) I could see by the light of the fire that his mind was oncommon solemnized. Says he to me, says he, "Silly." I says to him says I, "What?" He says to me, says he, *"We're all poor critters!"*

Aunt Maguire Continues Her Account of the Sewing Society

I wish to gracious you could attend one of our Sewin' Society meetin's. You never see nothin' to beat 'em, I'll be bound for 't. We've had tew now.

At the first one, at Squire Birsley's, ther was twenty-five present. Miss Birsley had got some shirts cut out o' Cappen Smalley's cloth, and as fast as they come in she sot 'em to work—at least she gin 'em some work, but ther was so much talkin' to dew ther was precious little sewin' done. Ther tongues went a good deal faster 'n ther fingers did, and the worst on 't was, they was all a runnin' at once. Ther was an everlastin' sight o' talkin', but it did seem as if they wouldent never come to no decision in creation. 'T wa'n't expected we should dew much at the first meetin' more 'n to elect the managers, and make up our minds how often we should meet— and I begun to think we shouldent dew even that much, there was such o' sight o' discussin' and disputin' about every thing. Some was for meetin' once a week, and some thought 't was altogether too often. Some was for stayin' to tea, and some was opposed to 't. Some thought 't would be a good plan to stay and work evenin's, and some was of opinion 't wouldn't pay, bein' as we'd have to burn so many candles and lamps. Ther wa'n't nothing said about what object we'd work for at the first meetin'— thought we'd leave that till next time.

Well, we talked and talked and talked, and the upshot on't was, Miss Birsley was appointed *president*—Miss Ben Stillman, Miss Dr. Lippincott and Miss Deacon Fustick, *managers*—Polly Mariar Stillman *secretary*, and Liddy Ann Buill, *treasurer*. Moreover, we agreed to meet once a fortnight, at tew o'clock in the afternoon, stay to tea an work till dark. When we'd got through with our bisness, we had tea—quite a plain tea. Miss Birsley don't approve o' makin' much fuss for Sewin' Society— because if ye dew, ther'll be some that'll feel as if they couldent afford to have it to their houses. She dident give us but one kind o' cake, but 't was light and good, and so was the bread; and we had sliced meat and cheese. Miss Birsley dident say nothing about it but she hoped the rest would foller her example. I made up my mind *I* would any how, whether the rest did or not.

Well the ladies all eat as if they liked it, and they praised up every thing at a wonderful rate. They *never* laid tooth to such bread in all their lives; the butter was superfine; the cold meat was *delicious;* and for the cake it *was* a mystery to them how Miss Birsley managed to *always* have such first-rate cake. Miss Deacon Peaboy declared she'd eat such a hearty supper she was afraid she should be sick. After tea, Miss Jo Gipson invited us to meet at their house next time, and then we went hum. While we was in the bedroom a puttin' on our things, I heerd Miss Peabody whisper to

Miss Stillman and say, "Did you ever see any thing to beat that tea in all your born days? No presarves at all!" "I never did," says Miss Stillman. "If I can't give 'em a better tea when they meet to our house, I'll give up."

Well, at the next meetin' ther was about the same number present, and we talked up what we'd dew with the money. The difficulty was, the members couldent agree upon nothin'—some wanted to work for *this* objict, and some wanted to work for *that*. Miss Skinner and some o' the rest thought we'd ought to sew for the missionaries, but most on 'em opposed it, 'cause they wanted to *see* what become o' the money. Miss Stubbles thought 't would be a good plan to establish a school for the colored sect—I s'pose the Professor put her up to 't—but nobody else dident seem to be in favor on 't; and Sister Bedott (she attended), she said *she* never'd agree to that, 't would be money throw'd away, for niggers would be niggers, dew what ye would to elevate 'em. Miss Fustick (she come in and sot a spell with her things on—said she couldent stay long, jest dropped in on her way to the Matarnal Society meetin'), she thought we couldent dew better'n to give the avails of our labor to the "Sons o' Temperance." "Sons o' yer granny," says Liddy Ann Buill, says she (you know she and Miss Fustick's a quarrelin'.) When she spoke up so, Miss Fustick looked awful mad, and got up to go: when she reached the door, she turned round and says she, "Perhaps Miss Buill would ruther work for the Old Maids' Consolation Society' that they talk o' formin'. Good afternoon, ladies!" and off she cut afore Liddy Ann had time to answer. The gals all tittered, and Liddy Ann lookt wonderful womblescropt. I don't know but she'd a cleared out if Miss Birsley hadent a smoothed it over in her cunnin' way; she laughed, and says she, "What, Miss Buill, you gals don't mean to help the old maids, I hope? I say let 'em take care o' themselves." Liddy Ann grinned and looked quite satisfied.

Well, they talked and talked and talked, jest as they did at the first meetin', to no more purpose neither only to git more ryled up than they did then. It seemed as if every one had got a partickler pint to carry and was detarmined the rest should yield to 't. I tried a number o' times to make a proposition I'd thought on, but ther was so many that talked louder and faster 'n what I could, that I couldent for the life o' me git nobody to listen tew me. At last I went to Miss Birsley and told her my idee, and axed her what she thought on 't. She said she liked the notion. "Well, then, you propose it," says I, "for I can't git 'em to listen to me if I try till Doomsday." So she spoke out, and says she, "Ladies!" but ther was such a racket nobody dident hear her. So she tried agin: "Ladies, I say!" but still they dident pay no attention. Then she took the tongs and knockt on the stove as loud as ever she could. "Order!" says she. They stoppt talkin' then, and lookt round to see what she wanted. "Ladies," says she, "Miss Magwire has proposed an object to work for that strikes me as an excellent one. She thinks we'd better raise enough to repair the meetin' house, and for my part, I think we couldent dew better: the meetin' house is in a miserable condition; the plasterin's a comin' off in ever so many places, and the pulpit's a forlorn old thing, away up in the air; it's enough to break a body's neck to look at the minister, and shakes like an old eggshell. Mr. Tuttle says he's a'most afeard to go into it. Don't you think 't would be a good plan to tear it down and build another? Now don't all speak at once. We never shall dew nothing in creation if we don't have some sort o' order. Miss Skinner, what's *your* opinion?"

Well, Miss Skinner was delighted with the idee, and so was the Grimeses, and the Fosters, and the Peabodys. Miss Peabody said the Baptists and the Episcopals was all a pintin' at us for lettin' our house o' worship be in such a condition. Miss John Brewster said she'd long thought our meetin' house was a disgrace to the village; she'd no doubt but what 't would be an advantage to the cause o' religion to repair it, for the Widder Pettibone told her how't if we'd had a decent meetin'-house *she* wouldent a went off and jined the Episcopals, but she got so disgusted with the old nasty house and so tired a stretchin' her neck to see the minister, that she couldent stan' it no longer.

"The dear me!" says Charity Grimes, "I want to know if she gives *that* as a reason! Why, every body knows she went there 'cause Curnel Dykeman's an Episcopal."

"Yes," says Polly Mariar Stillman, "I guess it's ginerally known what took *her* there."

"She's a wonderful oneasy critter," says Miss Peabody; "she's ben a Baptist and a Presbyterian, and now she's an Episcopal. I wonder what she'll be next."

"Well, it's cause she's a widder," says Glory Ann Billins. "I never know'd a widder yet but what was as oneasy as a fish out o' water. I raly believe it's nat'ral tew 'em."

"Jest so," says Liddy Ann Buill; "widders will be widders."

"Not if they can help it," says I. I was sorry as soon as I said it, Sister Bedott lookt so mad. I tell ye she gin me an awful blowin-up when we got hum—said every body in the room thought I meant her, and she dident mean to go to the meetin' no more. I don't know whether she will or not.

Well, they'd got hold o' the Widder Pettibone, and they dident let her drop right off: if her ears dident burn that afternoon, I'm mistaken. Some on 'em got so engaged talkin' about her they stopt sewin' intirely. Bymeby Miss Birsley got out o' patience, and knockt on the stove. "Order!" says she. When they got still, says she—"When the ladies have got the Widder Pettibone sufficiently done up, I'd like to have 'em take hold and dew up ther shirts." "Law me," says old Aunt Betsy Crocker, "they ain't a dewin' her up; they're a pickin' on her tew pieces." Aunt Betsy ain't no great talker, but when she does speak she always says somethin' to the pint. She's a real clever old soul, good to every body, dumb critters and all. She was disappinted when she was young, so she hain't never got married; lives all alone; nobody in the house but her and Gruff, her old dog. She thinks the world o' Gruff. I went in to see her one evenin' last winter. Gruff was asleep on a rug behind the stove, and ther was 'a great pan o' vittals settin' by him. I thought 't was somethin' she'd sot there to warm, so I says, say I, "Ain't you afeared Gruff'll be pokin' his nose into yer meat?" "Law me," says she, "that's there a purpose for him. I always set somethin' by him when he goes to bed, so he'll find it handy if he happens to wake up hungry in the night." "My sakes," says I, "I wouldent take all that pains for a dog." "Law me!" says she, "Gruff don't know he's a dog—he thinks he's *folks*."

"Well, ladies," says Miss Birsley, "if it's a possible thing, I'd like to have it decided whether we shall repair the meetin'-house or not. I think we'd better put it to vote. Them that's in favor on't will please to signify it by holdin' up their right hand." Well, all o' the members held up their right hand exceptin' Miss Ben Stillman and Polly Mariar. "Miss Stillman," says Miss Birsley, "I see that you and Polly Mariar don't hold up yer hands. Don't you approve of appropriatin' the money for that purpose?"

"Well, I can't say as I disapprove on 't," says Miss Stillman, "but I should think we'd better not be in a hurry about makin' up our minds what we'll dew with the money."

"What's the use o' waitin'?" says Miss Birsley. "For my part, I think we should go ahead with more sperrit if we had an object fixed on to work for." "I think so tew," says Miss Stillman; "but, you know, we'd ought to be unanimous." "Then why don't you agree with us?" says Miss Birsley; "that's the way to be unanimous."

"I mean," says Miss Stillman, says she, "that we'd ought to wait till ther's a full meetin' afore we vote."

"The land alive!" says Miss Birsley, "I don't know what you call a full meetin' if this ain't one."

"The fact is," says Polly Mariar, stretchin' her great mouth from ear to ear and displayin' all her big teeth—(Jeff says her mouth looks like an open sepulcher full o' dead men's bone)—"the fact is," says she, "mar and me's of opinion that we hadent ought to vote till Miss Samson Savage is consulted."

"Miss Samson Savage ain't a member o' the Society," says Miss Birsley, "and she don't go to meetin' once in six months. I don't know what we should want to consult her for, I'm sure."

"But you know," says Miss Stillman, "her means is such that she's able to contribbit a great deal to any object she approves of."

"And we'd ought to be careful about offendin' her," says Polly Mariar, "for, you know, she withdraw'd herself from the Baptists because their Sewin' Society dident dew as she wanted to have 'em."

"Did the Baptists break down after it?" says Miss Birsley. Jest then the door opened, and in marched Miss Samson Savage. But afore I go on, I'd ought to tell you something about her. She's one o' the *big bugs* here—that is, she's got more money than a'most any body else in town. She was a tailoress when she was a gal, and they say she used to make a dretful sight o' mischief among the folks where she sewed. But that was when she lived in Varmount. When Mr. Savage married her, he was one o' these ere specilators. Wonderful fellers to make money, them Varmounters. Husband says they come over the Green Mountains with a spellin'-book in one hand and a halter in t'other, and if they can't git a school to teach, they can steal a hoss. When they first come to our place, he was a follerin' the tin-peddlin' bisness; he used to go rumblin' round in his cart from house to house, and the rich folks ruther turned up their noses at him, or he consated they did, and it made him awful wrathy; so he determined he'd be richer'n any on 'em, and pay 'em off in their own coin. Old Smith says he's heerd him time and agin make his boast that he'd ride over all their heads some day—dident seem to have no higher end in view than to be the richest man in Scrabble Hill. He sot his heart and soul and body on 't, and knowin' how to turn every cent to the best advantage, and bein' wonderful sharp at a bargain, he succeeded; every thing he took hold of prospered, and without actilly bein' what you could call dishonest, afore many years every body allowed he was the richest man in the place. So he built a great big stun house and furnished it wonderful grand; his wife wouldent have a bit o' furnitewer made here—nothin' would dew but she must send away to Philadelphy for 't. And such furnitewer was never seen in the town afore! Such elegant sofys and cheers and curtins, and ever so many curus consarns that I don't know the name of, and I guess she don't neither. So she sot up for a lady. She was always a coarse, boisterous, high-tempered critter, and when her husband grow'd rich, she grow'd pompous and overbearin'. She made up her mind she'd rule th roast, no matter what it cost—she'd be the *first* in Scrabble Hill. She know'd she wa'n't a lady by natur nor by eddication, but she thought mabby other folks would be fools enough to think she was if she made a great parade. So she begun by dressin' more, and givin' bigger parties than any body else. Of course, them that thinks money's the main thing (and ther's plenty such here and every where), is ready to flatter her and made a fuss over her, and approve of all her dewin's. If ther's any body that *won't* knuckle tew her, I tell ye they have to take it *about east*. She abuses 'em to their faces and slanders 'em to their backs. Such conduct wouldent be put up with in a poor woman; but them that would be for drummin' *me* out o' town if I should act so, is ready to uphold Miss Samson Savage, and call it *independence* and *frankness* in her. She's got so she prides herself on it. She says *she* ain't afeard to tell folks what she think of 'em—if *she* don't like any body, they *know* it purty soon. Husband says she wouldent think it no harm to set her neighbor's house a fire if she done it in the *day-time*. She shows her independence in another way sometimes, by riggin' out in old duds that would disgrace a washerwoman, and trainin' round town, makin' calls and so forth, sometimes in an old wagin and sometimes afoot. It tickles her wonderfully to hear folks whisper as she goes along—"Jest see Miss Savage! that'll dew for *her,* but 't wouldent do for every body."

When she goes out in company, she 'nopolizes the hull o' the con-versation. She's determind that every body in the room shall have the benefit of all *she* has to say. So she talks up so awful loud that she drownds every body else's voice, and they have to listen tew her whether or no. I was to a party a spell ago where she was, and from the minnit she come in—(thank fortin' she never comes arly—always keeps the tea a waitin' for her)—I say, from the minnit she come till it broke up, she talked without ceesation. It did seem to me as if I should go distracted. In the course o' the evenin', somebody axed Pardon Pettibone's wife (she 't was Katy Carey) to play on the pianner and sing: she's a beautiful player, and I'm very fond o' hearin' her. When she sot down to the music, thinks me, Miss

Savage *will* hold her tongue now, I'm sure. But I was mistaken. *She* wa'n't a gwine to be put down by a pianner, not she, so she just pitched her voice a peg higher and went on with her stuff—all about her hired help—what Bets, the cook, done; how Suke, the chambermaid, managed, and how Nab, the washerwoman, carried sail. I couldent take no sense o' the music at all. Miss Stillman and Polly Mariar, and a few more, draw'd up round her and swallered all she said, but some o' the young folks that wanted to hear the music, lookt as if they wished Miss Samson Savage was furder.

But it's plain to be seen with all her pretensions she feels oneasy and oncomfortable the hull time. I've noticed that yer *codfish gentility* always dew. She knows she ain't the *ginniwine article,* and so she tries to make up for 't in brass and bluster. If any thing goes on without her bein' head man, she always tries to put it down. She was gone a journey when the Sewin' Society was started, and I s'pose she was awful mad to think we darst to git up such a thing without consultin' her. Miss Birsely called on her when she got hum, and axed her to jine. but she said she wouldent— she despised Sewin' Societies, dident want nothin' to dew with 'em. Miss Birsley dident tell nobody what she said but me; she know'd 't would make some o' the wimmin mad and scare the rest—but we both know'd 't wouldent be long afore she'd be pokin' her nose in among us.

Well, as I said afore, she came a marchin' into the room where we all sot. She's a great, tall, raw-boned woman, and she steps off like a trainer. She had on a dirty pink sun-bunnit, and an old ragged blue calicer open-gownd (what Jeff calls a *shelaly*) over her dress. She dident so much as say "How-de-dew" to nobody, but strammed right across the room and sot down; then she huv her old sun-bunnit onto the floor, and draw'd a long breath, and say she—"Well, I vow I'm tired—ben round a shoppin', and shoppin's no small bisness with me. I don't go into a shop and stan' an hour, and make the clerks haul down all ther goods, and then buy *tew-cents' worth,* as some folks dew"—here she lookt round at Miss Grimes and Charity—"when *I* trade, I trade to some amount, and no mistake. I was ruther tired afore I left hum—had company to dinner—dident think o' comin' here when I come out—" Caroline Gipson thought she was a gwine to apologize for her dress, so she says says she, "Oh, no apolgoies necessary—'t was jest as well to come in as you was." "What!" says she, "I hope ye don't think I'd a dressed up if I *had* a know'd I was a comin' here?—not I. I don't believe in riggin' up to come to a sewin' meeting' as some folks dew"—(here she squinted at the Skinners—they had on new plaid dresses)—"but 't ain't every body that can *afford* to wear an old double gownd. I says to Poll, my waitin'-maid, "Poll,' says I, 'go to the lumber-room and git my sun-bunnit and my blue calicer double gowned; I'm a gwine out.' 'Massy sakes!' says Poll says she, 'does Miss Savage know 't the blue double gownd has got one sleeve a' most ripped out, and the linnin's all tore so 't it hangs down below the outside round the bottom?' 'Poll," says I, 'if 't wa'n't that you've jest come out o' Pennsylvany woods, and don't know nothing' about manners yet, I'd discharge ye on the spot for darin' to question *me,* or make any remarks about what I order. I'll forgive ye this time on account o' yer ignorance, but if ever you dew it agin you'll git your walkin'-ticket on short order, as sure as my name's Miss Samson Savage. Now start yer stumps, and fetch them things quick meeter.' So she fetcht 'em, and I went and done my shoppin. On my way hum, it struck me that you was to meet here to-day, so thinks me, I'll jest step in and see what they're up tew." "Will you take some sewin'?" says Miss Birsley. "Not I," says she, "till I know what I'm a sewin' for. What do ye calculate to dew with the money ye raise?"

"We thought," says Miss Birsley, "that is, the majority of us thought 't would be a good idee to arn enough to repair the meetin'-house and build a new pulpit." "Murder!" says Miss Savage; "well, I vow if that wouldent be a *worthy* object." "So you don't approve on 't, hey?" says Miss Birsley. "Approve on 't?" says she; "not I."

"No more don't me and Polly Mariar," says Miss Stillman. Miss Savage went on: "I'd look purty, wouldent I, a workin' to fix up that meetin'-house for Tuttle to preach in!" "So you don't like Mr. Tuttle, hey?" says Miss Birsley. "Like him?" says she; "not I. He don't know nothin'—can't preach no more'n *that stove-pipe*"—(she hates Parson Tuttle 'cause he hain't never paid no more attention to her than he has to the rest o' the congregation)—"he's as green as grass and as flat as a pancake." "That's jest what mar and me thinks," says Polly Mariar Stillman. Miss Savage went on: "He don't know B from a broomstick, nor bran when the bag's open." "That's jest what I think," says Miss Stillman. "I says to Mr. Stillman last Sabbath, as we was a comin' from meetin', 'Mr. Stillman' say I"—But what 't was she said to Mr. Stillman, dear knows, for Miss Savage dident let her go on. "I say," says she, "I'd look beautiful a comin' to Sewin' Society and workin' the ends o' my fingers off to build a pulpit for Tuttle to be poked up in Sabbath after Sabbath, and preach off jest what he's a mind tew. No—ye don't ketch me a takin' a stich for such an object. I despise Tuttle, and I'll tell him so tew his face when I git a chance. Ye don't ketch me a slanderin' folks behind ther backs and then soft-soapin' 'em to their faces, as some folks dew"—(here she lookt at Miss Stillman and Polly Mariar.) "And where's his wife, I'd like to know? Why ain't *she* here to work to-day? A purty piece o' bisness, I must say, for you all to be here a diggin' away to fix up Tuttle's meetin'-house, when *she's* to hum a playin' *lady*." "Miss Tuttle ain't very well,' says I. "That's a likely story," says Miss Savage; and from that she went on and blazed away about Miss Tuttle at a terrible rate. Miss Stillman and Polly Mariar, and a number more o' the wimmin, sot tew and helped her whenever they could git a word in edgeways; and such a haulin' over as Miss Tuttle and the parson got, I never heerd afore in all the days o' my life.

While they was in the midst on 't, Miss Gipson come to the door and axed us to walk out to tea—she'd ben out all the afternoon a gittin' it reddy—so we put up our work and went out. We don't have the tea handed round at our meetin's as a gineral thing; we have the things sot on a long table; the woman o' the house pours tea at one end, and we all stan' round and help ourselves. It's very convenient, especially where they don't keep no help. Well, we all took hold, and for a while Parson Tuttle and his wife and every body else had a restin' spell, for even Miss Samson Savage had other use for her tongue. She believes in dewin' one thing to once. When *she* eats she *eats*—and when she talks she talks.

And we had a real nice tea, I tell ye—biscuit and butter, and crackers and cheese, and cold meat and pickles, and custard and whipt cream, and three kinds o' presarves, and four kinds o' cake, and what not! I couldent help o' thinkin' that the money laid out on that tea would a went a good way toward the new pulpit.

"What delightful biscuit," says Miss Grimes. "They are *so*," says Miss Skinner; "but Miss Gipson never has poor biscuit." "O shaw!" says Miss Gipson, "you ain't in arnest: my biscuits is miserable—not nigh so good as common. I don't think the flour's first rate." "Miss Gipson, how *dew* you make crackers?" says Miss Stillman; "I never tasted none so good." "Now you don't *mean* so," says Miss Gipson. "I *can* make good crackers, but them's very poor; the oven wa'n't jest right when I put 'em in." "I *must* have another piece o' this cheese, it's *so* good," says Miss Lippincott. "Where *did* you git it?" "Well, I got it of old Daddy Sharp: he ginerally makes excellent cheese, but I tell Mr. Gipson old Sharp's failed for once— that's what I call *poor* cheese." "Dew taste o' this plum sass, Miss Peabody," says Miss Brewster; "I never see the beat on 't." "I'd ruther have these peaches," says Miss Peabody; "they're *derlicious*. It is a mystery to me how Miss Gipson always has such luck with her presarves. I never dew, and I always take pound for pound tew." "This apple-jel's the clearest I ever see," says old Miss Parker. "How *did* you make it, Miss Gipson? Dident you dew it in the sun? I'm sure it don't look as if it ever was nigh the fire." "Now don't speak o' that jel," says Miss Gipson. "I told Carline I was ashamed o' my jell after seein' Miss Parker's, and I was a'most sorry I'd made any presarves since I'd eat some o' Miss Peabody's and Miss Skinner's, theirn was *so* much nicer." So they went on. The whipt cream and custard had to be gone over: Miss Gipson had to tell jest how 't was made—what flavorin' she used, and all that—though she declared she was ashamed on 't. The *cake* was praised up: they must know how much butter ther was in *this*, how many eggs it took for *that* and so forth. Miss Gipson, of course, run it down—she *could* make good cake, but somehow she failed that time. A person that dident know how wimmin always go on at such a place, would a thought that Miss Gipson had tried to have every thing the miserablest she possibly could, and that the rest on 'em had never had any thing to hum but what was miserabler yet.

Well, every thing arthly comes to an end, and so did that tea after a spell, and purty soon after we went hum. Miss Stillman invited us to meet to their house next time. She urged Miss Sampson Savage to come, and I don't doubt but what she will if she thinks ther's any chance for kickin' up a muss. I was in to Miss Birsley's the next day, and she and I talked it over. She says we hain't accomplished much yit, for some o' the work's done so miserable 't won't never sell in creation without it's picked out and done over better. The rest is put together wrong, and has got to be took to pieces whether or no. For my part, I feel eny most discouraged about the Sewin' Society.

Emily Dickinson
(1830–1886)

Long an almost mythic figure because of her life-long reclusiveness and the posthumous publication of the vast majority of her 1775 poems, Emily Dickinson has often been regarded as a poet obsessed by death and unrequited love. Yet her poetry is often playful, irreverent, even satiric, and reveals a probity and an active intelligence that belie the supposed insularity of her life. Dickinson lived all of her life in Amherst, Massachusetts; she traveled only occasionally during her youth, and spent one year at Mt. Holyoke Female Seminary, where the pressure to become a church member (which she—alone among the members of her family—never did) and an intense longing for her Amherst home combined to curtail her studies. Thereafter Dickinson stayed at home, observing life around her, speculating about love, passion, death, immortality, and friendship. Her poems are the record of these observations and speculations, set forth in a cryptic, highly metaphoric style. Her tone is by turns anguished, detached, and amused; she wrote about death with cool curiosity, and about loved ones with passionate longing. Dickinson's humorous poetry takes a skeptical view of a patriarchal conception of God, delights in minute details of the natural world, and satirizes—as had Frances Whitcher before her—the "cult of gentility" that affected the "gentlewomen" of her day. Her own refusal to be categorized—"I'm Nobody! Who are you?"—together with her insistence on an extremely private life has caused her to seem at times more enigma than poet, but since the publication of her *Complete Poems* in 1955 scholars have restored Dickinson to her rightful place as one of America's most innovative poets.

SOURCES   Juhasz, Suzanne. *The Undiscovered Country: Emily Dickinson and the Space of the Mind.* Bloomington: Indiana University Press, 1983; Sewall,

Richard B. *The Life of Emily Dickinson*. New York: Farrar, Straus and Giroux, 1974; Walker, Nancy. "Emily Dickinson and the Self: Humor as Identity." *Tulsa Studies in Women's Literature* 2:1 (Spring 1983): 57–68.

WORKS   *The Complete Poems of Emily Dickinson* (1955)

213

Did the Harebell loose her girdle
To the lover Bee
Would the Bee the Harebell *hallow*
Much as formerly?

Did the "Paradise"—persuaded—
Yield her moat of pearl—
Would the Eden *be* an Eden,
Or the Earl—an *Earl?*

288

I'm Nobody! Who are you?
Are you—Nobody—Too?
Then there's a pair of us?
Don't tell! they'd advertise—you know!

How dreary—to be—Somebody!
How public—like a Frog—
To tell one's name—the livelong June—
To an admiring Bog!

401

What Soft—Cherubic Creatures—
These Gentlewomen are—

One would as soon assault a Plush—
Or violate a Star—

Such Dimity Convictions—
A Horror so refined
Of freckled Human Nature—
Of Deity—ashamed—

It's such a common—Glory—
A Fisherman's—Degree—
Redemption—Brittle Lady—
Be so—ashamed of Thee—

987

The Leaves like Women interchange
Exclusive Confidence—
Somewhat of nods and somewhat
Portentous inference.

The Parties in both cases
Enjoining secrecy—
Inviolable compact
To notoriety.

1333

A little Madness in the Spring
Is wholesome even for the King,
But God be with the Clown—
Who ponders this tremendous scene—
This whole Experiment of Green—
As if it were his own!

1672

Lightly stepped a yellow star
To its lofty place—
Loosed the Moon her silver hat
From her lustral Face—
All of Evening softly lit
As an Astral Hall—
Father, I observed to Heaven,
You are punctual.

Harriet Beecher Stowe

(1811–1896)

It is probably apocryphal that following the record-setting sales of Stowe's *Uncle Tom's Cabin*, Abraham Lincoln greeted her as "the little lady who made this great big war," but Stowe's career as a writer was largely devoted to ethical and moral causes such as slavery. The Beecher family, in which nearly all the men were ministers, lived until 1832 in New England, where abolitionist feeling ran high, and then moved to Cincinnati, at the edge of "free" territory. While teaching at her sister Catherine's Western Female Institute, Harriet began writing sketches for periodicals and envisioned a literary career, but her marriage to Calvin Stowe in 1836 and the birth of five children in seven years slowed her progress. The religious and social zeal that caused her to write *Uncle Tom's Cabin*, however, unleashed a flood of productivity that lasted for more than twenty years; Stowe wrote essays on domestic life, sentimental novels, and sketches of New England customs and manners that antici-pated the regional realism of Mary Wilkins Freeman and Sarah Orne Jewett. The keen eye for detail and ear for dialect that made her anti-slavery novels so compelling is also evident in Stowe's New England stories, such as "The Minis-ter's Housekeeper." In these stories she adopts the narrative stance of Sam Lawson, a stereotypically lazy, kind storyteller complete with a nagging wife similar to Washington Irving's Dame Van Winkle. The tone of the stories is droll, in contrast to the polemical fervor of much of Stowe's work, but she uses the indirect method of humor to comment incisively on women's domestic lives and their relationships with men.

SOURCES   Adams, John R. *Harriet Beecher Stowe*. New York: D. Appleton-Century, 1963; Douglas, Ann. *The Feminization of American Culture*. New

York: Knopf, 1977; Rugoff, Milton. *The Beechers: An American Family in the Nineteenth Century*. New York: Harper & Row, 1981.

WORKS   *Oldtown Folks* (1869) and *Sam Lawson's Oldtown Fireside Stories* (1872)

from *Sam Lawson's Stories*

The Minister's Housekeeper

Donne—The shady side of a blueberry-pasture.—Sam Lawson with the boys, picking blueberries.-Sam, *loq.*

Wal, you see, boys, 'twas just here,—Parson Carryl's wife, she died along in the forepart o'March: my cousin Huldy, she undertook to keep house for him. The way on't was, that Huldy, she went to take care o' Mis'Carryl in the fust on't, when she fust took sick. Huldy was a tailoress by trade; but then she was one o' these 'ere facultised persons that has a gift for most anything, and that was how Mis Carryl come to set sech store by her, that, when she was sick, nothin' would do for her but she must have Huldy round all the time: and the minister, he said he'd make it good to her all the same, and she shouldn't lose nothin' by it. And so Huldy, she staid with Mis' Carryl full three months afore she died, and got to seein' to everything pretty much round the place.

"Wal, arter Mis' Carryl died, Parson Carryl, he'd got so kind o' used to hevin' on her 'round, takin' care o' things, that he wanted her to stay along a spell; and so Huldy, she staid along a spell, and poured out his tea, and mended his close, and made pies and cakes, and cooked and washed and ironed, and kep' every thing as neat as a pin. Huldy was a dreful chipper sort o'gal; and work sort o' rolled off from her like water off a duck's back. There warn't no gal in Sherburne that could put sich a sight o work through as Huldy; and yet, Sunday mornin', she always come out in the singers' seat like one o' these 'ere June roses, lookin' so fresh and smilin', and her voice was jest as clear and sweet as a meadow lark's—Lordy massy! I 'member how she used to sing some o' them 'are places where the treble and counter used to go together: her voice kind o' trembled a little, and it sort o' went thro' and thro' a feller! tuck him right where he lived!"

Here Sam leaned contemplatively back with his head in a clump of sweet fern, and refreshed himself with a chew of young wintergreen. "This 'ere young wintergreen, boys, is jest like a feller's thoughts o' things that happened when he was young: it comes up jest so fresh and tender every year, the longest time you hev to live; and you can't help chawin' on't tho' 'tis sort o' stingin'. I don't never get over likin' young wintergreen."

"But about Huldah, Sam?"

"Oh, yes! about Huldy. Lordy massy! when a feller is Indianin' round, these 'ere pleasant summer days, a feller's thoughts gits like a flock o' young partridges: they's up and down and everywhere; 'cause one place is jest about as good as another, when they's all so kind o' comfortable and nice. Wal, about Huldy,—as I was a sayin'. She was jest as handsome a gal to look at as a feller could have; and I think a nice, well-behaved young gal in the singers' seat of a Sunday is a means o' grace: it's sort o' drawin' to the unregenerate, you know. Why, boys, in them days, I've walked ten miles over to Sherburne of a Sunday mornin', jest to play the bass-viol in the same singers' seat with Huldy. She was very much respected, Huldy was; and, when she went out to tailorin', she was allers bespoke six months ahead, and sent for in waggins up and down for ten miles round; for the young fellers was allers 'mazin' anxious to be sent after Huldy, and was quite free to offer to go for her. Wal, after Mis' Carryl died, Huldy got to be sort o' housekeeper at the minister's, and saw to every thing, and did every thing: so that there warn't a pin out o' the way.

"But you know how 'tis in parishes: there allers is women that thinks the minister's affairs belongs to them, and they ought to have the rulin' and guidin' of 'em; and, if a minister's wife dies, there's folks that allers has their eyes open on providences,—lookin' out who's to be the next one.

"Now, there was Mis' Amaziah Pipperidge, a widder with snappin' black eyes, and a hook nose,—kind o like a hawk; and she was one o' them up-and-down commandin' sort o' women, that feel that they have a call to be seein' to every thing that goes on in the parish, and 'specially to the minister.

"Folks did say that Mis' Pipperidge sort o' sot her eye on the parson for herself: wal, now that 'are might a been, or it might not. Some folks thought it was a very suitable connection. You see she hed a good property of her own, right nigh to the minister's lot, and was allers kind o' active and busy; so, takin' one thing with another, I shouldn't wonder if

Mis' Pipperidge should a thought that Providence p'inted that way. At any rate, she went up to Deakin Blodgett's wife, and they two sort o' put their heads together a mournin' and condolin' about the way things was likely to go on at the minister's now Mis' Carryl was dead. Ye see, the parson's wife, she was one of them women who hed their eyes everywhere and on every thing. She was a little thin woman, but tough as Inger rubber, and smart as a steel trap; and there warn't a hen laid an egg, or cackled, but Mis' Carryl was right there to see about it; and she hed the garden made in the spring, and the medders mowed in summer, and the cider made, and the corn husked, and the apples got in the fall and the doctor, he hedn't nothin' to do but jest sit stock still a meditatin' on Jerusalem and Jericho and them things that ministers think about. But Lordy massy! he didn't know nothin' about where any thing he eat or drunk or wore come from or went to: his wife jest led him 'round in temporal things and took care on him like a baby.

"Wal, to be sure, Mis' Carryl looked up to him in spirituals, and thought all the world on him; for there warn't a smarter minister no where 'round. Why, when he preached on decrees and election, they used to come clear over from South Parish, and West Sherburn, and Old Town to hear him; and there was sich a row o' waggins tied along by the meetin'-house that the stables was all full, and all the hitchin'-posts was full clean up to the tavern, so that folks said the doctor made the town look like a gineral trainin'-day a Sunday.

"He was gret on texts, the doctor was. When he hed a p'int to prove, he'd jest go thro' the Bible, and drive all the texts ahead o' him like a flock o' sheep; and then, if there was a text that seemed agin him, why, he'd come out with his Greek and Hebrew, and kind o' chase it 'round a spell, jest as ye see a fellar chase a contrary bell-wether, and make him jump the fence arter the rest. I tell you, there wa'n't no text in the Bible that could stand agin the doctor when his blood was up. The year arter the doctor was app'inted to preach the 'lection sermon in Boston, he made such a figger that the Brattlestreet Church sent a committee right down to see if they couldn't get him to Boston; and then the Sherburne folks, they up and raised his salary; ye see, there ain't nothin' wakes folks up like somebody else's wantin' what you've got. Wal, that fall they made him a doctor o' Divinity at Cambridge College, and so they sot more by him than ever. Wal, you see, the doctor, of course he felt kind o' lonesome and afflicted when Mis' Carryl was gone; but railly and truly, Huldy was so up to every thing about house, that the doctor didn't miss nothin' in a temporal way. His shirt-bosoms was pleated finer than they ever was, and them ruffles 'round his wrist was kep' like the driven snow; and there warn't a brack in his silk stockin's, and his shoe buckles was kep' polished up, and his coats brushed, and then there warn't no bread and biscuit like Huldy's; and her butter was like solid lumps o' gold; and there wern't no pies to equal hers; and so the doctor never felt the loss o' Miss Carryl at table. Then there was Huldy allers oppisite to him, with her blue eyes and her cheeks like two fresh peaches. She was kind o' pleasant to look at; and the more the doctor looked at her the better he liked her; and so things seemed to be goin' on quite quiet and comfortable ef it hadn't been that Mis' Pipperidge and Mis' Deakin Blodgett and Mis' Sawin got their heads together a talkin' about things.

" 'Poor man,' says Mis' Pipperidge, 'what can that child that he's got there do towards takin' the care of all that place? It takes a mature woman,' she says, 'to tread in Mis' Carryl's shoes.'

" 'That it does,' said Mis' Blodgett; 'and, when things once get to runnin' down hill, there ain't no stoppin' on 'em,' says she.

"Then Mis' Sawin she took it up. (Ye see, Mis' Sawin used to go out to dress-makin', and was sort o jealous, 'cause folks sot more by Huldy than they did by her). 'Well,' says she, 'Huldy Peters is well enough at her trade. I never denied that, though I do say I never did believe in her way o' makin' button-holes; and I must say, if 't was the dearest friend I hed, that I thought Huldy tryin' to fit Mis' Kittridge's plumb-colored silk was a clear piece o' picsumption; the silk was jist spiled, so 'twarnt's fit to come into the meetin'-house. I must say, Huldy's a gal that's always too ventersome about takin' 'sponsibilities she don't know nothing' about.'

" 'Of course she don't," said Mis' Deakin Blodgett. 'What does she know about all the lookin' and seein' to that there ought to be in guidin' the minister's house. Huldy's well meanin', and she's good at her work, and good in the singers' seat; but Lordy massy! she hain't got no experience. Parson Carryl ought to have an experienced woman to keep house for him. There's the spring house-cleanin' and the fall house-cleanin' to be seen to, and the things to be put away from the moths; and then the gettin' ready for the association and all the ministers' meetin's; and the makin' the soap and the candles, and settin' the hens and turkeys, watchin' the calves, and seein' after the hired men and the garden; and there that 'are blessed man jist sets there at home as serene, and has nobody 'round but that 'are gal, and, don't even know how things must be a runnin' to waste!'

"Wal, the upshot on't was, they fussed and fuzzled and wuzzled till they'd drinked up all the tea in the teapot; and then they went down and called on the parson, and wuzzled him all up talkin' about this, that, and t'other that wanted lookin' to, and that it was no way to leave every thing to a young chit like Huldy, and that he ought to be looking' about for an experienced woman. The parson he thanked 'em kindly, and said he believed their motives was good, but he didn't go no further. He didn't ask Mis' Pipperidge to come and stay there and help him, nor nothin' o' that kind; but he said he'd attend to matters himself. The fact was, the parson had got such a likin' for havin' Huldy 'round, that he couldn't think o' such a thing as swappin' her off for the Widder Pipperidge.

"But he thought to himself, 'Huldy is a good girl; but I oughtn't to be a leavin' every thing to her,—it's too hard on her. I ought to be instructin' and guidin' and helpin' of her; 'cause 'taint everybody could be expected to know and do what Mis' Carryl did;' and so at it he went; and Lordy massy! didn't Huldy hev a time on't when the minister began to come out of his study, and want to tew 'round and see to things? Huldy, you see, thought all the world of the minister, and she was 'most afraid to laugh; but she told me she couldn't, for the life of her, help it when his back was turned, for he wuzzled things up in the most singular way. But Huldy she'd jest say 'Yes, sir,' and get him off into his study, and go on her own way.

" 'Huldy,' says the minister one day, 'you ain't experienced out doors; and, when you want to know any thing, you must come to me.'

" 'Yes, sir,' says Huldy.

" 'Now, Huldy,' says the parson, 'you must be sure to save the turkey-eggs, so that we can have a lot of turkeys for Thanksgiving.'

" 'Yes, sir,' says Huldy; and she opened the pantry-door, and showed him a nice dishful she'd been a savin' up. Wal, the very next day the parson's hen-turkey was found killed up to old Jim Scroggs's barn. Folks said Scroggs killed it; though Scroggs, he stood to it he didn't: at any rate, the Scroggses, they made a meal on't; and Huldy, she felt bad about it 'cause she'd set her heart on raisin' the turkeys; and says she, 'Oh, dear! I don't know what I shall do. I was just ready to set her.'

" 'Do, Huldy?' says the parson: 'why, there's the other turkey, out there by the door; and a fine bird, too, he is.'

Sure enough, there was the old tom-turkey a struttin' and a sidlin' and a quitterin',' and a floutin' his tail-feathers in the sun, like a lively young widower, all ready to begin life over again.

" 'But,' says Huldy, 'you know *he* can't set on eggs.'

" 'He can't? I'd like to know why,' says the parson. 'He *shall* set on eggs, and hatch 'em too.'

" 'O doctor!' says Huldy, all in a tremble; 'cause, you know, she didn't want to contradict the minister, and she was afraid she should laugh,—'I never heard that a tom-turkey would set on eggs.'

" 'Why, they ought to,' said the parson, getting quite 'arnest: 'what else be they good for? you just bring out the eggs, now, and put 'em in the nest, and I'll make him set on 'em.'

"So Huldy she thought there wern't no way to convince him but to let him try: so she took the eggs out, and fixed 'em all nice in the nest; and then she come back and found old Tom a skirmishin' with the parson pretty lively, I tell ye. Ye see, old Tom he didn't take the idee at all; and he flopped and gobbled, and fit the parson; and the parson's wig got 'round so that his cue stuck straight out over his ear, but he'd got his blood up. Ye see, the old doctor was used to carryin' his p'ints o' doctrine; and he hadn't fit the Arminians and Socinians to be beat by a tom-turkey; so finally he made a dive, and ketched him by the neck in spite o' his floppin', and stroked him down, and put Huldy's apron 'round him.

" 'There, Huldy,' he says, quite red in the face, 'we've got him now;' and he travelled off to the barn with him as lively as a cricket.

"Huldy came behind jist chokin' with laugh, and afraid the minister would look 'round and see her.

" 'Now, Huldy, we'll crook his legs, and set him down,' says the parson, when they got him to the nest: 'you see he is getting quiet, and he'll set there all right.'

"And the parson, he sot him down; and old Tom he sat there solemn enough, and held his head down all droopin', lookin' like a rail pious old cock, as long as the parson sot by him.

" 'There: you see how still he sets,' says the parson to Huldy.

"Huldy was 'most dyin' for fear she should laugh. 'I'm afraid he'll get up,' says she, 'when you do.'

" 'Oh, no, he won't!' says the parson, quite confident. 'There, there,' says he, layin' his hands on him, as if pronouncin' a blessin'. But when the parson riz up, old Tom he riz up too, and began to march over the eggs.

" 'Stop, now!' says the parson. 'I'll make him get down agin: hand me that corn-basket; we'll put that over him.'

"So he crooked old Tom's legs, and got him down agin; and they got the corn-basket over him, and then they both stood and waited.

" 'That'll do the thing, Huldy,' said the parson.

" 'I don't know about it,' says Huldy.

" 'Oh, yes, it will, child! I understand,' says he.

"Just as he spoke, the basket riz right up and stood, and they could see old Tom's long legs.

" 'I'll make him stay down, confound him,' says the parson; for, ye see, parsons is men, like the rest of us, and the doctor had got his spunk up.

" 'You jist hold him a minute, and I'll get something that'll make him stay, I guess;' and out he went to the fence, and brought in a long, thin, flat stone, and laid it on old Tom's back.

"Old Tom he wilted down considerable under this, and looked railly as if he was goin' to give in. He staid still there a good long spell, and the minister and Huldy left him there and come up to the house; but they hadn't more than got in the door before they see old Tom a hippin' along, as high-steppin' as ever, saying' 'Talk! talk! and quitter! quitter!' and struttin' and gobblin' as if he'd come through the Red Sea, and got the victory.

"Oh, my eggs!' says Huldy. 'I'm afraid he's smashed 'em!'

"And sure enough, there they was, smashed flat enough under the stone.

" 'I'll have him killed,' said the parson: 'we won't have such a critter 'round.'

"But the parson, he slep' on't, and then didn't do it: he only come out next Sunday with a tip-top sermon on the ' 'Riginal Cuss' that was pronounced on thing; in gineral, when Adam fell, and showed how every thing was allowed to go contrary ever since. There was pig-weed, and pusley, and Canady thistles, cut-worms, and bag-worms, and canker-worms, to say nothin' of rattlesnakes. The doctor made it very impressive and sort o' improvin'; but Huldy, she told me, goin' home, that she hardly could keep from laughin' two or three times in the sermon when she thought of old Tom a standin' up with the corn-basket on his back.

"Wal, next week Huldy she jist borrowed the minister's horse and side-saddle, and rode over to South Parish to her Aunt Bascome's,—Widder Bascome's, you know, that lives there by the trout-brook,—and got a lot o' turkey-eggs o' her, and come back and set a hen on 'em, and said nothin'; and in good time there was as nice a lot o' turkey-chicks as ever ye see.

"Huldy never said a word to the minister about his experiment, and he never said a word to her; but he sort o' kep' more to his books, and didn't take it on him to advise so much.

"But not long after he took it into his head that Huldy ought to have a pig to be a fattin' with the buttermilk. Mis' Pipperidge set him up to it; and jist then old Tim Bigelow, out to Juniper Hill, told him if he'd call over he'd give him a little pig.

"So he sent for a man, and told him to build a pig-pen right out by the well, and have it all ready when he came home with his pig.

"Huldy she said she wished he might put a curb round the well out there, because in the dark, sometimes, a body might stumble into it; and the parson, he told him he might do that.

"Wal, old Aikin, the carpenter, he didn't come till most the middle of the arternoon; and then he sort o' idled, so that he didn't get up the well-curb till sun down; and then he went off and said he'd come and do the pig-pen next day.

"Wal, arter dark, Parson Carryl he driv into the yard, full chizel, with his pig. He'd tied up his mouth to keep him from squeelin'; and he saw what he thought was the pig-pen,—he was rather near-sighted,—and so he ran and threw piggy over; and down he dropped into the water, and the minister put out his horse and pranced off into the house quite delighted.

" 'There, Huldy, I've got you a nice little pig.'

" 'Dear me!' says Huldy: 'where have you put him?'

" 'Why, out there in the pig-pen to be sure.'

" 'Oh, dear me!' says Huldy: 'that's the well-curb; there ain't no pig-pen built,' says she.

" 'Lordy massy!' says the parson: 'then I've thrown the pig in the well!'

"Wal, Huldy she worked and worked, and finally she fished piggy out in the bucket, but he was dead as a door-nail; and she got him out o' the way quietly, and didn't say much; and the parson, he took to a great Hebrew book in his study; and says he, 'Huldy, I ain't much in temporals,' says he. Huldy says she kind o' felt her heart go out to him, he was so sort o' meek and helpless and larned; and says she, 'Wal, Parson Carryl, don't trouble your head no more about it; I'll see to things;' and sure enough, a week arter there was a nice pen, all ship-shape, and two little white pigs that Huldy bought with the money for the butter she sold at the store.

" 'Wal, Huldy,' said the parson, 'you are a most amazin' child: you don't say nothin', but you do more than most folks.' "

"Arter that the parson set sich store by Huldy that he come to her and asked her about every thing, and it was amazin' how every thing she put her hand to prospered. Huldy planted marigolds and larkspurs, pinks and carnations, all up and down the path to the front door, and trained up mornin' glories and scarlet-runners round the windows. And she was always a gettin' a root here, and a sprig there, and a seed from somebody else: for Huldy was one o' them that has the gift, so that ef you jist give 'em the leastest sprig of any thing they make a great bush out of it right away; so that in six months Huldy had roses and geraniums and lilies, sich as it would a took a gardener to raise. The parson, he took no notice at fust; but when the yard was all ablaze with flowers he used to come and stand in a kind o' maze at the front door, and say, 'Beautiful, beautiful: why, Huldy, I never see any thing like it.' And then when her work was done arternoons, Huldy would sit with her sewin' in the porch, and sing and trill away till she'd draw the meadow-larks and the bobolinks, and the orioles to answer her, and the great big elm-tree overhead would get perfectly rackety with the birds; and the parson, settin' there in his study, would git to kind o' dreamin' about the angels, and golden harps, and the New Jerusalem; but he wouldn't speak a word, 'cause Huldy she was jist like them wood-thrushes, she never could sing so well when she thought folks was hearin'. Folks noticed, about this time, that the parson's sermons got to be like Aaron's rod, that budded and blossomed: there was things in 'em about flowers and birds, and more 'special about the music o' heaven. And Huldy she noticed, that ef there was a hymn run in her head while she was 'round a workin' the minister was sure to give it out next Sunday. You see, Huldy was jist like a bee: she always sung when she was workin', and you could hear her trillin', now down in the corn-patch, while she was pickin' the corn; and now in the buttery, while she was workin' the butter; and now she'd go singin' down cellar, and then she'd be singin' up over head, so that she seemed to fill a house chock full o' music.

"Huldy was so sort o'chipper and fair spoken, that she got the hired men all under her thumb: they come to her and took her orders jist as meek as so many calves; and she traded at the store, and kep' the accounts, and she hed her eyes everywhere, and tied up all the ends so tight that there want no gettin' 'round her. She wouldn't let nobody put nothin' off on Parson Carryl, 'cause he was a minister. Huldy was allers up to anybody that wanted to make a hard bargain; and, afore he knew jist what he was about, she'd got the best end of it, and everybody said that Huldy was the most capable gal that they'd ever traded with.

"Wal, come to the meetin' of the Association, Mis' Deakin Blodgett and

Mis' Pipperidge come callin' up to the parson's, all in a stew, and offerin' their services to get the house ready; but the doctor, he jist thanked 'em quiet, and turned 'em over to Huldy; and Huldy she told 'em that she'd got every thing ready, and showed 'em her pantries, and her cakes and her pies and her puddin's, and took 'em all over the house; and they went peekin' and pokin', openin' cupboard-doors, and lookin' into drawers; and they couldn't find so much as a thread out o' the way, from garret to cellar, and so they went off quite discontented. Arter that the women set a new trouble a brewin'. Then they begun to talk that it was a year now since Mis' Carryl died; and it r'ally wasn't proper such a young gal to be stayin' there, who everybody could see was a settin' her cap for the minister.

"Mis' Pipperidge said, that, so long as she looked on Huldy as the hired gal, she hadn't thought much about it; but Huldy was railly takin' on airs as an equal, and appearin' as mistress o' the house in a way that would make talk if it went on. And Mis' Pipperidge she driv 'round up to Deakin Abner Snow's, and down to Mis' 'Lijah Perry's, and asked them if they wasn't afraid that the way the parson and Huldy was a goin' on might make talk. And they said they hadn't thought on't before, but now, come to think on't, they was sure it would; and they all went and talked with somebody else, and asked them if they didn't think it would make talk. So come Sunday, between meetin's there warn't nothin' else talked about; and Huldy saw folks a noddin and a winkin', and a lookin' arter her, and she begun to feel drefful sort o' disagreeable. Finally Mis' Sawin she says to her, 'My dear, didn't you, never think folk would talk about you and the minister?'

" 'No: why should they?' says Huldy, quite innocent.

'Wal, dear,' says she, 'I think it's a shame; but they say you're tryin' to catch him, and that it's so bold and improper for you to be courtin' of him right in his own house,—you know folks will talk,—I thought I'd tell you 'cause I think so much of you,' says she.

"Huldy was a gal of spirit, and she despised the talk, but it made her drefful uncomfortable; and when she got home at night she sat down in the mornin'-glory porch, quite quiet, and didn't sing a word.

"The minister he had heard the same thing from one of his deakins that day; and, when he saw Huldy so kind o' silent, he says to her, 'Why don't you sing, my child?'

"He hed a pleasant sort o' way with him, the minister had, and Huldy had got to likin' to be with him, and it all come over her that perhaps she ought to go away; and her throat kind o' filled up so she couldn't hardly speak; and, says she, 'I can't sing to-night.'

"Says he, 'You don't know how much good you're singin' has done me, nor how much good *you* have done me in all ways, Huldy. I wish I knew how to show my gratitude.'

" 'O sir!' says Huldy, '*is* it improper for me to be here?'

" 'No, dear,' says the minister, 'but ill-natured folks will talk; but there is one way we can stop it, Huldy—if you will marry me. You'll make me very happy, and I'll do all I can to make you happy. Will you?'

"Wal, Huldy never told me jist what she said to the minister,—gals never does give you the particulars of them 'are things jist as you'd like 'em,—only I know the upshot and the hull on't was, that Huldy she did a consid'able lot o' clear starchin' and ironin' the next two days; and the Friday o' next week the minister and she rode over together to Dr. Lothrop's in Old Town; and the doctor, he jist made 'em man and wife, 'spite of envy of the Jews,' as the hymn says. Wal, you'd better believe there was a starin and a wonderin' next Sunday mornin' when the second bell was a tollin', and the minister walked up the broad aisle with Huldy, all in white, arm in arm with him, and he opened the minister's pew, and handed her in as if she was a princess; for, you see, Parson Carryl come of a good family, and was a born gentleman, and had a sort o' grand way o' bein' polite to women-folks. Wal, I guess there was a rus'lin' among the bunnets. Mis' Pipperidge gin a great bounce, like corn poppin' on a shovel, and her eyes glared through her glasses at Huldy as if they'd a sot her afire; and everybody in the meetin' house was a starin', I tell *yew*. But they couldn't none of 'em say nothin' agin Huldy's looks; for there wa'n't a crimp nor a frill about her that wa'n't jis' *so;* and her frock was white as the driven snow, and she had her bunnet all trimmed up with white ribbins; and all the fellows said the old doctor had stole a march, and got the handsomest gal in the parish.

"Wal, arter meetin' they all come 'round the parson and Huldy at the door, shakin' hands and laugh-in'; for by that time they was about agreed that they'd got to let putty well alone.

" 'Why, Parson Carryl,' says Mis' Deakin Blodgett, 'how you've come it over us.'

"Yes,' says the parson, with a kind o' twinkle in his eye. 'I thought,' says he, 'as folks wanted to talk about Huldy and me, I'd give 'em somethin' wuth talkin' about.' "

Josiah Allen's Wife
Marietta Holley (1836–1926)

At the turn of the twentieth century, American readers were
probably as familiar with Marietta Holley's character Samantha Allen as they were with any figure in American
humor. In more than twenty books published between 1873
and 1914, Samantha's blend of homespun common sense
and outspoken feminism amused and instructed readers on
issues of the day: female suffrage, temperance, fashions, race
relations, and much more. Samantha's is a moderate (she
calls it "meegum") but nontheless ardent feminism. In the
dialect of rural New York State, amidst the chaos of keeping
house for her husband, Josiah, and his two children from a
previous marriage, she calls for common sense to witness and
correct social injustices and frivolities, and she pits her
strength of mind and her 204 pounds against both the sexist
and the silly. Marietta Holley, like her character, lived in
upstate New York; unlike Samantha, Holley never married
and was quite shy, refusing many invitations to speak in
public on the women's rights issues that she so clearly
espoused in print. In her youth, Holley wrote pious, sentimental poetry, as does Samantha's fictional adversary Betsey
Bobbet, and throughout her life considered her poetry to be
more important than the "Samantha" books for which she
became widely known. As if to point up ironically women's
subordination to men, Holley used the pseudonym "Josiah
Allen's Wife" for many of her books, and she uses stereotypes
to subvert the cultural assumptions that lay behind them:
thus, Betsey Bobbet is the epitome of the sentimental, clinging female through whom Holley reveals the emptiness of
that behavior, and it is Samantha, rather than her husband
Josiah, who is strong of both body and mind.

SOURCES   Curry, Jane. *Samantha Rastles the Woman Question*. Urbana:
University of Illinois Press, 1983; Morris, Linda Ann Finton. "Women Vernacular

Humorists in Nineteenth Century America: Ann Stephens, Frances Whitcher, and Marietta Holley." Diss. University of California, Berkeley, 1978; Winter, Kate. *Marietta Holley: Life with "Josiah Allen's Wife."* Syracuse: Syracuse University Press, 1984.

WORKS   *My Opinions and Betsey Bobbet's* (1873); *Samantha at the Centennial* (1877); *Samantha at Saratoga* (1887); *Samantha on the Race Problem* (1892); *Samantha at the World's Fair* (1893); *Around the World with Josiah Allen's Wife* (1905) and *Samantha on the Woman Question* (1913)

from *My Opinions and Betsey Bobbet's*

Preface

Which is to be read, if it haint askin' too much of the kind hearted reader.

In the first days of our married life, I strained nearly every nerve to help my companion Josiah along and take care of his children by his former consort, the subject of black African slavery also wearin' on me, and a mortgage of 200 and 50 dollars on the farm. But as we prospered and the mortgage was cleared, and the children were off to school, the black African also bein' liberated about the same time of the mortgage, then my mind bein' free from these cares—the great subject of Wimmen's Rites kept a goarin' me, and a voice kept a sayin' inside of me,

"Josiah Allen's wife, write a book givin' your views on the great subject of Wimmen's Rites." But I hung back in spirit from the idea and says I, to myself, I never went to school much and don't know nothin' about grammer, and I never could spell worth a cent."

But still that deep voice kept a 'swaiden me—"Josiah Allen's wife, write a book."

Says I, "I cant write a book, I don't know no underground dungeons, I haint acquainted with no haunted houses, I never see a hero suspended over a abyss by his gallusses, I never beheld a heroine swoon away, I never see a Injun tommy hawked, nor a ghost; I never had any of these advantages; I cant write a book."

But still it kept a sayin' inside of my mind, "Josiah Allen's wife write a book about your life, as it passes in front of you and Josiah, daily, and your views on Wimmen's Rite's. The great publick wheel is a rollin' on slowly, drawin' the Femail Race into liberty; Josiah Allen's wife, put your shoulder blades to the wheel."

And so that almost hauntin' voice inside of me kept a' swaidin me, and finally I spoke out in a loud clear voice and answered it—

"I *will* put my shoulder blades to the wheel!"

I well remember the time I said it, for it skairt Josiah almost to death. It was night and we was both settin' by the fire relapsed into silence and he—not knowin the conversation goin' on inside of my mind, thought I was crazy, and jumped up as if he was shot, and says he, in tremblin' tones,

"What is the matter Samantha?"

Says I, "Josiah I am goin' to write a book."

This skairt him worse than ever—I could see, by his ghastly countenance—and he started off on the run for the camfire bottle.

Says I, in firm but gentle axcents, "camfire cant stop me Josiah, the book will be wrote."

He see by my pale but calm countenance, that I was not delirious any, and (by experience) he knows that when my mind is made up, I have got a firm and almost cast iron resolution. He said no more, but he sot down and sithed hevily; finally he spoke out in a desparin' tone, he is pretty close (but honest),

"Who will read the book Samantha? Remember if you write you have got to stand the brunt of it yourself—I haint no money to hire folks with to read it." And again he sithed two or three times. And he hadn't much more than got through sithein' when he asked me again in a tone of almost agony—

"Who will read the book Samantha after you write it?'

The same question was fillin' me with agonizin' apprehension, but I concealed it and answered with almost marble calm,

"I don't know Josiah, but I am determined to put my shoulder blades to the wheel and write it."

Josiah didn't say no more then, but it wore on him—for that night in the ded of night he spoke out in his sleep in a kind of a wild way,

"Who will read the book?"

I hunched him with my elbo' to wake him up, and he muttered—"I wont pay out one cent of my money to hire any body to read it."

I pitied him, for I was afraid it would end in the Night Mair, and I waked him up, and promised him then and there, that I never would ask him to pay out one cent to hire any body to read it. He has perfect confidence in me and he brightened up and haint never said a word sense against the idea, and that is the way this book come to be wrote.

A Day of Trouble

Sugerin' time come pretty late this year, and I told Josiah, that I didn't believe I should have a better time through the whole year, to visit his folks, and mother Smith, than I should now before we begun to make sugar, for I knew no sooner had I got that out of the way, than it would be time to clean house, and make soap. And then when the dairy work come on, I knew I never should get off. So I went. But never shall I forget the day I got back. I had been gone a week, and the childern bein' both off to school, Josiah got along alone. I have always said, and I say still, that I had jest as lives have a roarin' lion do my housework, as a man. Every thing that could be bottom side up in the house, was.

I had a fortnights washin' to do, the house to clean up, churnin' to do, and bakin'; for Josiah had eat up everything slick and clean, the buttery shelves looked like the dessert of Sarah. Then I had a batch of maple sugar to do off, for the trees begun to run after I went away and Josiah had syruped off—and some preserves to make, for his folks had gin me some pound sweets, and they was a spilein'. So it seemed as if everything come that day, besides my common housework—and well doth the poet say—"That a woman never gets her work done up," for she don't.

Now when a man ploughs a field, or runs up a line of figgers, or writes a serming, or kills a beef critter, there it is done—no more to be done over. But sposen a woman washes up her dishes clean as a fiddle, no sooner does she wash 'em up once, than she has to, right over and over agin, three times three hundred and 65 times every year. And the same with the rest of her work, blackin' stoves, and fillin' lamps, and washin' and moppin' floors, and the same with cookin'. Why jest the idee of paradin' out the table and teakettle 3 times 3 hundred and 65 times every year is enough to make a woman sweat. And then to think of all the cookin' utensils and ingredients—why if it wuzzn't for principle, no woman could stand the idee, let alone the labor, for it haint so much the muscle she has to lay out, as the strain on her mind.

Now last Monday, no sooner did I get my hands into the suds holt of one of Josiah's dirty shirts, than the sugar would mount up in the kettle and sozzle over on the top of the furnace in the summer kitchen—or else the preserves would swell up and drizzle over the side of the pan on to the stove—or else the puddin' I was a bakin' for dinner would show signs of scorchin', and jest as I was in the heat of the warfare, as you may say, who should drive up but the Editor of the Agur. He was a goin' on further, to engage a hired girl he had hearn of, and on his way back, he was goin' to stop and read that poetry, and eat some maple sugar; and he wanted to leave the twins till he come back.

Says he, "They won't be any trouble to you, will they?" I thought of the martyrs, and with a appearance of outward composure, I answered him in a sort of blind way; but I won't deny that I had to keep a sayin', John Rogers! John Rogers' over to myself all the time I was ondoin' of 'em, or I should have said somethin' I was sorry for afterwards. The poetry woried me the most, I won't deny.

After the father drove off, the first dive the biggest twin made was at the clock, he crep' up to that, and broke off the pendulum, so it haint been since, while I was a hangin' thier cloaks in the bedroom. And while I was a puttin' thier little oversocks under the stove to dry, the littlest one clim' up and sot down in a pail of maple syrup, and while I was a wringin' him out, the biggest one dove under the bed, at Josiah's tin trunk where he keeps a lot of old papers, and come a creepin' out, drawin' it after him like a hand-sled. There was a gography in it, and a Fox'es book of martyrs, and a lot of other such light reading' and I let the twins have 'em to recreate themselves on, and it kep 'em still most a minute.

I hadn't much more'n got my eye offen that Fox'es book of Martyrs—when there appeared before 'em a still more mournful sight, it was Betsey Bobbet come to spend the day.

I murmured dreamily to myself "John Rogers"—But that didn't do, I had to say to myself with a firmness—"Josiah Allen's wife, haint you ashamed of yourself, what are your sufferin's to John Roger'ses? Think of the agony of that man—think of his 9 children follerin' him, and the one at the breast, what are your sufferin's compared to his'en?" Then with a brow of calm I advanced to meet her. I see she had got over bein' mad about the surprise party, for she smiled on me once or twice, and as she looked at the twins, she smiled 2 times on each of 'em, which made 4 and says she in tender tones,

"You deah little motherless things." Then she tried to kiss 'em. But the biggest one gripped her by her false hair, which was flax, and I should think by a careless estimate, that he pulled out about enough to make half a knot of thread. The little one didn't do much harm, only I think he loosened her teeth a little, he hit her pretty near the mouth, and I thought as she arose she slipped 'em back in thier place. But she only said,

"Sweet, sweet little things, how ardent and impulsive they are, so like thier deah Pa."

She took out her work, and says she, "I have come to spend the day. I saw thier deah Pa bringin' the deah little twins in heah, aud I thought maybe I could comfort the precious little motherless things some, if I should come over heah. If there is any object upon the earth, Josiah Allen's wife, that appeals to a feelin' heart, it is the sweet little children of widowers. I cannot remember the time when I did not want to comfort them, and thier deah Pa's. I have always felt that it was woman's highest speah, her only mission to soothe, to cling, to smile, to coo. I have always felt it, and for yeah's back it has been a growin' on me. I feel that you do not feel as I do in this matter, you do not feel that it is woman's greatest privilege, her crowning blessing, to soothe lacerations, to be a sort of a poultice to the noble, manly breast when it is torn with the cares of life."

This was too much, in the agitated frame of mind I then was.

"Am I a poultice Betsey Bobbet; do I look like one?—am I in the condition to be one?" I cried turnin' my face, red and drippin' with prespiration towards her, and then attacked one of Josiah's shirt sleeves agin. "What has my sect done" says I, as I wildly rubbed his shirt sleeves, "That they have got to be lacerator soothers, when they have got everything else under the sun to do?" Here I stirred down the preserves that was a runnin' over, and turned a pail full of syrup into the sugar kettle. "Everybody says that men are stronger than women, and why should they be treated as if they was glass china, liable to break all to pieces if they haint handled careful. And if they have got to be soothed," says I in an agitated tone, caused by my emotions (and by pumpin' 6 pails of water to fill up the biler), "Why don't they get men to sooth'em? They have as much agin time as wimmen have; evenin's they don't have anything else to do, they might jest as well be a soothin' each other as to be a hangin' round grocery stores, or settin' by the fire whittlin'."

I see I was frightenin' her by my delerious tone and I continued more mildly, as I stirred down the strugglin' sugar with one hand—removed a cake from the oven with the other—watched my apple preserves with a eagle vision, and listened intently to the voice of the twins, who was playin' in the woodhouse.

"I had jest as soon soothe lacerations as not, Betsey, if I hadn't everything else to do. I had jest as lives set down and smile at Josiah by the hour, but who would fry him nut cakes? I could smoothe down his bald head affectionately, but who would do off this batch of sugar? I could coo at him day in and day out, but who would skim milk—wash pans—get vittles—wash and iron—and patch and scour—and darn and fry—and make and mend—and bake and bile while I was a cooin', tell me?" says I.

Betsey spoke not, but quailed, and I continued—

"Women haint any stronger than men, naturally; thier backs and thier nerves haint made of any stouter timber; their hearts are jest as liable to ache as men's are; so with their heads; and after doin a hard day's work when she is jest ready to drop down, a little smilin' and cooin' would do a woman jest as much good as a man. Not what," I repeated in the firm tone of principle "Not but what I am willin' to coo, if I only had time."

A pause enshued durin' which I bent over the washtub and rubbed with all my might on Josiah's shirt sleeve. I had got one sleeve so I could see streaks of white in it, (Josiah is awful hard on his shirt sleeves), and I lifted up my face and continued in still more reesonable tones, as I took out my rice puddin' and cleaned out the bottom of the oven, (the pudden had run over and was a scorchin' on), and scraped the oven bottom with a knife,

"Now Josiah Allen will go out into that lot," says I, glancein' out of the north window "and plough right straight along, furrow after furrow, no sweat of mind about it at all; his mind is in that free calm state that he could write poetry."

"Speaking of poetry, reminds me," said Betsey, and I see her pocket; I knew what was a comin', and I went on hurriedly, wavin' off what I knew must be, as long as I could. "Now, I, a workin' jest as hard as he accordin' to my strength, and havin' to look 40 ways to once, and 40 different strains on my mind, now tell me candidly, Betsey Bobbet, which is in the best condition for cooin', Josiah Allen or me? but it haint expected of him," says I in agitated tones, "I am expected to do all the smilin' and cooin' there is done, though you know," says I sternly, "that I haint no time for it."

"In this poem, Josiah Allen's wife, is embodied my views, which are widely different from yours."

I see it was vain to struggle against fate, she had the poetry in her hand. I rescued the twins from beneath a half a bushel of beans they had pulled over onto themselves—took off my preserves which had burnt to the pan while I was a rescuin', and calmly listened to her, while I picked up the beans with one hand, and held off the twins with the other.

"There is one thing I want to ask your advice about, Josiah Allen's wife. This poem is for the Jonesville Augah. You know I used always to write for the opposition papah, the Jonesville Gimlet, but as I said the othah day, since the Editah of the Augah lost his wife I feel that duty is a drawing of me that way. Now do you think that it would be any more pleasing and comforting to that deah Editah to have me sign my name Bettie Bobbet— or Betsey, as I always have?" And loosin' herself in thought she murmured dreamily to the twins, who was a pullin' each other's hair on the floor at her feet—

"Sweet little mothahless things, you couldn't tell me, could you, deahs, how your deah Pa would feel about it?"

Here the twins laid holt of each other so I had to part 'em, and as I did so I said to Betsey, "If you haint a fool you will hang on to the Betsey. You can't find a woman nowadays that answers to her true name. I expect," says I in a tone of cold and almost witherin' sarcasm, "that these old ears will yet hear some young minister preach abont Johnnie the Baptist, and Minnie Magdalen. Hang on to the Betsey; as for the Bobbet," says I, lookin' pityingly on her, "that will hang on for itself."

I was too well bread to interrupt her further, and I pared my potatoes, pounded my beefsteak, and ground my coffee for dinner, and listened. This commenced also as if she had been havin' a account with Love, and had come out in his debt.

OWED TO LOVE

Ah, when my deah future companion's heart with grief is rife,
With his bosom's smart, with the cares of life,
Ah, what higher, sweeter, bliss could be,
Than to be a soothing poultice unto he?

And if he have any companions lost—if they from earth have risen,
Ah, I could weep tears of joy—for the deah bliss of wiping away hisen;
Or if he (should happen to) have any twins, or othah blessed little ties,
Ah, *how willingly* on the altah of duty, B. Bobbet, herself would sacrifice.

I would (all the rest of) life to the cold winds fling,
And live for love—and live to cling.
Fame, victuals, away! away! our food shall be,
His smile on me—my sweet smile on he.

There was pretty near twenty verses of 'em, and as she finished she said to me—

"What think you of my poem, Josiah Allen's wife?"

Says I, fixin' my sharp grey eyes upon her keenly, "I have had more experience with men than you have, Betsey;" I see a dark shadow settlin' on her eye-brow, and I hastened to apologise—"you haint to blame for it, Betsey—we all know you haint to blame."

She grew calm, and I proceeded, "How long do you suppose you could board a man on clear smiles, Betsey—you jest try it for a few meals and you'd find out. I have lived with Josiah Allen 14 years, and I ought to know somethin' of the natur of man, which is about alike in all of 'em, and I say, and I contend for it, that you might jest as well try to cling to a bear as to a hungry man. After dinner, sentiment would have a chance, and you might smile on him. But then," says I thoughtfully, "there is the dishes to wash."

Jest at that minute the Editor of the Augur stopped at the gate, and Betsey, catchin' up a twin on each arm, stood up to the winder, smilin'.

He jumped out, and took a great roll of poetry out from under the buggy seat—I sithed as I see it. But fate was better to me than I deserved. For Josiah was jest leadin' the horse into the horse barn, when the Editor happened to look up and see Betsey. Josiah says he swore—says he "the d——!" I won't say what it was, for I belong to the meetin' house, but it wasn't the Diety though it begun with a D. He jumped into the buggy agin, and says Josiah,

"You had better stay to dinner, my wife is gettin' a awful good one—and the sugar is most done."

Josiah says he groaned, but he only said—

"Fetch out the twins."

Says Josiah, "You had better stay to dinner—you haint got no women folks to your house—and I know what it is to live on pancakes," and wantin' to have a little fun with him, says he, "Betsey Bobbet is here."

Josiah says he swore agin, and agin says he, "fetch out the twins." And he looked so kind o' wild and fearful towards the door, that Josiah started off on the run.

Betsey was determined to carry one of the twins out, but jest at the door he tore every mite of hair offen her head, and she, bein' bald naturally, dropped him. And Josiah carried 'em out, one on each arm, and he drove off with 'em fast. Betsey wouldn't stay to dinner all I could do and say, she acted mad. But one sweet thought filled me with such joyful emotion that I smiled as I thought of it—I shouldn't have to listen to any more poetry that day.

Gail Hamilton

Mary Abigail Dodge (1833–1896)

Although many women writers have used pseudonyms, Mary Abigail Dodge seems almost to have created a separate identity as "Gail Hamilton," an outspoken journalist and essayist who wrote for the *National Era,* the *Atlantic Monthly,* and the *New York Tribune* during a long and successful career. Mary Abigail Dodge, meanwhile, strenuously avoided publicity, and, though she never married, adhered to the dictates of "true womanhood" in her personal life. As Maurine Beasley puts it, Dodge was caught in a "personal cultural dilemma": "she rejected the totally domestic role that was the established ideal for women of her time," but "she still accepted the cultural ideal that a woman's place lay in the home." This split in consciousness is evident in her political writing as well: although she espoused many liberal causes, particularly abolition, which was the focus of the *National Era,* she was opposed to female suffrage, believing that voting would lower women to the level of men rather than allowing them to exert the influence of their finer natures. Yet one of her central themes was what came to be called "the war between the sexes," and in many of her witty essays for the *Atlantic Monthly* on this subject, she sounds very much like her near-contemporary "Fanny Fern," making fun of both genders for excessive and intolerant behavior. Dodge was born in Hamilton, Massachusetts, which probably inspired her pseudonym, and early in her life expressed dismay at the drudgery of her mother's life. In her mid-20s, Dodge went to Washington, DC, to become governess to the children of Gamaliel Bailey, editor of the *National Era,* and she quickly made a name for herself as one of a handful of female political journalists in pre-Civil War Washington. The subjects of her non-political writings range from religion to country life, and the latter is the topic in *Twelve Miles from a*

Lemon, which anticipates Betty MacDonald's 1945 *The Egg and I* in its depiction of the difficulties of housekeeping in a remote area. As MacDonald's narrator struggles with the recalcitrant "Stove," Hamilton's chases the elusive butcher for a piece of meat. Hamilton may have championed woman's "separate sphere," but she was also capable of seing the potential for slapstick comedy in the daily round of domestic duties as would Jean Kerr and Shirley Jackson nearly a century later.

SOURCES   Beasley, Maurine. "Mary Abigail Dodge: 'Gail Hamilton' and the Process of Social Change." *Essex Institute Historical Collections* 116:2 (April 1980): 82–100; Dodge, H. Augusta, ed. *Gail Hamilton's Life in Letters.* 2 vols. Boston: Lee & Shepard, 1901; "Mary Abigail Dodge." *American Authors: 1600–1900.* New York: H. H. Wilson, 1953. 220.

WORKS   *Twelve Miles from a Lemon* (1874)

from *Twelve Miles from a Lemon*

When Sydney Smith declared merrily that his living in Yorkshire was so far out of the way, that it was actually twelve miles from a lemon, all the world laughed. But the world little knows—the great, self-indulgent world, that dearly loves comfort and ease and pleasure, coolness in August and warmth in November—what it is to live twelve miles from a lemon. A lemon means ice and a market, all good things in their season, and all men eager to wait upon you.

You have been staying in Lemon, let us say, for months, preying upon your betters. You have become thoroughly demoralized by the delights of the lilies, toiling not, nor spinning, and taking no thought for the morrow. But the whirligig of time has brought about its revenges. Your betters, finding no other way to disembarrass themselves of you, have shut up their city house and gone, and you must go too, and take thought for the morrow, or be stranded on a desert island. As you are borne rapidly homeward you try to return once more to practical life, and make an intense mental effort to concentrate your thoughts, and remember what you have had for breakfast the last four months. Presently you chance upon a cracker-peddler. Crackers make a good pedestal for your wandering gods to alight on, and you buy a box.

"Do you go as far as The Old Elm?"

"Oh yes."

"Leave this box of crackers, then, in Leicester County, on the old stage road, right-hand side, low green house in a hollow, on the door-step. Never mind if the house seems closed. Leave them all the same."

You resume your journey with a light heart. Tomorrow shall take thought for the things of itself. One need never starve with a dozen pounds of crackers on the door-step.

Another stage of roar and rush, and dust and cinders, and the train leaves you at your own station. Unexpected, you are unawaited. Importunate hackmen know on which side their bread is buttered, and never stroll twelve miles from a lemon; so you leave your luggage, and walk, not reluctant, along the lovely path that was never so lovely as now—a deep, hard, straggling footpath, half hidden in the rank grass, green and dense under the gnarled old apple-trees. The slant sun, the ruddy sky, the bright, still, rich earth, alive with color, abloom with light, all the broad fields laughing with ripening harvests, all the birds mad with joy, and no war nor battle sound in all our borders—oh, the beautiful, beloved country!

But the pump will not go. Certainly not. A refractory and unprincipled pump from the beginning; and before I have shaken from my feet the dust of travel I must arise and depart again, for twelve miles from a lemon means fifteen miles from a plumber.

No more will the lamps burn. In one the wick refuses to budge a hairbreadth up or down. In the other it will go down, but not up. Of a third the chimney is broken. A fourth has lost the cement between globe and pedestal, and cants alarmingly. A fifth drops the wick, flame and all, down into the oil, as soon as it is lighted, and scares us out of our wits. There is one evening of a stray candle or two, and a horror of great darkness, and then another journey for a fresh supply. For ten miles from a lemon is twenty miles from a lamp.

The crackers come to time, the bread rises bravely, but my soul longeth for meat. This township swarms with butchers. "Malone, we will have some chickens. No, a tenderloin steak. Put out the sign." The sign is a crimson scarf tied around a post. "I put it out this morning," says Malone, "and he did not stop." "Put it out again to-morrow morning, and we will keep watch besides," I wake early, gnawed by many cares. I wonder if the bread has risen. Will Malone oversleep, and forget it, past the proper point. If that were off my mind I think I could go to sleep again. I creep softly down stairs and strike a bee-line for the breadpan, and Malone, who has also crept softly down her stairs for the same purpose, utters a little shriek. I withdraw, but not to sleep. We must have eggs. There is nothing to be done in the way of housekeeping without eggs. Perhaps Malone can get some at the milkman's. I will hear her when she goes out, and tell her. No; I will tell her now, and then it will be off my mind, and I shall go to sleep. "Malone," I call softly down the stairs, "try if the milkman has any eggs; and if he has, boil them for breakfast, and make a custard for dinner."

It is an hour before butcher-time, and I shall have a cozy nap. If I had only thought to buy some oat-meal in the lemon. Twelve miles away we get no nearer to it than oats. There is a rumble of wheels. It can not be the butcher. If it *should* be, and we lose our dinner to-day as we did yesterday! I may as well jump up and look, as thoroughly awake myself by fretting about it. It is not the butcher; but oh! it is the good-butter man; and I must stop him, at all costs; and Malone is gone for the milk; and oh! where is a wrapper? and what has become of my slippers? He is stone-deaf. Would he were also stone-blind! Here is a water-proof cloak. Will he think they wear water-proof morning dresses in lemons? Oh, joy! there is Malone coming. Thank Heaven, she is not deaf. "Malone!" with a deafening shriek, if any one could hear it; but the advantage of being twelve miles from a lemon is that you can do your marketing from the chamber windows and nobody the wiser—"Malone! stop the butter-man, and engage butter for the season." Malone rushes up to him like a freebooter, and I am happy.

Only casting about in my mind whether Malone put the cucumber in water—the cucumber which grew in Quincy Market, and which I had just room for in my lamp-journey—to be roused by her voice again. "What is it, Malone?"

"The milkman hadn't any eggs." Of course he had not. Hens do not lay eggs in the country. Eggs are laid in lemons, and you must go twelve miles to get them.

"Perhaps Mr. Meiggs has some."

"No. I went there Monday and got ten—all he had."

"Suppose you try the Briarses."

"I was there yesterday, and they only had a few that had been sot on."

"Very well. I am going to bed, Malone. Do the best you can without them."

I have not begun to doze. I do not expect so much as that—only a little quiet, preparatory to the day's campaign; but there is a rattle of wheels in the distance. It is early, but it sounds like the butcher's cart. It *is* the butcher's cart. Intrenched again in the water-proof, I fling up the sash ready to pounce upon him. "Butcher!" trying to soften a yell into a decorous call.

He turns neither to the right hand nor to the left. This will never do. Courage.

Butcher!"

He gives no sign. He is going by. I am desperate. I fling decorum to the winds.

"Butch-E-R-R-R!"

He does not hear the word, but the prolonged shriek pierces his ear. He stops. The household is aroused, and not exactly comprehending the situation, but each feeling a responsibility for the dinner, Babel ensues.

"Have you any tenderloin?" I cry.

Malone does not hear me from her wash-tub below, but she sees the butcher, and, feeling the whole care on her own shoulders, cries, in a voice to wake the dead,

"We want some—*tenderloin!*"

Simultaneously, Spitzbergen flings up another window, and entirely on her own account, calls vociferously for a "steak of *tenderloin!*" And even Tranquilla feels the necessity of action, and from the depths of the bed-clothes sends forth a muffled shriek for *"tenderloin!"* Thus suddenly, out of profound silence, the house resounds from turret to foundation-stone with the clangor of tenderloin, and the bewildered butcher stares blankly and can make out nothing for the hullaballoo. There is a short pause of exhaustion and experiment. I infer that the others have become, somehow, aware of the posture of affairs, and, taking advantage of the lull, begin to put my inquiry in a decent and Christian manner—to find that they have all arrived at the same conclusion, and are piping forth again a chaos of tenderloin; but Malone holds the key of the situation, marches to the front, extricates both butcher and tenderloin, and comes back brandishing her beefsteak triumphant. Whereupon the house subsides into its normal silence.

City folk undoubtedly believe that early vegetables spring from the soil, but we country dwellers know better. We look abroad upon the earth, and see the wide stretch of field and sky, and the ever-shifting panorama of the clouds, and the stately pomp of the sun on his daily march, and know perfectly well that it was all made to look at, and a good enough end is that. But when we want any thing to eat, we take a basket and go by rail twelve miles to the lemon. And it is not convenient. The country is perfect, if man could live by bread and meat alone, but he can not. He wants butter also, and fresh eggs, and early pease, and beets, and, lettuce, and above all, ice—the art preservative of all arts. . . .

That is the difference between living in a lemon and living twelve miles away from it. In the first case you are besought to buy. In the second you beseech others to sell.

"Why do you not raise things for youself, and be independent of butchers and bakers and butter-makers?" asks the astute and inexperienced Lemonite.

"Raise *things!* What, for instance?"

"Eggs, then, to begin with."

Because eggs are no sooner hatched than all the forces of nature rise up together to destroy them. Hatched, do I say? Before they are hatched the foe comes. While they are yet eggs the cats smell them out and suck them. When they have broken shell and become chickens, the first thing they do is to get lost. If there is a bit of late snow it shall go hard but they will roam around till they find it, and then they will stand still on it and shiver and die. If there is one grass-plot deeper and thicker and wetter than another, they will make a rush for that—anywhere so they can shiver and die. Then the hawks come down from the sky, and the skunks come up from the swamps, and the weasels come out of the woods, and the minks and the foxes and the woodchucks from their holes among the rocks, and make a dead set at the chickens. In vain the mother hen clucks alarm and hate. A hawk swoops down into your very door-yard and bears away a struggling chick in his talons. Now that the horse is stolen we will lock the stable-door. "Tranquilla, take your book into the piazza and keep watch." "A hawk! a hawk!" cries Tranquilla presently, in wild excitement, and we rush to the door with immense hootings and howlings, but no hawk is visible. The happy hen is peacefully brooding her young and gives no sign. "It must have been a mistake," you say, quite out of breath. "No, it was no mistake," exclaims Tranquilla. "It was a hawk; I saw him plainly; and he went 'caw! caw!'" "Oh! Tranquilla, go into the house." Foolishness is bound up in the heart of the Lemonite, and he never will know a hawk from a crow, though he see it twelve miles off! Now a thunder-cloud gathers. The forked lightnings flash red and angry. The thunder growls. The rain comes fast and furious. Of course the chickens are off in the far

pastures gobbling grasshoppers. There they come scampering home, terrified, in hot haste. Their wet feathers are tucked away from their little
sticks of legs, which look twice as long and twice as slender as they beat
home, frantic. And trotting placidly among them come four little skunks,
haud ignota loquor. Is this tempest, then, the beginning of the end of the
world, and does that quiet quartette presage the millennium—the lion
and the lamb, the chicken and the skunk, lying down together? Alas! no,
unless—as some one says—the one be inside the other. When the storm is
over the skunks will grow up and devour the neighbors' chickens—not
mine, for to-morrow morning I shall go out to find my chickens dead, one
and all, of rats; and that is why there are no eggs twelve miles from a
lemon.

But at least you might raise vegetables, which fox and weasel do not
devour, nor cats and rats break through and steal.

So you might, only labor all goes to Lemons, and twelve miles away
seven women have to lay hold of one man to get a beet-bed hoed, and then
find that, in the confusion of the moment, he has planted beans instead of
beets, and cabbages instead of sweet-corn. But there are early potatoes.
Yes, and earlier oxen who tear down your wall and leap into your garden,
and devour what they can and trample what they can not. You drive them
out with much brandishing of bean-poles and broomsticks—the beautiful
patient-eyed creatures, so strong and meek—and their master makes a
thousand apologies, and promises that they shall not trespass again; but
the black heifer from the next pasture does, and she too is repulsed in
force; and then comes a wail from Tranquilla, "Oh! the oxen are in
again!" and off you go, lance in rest, to find the trespassing oxen have
turned into neighbor Nelly's lovely Alderney cow, quietly feeding in her
own fields. "Tranquilla! Tranquilla! will you never have done discovering
mares' nests? Is not the way hard enough, but you must make mountains
of mole-hills?" But in two days your own eyes discern a horned beast
thrusting in among your vegetables, and your blood rises. You will see
whether there is to be any protection to life or property! "Who is the field-
driver?"

Nobody knows. I go to my friend the Forester. "Who is the field-
driver?"

"What's the matter? My cow got into your lot?"

"I never thought of its being your cow, but perhaps it is. It's a red cow."

"No, 'tain't mine. Mine is a Jersey."

"I am glad of that. Now I am tired of driving cows out of my yard. You make me pay taxes, and you won't let me vote; and the least you can do is to keep the cows out of my garden."

"That's so. Can't say nothin' agin that."

"Then who is the field-driver?"

"Well, there ain't exactly no field-driver, like. You see 'tain't no great of an office, and nobody hain't much hankering after it. So when they nominate 'em at town-meetin' they decline. So you have to fasten on somebody that ain't there, and they appointed Stephen Barrows. We got him there! But Stephen, you see, he ain't took the oath, an' won't take it, and so he hain't no responsibility; so we're kind of satisfied all round!"

"Beautiful legislation! How complicate, how wonderful, is man! Meanwhile, the cow's in the meadow, the sheep's in the corn, and isn't there any way to get them out except with bean-poles?"

"Well, yes. You can advertise in three towns that there is such a cow trespassing, and when the owner gets her you can make him pay her board, reckonin' in damages."

An easy way to turn a cow out of your garden! But that is why corn will not grow twelve miles from a lemon.

Louisa May Alcott
(1832–1888)

Since the 1940s, when Madeleine Stern and Leona Rostenberg discovered that the author of *Little Women* had written a number of Gothic thrillers using the pseudonym "A. M. Barnard," scholars have become gradually aware of the wide variety of Louisa May Alcott's work, from Gothic romance to stories for children. "Transcendental Wild Oats" is a satiric reflection on the Alcott family's brief sojourn in communal living at Fruitlands, an enterprise in which Henry David Thoreau was tangentially involved. Fruitlands was one of many attempts at the perfect life that Bronson Alcott, Louisa May's father, devised in lieu of supporting his family financially, and Louisa's early writing was motivated at least in part by economic necessity. As a young woman, she also earned money by teaching and sewing, but by the 1870s she was in demand as an author, not only of fiction, but also of articles on female suffrage, temperance, child labor, and other reformist topics about which her attitudes were formed by the liberal intellectual climate of Boston in which she grew up. Alcott's formal schooling was supplemented by books from Ralph Waldo Emerson's library, and both literature and her own experience inspired her writing. The publication of *Little Women* in 1868 brought her wide public recognition, establishing the reputation as a writer for young people that has largely defined her place in American literary history ever since. Yet Alcott based her character Jo in *Little Women* largely on herself, and Jo's rebellious, "masculine" qualities emerge in the tone of much of Alcott's work, as well as in her creation of strong women characters who live out passions that this "scribbling spinster" (Bronson Alcott's term) could only imagine, just as the idyllic circumstances of the four sisters in *Little Women* revise Alcott's own difficult, penurious childhood. The ironically-named Mrs. Hope, in

"Transcendental Wild Oats," is based loosely on Alcott's mother, Abba, who endured her husband's experiments with a stoic patience to which Louisa adds her own sense of irony.

SOURCES   *American Women Writers,* Vol 1; Saxton, Martha. *Louisa May: A Modern Biography of Louisa May Alcott.* Boston: Houghton Mifflin, 1977; Stern, Madeleine. Introduction. *Behind a Mask: The Unknown Thrillers of Louisa May Alcott.* New York: William Morrow, 1975.

WORKS   *Transcendental Wild Oats* (1872)

from *Silver Pitchers*

Transcendental Wild Oats

A Chapter from an Unwritten Romance.

On the first day of June, 184–, a large waggon, drawn by a small horse and containing a motley load, went lumbering over certain New England hills, with the pleasing accompaniments of wind, rain, and hail. A serene man with a serene child upon his knee was driving, or rather being driven, for the small horse had it all his own way. A brown boy with a William Penn style of countenance sat beside him, firmly embracing a bust of Socrates. Behind them was an energetic-looking woman, with a benevolent brow, satirical mouth, and eyes brimful of hope and courage. A baby reposed upon her lap, a mirror leaned against her knee, and a basket of provisions danced about at her feet, as she struggled with a large, unruly umbrella. Two blue-eyed little girls, with hands full of childish treasures, sat under one old shawl, chatting happily together.

In front of this lively party stalked a tall, sharp-featured man, in a long blue cloak; and a fourth small girl trudged along beside him through the mud as if she rather enjoyed it.

The wind whistled over the bleak hills; the rain fell in a despondent drizzle, and twilight began to fall. But the calm man gazed as tranquilly into the fog as if he beheld a radiant bow of promise spanning the grey sky. The cheery woman tried to cover every one but herself with the big umbrella. The brown boy pillowed his head on the bald pate of Socrates and slumbered peacefully. The little girls sang lullabies to their dolls in soft, maternal murmurs. The sharp-nosed pedestrian marched steadily on, with the blue cloak streaming out behind him like a banner; and the lively infant splashed through the puddles with a duck-like satisfaction pleasant to behold.

Thus these modern pilgrims journeyed hopefully out of the old world, to found a new one in the wilderness.

The editors of "The Transcendental Tripod" had received from Messrs. Lion and Lamb (two of the aforesaid pilgrims) a communication from which the following statement is an extract:—

"We have made arrangements with the proprietor of an estate of about a hundred acres which liberates this tract from human ownership. Here we shall prosecute our effort to initiate a Family in harmony with the primitive instincts of man.

"Ordinary secular farming is not our object. Fruit, grain, pulse, herbs, flax, and other vegetable products, receiving assiduous attention, will afford ample manual occupation, and chaste supplies for the bodily needs. It is intended to adorn the pastures with orchards, and to supersede the labour of cattle by the spade and the pruning-knife.

"Consecrated to human freedom, the land awaits the sober culture of devoted men. Beginning with small pecuniary means, this enterprise must be rooted in a reliance on the succours of an ever-bounteous Providence, whose vital affinities being secured by this union with uncorrupted field and unworldly persons, the cares and injuries of a life of gain are avoided.

"The inner nature of each member of the Family is at no time neglected. Our plan contemplates all such disciplines, culture, and habits as evidently conduce to the purifying of the inmates.

"Pledged to the spirit alone, the founders anticipate no hasty or numerous addition to their numbers. The kingdom of peace is entered only through the gates of self-denial; and felicity is the test and the reward of loyalty to the unswerving law of Love."

This prospective Eden at present consisted of an old red farm-house, a dilapidated barn, many acres of meadow-land, and a grove. Ten ancient apple-trees were all the "chaste supply" which the place offered as yet; but, in the firm belief that plenteous orchards were soon to be evoked from their inner consciousness, these sanguine founders had christened their domain Fruitlands.

Here Timon Lion intended to found a colony of Latter Day Saints, who, under his patriarchal sway, should regenerate the world and glorify his name for ever. Here Abel Lamb, with the devoutest faith in the high ideal which was to him a living truth, desired to plant a Paradise, where Beauty, Virtue, Justice, and Love might live happily together, without the possibility of a serpent entering in. And here his wife, unconverted, but faithful to the end, hoped, after many wanderings over the face of the earth, to find rest for herself and a home for her children.

"There is our new abode," announced the enthusiast, smiling with a satisfaction quite undamped by the drops dripping from his hat-brim, as they turned at length into a cart-path that wound along a steep hillside into a barren-looking valley.

"A little difficult of access," observed his practical wife, as she endeavoured to keep her various household gods from going overboard with every lurch of the laden ark.

"Like all good things. But those who earnestly desire and patiently seek will soon find us," placidly responded the philosopher from the mud, through which he was now endeavouring to pilot the much-enduring horse.

"Truth lies at the bottom of a well, Sister Hope," said Brother Timon, pausing to detach his small comrade from a gate, whereon she was perched for a clearer gaze into futurity.

"That's the reason we so seldom get at it, I suppose," replied Mrs. Hope, making a vain clutch at the mirror, which a sudden jolt sent flying out of her hands.

"We want no false reflections here," said Timon, with a grim smile, as he crunched the fragments under foot in his onward march.

Sister Hope held her peace, and looked wistfully through the mist at her promised home. The old red house with a hospitable glimmer at its windows cheered her eyes; and, considering the weather, was a fitter refuge than the sylvan bowers some of the more ardent souls might have preferred.

The new-comers were welcomed by one of the elect precious,—a regenerate farmer, whose idea of reform consisted chiefly in wearing white cotton raiment and shoes of untanned leather. This costume, with a snowy beard, gave him a venerable, and at the same time a somewhat bridal appearance.

The goods and chattels of the Society not having arrived, the weary family reposed before the fire on blocks of woods, while Brother Moses White regaled them with roasted potatoes, brown bread, and water, in two plates, a tin pan, and one mug; his table service being limited. But, having cast the forms and vanities of a depraved world behind them, the elders welcomed hardship with the enthusiasm of new pioneers, and the children heartily enjoyed this foretaste of what they believed was to be a sort of perpetual picnic.

During the progress of this frugal meal, two more brothers appeared. One a dark, melancholy man, clad in homespun, whose peculiar mission was to turn his name hind part before and use as few words as possible. The other was a bland, bearded Englishman, who expected to be saved by eating uncooked food and going without clothes. He had not yet adopted the primitive costume, however; but contented himself with meditatively chewing dry beans out of a basket.

"Every meal should be a sacrament, and the vessels used should be beautiful and symbolical," observed Brother Lamb, mildly, righting the tin pan slipping about on his knees. "I priced a silver service when in town, but it was too costly; so I got some graceful cup and vases of Britannia ware."

"Hardest things in the world to keep bright. Will whiting be allowed in the community?" inquired Sister Hope, with a housewife's interest in labour-saving institutions.

"Such trivial questions will be discussed at a more fitting time," answered Brother Timon sharply, as he burnt his fingers with a very hot potato. "Neither sugar, molasses, milk, butter, cheese, nor flesh are to be used among us, for nothing is to be admitted which has caused wrong or death to man or beast."

"Our garments are to be linen till we learn to raise our own cotton or some substitute for woollen fabrics," added Brother Abel, blissfully basking in an imaginary future as warm and brilliant as the generous fire before him.

"Haou abaout shoes?" asked Brother Moses, surveying his own with interest.

"We must yield that point till we can manufacture an innocent substitute for leather. Bark, wood, or some durable fabric will be invented in time. Meanwhile, those who desire to carry out our idea to the fullest extent can go barefooted," said Lion, who liked extreme measures.

"I never will, nor let my girls," murmured rebellious Sister Hope, under her breath.

"Haou do you cattle'ate to treat the ten-acre lot? Ef things ain't 'tended to right smart, we shan't hev no crops," observed the practical patriarch in cotton.

"We shall spade it," replied Abel, in such perfect good faith that Moses said no more, though he indulged in a shake of the head as he glanced at hands that had held nothing heavier than a pen for years. He was a paternal old soul, and regarded the younger men as promising boys on a new sort of lark.

"What shall we do for lamps, if we cannot use any animal substance? I do hope light of some sort is to be thrown upon the enterprise," said Mrs. Lamb, with anxiety, for in those days kerosene and camphene were not, and gas unknown in the wilderness.

"We shall go without till we have discovered some vegetable oil or wax to serve us," replied Brother Timon, in a decided tone, which caused Sister Hope to resolve that her private lamp should be always trimmed, if not burning.

"Each member is to perform the work for which experience, strength, and taste best fit him," continued Dictator Lion. "Thus drudgery and disorder will be avoided and harmony prevail. We shall rise at dawn, begin the day by bathing, followed by music, and then a chaste repast of fruit and bread. Each one finds congenial occupation till the meridian meal; when some deep-searching conversation gives rest to the body and development to the mind. Healthful labour again engages us till the last meal, when we assemble in social communion, prolonged till sunset, when we retire to sweet repose, ready for the next day's activity."

"What part of the work do you incline to yourself?" asked Sister Hope, with a humorous glimmer in her keen eyes.

"I shall wait till it is made clear to me. Being in preference to doing is the great aim, and this comes to us rather by a resigned willingness than a wilful activity, which is a check to all divine growth," responded Brother Timon.

"I thought so." And Mrs. Lamb sighed audibly, for during the year he had spent in her family Brother Timon had so faithfully carried out his idea of "being, not doing," that she had found his "divine growth" both an expensive and unsatisfactory process.

Here her husband struck into the conversation, his face shining with the light and joy of the splendid dreams and high ideals hovering before him.

"In these steps of reform, we do not rely so much on scientific reasoning or physiological skill as on the spirit's dictates. The greater part of man's duty consists in leaving alone much that he now does. Shall I stimulate with tea, coffee, or wine? No. Shall I consume flesh? Not if I value health. Shall I subjugate cattle? Shall I claim property in any created thing? Shall I trade? Shall I adopt a form of religion? Shall I interest myself in politics?

To how many of these questions—could we ask them deeply enough and could they be heard as having relation to our eternal welfare—would the response be 'Abstain'?"

A mild snore seemed to echo the last word of Abel's rhapsody, for Brother Moses had succumbed to mundane slumber and sat nodding like a massive ghost. Forest Absalom, the silent man, and John Pease, the English member, now departed to the barn; and Mrs. Lamb led her flock to a temporary fold, leaving the founders of the "Consociate Family" to build castles in the air till the fire went out and the symposium ended in smoke.

The furniture arrived next day, and was soon bestowed; for the principal property of the community consisted in books. To this rare library was devoted the best room in the house, and the few busts and pictures that still survived many flittings were added to beautify the sanctuary, for here the family was to meet for amusement, instruction, and worship.

Any housewife can imagine the emotions of Sister Hope, when she took possession of a large, dilapidated kitchen, containing an old stove and the peculiar stores out of which food was to be evolved for her little family of eleven. Cakes of maple sugar, dried peas and beans, barley and hominy, meal of all sorts, potatoes, and dried fruit. No milk, butter, cheese, tea, or meat, appeared. Even salt was considered a useless luxury, and spice entirely forbidden by these lovers of Spartan simplicity. A ten years' experience of vegetarian vagaries had been good training for this new freak, and her sense of the ludicrous supported her through many trying scenes.

Unleavened bread, porridge, and water for breakfast; bread, vegetables, and water for dinner; bread, fruit, and water for supper was the bill of fare ordained by the elders. No teapot profaned that sacred stove, no gory steak cried aloud for vengeance from her chaste gridiron; and only a brave woman's taste, time, and temper were sacrificed on that domestic altar.

The vexed question of light was settled by buying a quantity of bayberry wax for candles; and, on discovering that no one knew how to make them, pineknots were introduced, to be used when absolutely necessary. Being summer, the evenings were not long, and the weary fraternity found it no great hardship to retire with the birds. The inner light was sufficient for most of them. But Mrs. Lamb rebelled. Evening was the only time she had to herself, and while the tired feet rested the skilful hands mended torn frocks and little stockings, or anxious heart forgot its burden in a book.

So "mother's lamp" burned steadily, while the philosophers built a new heaven and earth by moonlight; and through all the metaphysical mists and philanthropic pyrotecnics of that period Sister Hope played her own little game of "throwing light," and none but the moths were the worse for it.

Such farming probably was never seen before since Adam delved. The band of brothers began by spading garden and field; but a few days of it lessened their ardour amazingly. Blistered hands and aching backs suggested the expediency of permitting the use of cattle till the workers were better fitted for noble toil by a summer of the new life.

Brother Moses brought a yoke of oxen from his farm,—at least, the philosophers thought so till it was discovered that one of the animals was a cow; and Moses confessed that he "must be let down easy, for he couldn't live on garden sarse entirely."

Great was Dictator Lion's indignation at this lapse from virtue. But time pressed, the work must be done; so the meek cow was permitted to wear the yoke and the recreant brother continued to enjoy forbidden draughts in the barn, which dark proceeding caused the children to regard him as one set apart for destruction.

The sowing was equally peculiar, for, owing to some mistake, the three brethren, who devoted themselves to this graceful task, found when about half through the job that each had been sowing a different sort of grain in the same field; a mistake which caused much perplexity, as it could not be remedied; but, after a long consultation and a good deal of laughter, it was decided to say nothing and see what would come of it.

The garden was planted with a generous supply of useful roots and herbs; but as manure was not allowed to profane the virgin soil, few of these vegetable treasures ever came up. Purslane reigned supreme, and the disappointed planters ate it philosophically, deciding that Nature knew what was best for them, and would generously supply their needs, if they could only learn to digest her "sallets" and wild roots.

The orchard was laid out, a little grafting done, new trees and vines set, regardless of the unfit season and entire ignorance of the husbandmen, who honestly believed that in the autumn they would reap a bounteous harvest.

Slowly things got into order, and rapidly rumours of the new experiment went abroad, causing many strange spirits to flock thither, for in those days communities were the fashion and transcendentalism raged wildly. Some came to look on and laugh, some to be supported in poetic idleness, a few to believe sincerely and work heartily. Each member was allowed to mount his favourite hobby and ride it to his heart's content. Very queer were some of the riders, and very rampant some of the hobbies.

One youth, believing that language was of little consequence if the spirit was only right, startled new comers by blandly greeting them with "Good morning, damn you," and other remarks of an equally mixed order. A second irrepressible being held that all the emotions of the soul should be freely expressed, and illustrated his theory by antics that would have sent him to a lunatic asylum, if, as an unregenerate wag said, he had not already been in one. When his spirit soared, he climbed trees and shouted; when doubt assailed him, he lay upon the floor and groaned lamentably. At joyful periods, he raced, leaped, and sang; when sad, he wept aloud; and when a great thought burst upon him in the watches of the night, he crowed like a jocund cockerel, to the great delight of the children and the great annoyance of the elders. One musical brother fiddled whenever so moved, sang sentimentally to the four little girls, and put a music-box on the wall when he hoed corn.

Brother Pease ground away at his uncooked food, or browsed over the farm on sorrel, mint, green fruit, and new vegetables. Occasionally he took his walks abroad, airily attired in an unbleached cotton *poncho*, which was the nearest approach to the primeval costume he was allowed to indulge in. At midsummer he retired to the wilderness, to try his plan where the woodchucks were without prejudices and huckleberry-bushes were hospitably full. A sunstroke unfortunately spoilt his plan, and he returned to semi-civilization a sadder and wiser man.

Forest Absalom preserved his Pythagorean silence, cultivated his fine dark locks, and worked like a beaver, setting an excellent example of brotherly love, justice, and fidelity by his upright life. He it was who helped overworked Sister Hope with her heavy washes, kneaded the endless succession of batches of bread, watched over the children, and did the many tasks left undone by the brethren, who were so busy discussing and defining great duties that they forgot to perform the small ones.

Moses White placidly plodded about, "chorin' raound," as he called it, looking like an old-time patriarch, with his silver hair and flowing beard, and saving the community from many a mishap by his thrift and Yankee shrewdness.

Brother Lion domineered over the whole concern; for, having put the most money into the speculation, he was resolved to make it pay,—as if anything founded on an ideal basis could be expected to do so by any but enthusiasts.

Abel Lamb simply revelled in the Newness, firmly believing that his dream was to be beautifully realized, and in time not only little Fruitlands, but the whole earth, be turned into a Happy Valley. He worked with every muscle of his body, for *he* was in deadly earnest. He taught with his whole head and heart; planned and sacrificed, preached and prophesied, with a soul full of the purest aspirations, most unselfish purposes, and desires for a life devoted to God and man, too high and tender to bear the rough usage of this world.

It was a little remarkable that only one woman ever joined this community. Mrs. Lamb merely followed wheresoever her husband led,—"as ballast for his balloon," as she said, in her bright way.

Miss Jane Gage was a stout lady of mature years, sentimental, amiable, and lazy. She wrote verses copiously, and had vague yearnings and graspings after the unknown, which led her to believe herself fitted for a higher sphere than any she had yet adorned.

Having been a teacher, she was set to instructing the children in the common branches. Each adult member took a turn at the infants; and, as each taught in his own way, the result was a chronic state of chaos in the minds of these much-afflicted innocents.

Sleep, food, and poetic musings were the desires of dear Jane's life, and she shirked all duties as clogs upon her spirit's wings. Any thought of lending a hand with the domestic drudgery never occurred to her; and when to the question, "Are there any beasts of burden on the place?" Mrs. Lamb answered, with a face that told its own tale, "Only one woman!" the buxom Jane took no shame to herself, but laughed at the joke, and let the stout-hearted sister tug on alone.

Unfortunately, the poor lady hankered after the flesh-pots, and endeavoured to stay herself with private sips of milk, crackers, and cheese, and on one dire occasion she partook of fish at a neighbour's table.

One of the children reported this sad lapse from virtue, and poor Jane was publicly reprimanded by Timon.

"I only took a little bit of the tail," sobbed the penitent poetess.

"Yes, but the whole fish had to be tortured and slain that you might tempt your carnal appetite with that one taste of the tail. Know ye not, consumers of flesh meat, that ye are nourishing the wolf and tiger in your bosoms?"

At this awful question and the peal of laughter which arose from the younger brethren, tickled by the ludicrous contrast between the stout sinner, the stern judge, and the naughty satisfaction of the young detective, poor Jane fled from the room, to pack her trunk and return to a world where fishes' tails were not forbidden fruit.

Transcendental wild oats were sown broadcast that year, and the fame thereof has not yet ceased in the land; for, futile as this crop seemed to outsiders, it bore an invisible harvest, worth much to those who planted in earnest. As none of the members of this particular community have ever recounted their experiences before, a few of them may not be amiss, since the interest in these attempts has never died out, and Fruitlands was the most ideal of all these castles in Spain.

A new dress was invented, since cotton, silk, and wool were forbidden as the product of slave-labour, worm-slaughter, and sheep-robbery. Tunics and trousers of brown linen were the only wear. The women's skirts were longer, and their straw hat-brims wider than the men's, and this was the only difference. Some persecution lent a charm to the costume, and the long-haired, linen-clad reformers quite enjoyed the mild martyrdom they endured when they left home.

Money was abjured, as the root of all evil. The produce of the land was to supply most of their wants, or be exchanged for the few things they could not grow. This idea had its inconveniences; but self-denial was the fashion, and it was surprising how many things one can do without. When they desired to travel, they walked, if possible, begged the loan of a vehicle, or boldly entered car or coach, and stating their principles to the officials, took the consequences. Usually their dress, their earnest frankness, and gentle resolution won them a passage; but now and then they met with hard usage, and had the satisfaction of suffering for their principles.

On one of these penniless pilgrimages they took passage on a boat, and, when fare was demanded, artlessly offered to talk instead of pay. As the boat was well under way and they actually had not a cent, there was no help for it. So Brothers Lion and Lamb held forth to the assembled passengers in their most eloquent style. There must have been something effective in this conversation, for the listeners were moved to take up a contribution for these inspired lunatics, who preached peace on earth good-will to man so earnestly, with empty pockets. A goodly sum was collected; but when the captain presented it the reformers proved that they were consistent even in their madness, for not a penny would they accept, saying, with a look at the group about them, whose indifference of contempt had changed to interest and respect, "You see how well we get on without money;" and so went serenely on their way, with their linen blouses flapping airily in the cold October wind.

They preached vegetarianism everywhere and resisted all temptations of the flesh, contentedly eating apples and bread at well-spread tables, and much afflicting hospitable hostesses by denouncing their food and taking away their appetites, discussing the "horrors of shambles," the "incorporation of the brute in man," and "on elegant abstinence the sign of a pure soul." But, when the perplexed or offended ladies asked what they should eat, they got in reply a bill of fare consisting of "bowls of sunrise for breakfast," "solar seeds of the sphere," "dishes from Plutarch's chaste table," and other viands equally hard to find in any modern market.

Reform conventions of all sorts were haunted by these brethren, who said many wise things and did many foolish ones. Unfortunately, these wanderings interfered with their harvest at home; but the rule was to do what the spirit moved, so they left their crops to Providence and went a-reaping in wider and, let us hope, more fruitful fields than their own.

Luckily, the earthly providence who watched over Abel Lamb was at hand to glean the scanty crop yielded by the "uncorrupted land," which, "consecrated to human freedom," had received "the sober culture of devout men."

About the time the grain was ready to house, some call of the Oversoul wafted all the men away. An easterly storm was coming up and the yellow stacks were sure to be ruined. Then Sister Hope gathered her forces. Three little girls, one boy (Timon's son), and herself, harnessed to clothes-baskets and Russia-linen sheets, were the only teams she could command; but with these poor appliances the indomitable woman got in the grain and saved food for her young, with the instinct and energy of a mother-bird with a brood of hungry nestlings to feed.

This attempt at regeneration had its tragic as well as comic side, though the world only saw the former.

With the first frosts, the butterflies, who had sunned themselves in the new light through the summer, took flight, leaving the few bees to see what honey they had stored for winter use. Precious little appeared beyond the satisfaction of a few months of holy living.

At first it seemed as if a chance to try holy dying was to be offered them. Timon, much disgusted with the failure of the scheme, decided to retire to the Shakers, who seemed to be the only successful community going.

"What is to become of us?" asked Mrs. Hope, for Abel was heart-broken at the bursting of his lovely bubble.

"You can stay here, if you like, till a tenant is found. No more wood must be cut, however, and no more corn ground. All I have must be sold to pay the debts of the concern, as the responsibility rests with me," was the cheering reply.

"Who is to pay us for what we have lost? I gave all I had,—furniture, time, strength, six months of my children's lives,—and all are wasted. Abel gave himself body and soul, and is almost wrecked by hard work and disappointment. Are we to have no return for this, but leave to starve and freeze in an old house, with winter at hand, no money, and hardly a friend left, for this wild scheme has alienated nearly all we had. You talk much about justice. Let us have a little, since there is nothing else left."

But the woman's appeal met with no reply but the old one: "It was an experiment. We all risked something, and must bear our losses as we can."

With this cold comfort, Timon departed with his son, and was absorbed into the Shaker brotherhood, where he soon found that the order of things was reversed, and it was all work and no play.

Then the tragedy began for the forsaken little family. Desolation and despair fell upon Abel. As his wife said, his new beliefs had alienated many friends. Some thought him mad, some unprincipled. Even the most kindly thought him a visionary, whom it was useless to help till he took more practical views of life. All stood aloof, saying, "Let him work out his own ideas, and see what they are worth."

He had tried, but it was a failure. The world was not ready for Utopia yet, and those who attempted to found it only got laughed at for their pains. In other days, men could sell all and give to the poor, lead lives devoted to holiness and high thought, and, after the persecution was over, find themselves honoured as saints or martyrs. But in modern times these things are out of fashion. To live for one's principles, at all costs, is a dangerous speculation; and the failure of an ideal, no matter how humane and noble, is harder for the world to forgive and forget than bank robbery or the grand swindles of corrupt politicians.

Deep waters now for Abel, and for a time there seemed no passage through. Strength and spirits were exhausted by hard work and too much thought. Courage failed when, looking about for help, he saw no sym-pathizing face, no hand outstretched to help him, no voice to say cheerily,—

"We all make mistakes, and it takes many experiences to shape a life. Try again, and let us help you."

Every door was closed, every eye averted, every heart cold, and no way open whereby he might earn bread for his children. His principles would not permit him to do many things that others did; and in the few fields where conscience would allow him to work, who would employ a man who had flown in the face of society, as he had done?

Then, this dreamer, whose dream was the life of his life, resolved to carry out his idea to the bitter end. There seemed no place for him here,— no work, no friend. To go begging conditions was as ignoble as to go begging money. Better perish of want than sell one's soul for the sustenance of his body. Silently he lay down upon his bed, turned his face to the wall, and waited with pathetic patience for death to cut the knot which he could not untie. Days and nights went by, and neither food nor water passed his lips. Soul and body were dumbly struggling together, and no word of complaint betrayed what either suffered.

His wife, when tears and prayers were unavailing, sat down to wait the end with a mysterious awe and submission; for in this entire resignation of all things there was an eloquent significance to her who knew him as no other human being did.

"Leave all to God," was his belief; and in this crisis the loving soul clung to this faith, sure that the All-wise Father would not desert this child who tried to live so near to Him. Gathering her children about her, she waited the issue of the tragedy that was being enacted in that solitary room, while the first snow fell outside, untrodden by the footprints of a single friend.

But the strong angels who sustain and teach perplexed and troubled souls came and went, leaving no trace without, but working miracles within. For, when all other sentiments had faded into dimness, all other hopes died utterly; when the bitterness of death was nearly over, when body was past any pang of hunger or thirst, and soul stood ready to depart, the love that outlives all else refused to die. Head had bowed to defeat, hand had grown weary with too heavy tasks, but heart could not grow cold to those who lived in its tender depths, even when death touched it.

"My faithful wife, my little girls,—they have not forsaken me, they are mine by ties that none can break. What right have I to leave them alone? What right to escape from the burden and the sorrow I have helped to bring? This duty remains to me, and I must do it manfully. For their sakes, the world will forgive me in time; for their sakes, God will sustain me now."

Too feeble to rise, Abel groped for the food that always lay within his reach, and in the darkness and solitude of that memorable night ate and drank what was to him the bread and wine of a new communion, a new dedication of heart and life to the duties that were left him when the dreams fled.

In the early dawn, when that sad wife crept fearfully to see what change had come to the patient face on the pillow, she found it smiling at her, saw a wasted hand outstretched to her, and heard a feeble voice cry bravely, "Hope!"

What passed in that little room is not to be recorded except in the hearts of those who suffered and endured much for love's sake. Enough for us to know that soon the wan shadow of a man came forth, leaning on the arm that never failed him, to be welcomed and cherished by the children, who never forgot the experiences of that time.

"Hope" was the watchword now; and, while the last logs blazed on the hearth, the last bread and apples covered the table, the new commander, with recovered courage, said to her husband,—

"Leave all to God—and me. He has done His part; now I will do mine."

"But we have no money, dear."

"Yes, we have. I sold all we could spare, and have enough to take us away from this snowbank."

"Where can we go?"

"I have engaged four rooms at our good neighbour Lovejoy's. There we can live cheaply till spring. Then for new plans and a home of our own, please God."

"But, Hope, your little store won't last long, and we have no friends."

"I can sew and you can chop wood. Lovejoy offers you the same pay as he gives his other men; my old friend, Mrs. Truman, will send me all the work I want; and my blessed brother stands by us to the end. Cheer up, dear heart, for while there is work and love in the world we shall not suffer."

"And while I have my good angel Hope, I shall not despair, even if I wait another thirty years before I step beyond the circle of the sacred little world in which I still have a place to fill."

So one bleak December day, with their few possessions piled on an ox-sled, the rosy children perched atop, and the parents trudging arm in arm behind, the exiles left their Eden and faced the world again.

"Ah, me! my happy dream. How much I leave behind that never can be mine again," said Abel, looking back at the lost Paradise, lying white and chill in its shroud of snow.

"Yes, dear; but how much we bring away," answered brave-hearted Hope, glancing from husband to children.

"Poor Fruitlands! The name was as great a failure as the rest!" continued Abel, with a sigh, as a frost-bitten apple fell from a leafless bough at his feet.

But the sigh changed to a smile as his wife added, in a half-tender, half-satirical tone,—

"Don't you you think Apple Slump would be a better name for it, dear?"

PART III
1900–1930:
Parodists, Suffragists, Feminists

Carolyn Wells
(1862–1942)

One of America's most acclaimed turn-of-the-century parodists, Carolyn Wells was considered the chief female humorist of the first two decades of the 1900s. An admirer of Lewis Carroll and Edward Lear, Wells also claimed Gelett Burgess and Oliver Herford as direct inspiration for her best-selling collections of verse. *Idle Idylls* (1900) is representative in both subject matter and style of Wells' work, which poked fun, through parody, at such popular pieces as *The Rubaiyat* of Omar Khayyam, Hamlet's soliloquy "To Be Or Not To Be," the popular song "The Old Oaken Bucket," and the sentimental and nature poetry of the period. The lightness of touch, lively fancy, and fluent rhythms for which early reviewers praised Wells are employed in this and subsequent volumes also to treat humorously such topics as love and courtship, women's fashions, images of the ideal woman, and feminine frailties and wiles. *A Phenomenal Fauna* (1902) and *Folly for the Wise* (1904) contain whimsical and nonsense verse about imagined creatures, such as the Clothes Horse and the Golf Lynx, and fanciful flora, such as Wild Oats, as well as parodies and limericks. These and other volumes emphasize Wells' verbal wit, delight in word play and puns, and ingenuity in reconciling incongruous combinations of images. *A Nonsense Anthology* (1902), her first effort as an anthologist of humorous verse, was followed by nine subsequent collections. In addition, she published books of games, puzzles, and brain teasers; verses and stories for children; two burlesque novels; and eighty-one mystery/detective novels. Her output and reputation were so prodigious that, as one reviewer stated, "to begin a sentence sharply with 'Carolyn Wells says' is to attract the attention of a whole tableful and silence any spasmodic, needless chatter that may be going on elsewhere around the board."

133

SOURCES   "Carolyn Wells." *Wilson Library Bulletin.* (April 1930): 366; Dresner, Zita Z. "Carolyn Wells." *Dictionary of Literary Biography,* Vol. 11, Part 2: 556–560; Masson, Thomas L. *Our American Humorists.* New York: Moffat, Yard, 1922. 303–23; Wells, Carolyn. *The Rest of My Life.* Philadelphia: Lippincott, 1937.

WORKS   *Idle Idylls* (1900); *A Phenomenal Fauna* (1902); *Folly for the Wise* (1904); *The Rubaiyat of a Motor Car* (1906) and *Baubles* (1917)

from *Idle Idylls*

To a Milkmaid

I hail thee, O milkmaid!
Goddess of the gaudy morn, hail!
Across the mead tripping,
Invariably across the mead tripping,
The merry mead with cowslips blooming,
With daisies blooming,
The milkmaid also more or less blooming!
I hail thee, O milkmaid!
I recognise the value of thy pail in literature and art.
What were a pastoral poet without thee?
Oh, I know thee, milkmaid!
I hail thy jaunty juvenescence.
I know thy eighteen summers and thy eternal springs.
Ay, I know thy trials!
I know how thou art outspread over pastoral poetry.
Rampant, ubiquitous, inevitable, thy riotings in pastoral poetry,
And in masterpieces of pastoral art!
How oft have I seen thee sitting;
On a tri-legged stool sitting;
On the wrong side of the cow sitting;
Garbed in all thy preposterous paraphernalia.
I know thy paraphernalia—
Yea, even thy impossible milkpail and thy improbable bodice.
Short-skirted siren!
Big-hatted beauty!

What were the gentle spring without thee!
I hail thee!
I hail thy vernality, and I rejoice in thy hackneyed ubiquitousness.
I hail the supriority of thy inferiorness, and
I lay at thy feet this garland of gratuitous
Hails!

The Poster Girl

The blessed Poster Girl leaned out
   From a pinky-purple heaven;
One eye was red and one was green;
   Her bangs were cut uneven;
She had three fingers on her hand,
   And the hairs on her head were seven.

Her robe, ungirt from clasp to hem,
   No sunflowers did adorn;
But a heavy Turkish portière
   Was very neatly worn;
And the hat that lay along her back
   Was yellow, like canned corn.

It was a kind of wobbly wave
   That she was standing on,
And high aloft she flung a scarf
   That must have weighed a ton.
And she was rather tall,—at least
   She reached up to the sun.
She curved and writhed, and then she said,
   Less green of speech than blue:
"Perhaps I *am* absurd—perhaps
   I *don't* appeal to you;
But my artistic worth depends
   Upon the point of view."

I saw her smile, although her eyes
   Were only smudgy smears;

And then she swished her swirling arms,
  And wagged her gorgeous ears.
She sobbed a blue-and-green checked sob,
  And wept some purple tears.

The Trailing Skirt

Oh, product of this vain and vapid age,
I would I could thy doom presage!
With righteous wrath it makes me rage
To think that in these late, enlightened years
Such an enormity appears
As thy lank length. I marvel and lament
That such a bane was sent.
Why cumberest thou the earth?
Of thee we have no need,
Even though thou'rt decreed
By Worth.
Thou trundling, trailing skirt!
Smearing thyself with dirt,
Forever catching in the swinging doors
As we go in and out of stores.
One should be a contortionist expert,
To manage a trained skirt.
Trained skirt, indeed! I would thou hadst been trained
To hold thyself up when it rained!
Perchance I pick thee up and carry thee,
Then see—
My arm
Shortly grows cramped and tired.
Where is thy charm,
O trailing skirt, that thou shouldst be desired?
Perchance I let thee trail,
A mass of cloth that drags
In rags
And tags
Like Dorothy Draggletail.

Then on thy folds a sturdy heel is placed.
Of course,
I'm stopped perforce.
(I feel thee parting from my waist!)
When I proceed 't is with the dread
That I shall tread
Upon some other victim's dragging gown,
And, peering down,
I pick my steps with care about the town.
I may not look to left or right,
I miss the sight
Of all that I came out to see;
I pass the friends who bow to me
Without a glance.

Or, if perchance
I shun the dangers of the muddy street
And in a crowded car lurch to a seat,
That dreadful train attacks the angry, vexed
Man who sits next!
And, like a living thing,
Contrives to writhe and cling
And twine itself completely round his feet.
Chagrined, I grab the floundering folds,
While every one beholds
The lining splashed and binding frayed
Of my best "tailor-made,"
Which, when I started, but an hour ago,
Was neat and trim and *comme il faut*.

Oh, how can rational women wear
Such awful things, nor dare
Even feebly to protest
Against the pest?
To be so blindly bound by Fashion's thralls,
Afraid to break her rules,
We must be silly fools!
At any rate,
We must be what Max Nordau calls
Degenerate!

A Ballade of Revolt

Washington's cherry-tree I prize,
　　And Jonah's whale—and how I hate
Iconoclasts who would revise
　　The old traditions, small or great.
　　Yet there be fools who idly prate
Of late research; and some buffoon
　　Declares the old man out of date,—
Now there's a woman in the moon.

Aggressive women I despise,
　　Yet they are everywhere of late;
Insistent, bold, and overwise,
　　They meddle with affairs of state.
　　Unending trouble they create,
And deem their services a boon;
　　Much grave disturbance I await,
Now there's a woman in the moon.

I know just how she'll scrutinise
　　Each timid lover and his mate;
She'll slyly peer with curious eyes,
　　When Dick and I shall stroll or skate;
　　I'm positive, at any rate,
I would n't even dare to spoon
　　With Robbie Smithers at the gate,
Now there's a woman in the moon.

L'ENVOI

Sweetheart, it is a cruel fate,
　　Her advent's most inopportune;
It spoils our moonlight tête-à-tête,
　　Now there's a woman in the moon.

Josephine Dodge Daskam Bacon

(1876–1961)

Although she is listed in reference works most commonly as Josephine Bacon, she wrote most of her fiction using her maiden name Daskam (a 1909 work, *Margarita's Soul: The Romantic Recollections of a Man of Fifty*, was written under the pseudonym Ingraham Lovell). A prolific author of short stories, novels, articles and poems, Daskam also compiled the *Girl Scout National Handbook* in 1920 and wrote the words to a "Hymn for the Nations" for the United Nations. Daskam's active life also included the raising of three children, and one of her most popular books was *The Memoirs of a Baby*, a satire on theories of child-raising published in 1904. Her career as a writer began while she was a student at Smith College, from which she graduated in 1898; *Smith College Stories* was published in 1900. In addition to writing poems of her own, she edited two volumes, one of nonsense verse and one titled *Truth o' Women: Last Words From Ladies Long Vanished* (1923). In the first decades of the century, Daskam was a contributor to *Collier's, Harper's Bazaar, Ladies' Home Journal,* and *Saturday Evening Post.* Her serious fiction usually features the "New Woman" of the turn of the century: single, independent, and making her way bravely in a man's world. The central characters of *Cassie-on-the-Job* (1937), *Kathy* (1934), and *Domestic Adventures* (1907) all support themselves, and although Daskam was not a radical feminist, she shared in the concern for woman's changing roles that also informed the work of Alice Duer Miller, Florence Guy Seabury, and Charlotte Perkins Gilman during the same period. *Fables for the Fair* is one of the earliest and most feminist of Daskam's works. These "cau-

139

tionary tales," as they are sub-titled, were written for the "new woman" who might be tempted to think that there was a "new man," also—one ready to accept her education, independence, and ambitions—but the moral of each fable is that this has not come to pass.

SOURCES   *Contemporary Authors*, Vols. 97–100; *New York Times.* 31 July 1961: 19.

WORKS   *The Memoirs of a Baby* (1904) and *Fables for the Fair: Cautionary Tales for Damsels Not Yet in Distress* (1901)

from *Fables for the Fair:*
Cautionary Tales for Damsels Not Yet in Distress

The Woman Who Used Her Theory

There was once a Woman who had a Theory that Men did Not Care for Too Much Intellectuality in her Sex. After this Theory she shaped her Actions, which Shows her to have been a Remarkable Woman. One day a Man asked her if she Belonged to her Sister's Ibsen Club.

"Oh, no," she answered," I Cannot understand Ibsen at all."

The Next Time he called he brought her a Bunch of Violets and asked her if she read Maeterlinck.

"No; I think it is Very Silly," she replied.

Then the Man brought her a Box of Chocolates, remarking, "Sweets to the Sweet'—do you not think Shakspere was Right?"

The Woman saw that she was Making Progress. Now was her Time to Stop, but this she Did Not Perceive.

"Shakspere?" said she. "Oh, yes, I have read a Little of His Works, but I do not see Much Sense in them, to tell the Truth."

"Nay, Nay," said the Man, "this is Too Much. Not to Understand Ibsen shows that you are a Good Woman; to think Maeterlinck Silly augurs Well for your Intelligence; but not to see Much Sense in Shakspere implies that you are Uneducated."

And he did not Call Again.

This teaches us that it is Possible to Get Too Much of a Good Thing.

The Woman Who Took Things Literally

There was once a Woman who Invited a Celebrated Scientist to Take Tea with her. After Tea a Beggar came to the Door and Asked for a Meal. She remembered the Last Page of the Celebrated Scientist's last Essay, and addressed the Beggar thus:

"While I Regret to see you Suffering from Hunger, I Realize that I Injure Society more in Catering to Your Idleness than I Hurt my Feelings in Refusing your intrinsically Vicious Request." And she Sent him Away.

"Great Heavens!" cried the Celebrated Scientist. "It is Hard Enough for Me to act Thus, and I am Forced to in Order to be Consistent. But a Woman, whose Every Instinct shold be Charity and Sympathy Incarnate—it is Disgusting!"

This teaches us that What is Sauce for the Gander may be Saucy for the Goose.

The Woman Who Had Broad Views

There was once a Woman who Held very Broad Views. Of these Views she Often Spoke, as is the Habit of Those who Hold them. But though she was Very Advanced, she had her Little Plans, just Like the Rest of Us. One Day she was Talking with a Man who was Interested in Her, and therefore, as she Thought, in Her Views. For even Advanced Women make this Error Occasionally.

"If I were Married," she said, "I should Never for One Moment expect My Husband to Confide his Past to me. I should Consider it to be None of My Business. Nor should I Feel that he was Necessarily Immoral if he Looked at Any Other Woman but Me. For that is Idiotic, considering that Men are only Human."

The Man smiled Approvingly.

"You are Quite Right," he said. "If More Women were Like You, the World would be a Happier Place. But Few are so Broad-minded."

"And then," said the Woman, "I should Expect the Same Tolerance from Him; for Women are Only Human, too."

The Man Drew away his Chair. "I Fear," said he, somewhat Coldly, "that you are Carrying Matters a Little Too Far. The Constitution of

Society requires Some Foundation. There are Certain Things a Man has a Right to Exact from His Wife."

And he Engaged Himself to a Recent Graduate of a Convent School.

This teaches us that the Broad Road is More than Likely to Lead to Destruction.

The Woman Who Caught the Idea

There was once a Woman whose Fiancé had a Decided Theory regarding the most Desirable Characteristics of the Sexes. This Theory, in a Word, was that a Woman should be Like a Clinging Vine, while a Man should Resemble a Sturdy Oak. For Many Years, therefore, the Woman had Practised Clinging with Great Success. One day, However, her Fiancé grew Critical of her Method and Addressed her thus:

"The Century is Progressing, and it Behooves Us to Progress with it. How can I Produce Great Works with no Mental Stimulus? I Want to be Criticised—appreciatively—Not Admired. March Abreast of Me and be my Spiritual Comrade, not my Slave. A Woman is the Noblest of God's Works. She Symbolizes a Number of Things. Let me Feel that your Blind Adulation has some Valuable Basis. Do you Catch the Idea?"

The Woman was Thunderstruck.

"I am Afraid Not," she said, sadly. "Not Immediately, at Least. I must Admit that though I Admire your Work Dreadfully I can Not Understand it At All. I have been Clinging too Long."

So they Broke off the Engagement. The Fiancé found a Progressive and Stimulating Woman who Agreed to Criticise him and March Abreast of him. The only Trouble with this was that Not Only did she March Abreast, but it Seemed Probable that she would Get Ahead. Also she had a Work of Her Own, which sometimes Interfered with His.

This was Hard to Bear, and the Fiancé Found that his Views had Changed, and this time Forever.

"I have been a Fool," he said, bravely. "I was Wrong. I will Go Back to my Old Love. She cannot Criticise, Thank Heaven, but she can Cling. I will Carry on my Work, and she will sit in a Low Chair with a Basket of Little Clothes and the Lamplight falling on her Hair in the Good Old Way.

And if she Cannot Understand my Work, what of that? I can. A Man wants Sympathy, not Criticism."

So he Returned to his Old Love and said, "Let All Be as it was Before."

"I am Afraid that can Not be," she replied, Sadly. "Since I Lost You I have Given Up Clinging, and I have Caught Your Idea. I had to Sympathize with Someone, so I have Taken Up a Work of My Own. Judging from your Tone I think you Would Fail to Comprehend it. The Century is Progressing and Things can Never Be as they Were Before."

This teaches us that It's Well to Be On with the Old Love Before you are Off with the New.

Anne Richmond Warner French

(1869–1913)

Little in Anne Warner's background suggests the folksy, rural quality of her "Susan Clegg" stories. She was born in St. Paul, Minnesota, but spent much of her adult life in Europe and England, where she died at the age of forty-four. At eighteen, she married Charles French, a Minneapolis businessman twenty-five years her senior, but although she had three children by French (one a daughter who died in infancy), she seems to have lived with him only rarely, spending most of her time in Germany and England. Warner's early work, in fact, deals with the European experience: *His Story, Their Letters* (1902) concerns a thwarted love affair between two young people in France, and *A Woman's Will* (1904) features an American widow and her relationship with a German musician. When Warner (who wrote as Anne French, Anne Richmond Warner French, and Anne Warner) created her Susan Clegg character in 1904, in *Susan Clegg and Her Friend Mrs. Lathrop,* she achieved instant success as a humorous writer in the tradition of the "local-color" authors Harriet Beecher Stowe (whose story "The Minister's House-keeper" is in this volume) and Ruth McEnery Stuart. The first "Susan Clegg" book was followed by four more collections of stories about the chatty spinster Susan, who takes care of her elderly father and gossips with her neighbor Mrs. Lathrop, a casual housekeeper (as Susan is not), about men, duty, and social events in their small town. Like Alice Childress' *Like One of the Family,* these selections are more nearly monologues than dialogues: Childress' Mildred never lets her friend Marge get a word in; Susan Clegg similarly anticipates Mrs. Lathrop's every laconic response. Yet both selections are evidence of the humorous exchange and sense of community that exists between women, white or black.

SOURCES   *American Women Writers*, Vol 2; *Dictionary of American Biography* (1964)

WORKS   *Susan Clegg and Her Friend Mrs. Lathrop* (1904); *Susan Clegg and Her Love Affairs* (1906); *Susan Clegg and Her Neighbors' Affairs* (1906) and *Susan Clegg and a Man in the House* (1907)

from *Susan Clegg and Her Friend Mrs. Lathrop*

The Marrying of Susan Clegg

Susan Clegg and Mrs. Lathrop were next-door neighbors and bosom friends. Their personalities were extremely congenial, and the theoretical relation which the younger woman bore to the elder was a further bond between them. Owing to the death of her mother some twenty years before, Susan had fallen into the position of a helpless and timid young girl whose only key to the problems of life in general had been the advice of her older and wiser neighbor. As a matter of fact Mrs. Lathrop was barely twelve years the senior, but she had married and as a consequence felt and was felt to be immeasurably the more ancient of the two.

Susan had never married, for her father—a bedridden paralytic—had occupied her time day and night for years. He was a great care and as she did her duty by him with a thoroughness which was praiseworthy in the extreme she naturally had very little leisure for society. Mrs. Lathrop had more, because her family consisted of but one son, and she was not given to that species of housekeeping which sweeps under the beds too often. It therefore came about that the one and only recreation which the friends could enjoy together to any great extent was visiting over the fence. Visiting over the fence is an occupation in which any woman may indulge without fear of unkind criticism.

If she takes occasion to run in next door, she is of course leaving the house which she ought to be keeping, but she can lean on the fence all day without feeling derelict as to a single duty. Then, too, there is something about the situation which produces a species of agreeable sub-consciousness that one is at once at home and abroad. It followed that

Susan and Mrs. Lathrop each wore a path from her kitchen door to the trysting-spot, and that all summer long they met there early and late.

Mrs. Lathrop did the listening while she chewed clover. Just beyond her woodpile red clover grew luxuriantly, and when she started for the place of meeting it was her invariable custom to stop and pull a number of blossoms so that she might eat the tender petals while devoting her attention to the business in hand.

It must be confessed that the business in hand was nearly always Miss Clegg's business, but since Mrs. Lathrop, in her position of experienced adviser, was deeply interested in Susan's exposition of her own affairs, that trifling circumstance appeared of little moment.

One of the main topics of conversation was Mr. Clegg. As Mr. Clegg had not quitted his bed for over a score of years, it might seem that his novelty as a subject of discussion would have been long since exhausted. But not so. His daughter was the most devoted of daughters, and his name was ever rife on her lips. What he required done for him and what he required done to him were the main ends of her existence, and the demands of his comfort, daily or annual, resulted in numerous phrases of a startling but thoroughly intelligible order. Of such a sort was her usual Saturday morning greeting to Mrs. Lathrop, "I'm sorry to cut you off so quick, but this 's father's day to be beat up and got into new pillow-slips," or her regular early-June remark, "Well, I thank Heaven 't father's had his hair picked over 'n' 't he's got his new tick for *this* year!"

Mrs. Lathrop was always interested, always sympathetic, and rarely ever startled; yet one July evening when Susan said suddenly, "I've finished my dress for father's funeral," she did betray a slight shock.

"You ought to see it," the younger woman continued, not noticing the other's start,—"it's jus' 's *nice*. I put it away in camphor balls, 'n' Lord knows I don't look forward to the gettin' it out to wear, f'r the whole carriage load'll sneeze their heads off whenever I move in that dress."

"Did you put newspaper—" Mrs. Lathrop began, mastering her earlier emotions.

"In the sleeves? Yes, I did, 'n' I bought a pair o' black gloves 'n' two handkerchiefs 'n' slipped 'em into the pockets. Everythin' is all fixed, 'n' there'll be nothin' to do when father dies but to shake it out 'n' lay it on the bed in his room. I say 'in his room,' 'cause o' course that day he'll be havin' the guest-room. I was thinkin' of it all this afternoon when I sat there by him hemmin' the braid on the skirt, 'n' I could n't but think 't if I sit 'n' wait very much longer I sh'll suddenly find myself pretty far advanced in years afore I know it. This world's made f'r the young 's well 's the old, 'n' you c'n believe me or not jus' 's you please, Mrs. Lathrop, but I've always meant to get married 's soon 's father was off my hands. I was countin' up to-day, though, 'n' if he lives to be a hunderd, I'll be nigh onto seventy 'n' no man ain't goin' to marry me at seventy. Not 'nless he was eighty, 'n' Lord knows I ain't intendin' to bury father jus' to begin on some one else, 'n' that's all it'd be."

Mrs. Lathrop chewed her clover.

"I set there thinkin' f'r a good hour, 'n' when I was putting' away the dress, I kep' on thinkin', 'n' the end was 't now that dress 's done I ain't got nothin' in especial to sew on 'n' so I may jus' 's well begin on my weddin' things. There's no time like the present, 'n' 'f I married this summer *he'd* have to pay f'r half of next winter's coal. 'N' so my mind's made up, 'n' you c'n talk yourself blind, 'f you feel so inclined, Mrs. Lathrop, but you can't change hide or hair o' my way o' thinkin'. I've made up my mind to get married, 'n' I'm goin' to set right about it. Where there's a will there's a way, 'n' I ain't goin' to leave a stone unturned. I went down town with the kerosene-can jus' afore tea, 'n' I bought me a new false front, 'n' I met Mrs. Brown's son, 'n' I told him 't I wanted him to come up to-morrow 'n' take a look at father."

"Was you thinkin' o' marryin' Mrs. Br—" Mrs. Lathrop gasped, taking her clover from her lips.

"Marryin' Mrs. Brown's son! Well, 'f your mind don't run queer ways! Whatever sh'd put such an idea into your head? I hope you'll excuse my sayin' so, Mrs. Lathrop, but I don't believe anybody but you would ever 'a' asked such a question, when you know's well 's everybody else does 't he's runnin' his legs off after Amelia Fitch. Any man who wants a little chit o' eighteen wouldn't suit my taste much, 'n' anyhow I never thought of him; I only asked him to come in in a friendly way 'n' tell me how long he thinks 't father may live. I don't see my way to makin' any sort o' plans with father so dreffle indefinite, 'n' a man who was fool enough to marry me, tied up like I am now, would n't have s'fficient brains to be worth lookin' over. Mrs. Brown's son 's learnin' docterin', 'n' he's been at it long enough so's to be able to see through anythin' 's simple 's father, *I* sh'd think. 'T any rate, 'f he don't know nothin' yet, Heaven help Amelia Fitch 'n' me, f'r he'll take us both in."

"Who was you thinkin' o'—" Mrs. Lathrop asked, resuming her former occupation.

"The minister," replied Miss Clegg. "I did n't stop to consider very much, but it struck me 's polite to begin with him. I c'd marry him without waitin' for father, too, 'cause a minister could n't in reason find fault over another man's bein' always to home. O' course he would n't be still like father is, but I ain't never been one to look gift-horses in the mouth, 'n' I d'n' know 's I'd ought to expect another man *jus'* like father in one life. Mother often said father's advantages was great, for you always knew where he was, 'n' 'f you drew down the shade you c'd tell him it was rainin' 'n' he could n't never contradick."

Mrs. Lathrop nodded acquiescently but made no comment.

Miss Clegg withdrew somewhat from her confidentially inclined attitude.

"I won't be out in the mornin'," she said. "I sh'll want to dust father — n' turn him out o' the window afore Mrs. Brown's son comes. After he's gone I'll wave my dish-towel, 'n' then you come out 'n' I'll tell you what he says."

They separated for the night, and Susan went to sleep with her own version of love's young dream.

Mrs. Brown's son arrived quite promptly the next morning. He drove up in Mr. Brown's buggy, and Amelia Fitch held the horse while he went inside to inspect Mr. Clegg. The visit did not consume more than ten minutes, and then he hurried out to the gate and was off.

The buggy was hardly out of sight up the road when Miss Clegg emerged from her kitchen door, her face bearing an imprint of deep and thorough disgust,

"Well, Mrs. Lathrop, I don't think much o' *that* young man," she announced in a tone of unmitigated disapproval; " 'peared to me like he was in a hurry to get done with father 's quick 's he could just so 's to be back beside Amelia Fitch. I'd venture a guess that 'f you was to ask him this minute he's forgot every word I said to him already. I asked him to set some sort of a figger on father, 'n' he would n't so much 's set down himself. Stood on one leg 'n' backed towards the door every other word, 'n' me, father's only child, standin' there at his mercy. Said 't last 's he *might* die to-morrow 'n' *might* live twenty years. I tell you my patience pretty near went at that. I don't call such a answer no answer a *tall*. I've often thought both them things myself, 'n' me no doctor. Particularly about the twenty years. Father's lived seventy-five years—I must say 't to my order o' thinkin' he's pretty well set a-goin', 'n' that the life he leads ain't drainin' his vitality near 's much 's it's drainin' mine."

Miss Clegg stopped and shook her head impatiently.

"I d'n' know when I've felt as put out 's this. 'N' me with so much faith in doctors too. It's a pretty sad thing, Mrs. Lathrop, when all the comfort you c'n get out of a man is the thinkin' 't perhaps God in his mercy has made him a fool. I had a good mind to tell that very thing to Mrs. Brown's son, but I thought maybe he'd learn better later. Anyway I'm goin' right ahead with my marriage. It'll have to be the minister now, 'n' I can't see what I've ever done 't I sh'd have two men around the house 't once like they'll be, but that 's all in the hands o' Fate, 'n' so I jus' took the first step 'n' told Billy when he brought the milk to tell his father 't if he'd come up here to-night I'd give him a quarter for the Mission fund. I know the quarter 'll bring him, 'n' I can't help kind o' hopin' 't to-morrow 'll find the whole thing settled 'n' off my mind."

The next morning Mrs. Lathrop laid in an unusually large supply of fodder and was very early at the fence. Her son—a placid little innocent of nine-and-twenty years—was still in bed and asleep. Susan was up and washing her breakfast dishes, but the instant that she spied her friend she abruptly abandoned her task and hastened to the rendezvous.

"Are you goin' t'—" Mrs. Lathrop called eagerly.

"No, I ain't," was the incisive reply.

Then they both adjusted their elbows comfortably on the top rail of the fence, and Miss Clegg began, her voice a trifle higher pitched than usual.

"Mrs. Lathrop, it's a awful thing for a Christian woman to feel forced to say, 'n' Lord knows I would n't say it to no one but you, but it's true 'n' beyond a question so, 'n' therefore I may 's well be frank 'n' open 'n' remark 't our minister ain't no good a *tall*.—'N' I d'n' know but I'll tell, any one 's asks me the same thing, f'r it certainly ain't nothin' f'r me to weep over, 'n' the blood be on his head from on."

Miss Clegg paused briefly, and her eyes became particularly wide open. Mrs. Lathrop was all attention.

"Mrs. Lathrop, you ain't lived next to me 'n' known me in 'n' out 'n' hind 'n' front all these years not to know 't I'm pretty sharp. I ain't been cheated mor' 'n twice 'n my life, 'n' one o' them times was n't my fault, for it was printed on the band 't it would wash. Such bein' the case, 'n' takin' the minister into consideration, I do consider 't *no* man would 'a' supposed 't he could get the better o' me. It's a sad thing to have to own to, 'n' if I was anybody else in kingdom come I'd never own to it till I got there; but my way is to live open 'n' aboveboard, 'n' so to my shame be 't told 't the minister—with all 't he's got eight children 'n' I ain't even married—is certainly as sharp as me. Last night when I see him comin' up the walk I never 'd 'a' believed 's he c'd get away again so easy, but it just goes to show what a world o' deceit this is, 'n' seein 's 's I have father to clean from his windows aroun' to-day, I'll ask you to excuse me 'f I don't draw the subjeck out none, but jus' remark flat 'n' plain 't there ain't no chance o' my *ever* marryin' the minister. You may consider that a pretty strong statement, Mrs. Lathrop, 'n' I don't say myself but 't with any other man there might be a hereafter, but it was me 'n' not anybody else as see his face last night, 'n' seein' his face 'n' bein' a woman o' more brains 'n falls to the lot of yourself 'n' the majority, I may just as well say once for all that, 's far 's the minister's concerned, I sh'll never be married to *him*."

"What did he—" began Mrs. Lathrop.

"All 't was necessary 'n' more too. He did n't give me hardly time to state 't I was single afore he come out strong 't we'd both better stay so. I spoke right out to his face then, 'n' told him 't my shingles was new last year 'n' it was a open question whether his 'd ever be, but he piped up f'r all the world like some o' the talkin' was his to do, 'n' said 't he had a cistern 'n' I'd only got a sunk hogshead under the spout. I did n't see no way to denyin' *that*, but I went right on 'n' asked him 'f he could in his conscience deny 't them eight children stood in vital need of a good mother, 'n' he spoke up 's quick 's scat 'n' said 't no child stood in absolute vital need of a mother after it was born. 'N' then he branched out 'n' give me to understand 't he had a wife till them eight children all got themselves launched 'n' 't it was n't his fault her dyin' o' Rachel Rebecca. When he said 'dyin',' I broke in 'n' said 't it was Bible-true 's there was 's good fish in the sea 's ever was caught out of it, 'n' he was impolite enough to interrupt 'n' tell me to my face 'Yes, but when a man had been caught once he was n't easy caught again.' I will own 't I was more 'n put out 't that, for o' course when I said *fish* I meant his wife 'n' me, but when he pretended to think 't I meant him I begin to doubt 's it was worth while to tackle him further. One man can lead a horse to water, but a thousand can't get him to stick his nose in 'f he don't want to, 'n' I thank my stars 't I ain't got nothin' 'n me as craves to marry a man 's appears dead-set ag'in' the idea. I asked him 'f he did n't think 's comin' into property was always a agreeable feelin', 'n' he said, 'Yes, but not when with riches come a secret thorn in the flesh,' 'n' at that I clean give up, 'n' I hope it was n't to my discredit, for no one on the face of the earth could 'a' felt 't there 'd be any good in keepin' on. But it was no use, 'n' you know 's well as I do 't I never was give to wastin' my breath, so I out 'n' told him 't I was n't giv' to wastin' my time either, 'n' then I stood up 'n' he did too. 'N' *then* I got even with him, 'n' I c'n assure you 't I enjoyed it, f'r I out 'n' told him 't I'd changed my mind about the quarter. So he had all that long walk for nothin', 'n' I can't in conscience deny 't I was more 'n rejoiced, for Lord knows I did n't consider 't he had acted very obligin'."

Mrs. Lathrop ceased to chew and looked deeply sympathetic.

There was a brief silence, and then she asked, "Was you thinkin' o' tryin' any—"

Mrs. Clegg stared at her in amazement.

"Mrs. Lathrop! Do you think I'd give up now, 'n' let the minister see 't my marryin' depended on *his* say-so? Well, I guess not! I'm more dead-set 'n' ever, 'n' I vow 'n' declare 't I'll never draw breath till after I've stood up right in the face o' the minister 'n' the whole congregation 'n' had 'n' held some man, no matter who nor when nor where. Marryin' was goin' to have been a pleasure, now it's a business. I'm goin' to get a horse 'n' buggy this afternoon 'n' drive out to Farmer Sperrit's. I've thought it all over, 'n' I c'n tell father 't I'll be choppin' wood; then 'f he says afterwards 't he called 'n' called, I c'n say 't I was makin' so much noise 't I did n't hear him."

"You'll have to hire—" suggested Mrs. Lathrop.

"I know, but it won't cost but fifty cents, 'n' I saved a quarter on the minister, you know. I'd like to ask you to drive out with me, Mrs. Lathrop, but if Mr. Sperrit's got it in him to talk like the minister did, I'm free to confess 't, I'd rather be alone to listen. 'N' really, Mrs. Lathrop, I must go in now. I've got bread a-risin' 'n' dishes to do, 'n', as I told you before, this is father's day to be all but scraped 'n' varnished."

Mrs. Lathrop withdrew her support from the fence, and Miss Clegg did likewise. Each returned up her own path to her own domicile, and it was long after that day's tea-time before the cord of friendship got knotted up again.

"Did you go to the farm?" Mrs. Lathrop asked. "I was to the Sewin' So—"

"Yes, I went," said Miss Clegg, her air decidedly weary; "oh, yes, I went. I had a nice ride too, 'n' I do believe I saw the whole farm, from the pigs to the punkins."

There was a pause, and Mrs. Lathrop filled it to the brim with expectancy until she could wait no longer.

"Are you—" she finally asked.

"No," said her friend, sharply, "I ain't. He was n't a bit spry to hop at the chance, 'n' Lord knows there wa'n't no great urgin' on my part. I asked him why he ain't never married, 'n' he laughed like it was a funny subjeck, 'n' he said 's long 's he never did 't that was the least o' *his* troubles. I did n't call that a very encouragin' beginnin', but my mind was made up not to let it be *my* fault 'f the horse was a dead waste o' fifty cents, 'n' so I said to him 't if he'd marry any woman with a little money he could easy buy the little Jones farm right next him, 'n' then 't 'd be 's clear 's day that it 'd be his own fault if he did n't soon stretch right from the brook to the road. He laughed some more 't that, 'n' said 't I did n't seem to be aware 't he owned a mortgage on the Jones farm 'n' got all 't it raised now 'n' would get the whole thing in less 'n two years."

Mrs. Lathrop stopped chewing.

"They was sayin' in the Sewin' Society 's he 's goin' to marry Eliza Gr—" she said mildly.

Miss Clegg almost screamed.

"Eliza Gringer, as keeps house for him?"

Her friend nodded.

Miss Clegg drew in a sudden breath.

"Well! 'f I'd knowed *that,* I'd never 'a' paid fifty cents for that horse 'n' buggy! Eliza Gringer! why, she's older 'n' I am,—she was to 'Cat' when I was only to 'M.' 'N' he 's goin' to marry her! Oh, well, I d'n' know 's it makes any difference to me. In my opinion a man as 'd be fool enough to be willin' to marry a woman 's ain't got nothin' but herself to give him, 's likelier to be happier bein' her fool 'n he ever would be bein' mine."

There was a pause.

"Your father's just the—" Mrs. Lathrop said at last.

"Same? Oh yes, he's just the same. Seems 't I can't remember when he was n't just the same."

Then there was another pause.

"I ain't discouraged," Susan announced suddenly, almost aggressively,—"I ain't discouraged 'n' I won't give up. I'm goin' to see Mr. Weskin, the lawyer, to-morrow. They say—'n' I never see nothin' to lead me to doubt 'em—'t he's stingy 'n' mean for all he's forever makin' so merry at other folks' expense; but I believe 't there's good in everythin' 'f you 're willin' to hunt for it 'n' Lord knows 't if this game keeps up much longer I'll get so used to huntin' 't huntin' the good in Lawyer Weskin 'll jus' be child's play to me."

"I was thinkin'—" began Mrs. Lathrop.

"It ain't no use if you are," said her neighbor; "the mosquitoes is gettin' too thick. We'd better in."

And so they parted for the night.

The following evening was hot and breathless, the approach of Fourth of July appearing to hang heavily over all. Susan brought a palm-leaf fan with her to the fence and fanned vigorously.

"It ain't goin' to be the lawyer, either," she informed the expectant Mrs. Lathrop, " 'n' I hav' n't no tears to shed over *that*. I went there the first thing after dinner, 'n' he give me a solid chair 'n' whirled aroun' in one 't twisted, 'n' I did n't fancy such manners under such circumstances a *tall*. I'd say suthin' real serious 'n' he'd brace himself ag'in his desk 'n' take a spin 's if I did n't count for sixpence. I could n't seem to bring him around to the seriousness of the thing nohow. 'N' I come right out square 'n' open in the very beginnin' too, for Lord knows I'm dead sick o' beatin' around the bush o' men's natural shyness. He whirled himself clean around two times 'n' then said 's long 's I was so frank with him 't it 'd be nothin' but a joy for him to be equally frank with me 'n' jus' say 's he'd rather not. I told him he'd ought to remember 's he'd have a lot o' business when father died 'f he kept my good will, but he was lookin' over 'n' under himself to see how near to unscrewed he was 'n' if it was safe to keep on turnin' the same way any longer, 'n' upon my honor, Mrs. Lathrop, I was nigh to mad afore he got ready to remark 's father 'd left him a legacy on condition 't he did n't charge nothin' for probatin'."

Mrs. Lathrop chewed her clover.

"So I come away, 'n' I declare my patience is nigh to gin out. This gettin' married is harder 'n' house-paintin' in fly-time. I d'n' know when I've felt so tired. Here's three nights 't I've had to make my ideas all over new to suit a different husband each night. It made my very bones ache to think o' pilin' them eight children 'n' the minister on top o' father, 'n' then the next night it was a good jump out to that farm, f'r I never was one to know any species o' fellow-feelin' with pigs 'n' milkin'. 'N' last night!—Well, you know I never liked Mr. Weskin anyhow. But I d'n' know who I *can* get now. There's Mrs. Healy's husband, o' course; but when a woman looks happier in her coffin 'n she ever looked out of it's more 'n a hint to them 's stays behind to fight shy o' her husband. They say he used to throw dishes at her, 'n' I never could stand that—I'm too careful o' my china to risk any such goin's on."

Mrs. Lathrop started to speak, but got no further.

"There's a new clerk in the drug-store,—I see him through the window when I was comin' home to-day. He looked to be a nice kind o' man, but I can't help feelin' 't it 'd be kind o' awkward to go up to him 'n' have to begin by askin' him what my name 'd be 'f I married him. Maybe there's them 's could do such a thing, but I've never had nothin' about me 's 'd lead me to throw myself at the head o' any man, 'n' it 's too late in the day f'r me to start in now."

Mrs. Lathrop again attempted to get in a word and was again unsuccessful.

"I don't believe 't there's another free man in the town. I've thought 'n' thought 'n' I can't think o' one." She stopped and sighed.

"There's Jathrop!" said Mrs. Lathrop, with sudden and complete success. Jathrop was her son, so baptized through a fearful slip of the tongue at a critical moment. He was meant to have been John.

Miss Clegg gave such a start that she dropped her fan over the fence.

"Well, Heaven forgive me!" she cried,—" 'n' me 't never thought of him once, 'n' him so handy right on the other side of the fence! Did I ever!"

"He ain't thir—" said Mrs. Lathrop, picking up the fan.

"I don't care. What's twelve years or so when it's the woman 's 'as got the property? Well, Mrs. Lathrop, I certainly *am* obliged to you for mentionin' him, for I don't believe he ever would 'a' occurred to me in kingdom come. 'N' here I've been worryin' my head off ever since suppertime 'n' all for suthin' 's close 's Jathrop Lathrop. But I had good cause to worry, 'n' now 't it's over I don't mind mentionin' the reason 'n' tellin' you frank 'n' plain 't I'd begun on my things. I cut out a pink nightgown last night, a real fussy one, 'n' I felt sick all over 't the thought 't perhaps I'd wasted all that cloth. There wan't nothin' foolish about cuttin' out the nightgown, for I'd made up my mind 't if it looked too awful fancy on 't I'd just put it away for the oldest girl when she gets married, but o' course 'f I can't get a husband stands to reason there'll be no oldest girl, 'n' all that ten cent gingham 't Shores is sellin' off 't five 'd be a dead waste o' good stuff."

Mrs. Lathrop chewed her clover.

"Do you suppose there'll be any trouble with Jathrop? Do you suppose it 'll matter any to him which side o' the fence he lives on?"

Mrs. Lathrop shook her head slowly.

"I sh'd think he ought to be only too pleased to marry me 'f I want him to, all the days 't I tended him when he was a baby! My, but he *was* a cute little fellow! Everybody was lookin' for him to grow up a real credit to you *then*. Well, 's far 's that goes, it's a ill wind 't blows no good, 'n' no one c'n deny 't he's been easy for you to manage, 'n' what's sauce f'r the goose is sauce f'r the gander, so I sh'll look to be equally lucky."

Mrs. Lathrop looked proud and pleased.

"Why can't you ask him to-night 'n' let me know the first thing in the mornin'? That'll save me havin' to come 'way aroun' by the gate, you know."

Mrs. Lathrop assented to the obvious good sense of this proposition with one emphatic nod of her head.

" 'N' I'll come out jus' 's quick 's I can in the mornin' 'n' hear what he said; I 'll come 's soon 's ever I can get father 'n' the dishes washed up. I hope to Heaven father'll sleep more this night 'n he did last. He was awful restless last night. He kept callin' f'r things till finally I had to take a pillow and go down on the dinin'-room lounge to keep from bein' woke up any more."

"Do you think he's—"

"No, I don't think he's worse; not 'nless wakin' up 'n' askin' f'r things jus' to be aggravatin' is worse. If it is, then he is too. But, lor, there ain't no manner o' use in talkin' o' father! A watched pot *never* boils! Jathrop 's more to the point right now."

Upon this hint Mrs. Lathrop de-fenced herself, so to speak, and the friendly chat ended for that time.

The morning after Miss Clegg was slow to appear at the summons of her neighbor. When she did approach the spot where the other stood waiting, her whole face and figure bore a weary and fretful air.

"Father jus' about kept me up this whole blessed night," she began as soon as she was within easy hearing. "I d'n' know what I want to get married f'r, when I'm bound to be man-free in twenty-five years 'f I c'n jus' make out to live that long."

Mrs. Lathrop chewed and listened.

"If there was anythin' in the house 't father did n't ask f'r 'n' 't I did n't get him last night, it must 'a' been the cook-stove in the kitchen. I come nigh to losin' a toe in the rat-trap the third time I was down cellar, 'n' I clum that ladder to the garret so many times I do believe I dusted all overhead with my hair afore mornin'. My ears is full o' cobwebs too, 'n' you know 's well 's I do 't I never was one to fancy cobwebs about me. They say 't every cloud has a silver linin', but I can't see no silver linin' to a night like last night. When the rooster crowed f'r the first time this mornin', I had it in my heart to march right out there 'n' hack off his head. If it'd 'a' been Saturday, I'd 'a' done 't too, 'n' relished him good at Sunday dinner!"

Miss Clegg paused and compressed her lips firmly for a few seconds; then she gave herself a little shake and descended to the main question of the day.

"Well, what did Jathrop say?"

Mrs. Lathrop looked very uncomfortable indeed, and in lieu of an answer swallowed her clover.

"You asked him, did n't you?"

"Yes, I—"

"Well, what 'd he say?"

"He ain't very—"

"My soul 'n' body! What reason did he give?"

"He's afraid your father's livin' on a annu—"

"Well, he ain't." Susan's tone was more than a little displeased. "Whatever else father may 'a' done, he never played no annuity tricks. He's livin' on his own property, 'n' I'll take it very kindly o' you, Mrs. Lathrop, to make that piece o' news clear to your son. My father's got bank-stock, 'n' he owns them two cottages across the bridge, 'n' the blacksmith-shop belongs to him too. There! I declare I never thought o' the blacksmith,— his wife died last winter."

"Jathrop asked me what I th—"

"Well, what 'd you tell him?"

"I said 't if your father was some older—"

Miss Clegg's eyebrows moved understandingly.

"How long is it since you 've seen father?" she asked without waiting for the other to end her sentence.

"Not since your mother died, I guess; I was—"

"I wish you c'd come over 'n' take a look at him now 'n' tell me your opinion. Why can't you?"

Mrs. Lathrop reflected.

"I don't see why I can't. I'll go in 'n' take off—"

"All right, 'n' when you've got it off, come right over 'n' you'll find me in the kitchen waitin' for you."

Mrs. Lathrop returned to her own house to shed her apron and wash her hands, and then sallied over to view Mr. Clegg. The two friends mounted the stair together, and entered the old man's room.

It was a scrupulously clean and bright and orderly room, and the invalid in the big white bed bore evidence to the care and attention so dutifully lavished on him. He was a very wizened little old man, and his features had been crossed and recrossed by the finger of Time until their original characteristics were nearly obliterated. The expression upon his face resembled nothing so much as a sketch which has been done over so many times that its first design is altogether lost, and if there was any answer to the riddle, it was not the mental perception of Mrs. Lathrop that was about to seize upon it.

Instead, that kindly visitor stood lost in a species of helpless contemplation, until at last a motion of Susan's, directed towards the ordering of an unsightly fold in the wide smoothness of the counterpane, led to her bending herself to do a similar kindness upon her side of the bed. The action resulted in a slight change in her expression which Susan's watchfulness at once perceived.

"Was it a needle?" she asked quickly. "Sometimes I stick 'em in while I'm sewin'. You see, his havin' been paralyzed so many years has got me where I'm awful careless about leavin' needles in his bed."

"No," said Mrs. Lathrop; "it wasn't a—"

"Come on downstairs again," said the hostess; "we c'n talk there."

They went down into the kitchen, and there Mrs. Lathrop seated herself and coughed solemnly.

"What is it, anyhow?" the younger woman demanded.

Mrs. Lathrop coughed again.

"Susan, did I feel a feather—"

"Yes," said Susan, in great surprise; "he likes one."

"I sh'd think it was too hot this—"

"He don't never complain o' the heat, 'n' he hates the chill o' rainy days."

Mrs. Lathrop coughed again.

Miss Clegg's interest bordered on impatience.

"Now, Susan, I ain't sayin' as it's noways true, but I *have* heard as there's them's can't die on—"

"On feathers?" cried the daughter.

"Yes; they say they hold the life right in 'n'—"

Miss Clegg's eyes opened widely.

"But I couldn't take it away from him, anyhow," she said, with a species of determined resignation in her voice. "I'd have to wait 'till he wanted it took."

Mrs. Lathrop was silent. Then she rose to go. Susan rose too. They went out the kitchen door together, and down the steps. There they paused to part.

"Do you believe 't it 'd be any use me thinkin' o' Lathrop any more?" the maiden asked the matron.

"I believe I'd try the blacksmith if I was you; he looks mighty nice Sundays."

Miss Clegg sighed heavily and turned to re-enter the house.

Mrs. Lathrop went "round by the gate" and became again an inmate of her own kitchen. There the thought occurred to her that it was an excellent morning to clean the high-shelf over the sink. For years past whenever she had had occasion to put anything up there, showers of dust and rolls of lint had come tumbling down upon her head. Under such circumstances it was but natural that a determination to some day clean the shelf should have slowly but surely been developed. Accordingly she climbed up on the edge of the sink and undertook the initiatory proceedings. The lowest stratum of dirt was found to rest upon a newspaper containing an account of one day of Guiteau's trial. Upon the discovery of the paper Mrs. Lathrop suddenly abandoned her original plan, got down from the sink, ensconced herself in her kitchen rocker, and plunged into bliss forthwith.

An hour passed pleasantly and placidly by. Bees buzzed outside the window, the kettle sizzled sweetly on the stove, the newspaper rustled less and less, Mrs. Lathrop's head sank sideways, and the calm of perfect peace reigned in her immediate vicinity.

This state of things endured not long.

Its gentle Paradise was suddenly broken in upon and rent apart by a succession of the most piercing shrieks that ever originated in the throat of a human being. Mrs. Lathrop came to herself with a violent start, sprang to her feet, ran to the door, and then stood still, completely dazed and at first unable to discern from which direction the ear-splitting screams proceeded. Then, in a second, her senses returned to her, and she ran as fast as she could to the fence. As she approached the boundary, she saw Susan standing in one of her upstairs windows and yelling at the top of her voice. Mrs. Lathrop paused for no conventionalities of civilization. She hoisted herself over the fence in a fashion worthy a man or a monkey, ran across the Clegg yard, entered the kitchen door, stumbled breathlessly up the dark back stairs, and gasped, grabbing Susan hard by the elbow,—

"What *is* it, for pity's—"

Susan was all colors and shaking as if with the ague.

"You never told me 's it 'd work so quick," she cried out.

"What would—"

"The feathers!"

"Whose feathers?"

"Father's feathers."

"Lord have mercy, Susan, you don't mean—"

"Yes, I do."

"He ain't never—"

"Yes, he is."

Mrs. Lathrop stood stricken.

Susan wiped her eyes with her apron and choked.

After a while the older woman spoke feebly.

"What did hap—"

Miss Clegg cut the question off in its prime.

"I don't know as I c'n ever tell you; it's too awful even to think of."

"But you—"

"I know, 'n' I'm goin' to. But I tell you once for all, Mrs. Lathrop, 't this'll be a lesson to me forever after 's to takin' the say-so o' other folks unto myself. 'N' I didn't really consider 't I was doin' so this time, f'r if I had, Lord knows I'd 'a' landed three beds atop o' him afore I'd 'a' ever—" She stopped and shook convulsively.

"Go on," said Mrs. Lathrop, her curiosity getting the better of her sympathy, and her impatience ranking both.

Susan ceased sobbing, and essayed explanation.

"You see, after you was gone, he said 't he *was* pretty hot these last nights, 'n' 't that was maybe what kept him so awfully awake. I asked him if—if—maybe the feather-bed 'n'—well, Mrs. Lathrop, to put the whole in a nut-shell, we settled to move him, 'n' I moved him. I know I didn't hurt him one bit, for I'm 's handy with—at least, I *was* 's handy with him 's I am with a broom. 'N' I laid him on the lounge, 'n' dumped that bed out into the back hall. I thought I'd sun it 'n' put it away this afternoon, f'r *you* know 's I'm never no hand to leave nothin' lyin' aroun'. Well, I come back 'n' got out some fresh sheets, 'n' jus' 's I was—"

The speaker halted, and there was a dramatic pause.

"Where is—" Mrs. Lathrop asked at last.

"Back in the feathers. My heaven alive! When I see what I'd done, I was that upset 't I just run 's quick 's ever I could, 'n' got the bed, 'n' dumped it right atop of him!"

There was another dramatic silence, finally broken by Mrs. Lathrop's saying slowly and gravely,—

"Susan, 'f I was you I wouldn't never say—"

"I ain't goin' to. I made up my mind to never tell a livin' soul the very first thing. To think o' me doin' it! To think o' all these years 't I've tended father night 'n' day, 'n' then to accidentally go 'n' do a thing like that! I declare, it fairly makes me sick all over!"

"Well, Susan, you know what a good daughter you've—"

"I know, 'n' I've been thinkin' of it. But somehow nothin' don't seem to comfort me none. Perhaps you'd better make me some tea, 'n' while I'm drinkin' it, Jathrop c'n go down town 'n'—"

"Yes," said Mrs. Lathrop, " 'n' I'll go right 'n'—"

"That's right," said the bereaved, " 'n' hurry."

It was a week later—a calm and lovely evening—and the two friends stood by the fence. The orphan girl was talking, while Mrs. Lathrop chewed her clover.

"It don't seem like only a week!—seems more like a month or even a year. Well, they say sometimes, folks live a long ways ahead in a very short time, 'n' I must say 't, as far's my observation 's extended, comin' into property always leads to experience, so I could n't in reason complain 't not bein' no exception. This 's been the liveliest week o' my life, 'n' I'm free to confess 't I haven't cried anywhere near 's much 's I looked to. My feelin's have been pretty agreeable, take it all in all, 'n' I'd be a born fool 'f I didn't take solid comfort sleepin' nights, 'n' I never was a fool—never was 'n' never will be. The havin' somebody to sleep in the house 's been hard, 'n' Mrs. Macy's fallin' through the cellar-flap giv' me a bad turn, but she's doin' nicely, 'n' the minister makes up f'r anythin'. I do wish 't you'd seen him that afternoon, Mrs. Lathrop; he did look *so* most awful sheepish, 'n' his clean collar give him dead away afore he ever opened his mouth. He set out by sayin' 't the consolations of religion was mine f'r the askin', but I didn't take the hint, 'n' so he had to jus' come out flat 'n' say 't he'd been thinkin' it over 'n' he'd changed his mind. I held my head good 'n' high 't that, I c'n assure you, 'n' it was a pretty sorry look he give me when I said 't I'd been thinkin' it over too, 'n' I'd changed my mind too. He could 'a' talked to me till doomsday about his bein' a consolation, I'd know it was nothin' 't changed him but me comin' into them government bonds. No man alive could help wantin' me after them bonds was found, 'n' I had the great pleasure o' learnin' that fact out o' Lawyer Weskin himself. All his species o' fun-makin' 't nobody but hisself ever sees any fun in, jus' died right out when we unlocked father's old desk 'n' come on that bundle o' papers. He give one look 'n' then all his gay spinniness oozed right out o' him, 'n' he told me 's serious 's a judge 't a woman 's rich 's I be needed a good lawyer to look out f'r her 'n' her property right straight along. Well I was 's quick to reply 's he was to speak. 'N' I was to the point too. I jus' up 'n' said, Yes, I thought so myself, 'n' jus' 's soon 's I got things to rights I was goin' to the city 'n' get me one."

Miss Clegg paused to frown reminiscently; Mrs. Lathrop's eyes never quitted the other's face.

"There was Mr. Sperrit too. Come with a big basket o' fresh vegetables 't he said he thought 'd maybe tempt my appetite. I d'n' know 's I ever enjoyed rappin' no one over the knuckles more 'n I did him. I jus' stopped to take in plenty o' breath 'n' then I let myself out, 'n' I says to him flat 'n' plain, I says, 'Thank you kindly, but I guess no woman in these parts 's better able to tempt her own appetite 'n' I be now, 'n' you'll be doin' me the only kindness 't it's in you to do me now if you'll jus' take your garden stuff 'n' give it to some one 's is poor 'n' needin'.' He looked so crestfallen 't I made up my mind 't it was then or never to settle my whole score with him, so I up 'n' looked him right in the eye 'n' I says to him, I says, 'Mr. Sperrit, you did n't seem to jus' realize what it meant to me that day 't I took that horse 'n' buggy 'n' drove 'way out to your farm to see you; you didn't seem to think what it meant to me to take that trip: but I c'n tell you 't it costs suthin' for a woman to do a thing like that; it cost me a good deal—it cost me fifty cents.' He went away then, 'n' he can marry Eliza Gringer if he likes, 'n' I'll wish 'em both joy 'n' consider myself the luckiest o' the three."

Mrs. Lathrop chewed her clover.

" 'N' then there's Jathrop!" continued the speaker, suddenly transfixing her friend with a piercing glance,—"there's even Jathrop! under my feet night 'n' day. I declare to you 't upon my honor I ain't turned around four times out o' five this week without almost fallin' over Jathrop wantin' me to give him a chance to explain his feelin's. I don't wish to hurt *your* feelin's, Mrs. Lathrop, 'n' it's natural 't, seein' you can't help yourself, you look upon him 's better 'n' nothin', but still I will remark 't Jathrop's the last straw on top o' my hump, 'n' this mornin' when I throwed out the dish-water 'n' hit him by accident jus' comin' in, my patience clean gin out. I didn't feel no manner o' sympathy over his soapy wetness, 'n' I spoke my mind right then 'n' there. 'Jathrop Lathrop,' I says to him, all forgettin' how big he'd got 'n' only rememberin' what a bother he's always been, 'Jathrop Lathrop, you let that soakin' be a lesson to you 'n' march right straight home this instant, 'n' 'f you want to think of me, think 't if I hear any more about your feelin's the feelin' you'll have best cause to talk about 'll be the feelin' o' gettin' spanked.' "

Mrs. Lathrop sighed slightly.

Miss Clegg echoed the sigh.

"There never was a truer sayin' 'n' the one 't things goes by contraries," she continued presently. "Here I've been figgerin' on bein' so happy married, 'n' instid o' that I find myself missin' father every few minutes. There was lots o' good about father, particular when he was asleep. I'd got so used to his stayin' where I put him 't I don't know 's I c'd ever get used to a man 's could get about. 'F I wanted to talk, father was always there to listen, 'n' 'f he wanted to talk I c'd always go downstairs. He didn't never have but one button to keep sewed on 'n' no stockings to darn a *tall*. 'N' all the time there was all them nice gover'ment bonds savin' up for me in his desk! No, I sha'n't consider no more as to gettin' married. While it looked discouragin' I hung on 'n' never give up hope, but I sh'd be showin' very little o' my natural share o' brains 'f I did n't know 's plain 's the moon above 't 'f I get to be eighty 'n' the fancy takes me I c'n easy get a husband any day with those bonds. While I could n't seem to lay hands on no man I was wild to have one—now 't I know I c'n have any man 't I fancy, I don't want no man a *tall*. It'll always be a pleasure to look back on my love-makin', 'n' I would n't be no woman 'f down in the bottom of my heart I was n't some pleased over havin' 's good 's had four offers inside o' the same week. But I might o' married, Mrs. Lathrop, 'n' Heaven might o' seen fit to give me such a son's he give you, 'n' 'f I had n't no other reason for remainin' single that alone 'd be s'fficient. After all, the Lord said 'It is not good for a man to be alone,' but He left a woman free to use her common sense 'n' I sh'll use mine right now. I've folded up the pink nightgown, 'n' I'm thinkin' very seriously o' givin' it to Amelia Fitch, 'n' I'll speak out frank 'n' open 'n' tell her 'n' everybody else 't I don't envy no woman—not now 'n' not never."

Mrs. Lathrop chewed her clover.

Gertrude Stein

(1874–1946)

Called "one of the most arcane of modernists" by Wendy
Steiner, Gertrude Stein was born in Allegheny, Pennsylvania,
the youngest of seven children of German-Jewish parents.
After spending her early years first in Vienna and Paris and
then in Oakland, California, Stein moved to Baltimore in
1892. She graduated from Radcliffe and attended the Johns
Hopkins University Medical School, but instead of complet-
ing her studies she joined her brother Leo in Italy in 1902
and settled with him in Paris in 1903, where they established
friendships with and collected paintings by the modern
artists Cezanne, Gaugin, Rousseau, Matisse, Braque, and
Picasso. Influenced by cubism, cinema, and the theories of
William James, Stein argued against traditional narrative
structures, using repetition in an attempt to achieve imme-
diacy and convey essences. Her first published work, *Three
Lives* (1909), reflects her initial efforts to translate her ideas
into literature. However, the enigmatic linguistic patterns and
extravagant verbal experiments for which she was both
praised and ridiculed were first introduced in *Tender Buttons,* published in 1914. With *The Autobiography of
Alice B. Toklas* (1933), the life of Gertrude Stein as told in
the voice of Alice B. Toklas, her companion from 1911 until
her death, Stein enjoyed her first commercial success and
became celebrated for her wit. However, Neil Schmitz asserts
that "Stein's humorous style originates in the double-talk of
Tender Buttons, in that humor that freely traverses the
primary symbolic orders in discourse: the realm of the
Mother (household speech), the sphere of the Father (philosophical writing)," and that the motive behind Stein's stylistic
experiments was consistently "to keep Gertrude Stein, as a
writer, out of the fixation of a particular identity, *he said she
said . . .,*" which is also political: to deconstruct, through

irony, the ways in which men and women are identified. Acclaimed performances in New York in 1933 of Virgil Thompson's musical setting of her opera *Four Saints in Three Acts* furthered her reputation and led to a highly successful American lecture tour in 1934 and a book about that experience, *Everybody's Autobiography* (1937). During and after the German occupation of France, she continued to write novels, plays, and memoirs, as well as to enjoy the attention of admirers, "pilgrims," and the American press.

SOURCES   Day, Donald. "Gertrude Stein." *Notable American Women*. Vol. 3: 355–359; Gilbert, Sandra M. and Susan Gubar, eds. *The Norton Anthology of Literature by Women*. New York: Norton, 1985. 1304–1307 and 2424–2425; Schmitz, Neil. *Of Huck and Alice: Humorous Writing in American Literature*. Minneapolis: University of Minnesota Press, 1983; Steiner, Wendy. Introduction to *Lectures in America* by Gertrude Stein. Boston: Beacon, 1985; Van Vechten, Carl, ed. *The Yale Edition of the Unpublished Writings of Gertrude Stein*. 8 vols. New Haven: Yale University Press, 1951–1958.

WORKS   *Three Lives* (1909); *G.M.P and Two Shorter Stories* (1910); *Tender Buttons* (1914); *The Autobiography of Alice B. Toklas* (1933) and *Everybody's Autobiography* (1937)

from *G.M.P. and Two Shorter Stories*

from "Many Many Women"

In being one satisfying every one that that one is some one some one is satisfying every one that she is some one. She is that one. She is one and satisfying any one that she is some one. She is one. She is some one. She is satisfying, she is satisfying every one that she is some one.

She, she could feel in being that one, was feeling in being that some one who was satisfying every one that she was some one. Feeling was delivering that she was giving everything that she was getting.

Effecting that she had been learning she completed keeping what she had been getting. She was and is one restraining what she could see moving. She was one feeling. She is one feeling.

She was continuing and was not burying what was not growing. She is continuing and what is growing is filling and what is filling is burrowing and what is burrowing is what is moving and what is moving is showing that moving is not steadying. She is one and she is convincing any one that she was that one. She is one and satisfying every one that she is some one is something.

She, she was expecting what she had been saying, she was attacking what she was expecting, was one satisfying every one of being one, she being one, believing what attacking, what expecting, what believing, what saying is meaning. She had begun and what she had begun was what was meaning to be what she, satisfying every one that she was some one, was expressing in believing that attacking, that believing, that expecting, that giving what she would be receiving was meaning.

She satisfying every one that she was some one in saying what was coming was saying what she was expecting to be saying in attacking what she was attacking in believing what she was believing in meaning meaning what was winning in giving what she would be receiving.

She satisfying every one that she was some one was satisfying herself then that she was saying what expecting to be saying was attacking whom she was attacking in subduing what she was subduing in believing that she was meaning what she was meaning in giving what she would be receiving and in giving what she was giving. She satisfying every one that she was some one was satisfying herself that saying what she was expecting to be saying was subduing what she was expecting to be subduing, and she being one satisfying every one that she was some one was one feeling what she was feeling in giving what she would be receiving, and she being one satisfying every one that she was some one was believing what she was believing in giving what she was giving, and she being one satisfying every one that she was some one was one being one being one not having moving what was not moving and being one feeling that what was not moving was being what it was being and she being one satisfying every one that she was one feeling that she was not burying what she was not burying, and she being one satisfying every one that she was some one was being what she was being she being one satisfying every one that she was some one.

She, she working was arranging that having teaching was what she had not been burying in not burying what she was not burying, cleaning was continuing that she was arranging what she would be arranging in being one satisfying what she was satisfying in being one and satisfying every one that being one she was some one who was some one.

She in satisfying every one was satisfying every one that she was some one and in satisfying every one in satisfying every one that she was some one was satisfying every one that she was some one and in satisfying every one that she was some one she was one who was, in satisfying every one that she was some one, was satisfying every one that she was some one.

She, she was expecting what she was arranging and was arranging to be saving what she was saving, giving what she would be receiving was feeling what she was receiving in giving what she was receiving. She was believing what she was giving in receiving, and giving what she was receiving and receiving what she was giving she was feeling what she was believing. Feeling what she was believing she was not burying what she was not burying, she was not feeling what she was not feeling, she was believing what she was believing, she was expecting what she was arranging, she was satisfying in satisfying and in satisfying she was satisfying every one that she was some one.

In developing, and she had been developing that she developing was developing, in developing, and she had been developing in continuing believing and she was believing, in developing she had developed and having developed she was being what in being is meaning that she is being. She being and meaning being in being she was being and she being being was meaning and she being was meaning what she being was meaning. She being she was meaning. She was meaning and she was being. She was being what in being is meaning that she is being.

She, she was being and being was meaning that she was being and meaning what she was being, she continuing was remaining and having been remaining something was not coming and something not coming she was being and she being she was meaning and meaning she was meaning what she was being. She was satisfying every one that she was some one.

When she came to having been and being and continuing being that one she was one and being that one was meaning to be that one and was meaning being that one and was satisfying and satisfying was satisfying every one and satisfying every one was satisfying every one that she was some one. In having come to be that one and continuing and being that one and not burying anything in not burying anything and being that one in meaning that thing in meaning being that one and being one satisfying in meaning, in being that one who was one who was satisfying every one that she was some one in continuing having come to be that one she was one coming to be expecting to not bury what she was not burying and in expecting that thing she was not expecting what she was not expecting, she was not expecting and not expecting she was not expecting and she was not expecting and not expecting and giving what she was receiving she was not burying what she was not burying and she was not expecting and she was satisfying every one that she was some one and satisfying every one that she was some one and being one and meaning and believing she was satisfying every one that she was some one and she was not expecting and she was giving what she was receiving and she was being what in being is meaning that she is being and she is being meaning what she is meaning in being and she is being and being she is satisfying every one that she is some one.

In coming to be one needing to be burying what she would be burying she was one coming to not burying what she was uncovering. That being uncovered was being what she would be burying if she could come to be burying what she was not coming to be burying. She was changing, that is in satisfying every one that she was some one she was satisfying every one that she was continuing being some one and in satisfying every one that she was continuing being some one she was satisfying herself that she was satisfying every one that she was some one. She was some one, she was satisfying herself in satisfying every one that she was some one. She was satisfying herself that she was continuing satisfying every one that she was some one. She was satisfying every one that she was some one.

In arranging, and she was arranging in believing what she was believing, in arranging she was continuing arranging what she was arranging in believing what she was believing. In arranging she was continuing in arranging and in continuing in arranging she was believing what she was believing. She was believing what she was believing. She was arranging in arranging and she was continuing in arranging and she was believing what she was believing and she was arranging in arranging. She was satisfying every one that she was some one. She was satisfying herself that she was satisfying every one that she was some one. She was believing what she was believing. She was arranging and believing what she was believing. She was believing what she was believing.

If she was one satisfying every one that she was some one, and she was one satisfying every one that she was one, she was one and she was satisfying every one that she was some one, if she was that one she would be changing in coming to be the one she was being when she was being the one she was being in being one who was being that one. In being the one she was being in being the one she was when she was the one she was she was being one and looking she was feeling what being that one she was feeling. She was showing all of this thing and showing all of this thing and showing anything she was showing all of being the one being the one she was and being that one. In showing all of being that one she was looking and looking she was feeling that being one showing anything she was being the one having what she was having, and having what she was having she was one to be continuing, if showing anything is meaning nothing, she was one to be continuing having what she was having, she being one believing what she was believing and being one satisfying every one that she was some one.

If any one continuing is coming to be a dead one they could then have come to be what they had come to be but if they had not come to be a dead one they had not come to be what they had come to be. She had not come to be a dead one. She had not come to be what she would come to be.

Each one is one, there are many of them. Each one, every one, all of them, any of them, one of them, one of them, each one being, every one being, any one is the one and the one is the one and any history is the meaning of the one not meaning what any meaning is meaning.

Charlotte Perkins Gilman

(1860–1935)

It may seem odd to refer to Charlotte Perkins Gilman, social
activist and author of *Women and Economics* (1898), as a
humorist, and yet to see, as she did, the vast discrepancies
between the rights and freedoms of women and men at the
turn of the twentieth century requires a sense of irony that
informs many of Gilman's works, including her utopian novel
Herland (1915) and even her widely-anthologized story "The
Yellow Wallpaper." Gilman was well aware not only of the
broad and deep discrimination against women that affected
them socially, economically, and politically, but also of the
power of rhetoric and social nuance to proscribe women's
activities and aspirations. Thus when Mollie Mathewson, in
"If I Were a Man," imagines wearing her husband's clothes,
she immediately feels the greater freedom and potential for
action afforded by men's clothing. Gilman's attentiveness to
such telling details characterizes both her fiction and her nonfiction work and gives force to her many volumes of social
criticism. Charlotte Perkins was born in 1860 in Connecticut,
attended the Rhode Island School of Design, and in 1884
married Charles W. Stetson, from whom she was separated in
1888 and divorced in 1894. The divorce, and especially the
fact that she preferred that her daughter live with her former
husband and his second wife, caused her to be regarded as
"unnatural" by a public that defined woman's "natural" role
as that of wife and mother. It is this concept of woman's
"appropriate" behavior that Gilman treats ironically at the
beginning of "If I Were a Man" when she describes Mollie
Mathewson as a "true woman." By 1900, Charlotte had
published *Women and Economics,* had married Charles
Houghton Gilman, and was launched on a demanding career
as journalist, activist, and proponent of women's rights that
took her to Europe several times for speaking tours and

international conferences on women. Between 1909 and 1916 she single-handedly wrote and published a monthly magazine, the *Forerunner,* in addition to writing several novels. In 1935 she committed suicide in preference to succumbing to an inoperable cancer that had been diagnosed several years earlier.

SOURCES   Gilman, Charlotte Perkins. *The Living of Charlotte Perkins Gilman.* 1935. Rpt. New York: Arno Press, 1971; Lane, Ann J. Introduction. *The Charlotte Perkins Gilman Reader.* New York: Pantheon, 1980; Scharnhorst, Gary. *Charlotte Perkins Gilman.* Boston: Twayne, 1985.

WORKS   *Herland* (1915) and *The Charlotte Perkins Gilman Reader* (1980)

If I Were a Man

"If I were a man, . . ." that was what pretty little Mollie Mathewson always said when Gerald would not do what she wanted him to—which was seldom.

That was what she said this bright morning, with a stamp of her little high-heeled slipper, just because he had made a fuss about that bill, the long one with the "account rendered," which she had forgotten to give him the first time and been afraid to the second—and now he had taken it from the postman himself.

Mollie was "true to type." She was a beautiful instance of what is reverentially called "a true woman." Little, of course—no true woman may be big. Pretty, of course—no true woman could possibly be plain. Whimsical, capricious, charming, changeable, devoted to pretty clothes and always "wearing them well," as the esoteric phrase has it. (This does not refer to the clothes—they do not wear well in the least—but to some special grace of putting them on and carrying them about, granted to but few, it appears.)

She was also a loving wife and a devoted mother possessed of "the social gift" and the love of "society" that goes with it, and, with all these was fond and proud of her home and managed it as capably as—well, as most women do.

If ever there was a true woman it was Mollie Mathewson, yet she was wishing heart and soul she was a man.

And all of a sudden she was!

She was Gerald, walking down the path so erect and square-shouldered, in a hurry for his morning train, as usual, and, it must be confessed, in something of a temper.

Her own words were ringing in her ears—not only the "last word," but several that had gone before, and she was holding her lips tight shut, not to say something she would be sorry for. But instead of acquiescence in the position taken by that angry little figure on the veranda, what she felt was a sort of superior pride, a sympathy as with weakness, a feeling that "I must be gentle with her," in spite of the temper.

A man! Really a man—with only enough subconscious memory of herself remaining to make her recognize the differences.

At first there was a funny sense of size and weight and extra thickness, the feet and hands seemed strangely large, and her long, straight, free legs swung forward at a gait that made her feel as if on stilts.

This presently passed, and in its place, growing all day, wherever she went, came a new and delightful feeling of being *the right size*.

Everything fitted now. Her back snugly against the seat-back, her feet comfortably on the floor. Her feet? . . . His feet! She studied them carefully. Never before, since her early school days, had she felt such freedom and comfort as to feet—they were firm and solid on the ground when she walked; quick, springy, safe—as when, moved by an unrecognizable impulse, she had run after, caught, and swung aboard the car.

Another impulse fished in a convenient pocket for change—instantly, automatically, bringing forth a nickel for the conductor and a penny for the newsboy.

These pockets came as a revelation. Of course she had known they were there, had counted them, made fun of them, mended them, even envied them; but she never had dreamed of how it *felt* to have pockets.

Behind her newspaper she let her consciousness, that odd mingled consciousness, rove from pocket to pocket, realizing the armored assurance of having all those things at hand, instantly get-at-able, ready to meet emergencies. The cigar case gave her a warm feeling of comfort—it was full; the firmly held fountain pen, safe unless she stood on her head; the keys, pencils, letters, documents, notebook, checkbook, bill folder— all at once, with a deep rushing sense of power and pride, she felt what she had never felt before in all her life—the possession of money, of her own earned money—hers to give or to withhold, not to beg for, tease for, wheedle for—hers.

That bill—why, if it had come to her—to him, that is—he would have paid it as a matter of course, and never mentioned it—to her.

Then, being he, sitting there so easily and firmly with his money in his pockets, she wakened to his life-long consciousness about money. Boyhood—its desires and dreams, ambitions. Young manhood—working tremendously for the wherewithal to make a home—for her. The present years with all their net of cares and hopes and dangers; the present moment, when he needed every cent for special plans of great importance, and this bill, long overdue and demanding payment, meant an amount of inconvenience wholly unnecessary if it had been given him when it first came; also, the man's keen dislike of that "account rendered."

"Women have no business sense!" she found herself saying. "And all that money just for hats—idiotic, useless, ugly things!"

With that she began to see the hats of the women in the car as she had never seen hats before. The men's seemed normal, dignified, becoming, with enough variety for personal taste, and with distinction in style and in age, such as she had never noticed before. But the women's—

With the eyes of a man and the brain of a man; with the memory of a whole lifetime of free action wherein the hat, close-fitting on cropped hair, had been no handicap; she now perceived the hats of women.

The massed fluffed hair was at once attractive and foolish, and on that hair, at every angle, in all colors, tipped, twisted, tortured into every crooked shape, made of any substance chance might offer, perched these formless objects. Then, on their formlessness the trimmings—these squirts of stiff feathers, these violent outstanding bows of glistening ribbon, these swaying, projecting masses of plumage which tormented the faces of bystanders.

Never in all her life had she imagined that this idolized millinery could look, to those who paid for it, like the decorations of an insane monkey.

And yet, when there came into the car a little woman, as foolish as any, but pretty and sweet-looking, up rose Gerald Mathewson and gave her his seat. And, later, when there came in a handsome red-cheeked girl, whose hat was wilder, more violent in color and eccentric in shape than any other—when she stood nearby and her soft curling plumes swept his cheek once and again—he felt a sense of sudden pleasure at the intimate tickling touch—and she, deep down within, felt such a wave of shame as might well drown a thousand hats forever.

When he took his train, his seat in the smoking car, she had a new surprise. All about him were the other men, commuters too, and many of them friends of his.

To her, they would have been distinguished as "Mary Wade's husband," "the man Belle Grant is engaged to," "that rich Mr. Shopworth," or "that pleasant Mr. Beale." And they would all have lifted their hats to her, bowed, made polite conversation if near enough—especially Mr. Beale.

Now came the feeling of open-eyed acquaintance, of knowing men—as they were. The mere amount of this knowledge was a surprise to her—the whole background of talk from boyhood up, the gossip of barber-shop and club, the conversation of morning and evening hours on trains, the knowledge of political affiliation, of business standing and prospects, of character—in a light she had never known before.

They came and talked to Gerald, one and another. He seemed quite popular. And as they talked, with this new memory and new understanding, an understanding which seemed to include all these men's minds, there poured in on the submerged consciousness beneath a new, a startling knowledge—what men really think of women.

Good, average, American men were there; married men for the most part, and happy—as happiness goes in general. In the minds of each and all there seemed to be a two-story department, quite apart from the rest of their ideas, a separate place where they kept their thoughts and feelings about women.

In the upper half were the tenderest emotions, the most exquisite ideals, the sweetest memories, all lovely sentiments as to "home" and "mother," all delicate admiring adjectives, a sort of sanctuary, where a veiled statue, blindly adored, shared place with beloved yet commonplace experiences.

In the lower half—here that buried consciousness woke to keen distress—they kept quite another assortment of ideas. Here, even in this clean-minded husband of hers, was the memory of stories told at men's dinners, of worse ones overheard in street or car, of base traditions, coarse epithets, gross experiences—known, though not shared.

And all these in the department "woman," while in the rest of the mind—here was new knowledge indeed.

The world opened before her. Not the world she had been reared in— where Home had covered all the map, almost, and the rest had been "foreign," or "unexplored country," but the world as it was—man's world, as made, lived in, and seen, by men.

It was dizzying. To see the houses that fled so fast across the car window, in terms of builders' bills, or of some technical insight into materials and methods; to see a passing village with lamentable knowledge of who "owned it" and of how its Boss was rapidly aspiring in state power, or of how that kind of paving was a failure; to see shops, not as mere exhibitions of desirable objects, but as business ventures, many mere sinking ships, some promising a profitable voyage—this new world bewildered her.

She—as Gerald—had already forgotten about that bill, over which she—as Mollie—was still crying at home. Gerald was "talking business" with this man, "talking politics" with that, and now sympathizing with the carefully withheld troubles of a neighbor.

Mollie had always sympathized with the neighbor's wife before.

She began to struggle violently with this large dominant masculine consciousness. She remembered with sudden clearness things she had read, lectures she had heard, and resented with increasing intensity this serene masculine preoccupation with the male point of view.

Mr. Miles, the little fussy man who lived on the other side of the street, was talking now. He had a large complacent wife; Mollie had never liked her much, but had always thought him rather nice—he was so punctilious in small courtesies.

And here he was talking to Gerald—such talk!

"Had to come in here," he said. "Gave my seat to a dame who was bound to have it. There's nothing they won't get when they make up their minds to it—eh?"

"No fear!" said the big man in the next seat. "They haven't much mind to make up, you know—and if they do, they'll change it."

"The real danger," began the Rev. Alfred Smythe, the new Episcopal clergyman, a thin, nervous, tall man with a face several centuries behind the times, "is that they will overstep the limits of their God-appointed sphere."

"Their natural limits ought to hold 'em, I think," said cheerful Dr. Jones. "You can't get around physiology, I tell you."

"I've never seen any limits, myself, not to what they want, anyhow," said Mr. Miles. "Merely a rich husband and a fine house and no end of bonnets and dresses, and the latest thing in motors, and a few diamonds—and so on. Keeps us pretty busy."

There was a tired gray man across the aisle. He had a very nice wife, always beautifully dressed, and three unmarried daughters, also beautifully dressed—Mollie knew them. She knew he worked hard, too, and she looked at him now a little anxiously.

But he smiled cheerfully.

"Do you good, Miles," he said. "What else would a man work for? A good woman is about the best thing on earth."

"And a bad one's the worst, that's sure," responded Miles.

"She's a pretty weak sister, viewed professionally," Dr. Jones averred with solemnity, and the Rev. Alfred Smythe added, "She brought evil into the world."

Gerald Mathewson sat up straight. Something was stirring in him which he did not recognize—yet could not resist.

"Seems to me we all talk like Noah," he suggested drily. "Or the ancient Hindu scriptures. Women have their limitations, but so do we, God knows. Haven't we known girls in school and college just as smart as we were?"

"They cannot play our games," coldly replied the clergyman.

Gerald measured his meager proportions with a practiced eye.

"I never was particularly good at football myself," he modestly admitted, "but I've known women who could outlast a man in all-round endurance. Besides—life isn't spent in athletics!"

This was sadly true. They all looked down the aisle where a heavy ill-dressed man with a bad complexion sat alone. He had held the top of the columns once, with headlines and photographs. Now he earned less than any of them.

"It's time we woke up," pursued Gerald, still inwardly urged to unfamiliar speech. "Women are pretty much *people,* seems to me. I know they dress like fools—but who's to blame for that? We invent all those idiotic hats of theirs, and design their crazy fashions, and, what's more, if a woman is courageous enough to wear common-sense clothes—and shoes—which of us wants to dance with her?

"Yes, we blame them for grafting on us, but are we willing to let our wives work? We are not. It hurts our pride, that's all. We are always criticizing them for making mercenary marriages, but what do we call a girl who marries a chump with no money? Just a poor fool, that's all. And they know it.

"As for Mother Eve—I wasn't there and can't deny the story, but I will say this. If she brought evil into the world, we men have had the lion's share of keeping it going ever since—how about that?"

They drew into the city, and all day long in his business, Gerald was vaguely conscious of new views, strange feelings, and the submerged Mollie learned and learned.

"If I Were a Man" was published in the July 1914 issue of *Physical Culture,* 31–34.

Mary Roberts Rinehart
(1876–1958)

Trained as a nurse, Mary Roberts Rinehart first published children's verses and satiric poems in 1904. These were soon followed by stories of all kinds—comic, romantic, grotesque—until her first serial, *The Man in Lower 10* (1906), launched her long and successful career as a mystery writer. In addition to her detective novels, Rinehart also wrote plays, popular fiction in the social melodrama vein, numerous articles and interviews on social and political topics, and humorous stories about her indomitable spinster character, Letitia Carberry. The first "Tish" story was published in *The Saturday Evening Post* in 1910; the last, in 1937. In between, the Tish stories were collected in a number of volumes: *The Amazing Adventures of Letitia Carberry* (1911), *Tish* (1916), *More Tish* (1921), *Tish Plays the Game* (1926), *The Book of Tish* (1931), and *Tish Marches On* (1937). In a brief "Preface" to the 1955 collection *The Best of Tish*, Rinehart's sons suggest that Tish was the woman Rinehart would have liked to be if she had remained single. While Tish has many traits in common with Miss Rachel Innes, the narrator of Rinehart's enduringly popular mystery *The Circular Staircase* (1907), both characters recall Rinehart herself in their mixture of old-fashioned ideals and independent behavior, their genteel style and irresistible attraction to adventure. In fact, most of the adventures that Tish and her cohorts go through had been experienced by Rinehart herself. As a correspondent for *The Saturday Evening Post*, she was the only woman reporter to visit the Front during World War I; she was also the first woman to venture through Glacier National Park when it was opened in 1915. Despite Rinehart's reputation as a best-selling mystery novelist, Tish was considered by some to be one of her finest achievements, and she remains a unique and vibrant character in American humor.

SOURCES   Cohn, Jan. *Improbable Fiction: The Life of Mary Roberts Rienhart*. Pittsburgh: University of Pittsburgh Press, 1980; Rinehart, Mary Roberts. *My Story*. New York: Farrar and Rinehart, 1931; Walker, Nancy. "Susan and Tish: Women's Humor at the Turn of the Century." *Turn-of-the-Century Women* 2:2 (Winter 1985): 50–54.

WORKS   *The Amazing Adventures of Letitia Carberry* (1911); *Tish* (1916); *More Tish* (1921); *Tish Plays the Game* (1926); *The Book of Tish* (1931); *Tish Marches On* (1937) and *The Best of Tish* (1955)

Mind Over Motor

How Tish Broke the Law and some Records

So many unkind things have been said of the affair at Morris Valley that I think it best to publish a straightforward account of everything. The ill nature of the cartoon, for instance, which showed Tish in a pair of khaki trousers on her back under a racing car was quite uncalled for. Tish did not wear the khaki trousers; she merely took them along in case of emergency. Nor was it true that Tish took Aggie along as a mechanician and brutally pushed her off the car because she was not pumping enough oil. The fact was that Aggie sneezed on a curve and fell out of the car, and would no doubt have been killed had she not been thrown into a pile of sand.

It was in early September that Eliza Bailey, my cousin, decided to go to London, ostensibly for a rest, but really to get some cretonne at Liberty's. Eliza wrote me at Lake Penzance asking me to go to Morris Valley and look after Bettina.

I must confess that I was not eager to do it. We three were very comfortable at Mat Cottage, "Mat" being the name Charlie Sands, Tish's nephew, had given it, being the initials of "Middle-Aged Trio." Not that I regard the late forties as middle-aged. But Tish, of course, is fifty. Charlie Sands, who is on a newspaper, calls us either the "M.A.T." or the "B.A.'s," for "Beloved Aunts," although Aggie and I are not related to him. Bettina's mother's note:

> Not that she will allow you to do it, or because she isn't entirely able to take care of herself; but because the people here are a talky lot. Bettina will probably

look after you. She has come from college with a feeling that I am old and decrepit and must be cared for. She maddens me with pillows and cups of tea and woolen shawls. She thinks Morris Valley selfish and idle, and is disappointed in the church, preferring her Presbyterianism pure. She is desirous now of learning how to cook. If you decide to come I'll be grateful if you can keep her out of the kitchen.

Devotedly, ELIZA.

P.S. If you can keep Bettina from getting married while I'm away I'll be very glad. She believes a woman should marry and rear a large family! E.

We were sitting on the porch of the cottage at Lake Penzance when I received the letter, and I read it aloud.

"Humph!" said Tish, putting down the stocking she was knitting and looking over her spectacles at me—"Likes her Presbyterianism pure and believes in a large family! How old is she? Forty?"

"Eighteen or twenty," I replied, looking at the letter. "I'm not anxious to go. She'll probably find me frivolous."

Tish put on her spectacles and took the letter.

"I think it's your duty, Lizzie," she said when she'd read it through. "But that young woman needs handling. We'd better all go. We can motor over in half a day."

That was how it happened that Bettina Bailey, sitting on Eliza Bailey's front piazza, decked out in chintz cushions,—the piazza, of course,—saw a dusty machine come up the drive and stop with a flourish at the steps. And from it alight, not one chaperon, but three.

After her first gasp Bettina was game. She was a pretty girl in a white dress and bore no traces in her face of any stern religious proclivities.

"I didn't know—" she said, staring from one to the other of us. "Mother said—that is—won't you go right upstairs and have some tea and lie down?" She had hardly taken her eyes from Tish, who had lifted the engine hood and was poking at the carburetor with a hairpin.

"No, thanks," said Tish briskly. "I'll just go around to the garage and oil up while I'm dirty. I've got a short circuit somewhere. Aggie, you and Lizzie get the trunk off."

Bettina stood by while we unbuckled and lifted down our traveling trunk. She did not speak a word, beyond asking if we wouldn't wait until the gardener came. On Tish's saying she had no time to wait, because she wanted to put kerosene in the cylinders before the engine cooled, Bettina lapsed into silence and stood by watching us.

Bettina took us upstairs. She had put Drummond's *Natural Law in the*

Spiritual World on my table and a couch was ready with pillows and a knitted slumber robe, Very gently she helped us out of our veils and dusters and closed the windows for fear of drafts.

"Dear mother is so reckless of drafts," she remarked. "Are you sure you won't have tea?"

"We had some blackberry cordial with us," Aggie said, "and we all had a little on the way. We had to change a tire and it made us thirsty."

"Change a tire!"

Aggie had taken off her bonnet and was pinning on the small lace cap she wears, away from home, to hide where her hair is growing thin. In her cap Aggie is a sweet-faced woman of almost fifty, rather ethereal. She pinned on her cap and pulled her crimps down over her forehead.

"Yes," she observed. "A bridge went down with us and one of the nails spoiled a new tire. I told Miss Carberry the bridge was unsafe, but she thought, by taking it very fast—"

Bettina went over to Aggie and clutched her arm. "Do you mean to say," she quavered, "that you three women went through a bridge—"

"It was a small bridge," I put in, to relieve her mind, "and only a foot or two of water below. If only the man had not been so disagreeable—"

"Oh," she said, relieved, "you had a man with you!"

"We never take a man with us," Aggie said with dignity. "This one was fishing under the bridge and he was most ungentlemanly. Quite refused to help, and tried to get the license number so he could sue us."

"Sue you!"

"He claimed his arm was broken, but I distinctly saw him move it." Aggie, having adjusted her cap, was looking at it in the mirror. "But dear Tish thinks of everything. She had taken off the license plates."

Bettina had gone really pale. She seemed at a loss, and impatient at herself for being so. "You—you won't have tea?" she asked.

"No, thank you."

"Would you—perhaps you would prefer whiskey and soda."

Aggie turned on her a reproachful eye. "My dear girl," she said, "with the exception of a little homemade wine used medicinally we drink nothing. I am the secretary of the Woman's Prohibition Party."

Bettina left us shortly after that to arrange for putting up Letitia and Aggie. She gave them her mother's room, and whatever impulse she may have had to put the Presbyterian Psalter by the bed, she restrained it. By midnight Drummond's *Natural Law* had disappeared from my table and a novel had taken its place. But Bettina had not lost her air of bewilderment.

That first evening was very quiet. A young man in white flannels called, and he and Letitia spent a delightful evening on the porch talking spark-plugs and carburetors. Bettina sat in a corner and looked at the moon. Spoken to, she replied in monosyllables in a carefully sweet tone. The young man's name was Jasper McCutcheon.

It developed that Jasper owned an old racing car which he kept in the Bailey garage, and he and Tish went out to look it over. They very politely asked us all to go along, but Bettina refusing, Aggie and I sat with her and looked at the moon.

Aggie in her capacity as chaperon, or as one of an association of chaperons, used the opportunity to examine Bettina on the subject of Jasper.

"He seems a nice boy," she remarked. Aggie's idea of a nice boy is one who in summer wears fresh flannels outside, in winter less conspicuously. "Does he live near?"

"Next door," sweetly but coolly.

"He is very good-looking."

"Ears spoil him—too large."

"Does he come around—er—often?"

"Only two or three times a day. On Sunday, of course, we see more of him."

Aggie looked at me in the moonlight. Clearly the young man from next door needed watching. It was well we had come.

"I suppose you like the same things?" she suggested. "Similar tastes and—er—all that?"

Bettina stretched her arms over head and yawned.

"Not so you could notice it," she said coolly. "I can't think of anything we agree on. He is an Episcopalian; I'm a Presbyterian. He approves of suffrage for women; I do not. He is a Republican; I'm a Progressive. He disapproves of large families; I approve of them, if people can afford them."

Aggie sat straight up. "I hope you don't discuss that!" she exclaimed.

Bettina smiled. "How nice to find that you are really just nice elderly ladies after all!" she said. "Of course we discuss it. It is anything to be ashamed of?"

"When I was a girl." I said tartly, "we married first and discussed those things afterward."

"Of course you did, Aunt Lizzie," she said, smiling alluringly. She was the prettiest girl I think I have ever seen, and that night she was beautiful.

"And you raised enormous families who religiously walked to church in their bare feet to save their shoes!"

"I did nothing of the sort," I snapped.

"It seems to me," Aggie put in gently, "that you make very little of love." Aggie was once engaged to be married to a young man named Wiggins, a roofer by trade, who was killed in the act of inspecting a tin gutter, on a rainy day. He slipped and fell over, breaking his neck as a result.

Bettina smiled at Aggie. "Not at all," she said. "The day of blind love is gone, that's all—gone like the day of the chaperon."

Neither of us cared to pursue this, and Tish at that moment appearing with Jasper, Aggie and I made a move toward bed. But Jasper not going, and none of us caring to leave him alone with Bettina, we sat down again.

We sat until one o'clock.

At the end of that time Jasper rose, and saying something about its being almost bedtime strolled off next door. Aggie was sound asleep in her chair and Tish was dozing. As for Bettina, she had said hardly a word after eleven o'clock.

Aggie and Tish, as I have said, were occupying the same room. I went to sleep the moment I got into bed, and must have slept three or four hours when I was awakened by a shot. A moment later a dozen or more shots were fired in rapid succession and I sat bolt upright in bed. Across the street someone was raising a window, and a man called "What's the matter?" twice.

There was no response and no further sound. Shaking in every limb, I found the light switch and looked at the time. It was four o'clock in the morning and quite dark.

Someone was moving in the hall outside and whimpering. I opened the door hurriedly and Aggie half fell into the room.

"Tish is murdered, Lizie!" she said, and collapsed on the floor in a heap.

"Nonsense!"

"She's not in her room or in the house, and I heard shots!"

Well, Aggie was right. Tish was not in her room. There was a sort of horrible stillness everywhere as we stood there clutching at each other and listening.

"She's heard burglars downstairs and has gone down after them, and this is what has happened! Oh, Tish! brave Tish!" Aggie cried hysterically.

And at that Bettina came in with her hair over her shoulders and asked us if we had heard anything. When we told her about Tish, she insisted on going downstairs, and with Aggie carrying her first-aid box and I carrying the blackberry cordial, we went down.

The lower floor was quiet and empty. The man across the street had put down his window and gone back to bed, and everything was still. Bettina in her dressing gown went out on the porch and turned on the light. Tish was not there, nor was there a body lying on the lawn.

"It was back of the house by the garage," Bettina said. "If only Jasper—"

And at that moment Jasper came into the circle of light. He had a Norfolk coat on over his pajamas and a pair of slippers, and he was running, calling over his shoulder to someone behind as he ran.

"Watch the drive!" he yelled. "I saw him duck round the corner."

We could hear other footsteps now and somebody panting near us. Aggie was sitting huddled in a porch chair, crying, and Bettina, in the hall, was trying to get down from the wall a Moorish knife that Eliza Bailey had picked up somewhere.

"John!" we heard Jasper calling. "John! Quick! I've got him!"

He was just at the corner of the porch. My heart stopped and then rushed on a thousand a minute. Then:—

"Take your hands off me!" said Tish's voice.

The next moment Tish came majestically into the circle of light and mounted the steps. Jasper, with his mouth open, stood below looking up, and a hired man in what looked like a bed quilt was behind in the shadow.

Tish was completely dressed in her motoring clothes, even to her goggles. She looked neither to the right nor left, but stalked across the porch into the house and up the stairway. None of us moved until we heard the door of her room slam above.

"Poor old dear!" said Bettina. "She's been walking in her sleep!"

"But the shots!" gasped Aggie. "Someone was shooting at her!"

Conscious now of his costume, Jasper had edged close to the veranda and stood in its shadow.

"Walking in her sleep, of course!" he said heartily. "The trip today was too much for her. But think of her getting into that burglar-proof garage with her eyes shut—or do sleepwalkers have their eyes shut?—and actually cranking up my racer!"

Aggie looked at me and I looked at Aggie.

"Of course," Jasper went on, "there being no muffler on it, the racket wakened her as well as the neighborhood. And then the way we chased her!"

"Poor old dear!" said Bettina again. "I'm going in to make her some tea."

"I think," said Jasper, "that I need a bit of tea too. If you will put out the porch lights I'll come up and have some."

But Aggie and I said nothing. We knew Tish never walked in her sleep. She had meant to try out Jasper's racing car at dawn, forgetting that racers have no mufflers, and she had been, as one may say, hoist with her own petard—although I do not know what a petard is and have never been able to find out.

We drank our tea, but Tish refused to have any or to reply to our knocks, preserving a sulky silence. Also she had locked Aggie out and I was compelled to let her sleep in my room.

I was almost asleep when Aggie spoke:—

"Did you think there was anything queer about the way that Jasper boy said good night to Bettina?" she asked drowsily.

"I didn't hear him say good night."

"That was it. He didn't. I think"—she yawned—"I think he kissed her."

Tish was down early to breakfast that morning and her manner forbade any mention of the night before. Aggie, however, noticed that she ate her cereal with her left hand and used her right arm only when absolutely necessary. Once before Tish had almost broken an arm cranking a car and had been driven to arnica compresses for a week; but this time we dared not suggest anything.

Shortly after breakfast she came down to the porch where Aggie and I were knitting.

"I've hurt my arm, Lizzie," she said. "I wish you'd come out and crank the car."

"You'd better stay at home with an arm like that," I replied stiffly.

"Very well, I'll crank it myself."

"Where are you going?"

"To the drugstore for arnica."

Bettina was not there, so I turned on Tish sharply. "I'll go, of course," I said; "but I'll not go without speaking my mind, Letitia Carberry. By and large, I've stood by you for twenty-five years, and now in the weakness of your age I'm not going to leave you. But I warn you, Tish, if you touch that racing car again, I'll send for Charlie Sands."

"I haven't any intention of touching it again," said Tish, meekly enough. "But I wish I could buy a second-hand racer cheap."

"What for?" Anggie demanded.

Tish looked at her with scorn. "To hold flowers on the dining table," she snapped.

It being necessary, of course, to leave a chaperon with Bettina, because of the Jasper person's habit of coming over at any hour of the day, we left Aggie with instructions to watch them both.

Tish and I drove to the drugstore together, and from there to a garage for gasoline. I have never learned to say "gas" for gasoline. It seems to me as absurd as if I were to say "but" for butter. Considering that Aggie was quite sulky at being left, it is absurd for her to assume an air of virtue over what followed that day. Aggie was only like a lot of people—good because she was not tempted; for it was at the garage that we met Mr. Ellis.

We had stopped the engine and Tish was quarreling with the man about the price of gasoline when I saw him—a nice-looking young man in a black-and-white checked suit and a Panama hat. He came over and stood looking at Tish's machine.

"Nice lines to that car," he said. "Built for speed, isn't she? What do you get out of her?"

Tish heard him and turned.

"Get out of her?" she said. "Bills mostly."

"Well, that's the way with most of them," he remarked, looking steadily at Tish. "A machine's a rich man's toy. The only way to own one is to have it endowed like a university. But I meant speed. What can you make?"

"Never had a chance to find out," Tish said grimly. "Between nervous women in the machine and constables outside I have the twelve-miles-an-hour habit. I'm going to exchange the speedometer for a vacuum bottle."

He smiled. "I don't think you're fair to yourself. Mostly—if you'll forgive me—I can tell a woman's driving as far off as I can see the machine; but you are a very fine driver. The way you brought that car in here impressed me considerably."

"She need not pretend she crawls along the road," I said with some sarcasm. "The bills she complains of are mostly fines for speeding."

"No!" said the young man, delighted. "Good! I'm glad to hear it. So are mine!"

After that we got along famously. He had his car there—a low gray thing that looked like an armored cruiser.

"I'd like you ladies to try her," he said. "She can move, but she is as gentle as a lamb. A lady friend of mine once threaded a needle as an experiment while going sixty-five miles an hour."

"In this car?"

"In this car."

Looking back, I do not recall just how the thing started. I believe Tish expressed a desire to see the car go, and Mr. Ellis said he couldn't let her out on the roads, but that the race track at the fair grounds was open and if we cared to drive down there in Tish's car he would show us her paces, as he called it. From that to going to the race track, and from that to Tish's getting in beside him on the mechanician's seat and going round once or twice, was natural. I refused; I didn't like the look of the thing.

Tish came back with a cinder in her eye and full of enthusiasm. "It was magnificent, Lizzie," she said. "The only word for it is sublime. You see nothing. There is just the rush of the wind and the roar of the engine and a wonderful feeling of flying. Here! See if you can find this cinder."

"Won't you try it, Miss—er—Lizzie?"

"No, thanks," I replied. "I can get all the roar and rush of wind I want in front of an electric fan, and no danger."

He stood by, looking out over the oval track while I took three cinders from Tish's eye.

"Great track!" he said. "It's a horse track, of course, but it's in bully shape—the county fair is held there and these fellows make a big feature of their horse races. I came up here to persuade them to hold an automobile meet, but they've got cold feet on the proposition."

"What was the proposition?" asked Tish.

"Well," he said, "it was something like this. I've been turning the trick all over the country and it works like a charm. The town's ahead in money and business, for an automobile race always brings a big crowd; the track owners make the gate money and the racing cars get the prizes. Everybody's ahead. It's a clean sport too."

"I don't approve of racing for money," Tish said decidedly.

But Mr. Ellis shrugged his shoulders. "It's really hardly racing for money," he explained. "The prizes cover the expenses of the racing cars, which are heavy naturally. The cars alone cost a young fortune."

"I see," said Tish. "I hadn't thought of it in that light. Well, why didn't Morris Valley jump at the chance?"

He hesitated a moment before he answered. "It was my fault really," he said. "They were willing enough to have the races, but it was a matter of money. I made them a proposition to duplicate whatever prize money they offered, and in return I was to have half the gate receipts and the betting privileges."

Tish quite stiffened. "Clean sport!" she said sarcastically. "With betting privileges!"

"You don't quite understand, dear lady," he explained. "Even in the cleanest sport we cannot prevent a man's having an opinion and backing it with his own money. What I intended to do was to regulate it. Regulate it."

Tish was quite mollified. "Well, of course," she said, "I suppose since it must be, it is better—er—regulated. But why haven't you succeeded?"

"An unfortunate thing happened just as I had the deal about to close," he replied, and drew a long breath. "The town had raised twenty-five hundred. I was to duplicate the amount. But just at that time a—a young brother of mine in the West got into difficulties, and I—but why go into family matters? It would have been easy enough for me to pay my part of the purse out of my share of the gate money; but the committee demands cash on the table. I haven't got it."

Tish stood up in her car and looked out over the track.

"Twenty-five hundred dollars is a lot of money, young man."

"Not so much when you realize that the gate money will probably amount to twelve thousand."

Tish turned and surveyed the grandstand.

"That thing doesn't seat twelve hundred."

"Two thousand people in the grandstand—that's four thousand dollars. Four thousand standing inside the ropes at a dollar each, four thousand more. And say eight hundred machines parked in the oval there at five dollars a car, four thousand more. That's twelve thousand for the gate money alone. Then there are the concessions to sell peanuts, toy balloons, lemonade and palm-leaf fans, the lunch-stands, merry-go-round and moving-picture permits. It's a bonanza! Fourteen thousand anyhow."

"Half of fourteen thousand is seven," said Tish dreamily. "Seven thousand less twenty-five hundred is thirty-five hundred dollars profit."

"Forty-five hundred, dear lady," corrected Mr. Ellis, watching her. "Forty-five hundred dollars profit to be made in two weeks, and nothing to do to get it but sit still and watch it coming!"

I can read Tish like a book and I saw that was in her mind. "Letitia Carberry!" I said sternly. "You take my warning and keep clear of this foolishness. If money comes as easy as that it ain't honest."

"Why not?" demanded Mr. Ellis. "We give them their money's worth, don't we? They'd pay two dollars for a theater seat without half the thrills—no chances of seeing a car turn turtle or break its steering knuckle and dash into the side lines. Two dollars' worth? It's twenty!"

But Tish had had a moment to consider, and the turning-turtle business settled it. She shook her head. "I'm not interested, Mr. Ellis," she said coldly. "I couldn't sleep at night if I thought I'd been the cause of anything turning turtle or dashing into the side lines."

"Dear lady!" he said, shocked. "I had no idea of asking you to help me out of my difficulties. Anyhow, while matters are at a standstill probably some shrewd money-maker here will come forward before long and make a nice profit on a small investment."

As we drove away from the fair grounds Tish was very silent; but just as we reached the Bailey place, with Bettina and young Jasper McCutcheon batting a ball about on the tennis court, Tish turned to me.

"You needn't look like that, Lizzie," she said. "I'm not even thinking of backing an automobile race—although I don't see why I shouldn't, so far as that goes. But it's curious, isn't it, that I've got twenty-five hundred dollars from Cousin Angeline's estate not even earning four per cent?"

I got out grimly and jerked at my bonnet strings.

"You put it in a mortgage, Tish," I advised her with severity in every tone. "It may not be so fast as an automobile race or so likely to turn turtle or break its steering knuckle, but it's safe."

"Huh!" said Tish, reaching for the gear lever. "And about as exciting as a cold pork chop."

"And furthermore," I interjected, "if you go into this thing now that your eyes are open, I'll send for Charlie Sands!"

"You and Charlie Sands," said Tish viciously, jamming at her gears, "ought to go and live in an old ladies' home away from this cruel world."

Aggie was sitting under a sunshade in the broiling sun at the tennis court. She said she had not left Bettina and Jasper for a moment, and that they had evidently quarreled, although she did not know when, having listened to every word they said. For the last half-hour, she said, they had not spoken at all.

"Young people in love are very foolish," she said, rising stiffly. "They should be happy in the present. Who knows what the future may hold?"

I knew she was thinking of Mr. Wiggins and the wet roof, so I patted her shoulder and sent her up to put cold cloths on her head for fear of sunstroke. Then I sat down in the broiling sun and chaperoned Bettina until luncheon.

Jasper took dinner with us that night. He came across the lawn, freshly shaved and in clean white flannels, just as dinner was announced, and said he had seen a chocolate cake cooling on the kitchen porch and that it was a sort of unwritten social law that when the Baileys happened to have a chocolate cake at dinner they had him also.

There seemed to be nothing to object to in this. Evidently he was right for we found his place laid at the table. The meal was quite cheerful, although Jasper ate the way some people play the piano, by touch, with his eyes on Bettina. And he gave no evidence at the dessert of a fondness for chocolate cake sufficient to justify a standing invitation.

After dinner we went out on the veranda, and under cover of showing me a sunset Jasper took me round the corner of the house. Once there, he entirely forgot the sunset.

"Miss Lizzie," he began at once, "what have I done to you to have you treat me like this?"

"I?" I asked, amazed.

"All three of you. Did—did Bettina's mother warn you against me?"

"The girl has to be chaperoned."

"But not jailed, Miss Lizzie, not jailed! Do you know that I haven't had a word with Bettina alone since you came?"

"Why should you want to say anything we cannot hear?"

"Miss Lizzie," he said desperately, "do you want to hear me propose to her? For I've reached the point where if I don't propose to Bettina soon, I'll—I'll propose to somebody. You'd better be warned in time. It might be you or Miss Aggie."

I weakened at that. The Lord never saw fit to send me a man I could care enough about to marry, or one who cared enough about me, but I couldn't look at the boy's face and not be sorry for him.

"What do you want me to do?" I asked.

"Come for a walk with us," he begged. "Then sprain your ankle or get tired, I don't care which. Tell us to go on and come back for you later. Do you see? You can sit down by the road somewhere."

"I won't lie," I said firmly. "If I really get tired I'll say so. If I don't—"

"You will." He was gleeful. "We'll walk until you do! You see it's like this, Miss Lizzie. Bettina was all for me, in spite of our differing on religion and politics and—"

"I know all about your differences," I put in hastily.

"Until a new chap came to town—a fellow named Ellis. Runs a sporty car and has every girl in the town lashed to the mast. He's a novelty and I'm not. So far I have kept him away from Bettina, but at any time they may meet, and it will be one-two-three with me."

I am not defending my conduct: I am only explaining. Eliza Bailey herself would have done what I did under the circumstances. I went for a walk with Bettina and Jasper shortly after my talk with Jasper, leaving Tish with the evening paper and Aggie inhaling a cubeb cigarette, her hay fever having threatened a return. And what is more, I tired within three blocks of the house, where I saw a grassy bank beside the road.

Bettina wished to stay with me, but I said, in obedience to Jasper's eyes, that I liked to sit alone and listen to the crickets, and for them to go on. The last I saw of them Jasper had drawn Bettina's arm through his and was walking beside her with his head bent, talking.

I sat for perhaps fifteen minutes and was growing uneasy about dew and my rheumatism when I heard footsteps and, looking up, I saw Aggie coming toward me. She was not surprised to see me and addressed me coldly.

"I thought as much!" she said. "I expected better of you, Lizzie. That boy asked me and I refused. I dare say he asked Tish also. For you, who pride yourself on your strength of mind—"

"I was tired," I said.

"I was to sprain my ankle," she observed sarcastically. "I just thought as I was sitting there alone—"

"Where's Tish?"

"A young man named Ellis came and took her out for a ride," said Aggie. "He couldn't take us both, as the car holds only two."

I got up and stared at Aggie in the twilight. "You come straight home with me, Aggie Pilkington," I said sternly.

"But what about Bettina and Jasper?"

"Let 'em alone," I said; "they're safe enough. What we need to keep an eye on is Letitia Carberry and her Cousin Angeline's legacy."

But I was too late. Tish and Mr. Ellis whirled up to the door at half-past eight and Tish did not even notice that Bettina was absent. She took off her veil and said something about Mr. Ellis's having heard a grinding in the differential of her car that afternoon and that he suspected a chip of steel in the gears. They went out together to the garage, leaving Aggie and me staring at each other. Mr. Ellis was carrying a box of tools.

Jasper and Bettina returned shortly after, and even in the dusk I knew things had gone badly for him. He sat on the steps, looking out across the dark lawn, and spoke in monosyllables. Bettina, however, was very gay.

It was evident that Bettina had decided not to take her Presbyterianism into the Episcopal fold. And although I am a Presbyterian myself I felt sorry.

Tish and Mr. Ellis came round to the porch about ten o'clock and he was presented to Bettina. From that moment there was no question in my mind as to how affairs were going, or in Jasper's either. He refused to move and sat doggedly on the steps, but he took little part in the conversation.

Mr. Ellis was a good talker, especially about himself.

"You'll be glad to know," he said to me, "that I've got this race matter fixed up finally. In two weeks from now we'll have a little excitement here."

I looked toward Tish, but she said nothing.

"Excitement is where I live," said Mr. Ellis. "If I don't find any waiting I make it."

"If you are looking for excitement, we'll have to find you some," Jasper said pointedly.

Mr. Ellis only laughed. "Don't put yourself out, dear boy," he said. "I have enough for present necessities. If you think an automobile race is an easy thing to manage, try it. Every man who drives a racing car has a coloratura soprano beaten to death for temperament. Then every racing car has quirky spells; there's the local committee to propitiate; the track to look after; and if that isn't enough, there's the promotion itself, the advertising. That's my stunt—the advertising."

"It's a wonderful business, isn't it?" asked Bettina. "To take a mile or so of dirt track and turn it into a sort of stage, with drama every minute and sometimes tragedy!"

"Wait a moment," said Mr. Ellis. "I want to put that down. I'll use it somewhere in the advertising." He wrote by the light of a match, while we all sat rather stunned by both his personality and his alertness. "Everything's grist that comes to my mill. I suppose you all remember when I completed the speedway at Indianapolis and had the Governor of Indiana lay a gold brick at the entrance? Great stunt that! But the best part of that story never reached the public."

Bettina was leaning forward, all ears and thrills. "What was that?" she asked.

"I had the gold brick stolen that night—did it myself and carried the brick away in my pocket—only gold-plated, you know. Cost eight or nine dollars, all told, and brought a million dollars in advertising. But the papers were sore about some passes and wouldn't use the story. Too bad we can't use the brick here. Still have it kicking about somewhere."

It was then, I think, that Jasper yawned loudly, apologized, said good night and lounged away across the lawn. Bettina hardly knew he was going. She was bending forward, her chin in her palms, listening to Mr. Ellis tell about a driver in a motor race breaking his wrist cranking a car, and how he—Ellis—had jumped into the car and driven it to victory. Even Aggie was enthralled. It seemed as if, in the last hour, the great world of stress and keen wits and endeavor and mad speed had sat down on our doorstep.

As Tish said when we were going up to bed, why shouldn't Mr. Ellis brag? He had something to brag about.

Although I felt quite sure that Tish had put up the prize money for Mr. Ellis, I could not be certain. And Tish's attitude at that time did not invite inquiry. She took long rides daily with the Ellis man in his gray car, and I have reason to believe that their objective point was always the same—the race track.

Mr. Ellis was the busiest man in Morris Valley. In the daytime he was superintending putting the track in condition, writing what he called "promotion stuff," securing entries and forming the center of excited groups at the drugstore and one or another of the two public garages. In the evenings he was generally to be found at Bettina's feet.

Jasper did not come over any more. He sauntered past, evening after evening, very much white-flanneled and carrying a tennis racket. And once or twice he took out his old racing car, and later shot by the house with a flutter of veils and a motor coat beside him.

Aggie was exceedingly sorry for him, and even went the length of having the cook bake a chocolate cake and put it on the window sill to cool. It had, however, no perceptible effect, except to draw from Mr. Ellis, who had been round at the garage looking at Jasper's old racer, a remark that he was exceedingly fond of cake, and if he were urged—

That was, I believe, a week before the race. The big city papers had taken it up, according to Mr. Ellis, and entries were pouring in.

"That's the trouble on a small track," he said—"we can't crowd 'em. A dozen cars will be about the limit. Even with using the cattle pens for repair pits we can't look after more than a dozen. Did I tell you Heckert had entered his Bonor?"

"No!" we exclaimed. As far as Aggie and I were concerned, the Bonor might have been a new sort of dog.

"Yes, and Johnson his Sampler. It's going to be some race—eh, what!"

Jasper sauntered over that evening, possibly a late result of the cake, after all. He greeted us affably, as if his defection of the past week had been merely incidental, and sat down on the steps.

"I've been thinking, Ellis," he said, "that I'd like to enter my car."

"What!" said Ellis, "Not that—"

"My racer I'm not much for speed, but there's a sort of feeling in the town that the locality ought to be represented. As I'm the only owner of a speed car—"

"Speed car!" said Ellis, and chuckled. "My dear boy, we've got Heckert with his ninety-horse-power Bonor!"

"Never heard of him." Jasper lighted a cigarette. "Anyhow, what's that to me? I don't like to race. I've got less speed mania than any owner of a race car you ever met. But the honor of the town seems to demand a sacrifice, and I'm it."

"You can try out for it anyhow," said Ellis. "I don't think you'll make it; but, if you qualify, all right. But don't let any other town people, from a sense of mistaken local pride, enter a street roller or a traction engine."

Jasper colored, but kept his temper.

Aggie, however, spoke up indignantly. "Mr. McCutcheon's car was a very fine racer when it was built."

"De mortius nil nisi bonum," remarked Mr. Ellis, and getting up said good night.

Jasper sat on the steps and watched him disappear. Then he turned to Tish.

"Miss Letitia," he said, "do you think you are wise to drive that racer of his the way you have been doing?"

Aggie gave a little gasp and promptly sneezed, as she does when she is excited.

"I?" said Tish.

"You!" from Aggie.

"—you were fortunate. But when a racer turns over the results are not pleasant."

"As a matter of fact," said Tish coldly, "it was a wheat field, not a ditch."

Jasper got up and threw away his cigarette. "Well, our departing friend is not the only one who can quote Latin," he said. *"Verbum sap.,* Miss Tish. Good night, everybody. Good night, Bettina."

Bettina's good night was very cool. As I went up to bed that night, I thought Jasper's chances poor indeed. As for Tish, I endeavored to speak a few words of remonstrance to her, but she opened her Bible and began to read the lesson for the day and I was obliged to beat a retreat.

It was that night that Aggie and I, having decided the situation was beyond us, wrote a letter to Charlie Sands asking him to come up. Just as I was sealing it Bettina knocked and came in. She closed the door behind her and stood looking at us both.

"Where is Miss Tish?" she asked.

"Reading her Bible," I said tartly. "When Tish is up to some mischief, she generally reads an extra chapter or two as atonement."

"Is she—is she always like this?"

"The trouble is," explained Aggie gently, "Miss Letitia is an enthusiast. Whatever she does, she does with all her heart."

"I feel so responsible," said Bettina. "I try to look after her, but what can I do?"

"There is only one thing to do," I assured her—"let her alone. If she wants to fly, let her fly; if she wants to race, let her race—and trust in Providence."

"I'm afraid Providence has its hands full!" said Bettina, and went to bed.

For the remainder of that week nothing was talked of in Morris Valley but the approaching race. Some of Eliza Bailey's friends gave fancy-work parties for us, which Aggie and I attended. Tish refused, being now openly at the race track most of the day. Morris Valley was much excited. Should it wear motor clothes, or should it follow the example of the English Derby and the French races and wear its afternoon reception dress with white kid gloves? Or—it being warm—wouldn't lingerie clothes and sunshades be most suitable?

Some of the gossip I retailed to Jasper, oil-streaked and greasy, in the Baileys' garage where he was working over his car.

"Tell 'em to wear mourning," he said pessimistically. "There's always a fatality or two. If there wasn't a fair chance of it nothing would make 'em sit for hours watching dusty streaks going by."

The race was scheduled for Wednesday. On Sunday night the cars began to come in. On Monday Tish took us all, including Bettina, to the track. There were half a dozen tents in the oval, one of them marked with a huge red cross.

"Hospital tent," said Tish calmly.

We even, on permission from Mr. Ellis, went round the track. At one spot Tish stopped the car and got out.

"Nail," she said briefly. "It's been a horse-racing track for years, and we've gathered a bushel of horseshoe nails."

Aggie and I said nothing, but we looked at each other. Tish had said "we." Evidently Cousin Angeline's legacy was not going into a mortgage.

The fairgrounds were almost ready. Peanut and lunch stands had sprung up everywhere. The oval, save by the tents and the repair pits, was marked off into parking spaces numbered on tall banners. Groups of dirty men in overalls, carrying machine wrenches, small boys with buckets of water, onlookers round the tents and track rollers made the place look busy and interesting. Some of the excitement, I confess, got into my blood. Tish, on the contrary, was calm and businesslike. We were sorry we had sent for Charlie Sands. She no longer went out in Mr. Ellis's car, and that evening she went back to the kitchen and made a boiled salad dressing.

We were all deceived.

Charlie Sands came the next morning. He was on the veranda reading a paper when we got down to breakfast. Tish's face was a study.

"Who sent for you?" she demanded.

"Sent for me! Why, who would send for me? I'm here to write up the race. I thought, if you haven't been out to the track, we'd go out this morning."

"We've been out," said Tish shortly, and we went in to breakfast. Once or twice during the meal I caught her eye on me and on Aggie and she was short with us both. While she was upstairs I had a word with Charlie Sands.

"Well," he said, "what is it this time? Is she racing?"

"Worse than that," I replied. "I think she's backing the thing!"

"No!"

"With her cousin Angeline's legacy." With that I told him about our meeting Mr. Ellis and the whole story. He listened without a word.

"So that's the situation," I finished. "He has her hypnotized, Charlie. What's more, I shouldn't be surprised to see her enter the race under an assumed name."

Charlie Sands looked at the racing list in the Morris Valley *Sun*.

"Good cars all of them," he said. "She's not here among the drivers, unless she's—Who are these drivers anyhow? I never heard of any of them."

"It's a small race," I suggested. "I dare say the big men—"

"Perhaps." He put away his paper and got up. "I'll just wander round the town for an hour or two, Aunt Lizzie," he said. . . .

When he came back about noon, however, he looked puzzled. I drew him aside.

"It seems on the level," he said. "It's so darned open it makes me suspicious. But she's back of it all right. I got her bank on the long-distance 'phone."

We spent that afternoon at the track, with the different cars doing what I think they called "trying out heats." It appeared that a car, to qualify, must do a certain distance in a certain time. It grew monotonous after a while. All but one entry qualified and Jasper just made it. The best showing was made by the Bonor car, according to Charlie Sands.

Jasper came to our machine when it was over, smiling without any particular good cheer.

"I've made it and that's all," he said. "I've got about as much chance as a watermelon at a . . . picnic. I'm being slaughtered to make a Roman holiday."

"If you feel that way why do you do it?" demanded Bettina coldly. "If you go in expecting to be slaughtered—"

He was leaning on the side of the car and looked up at her with eyes that made my heart ache, they were so wretched.

"What does it matter?" he said. "I'll probably trail in at the last, sound in wind and limb. If I don't what does it matter?"

He turned and left us at that, and I looked at Bettina. She had her lips shut tight and was blinking hard. I wished that Jasper had looked back.

Charlie Sands announced at dinner that he intended to spend the night at the track.

Tish put down her fork and looked at him. "Why?" she demanded.

"I'm going to help the boy next door watch his car," he said calmly. "Nothing against your friend Mr. Ellis, Aunt Tish, but some enemy of true sport might take a notion in the night to slip a dope pill into the mouth of friend Jasper's car and have her go to sleep on the track tomorrow."

We spent a quiet evening. Mr. Ellis was busy, of course, and so was Jasper. The boy came to the house to get Charlie Sands and, I suppose, for a word with Bettina, for when he saw us all on the porch he looked, as you may say, thwarted.

When Charlie Sands had gone up for his pajamas and dressing gown, Jasper stood looking up at us.

"Oh, Association of Chaperons!" he said, "is it permitted that my lady walk to gate with me—alone?"

"I am not your lady," flashed Bettina.

"You've nothing to say about that," he said recklessly. "I've selected you; you can't help it. I haven't claimed that you have selected me."

"Anyhow, I don't wish to go to the gate," said Bettina.

He went rather white at that, and Charlie Sands coming down at that moment with a pair of red-and-white pajamas under his arm and a toothbrush sticking out of his breast pocket, romance, as Jasper said later in referring to it, "was buried in Sands."

Jasper went up to Bettina and held out his hand. "You'll wish me luck, won't you?"

"Of course." She took his hand. "But I think you're a bit of a coward, Jasper!"

He eyed her. "Coward!" he said. "I'm the bravest man you know. I'm doing a thing I'm scared to death to do!"

The race was to begin at two o'clock in the afternoon. There were small races to be run first, but the real event was due at three.

From early in the morning a procession of cars from out of town poured in past Eliza Bailey's front porch, and by noon her cretonne cushions were thick with dust. And not only automobiles came, but hay wagons, side-bar buggies, delivery carts—anything and everything that could transport the crowd.

At noon Mr. Ellis telephoned Tish that the grandstand was sold out and that almost all the parking places that had been reserved were taken. Charlie Sands came home to luncheon with a curious smile on his face.

"How are you betting, Aunt Tish?" he asked.

"Betting!"

"Yes. Has Ellis let you in on the betting?"

"I don't know what you are talking about," Tish said sourly. "Mr. Ellis controls the betting so that it may be done in an orderly manner. I am sure I have nothing to do with it."

"I'd like to bet a little, Charlie," Aggie put in with an eye on Tish. "I'd put all I win on the collection plate on Sunday."

"Very well." Charlie Sands took out his notebook. "On what car and how much?"

"Ten dollars on the Fein. It made the best time at the trial heats."

"I wouldn't if I were you," said Charlie Sands. "Suppose we put it on our young friend next door."

Bettina rather sniffed. "On Jasper!" she exclaimed.

"On Jasper," said Charlie Sands gravely.

Tish, who had hardly heard us, looked up from her plate.

"Betting is betting," she snapped. "Putting it on the collection plate doesn't help any." But with that she caught Charlie Sands' eye and he winked at her. Tish colored. "Gambling is one thing, clean sport is another," she said hotly.

I believe, however, that whatever Charlie Sands may have suspected, he really knew nothing until the race had started. By that time it was too late to prevent it, and the only way he could think of to avoid getting Tish involved in a scandal was to let it go on.

We went to the track in Tish's car and parked in the oval. Not near the grandstand, however. Tish had picked out for herself a curve at one end of the track which Mr. Ellis had said was the worst bit on the course.

"He says," said Tish, as we put the top down and got out the vacuum bottle—oh, yes, Mr. Ellis had sent Tish one as a present—"that if there are any smashups they'll occur here."

Aggie is not a bloodthirsty woman ordinarily, but her face quite lit up. "Not really!" she said.

"They'll probably turn turtle," said Tish. "There is never a race without a fatality or two. No racer can get any life insurance. Mr. Ellis says four men were killed at the last race he promoted."

"Then I think Mr. Ellis is a murderer," Bettina cried. We all looked at her. She was limp and white and was leaning back among the cushions with her eyes shut. "Why didn't you tell Jasper about this curve?" she demanded of Tish.

But at that moment a pistol shot rang out and the races were on.

The Fein won two of the three small races. Jasper was entered only for the big race. In the interval before the race was on, Jasper went round the track slowly, looking for Bettina. When he saw us he waved, but did not stop. He was number thirteen. I shall not describe the race. After the first round or two, what with dust in my eyes and my neck aching from turning my head so rapidly, I just sat back and let them spin in front of me.

It was after a dozen laps or so, with number thirteen doing as well as any of them, that Tish was arrested.

Charlie Sands came up beside the car with a gentleman named Atkins, who turned out to be a county detective. Charlie Sands was looking stern and severe, but the detective was rather apologetic.

"This is Miss Carberry," said Charlie Sands. "Aunt Tish, this gentleman wishes to speak to you."

"Come around after the race," Tish observed calmly.

"Miss Carberry," said the detective gently, "I believe you are back of this race, aren't you?"

"What if I am?" demanded Tish.

Charlie Sands put a hand on the detective's arm. "It's like this, Aunt Tish," he said; "you are accused of practicing a short-change game, that's all. This race is sewed up. You employ those racing cars with drivers at an average of fifty dollars a week. They are hardly worth it, Aunt Tish. I could have got you a better string for twenty-five."

Tish opened her mouth and shut it again without speaking.

"You also control the betting privileges. As you own all the racers you have probably known for a couple of weeks who will win the race. Having made the Fein favorite, you can bet on a Brand or a Bonor, or whatever one you chance to like, and win out. Only I take it rather hard of you, Aunt Tish, not to have let the family in. I'm hard up as the dickens."

"Charlie Sands!" said Tish impressively. "If you are joking—"

"Joking! Did you ever know a county detective to arrest a prominent woman at a race track as a little jest between friends? There's no joke, Aunt Tish. You've financed a phony race. The permit is taken in your name—L. Carberry. Whatever car wins, you and Ellis take the prize money, half the gate receipts, and what you have made out of the betting—"

Tish rose in the machine and held out both her hands to Mr. Atkins.

"Officer, perform your duty," she said solemnly. "Ignorance is no defense and I know it. Where are the handcuffs?"

"We'll not bother about them, Miss Carberry," he said. "If you like I'll get into the car and you can tell me all about it while we watch the race. Which car is to win?"

"I may have been a fool, Mr. County Detective," she said coldly, "but I'm not a knave. I have not bet a dollar on the race."

We were very silent for a time. The detective seemed to enjoy the race very much and ate peanuts out of his pocket. He even bought a red-and-black pennant, with "Morris Valley Races" on it, and fastened it to the car. Charlie Sands, however, sat with his arms folded, still and severe.

Once Tish bent forward and touched his arm.

"You—you don't think it will get in the papers, do you?" she quavered.

Charlie Sands looked at her with gloom. "I shall have to send it myself, Aunt Tish," he said. "It is my duty to my paper. Even my family pride, hurt to the quick and quivering as it is, must not interfere with my duty."

It was Bettina who suggested a way out—Bettina, who had sat back as pale as Tish and heard that her Mr. Ellis was, as Charlie Sands said later, as crooked as a pretzel.

"But Jasper was not—not subsidized," she said. "If he wins, it's all right, isn't it?"

The county detective turned to her.

"Jasper?" he said.

"A young man who lives here." Bettina colored.

"He is—not to be suspected?"

"Certainly not," said Bettina haughtily. "He is above suspicion. Besides, he—he and Mr. Ellis are not friends."

Well, the county detective was no fool. He saw the situation that minute, and smiled when he offered Bettina a peanut. "Of course," he said cheerfully, "if the race is won by a Morris Valley man, and not by one of the Ellis cars, I don't suppose the district attorney would care to do anything about it. In fact," he said smiling at Bettina, "I don't know that I'd put it up to the district attorney at all. A warning to Ellis would get him out of the State."

It was just at that moment that car number thirteen, coming round the curve, skidded into the field, threw out both Jasper McCutcheon and his mechanician, and after standing on two wheels for an appreciable moment of time, righted herself, panting, with her nose against a post.

Jasper sat up almost immediately and caught at his shoulder. The mechanician was stunned. He got up, took a step or two and fell down, weak with fright.

I do not recall very distinctly what happened next. We got out of the machine, I remember, and Bettina was cutting off Jasper's sweater with Charlie Sands' penknife, and crying as she did it. And Charlie Sands was trying to prevent Jasper from getting back into his car, while Jasper was protesting that he could win in two or more laps and that he could drive with one hand—he'd only broken his arm.

The crowd had gathered round us, thick. Suddenly they drew back, and in a sort of haze I saw Tish in Jasper's car, with Aggie, as white as death, holding to Tish's sleeve and begging her not to get in. The next moment Tish let in the clutch of the racer and Aggie took a sort of flying leap and landed beside her in the mechanician's seat.

Charlie Sands saw it when I did, but we were both too late. Tish was crossing the ditch into the track again, and the moment she struck level ground she put up the gasoline.

It was just then that Aggie fell out, landing, as I have said before, in a pile of sand. Tish said afterward that she never missed her. She had just discovered that this was not Jasper's old car, which she knew something about, but a new racer with the old hood and seat put on in order to fool Mr. Ellis. She didn't know a thing about it.

Well, you know the rest—how Tish, trying to find how the gears worked, sideswiped the Bonor car and threw it off the field and out of the race; how, with the grandstand going crazy, she skidded off the track into the field, turned completely round twice, and found herself on the track again facing the way she wanted to go; how; at the last lap, she threw a tire and, without cutting down her speed, bumped home the winner, with the end of her tongue nearly bitten off and her spine fairly driven up into her skull.

All this is well known now, as is also the fact that Mr. Ellis disappeared from the judges' stand after a word or two with Mr. Atkins, and was never seen at Morris Valley again.

Tish came out of the race ahead by half the gate money—six thousand dollars—by a thousand dollars from concessions, and a lame back that she kept all winter. Even deducting the twenty-five hundred she had put up, she was forty-five hundred dollars ahead, not counting the prize money. Charlie Sands brought the money from the track that night, after having paid off Mr. Ellis's racing string and given Mr. Atkins a small present. He took over the prize money to Jasper and came back with it, Jasper maintaining that it belonged to Tish, and that he had only raced for the honor of Morris Valley. For some time the money went begging, but it settled itself naturally enough, Tish giving it to Jasper in the event of—but that came later.

On the following evening—Bettina, in the pursuit of learning to cook, having baked a chocolate cake—we saw Jasper, with his arm in a sling, crossing the side lawn.

Jasper stopped at the foot of the steps. "I see a chocolate cake cooling on the kitchen porch," he said. "Did you order it, Miss Lizzie?"

I shook my head.

"Miss Tish? Miss Aggie?"

"I ordered it," said Bettina defiantly—"or rather I baked it."

"And you did that, knowing what it entailed?" He was coming up the steps slowly and with care.

"What does it entail?" demanded Bettina.

"Me."

"Oh, that!" said Bettina. "I knew that."

Jasper threw his head back and laughed. Then:—

"Will the Associated Chaperons," he said, "turn their backs?"

"Not at all," I began stiffly. "If I—"

"She baked it herself!" said Jasper exultantly. "One—two. When I say three I shall kiss Bettina."

And I have every reason to believe he carried out his threat.

Eliza Bailey forwarded me this letter from London, where Bettina had sent it to her:

Dearest Mother: I hope you are coming home soon. I really think you should. Aunt Lizzie is here and she brought two friends, and, Mother, I feel so responsible for them! Aunt Lizzie is sane enough, if somewhat cranky; but Miss Tish is almost more than I can manage—I never know what she is going to do next—and I am worn out with chaperoning her. And Miss Aggie, although she is very sweet, is always smoking cubeb cigarettes for hay fever, and it looks terrible! The neighbors do not know they are cubeb, and, anyhow, that's a habit, Mother. And yesterday Miss Tish was arrested, and ran a motor race and won it, and today she is knitting a stocking and reciting the Twenty-third Psalm. Please, Mother, I think you should come home.

Lovingly, BETTINA.

P.S. I think I shall marry Jasper after all. He says he likes the Presbyterian service.

I looked up from reading Eliza's letter. Tish was knitting quietly and planning to give the money back to the town in the shape of a library, and Aggie was holding a cubeb cigarette to her nose. Down on the tennis court Jasper and Bettina were idly batting a ball round.

"I'm glad the Ellis man did not get her," said Aggie. And then, after a sneeze, "How Jasper reminds me of Mr. Wiggins."

The library did not get the money after all. Tish sent it, as a wedding present, to Bettina.

Alice Duer Miller
(1874–1942)

At the time of her death in 1942, Alice Duer Miller was best known for *The White Cliffs* (1940), a romantic story in verse of an American girl married to a British soldier during World War II that sold more than 700,000 copies before the end of the war. Yet during most of her career Miller was known for her lighthearted, sometimes satiric novels, stories, and newspaper column, "Are Women People?," which ran in the *New York Tribune* from 1914 to 1917. The column, and a collection of satiric verses with the same title published in 1915, reflect Miller's deep feminist convictions: in 1916 she chaired the committee on resolutions of the National American Women Suffrage Association. During the 1920s she was a member of the Algonquin Round Table group along with Dorothy Parker and Alexander Woollcott, and in 1927 she was the subject of a *New Yorker* "Profile." Miller's success as a writer and her husband's success as a Wall Street broker restored her to the social prominence of her childhood, before the Duer family fortune was lost in a bank crisis just after her social debut. With what proved to be characteristic though non-traditional ambition, Alice Duer decided at that point to go to college, and graduated from Barnard with a degree in mathematics in 1899. She began to publish fiction and poetry while her husband, Henry Wise Miller, worked his way up to a seat on the New York Stock Exchange, and she quickly became a central figure in American popular literature, publishing regularly in the *Saturday Evening Post* from 1916 until the 1930s. Several of the novels that were serialized in the *Post*—including *The Charm School* (1919), *Manslaughter* (1921), and *Gowns by Roberta* (1933)—were made into films, and Miller several times went to Hollywood as a consultant. The very popularity of her work, and the fact that she wrote primarily about the upper classes, overshadowed even in her own lifetime the depth of her political convictions: some of her early work was published in Max Eastman's socialist magazine *The Masses,* and she was a member of Heterodoxy, a group of radical feminists that met in Greenwich Village from 1912 to 1940. In her prosuffrage satires, Miller recalls Marietta Holley and other nineteeth-century feminist writers who found women's oppression patently absurd.

SOURCES   *Notable American Women: 1607–1950.* Cambridge: Belknap Press, 1971. 538–40; O'Higgins, Harvey. "A Lady Who Writes." *The New Yorker.* 19 February 1927: 25–27; Overton, Grant. *The Women Who Make Our Novels.* New York: Dodd, Mead, 1931. 206–213; Schwarz, Judith. *Radical Feminists of Heterodoxy: Greenwich Village 1912–1940.* Lebanon, NH: New Victoria Publishers, 1982.

WORKS   *Are Women People? A Book of Rhymes for Suffrage Times* (1915) and *Women Are People!* (1917)

from *Are Women People? A Book of Rhymes for Suffrage Times*

Introduction

Father, what is a Legislature?
A representative body elected by the people of the state.
Are women people?
No, my son, criminals, lunatics and women are not people.
Do legislators legislate for nothing?
Oh, no; they are paid a salary.
By whom?
By the people.
Are women people?
Of course, my son, just as much as men are.

The Newer Lullaby

("Good heavens, when I think what the young boy of to-day is growing up to I gasp. He has too many women around him all the time. He has his mother when he is a baby."—*Bernard Fagin, Probation Officer.*)

Hush-a-bye, baby,
 Feel no alarm,
Gunmen shall guard you,
 Lest Mother should harm.
Wake in your cradle,
 Hear father curse!
Isn't that better
 Than Mother or Nurse?

The Protected Sex

With apologies to James Whitcomb Riley.

("The result of taking second place to girls at school is that the boy feels a sense of inferiority that he is never afterward able entirely to shake off."—*Editorial in London Globe against co-education.*)

There, little girl, don't read,
You're fond of your books, I know,
But Brother might mope
If he had no hope
Of getting ahead of you.
It's dull for a boy who cannot lead.
There, little girl, don't read.

Why We Oppose Votes for Men

1. Because man's place is the armory.

2. Because no really manly man wants to settle any question otherwise than by fighting about it.

3. Because if men should adopt peaceable methods women will no longer look up to them.

4. Because men will lose their charm if they step out of their natural sphere and interest themselves in other matters than feats of arms, uniforms and drums.

5. Because men are too emotional to vote. Their conduct at baseball

games and political conventions shows this, while their innate tendency to appeal to force renders them peculiarly unfit for the task of government.

Many Men to Any Woman

If you have beauty, charm, refinement, tact,
If you can prove that should I set you free,
You would not contemplate the smallest act
That might annoy or interfere with me.
If you can show that women will abide
By the best standards of their womanhood—
(And I must be the person to decide
What in a woman is the highest good);
If you display efficiency supreme
In philanthropic work devoid of pay;
If you can show a clearly thought-out scheme
For bringing the millennium in a day;
    Why, then, dear lady, at some time remote,
    I might consider giving you the vote.

The Revolt of Mother

("Every true woman feels——"
—*Speech of almost any Congressman.*)

I am old-fashioned, and I think it right
    That man should know, by Nature's laws eternal,
The proper way to rule, to earn, to fight,
    And exercise those functions called paternal;
But even I a little bit rebel
At finding that he knows my job as well.

At least he's always ready to expound it,
    Especially in legislative hall,
The joys, the cares, the halos that surround it,
    "How women feel"—he knows that best of all.

In fact his thesis is that no one can
Know what is womanly except a man.

I am old-fashioned, and I am content
    When he explains the world of art and science
And government—to him divinely sent—
    I drink it in with ladylike compliance.
But cannot listen—no, I'm only human—
While he instructs me how to be a woman.

The Gallant Sex

(A woman engineer has been dismissed by the Board of Education, under their
new rule that women shall not attend high pressure boilers, although her work
has been satisfactory and she holds a license to attend such boilers from the
Police Department.)

Lady, dangers lurk in boilers,
    Risks I could not let you face.
Men were meant to be the toilers,
    Home, you know, is woman's place.
Have no home? Well, is that so?
Still, it's not my fault, you know.

Charming lady, work no more;
    Fair you are and sweet as honey;
Work might make your fingers sore,
    And, besides, I need the money.
Prithee rest,—or starve or rob—
Only let me have your job!

Agnes Repplier
(1855 [58?]–1950)

In 1946, Edward Wagenknecht called Agnes Repplier "our dean of essayists." Repplier was a prolific and well-known writer in the late nineteenth and early twentieth century, the author of more than twenty-five volumes of biography, history, and essays on literature and current events between 1888 and 1937. She is one of those almost-forgotten women writers about whom their contemporary commentators so often say, maddeningly, something like, "Her work is so well-known that I hardly need say much about it." Reliable information about Repplier's life (including her birth date) is sketchy. She was born in and died in Philadelphia, but lived for long periods of time in Europe. She reportedly did not learn to read until she was almost ten, and was dismissed from two private schools for "independent behavior," but she apparently had a talent for self-education, because at sixteen she began publishing essays in Philadelphia newspapers and in 1886 published the first of what would be ninety essays in the *Atlantic Monthly*. A contradictory figure, Repplier was a devoted Catholic who wrote biographies of three American Catholic leaders, yet she believed in the feminist cause and argued against American neutrality before America entered World War I. *In Pursuit of Laughter* (1936) is an informal (in a scholarly sense) but well-informed survey of the nature and importance of humor in Western culture, written by one for whom elegance of phrasing is more important than precise documentation. Despite her advocacy of political stances, Repplier had little patience with reformers, including feminist activists, because of what she viewed as simplistic zealotry. "Woman Enthroned," first published in the *Atlantic Monthly* and collected in *Points of Friction* (1920), is a witty exploration of the relationship between women and power, in

207

which Repplier repudiates the notion that women are inherently "purer" than men.

SOURCES   *American Women Writers,* Vol. 3; Millett, Fred B. *Contemporary American Authors.* New York: Harcourt, Brace, 1940. 537–539; Wagenknecht, Edward, ed. *When I Was a Child.* New York: E. P. Dutton, 1946. 327–337 (selections from Repplier's autobiographical essay "Small Tragedies").

WORKS   *Compromises* (1904); *Points of Friction* (1920) and *In Pursuit of Laughter* (1936)

from *Points of Friction*

Woman Enthroned

The Michigan magistrate who gave orders that a stalwart male angel presiding over the gateway of a cemetery should be recast in feminine mould may have been an erring theologian and a doubtful art-critic; but that he was a sound-hearted American no one can deny. He was not thinking of Azrael the mighty who had garnered that little harvest of death; or of Michael, great leader of the "fighting seraphim," whose blade "smote and felled Squadrons at once"; or of Gabriel the messenger. Holy Writ was as remote from his mental vision as was Paradise Lost. He was thinking very properly of the "angel in the house," and this feminine ideal was affronted by the robust outlines, no less than by the robust virtues, associated with the heavenly host. Cowley's soothing compromise, which was designed as a compliment to a lady, and which, instead of unsexing angels, endowed them with a double line of potencies,—"They are than Man more strong, and more than Woman sweet,"—is not easily expressed in art. The very gallant Michigan gentleman simplified the situation by eliminating the masculine element. He registered his profession of faith in the perfectibility of women.

It is awkward to be relegated to the angelic class, and to feel that one does not fit. Intelligent feminists sometimes say that chivalry—that inextinguishable point of view which has for centuries survived its own death-notices—is more disheartening than contempt. Chivalry is essentially protective. It is rooted in the consciousness of superior strength. It is expansively generous and scrimpingly just. It will not assure to women a fair field and no favours, which is the salvation of all humanity; but it will protect them from the consequences of their own deeds, and that way lies perdition.

Down through the ages we see the working of this will. Rome denied to women all civic rights, but allowed them many privileges. They were not permitted to make any legal contract. They were not permitted to bequeath their own fortunes, or—ordinarily—to give testimony in court. But they might plead ignorance of the law, "as a ground for dissolving an obligation," which, if often convenient, was always demoralizing. Being somewhat contemptuously absolved from the oath of allegiance in the Middle Ages, they were as a consequence immune from outlawry. On the other hand, the severity with which they were punished for certain crimes which were presumed to come easy to them—poisoning, husband-murder, witchcraft (King Jamie was not the only wiseacre who marvelled that there should be twenty witches to one warlock)—is evidence of fear on the legislators' part. The oldest laws, the oldest axioms which antedate all laws, betray this uneasy sense of insecurity. "Day and night must women be held by their protectors in a state of dependence," says Manu, the Hindu Noah, who took no female with him in his miraculously preserved boat, but was content with his own safety, and trusted the continuance of the race to the care and ingenuity of the gods.

In our day, and in our country, women gained their rights (I use the word "rights" advisedly, because, though its definition be disputed, every one knows what it implies) after a prolonged, but not embittered struggle. Certain States moved so slowly that they were overtaken by a Federal Amendment. Even with the franchise to back them, American women have a hard time making their way in the professions, though a great deal of courtesy is shown them by professional men. They have a hard time making their way in trades, where the unions block their progress. They have a very small share of political patronage, and few good positions on the civil lists. Whether the best interests of the country will be advanced or retarded by a complete recognition of their claims—which implies giving them an even chance with men—is a point on which no one can speak with authority. The absence of data leaves room only for surmise. Women are striving to gain this "even chance" for their own sakes, which is lawful and reasonable. Their public utterances, it is true, dwell pointedly on the regeneration of the world. This also is lawful and reasonable. Public utterances have *always* dwelt on the regeneration of the world, since the apple was eaten and Paradise closed its gates.

Meanwhile American chivalry, a strong article and equal to anything Europe ever produced, clings passionately and persistently to its inward vision. Ellen Key speaks casually of "the vices which men call woman's nature." If Swedish gentlemen permit themselves this form of speech, it finds no echo in our loyal land. Two things an American hates to do,—hold a woman accountable for her misdeeds, and punish her accordingly. When Governor Craig of North Carolina set aside the death-sentence which had been passed upon a murderess, and committed her to prison for life, he gave to the public this plain and comprehensive statement: "There is no escape from the conclusion that Ida Bell Warren is guilty of murder, deliberate and premeditated. Germany executed the woman spy; England did not. The action of the military Governor of Belgium was condemned by the conscience of the world. The killing of this woman would send a shiver through North Carolina."

Apart from the fact that Edith Cavell was not a spy, and that her offence was one which has seldom in the world's history been so cruelly punished, Governor Craig's words deserve attention. He explicitly exempted a woman, because she was a woman, from the penalty which would have been incurred by a man. Incidentally he was compelled to commute the death-sentence of her confederate, as it was hardly possible to send the murderous wife to prison, and her murderous accomplice to the chair. That the execution of Mrs. Warren would have sent a "shiver" though North Carolina is doubtless true. The Governor had received countless letters and telegrams protesting against the infliction of the death-penalty on a woman.

One of the reasons which has been urged for the total abolition of this penalty is the reluctance of juries to convict women of crimes punishable by death. The number of wives who murder their husbands, and of girls who murder their lovers, is a menace to society. Our sympathetic tolerance of these *crimes passionnés,* the sensational scenes in court, and the prompt acquittals which follow, are a menace to law and justice. Better that their perpetrators should be sent to prison, and suffer a few years of corrective discipline, until soft-hearted sentimentalists circulate petitions, and secure their pardon and release.

The right to be judged as men are judged is perhaps the only form of equality which feminists fail to demand. Their attitude to their own *errata* is well expressed in the solemn warning addressed by Mr. Louis Untermeyer's Eve to the Almighty, "Pause, God, and ponder, ere Thou judgest me!" The right to be punished is not, and has never been, a popular prerogative with either sex. There was, indeed, a London baker who was sentenced in the year 1816 to be whipped and imprisoned for vagabondage. He served his term; but, whether from clemency or from oversight, the whipping was never administered. When released, he promptly brought action against the prison authorities because he had not been whipped, "according to the statute," and he won his case. Whether or not the whipping went with the verdict is not stated; but it was a curious joke to play with the grim realities of British law.

American women are no such sticklers for code. They acquiesce in their frequent immunity from punishment, and are correspondingly, and very naturally, indignant when they find themselves no longer immune. There was a pathetic ring in the explanation offered some years ago by Mayor Harrison of Chicago, whose policemen were accused of brutality to female strikers and pickets. "When the women do anything in violation of the law," said the Mayor to a delegation of citizens, "the police arrest them. And then, instead of going along quietly as men prisoners would, the women sit down on the sidewalks. What else can the policemen do but lift them up?"

If men "go along quietly," it is because custom, not choice, has bowed their necks to the yoke of order and equity. They break the law without being prepared to defy it. The lawlessness of women may be due as much to their long exclusion from citizenship, "Some reverence for the laws ourselves have made," as to the lenity shown them by men,—a lenity which they stand ever ready to abuse. We have to only to imagine what would have happened to a group of men who had chosen to air a grievance by picketing the White House, the speed with which they would have been arrested, fined, dispersed, and forgotten, to realize the nature of the tolerance granted to women. For months these female pickets were unmolested. Money was subscribed to purchase for them umbrellas and overshoes. The President, whom they were affronting, sent them out coffee on cold mornings. It was only when their utterances became treasonable, when they undertook to assure our Russian visitors that Mr. Wilson and Mr. Root were deceiving Russia, and to entreat these puzzled foreigners to help them free our nation, that their sport was suppressed, and they became liable to arrest and imprisonment.

Much censure was passed upon the unreasonable violence of these women. The great body of American suffragists repudiated their action, and the anti-suffragists used them to point stern morals and adorn vivacious tales. But was it quite fair to permit them in the beginning a liberty which would not have been accorded to men, and which led inevitably to licence? Were they not treated as parents sometimes treat children, allowing them to use bad language because, "if you pay no attention to them, they will stop it of their own accord"; and then, when they do not stop it, punishing them for misbehaving before company? When a sympathetic gentleman wrote to a not very sympathetic paper to say that the second Liberty Loan would be more popular if Washington would "call off the dogs of war on women," he turned a flashlight upon the fathomless gulf with which sentimentalism has divided the sexes. No one dreams of calling policemen and magistrates "dogs of war" because they arrest and punish men for disturbing the peace. If men claim the privileges of citizenship, they are permitted to suffer its penalties.

A few years before the war, a rage of compiling useless statistics swept over Europe and the United States. When it was at its height, some active minds bethought them that children might be made to bear their part in the guidance of the human race. Accordingly a series of questions—some sensible and some foolish—were put to English, German, and American school-children, and their enlightening answers were given to the world. One of these questions read: "Would you rather be a man or a woman, and why?" Naturally this query was of concern only to little girls. No sane educator would ask it of a boy. German pedagogues struck it off the list. They said that to ask a child, "Would you rather be something you must be, or something you cannot possibly be?" was both foolish and useless. Interrogations concerning choice were of value only when the will was a determining factor.

No such logical inference chilled the examiners' zeal in this inquisitive land. The question was asked and was answered. We discovered, as a result, that a great many little American girls (a minority, to be sure, but a respectable minority) were well content with their sex; not because it had its duties and dignities, its pleasures and exemptions; but because they plainly considered that they were superior to little American boys, and were destined, when grown up, to be superior to American men. One small New England maiden wrote that she would rather be a woman because "Women are always better than men in morals." Another, because "Women are of more use in the world." A third, because "Women learn things quicker than men, and have more intelligence." And so on through varying degrees of self-sufficiency.

These little girls, who had no need to echo the Scotchman's prayer, "Lord, gie us a gude conceit o' ourselves!" were old maids in the making.

They had stamped upon them in their tender childhood the hall-mark of the American spinster. "The most ordinary cause of a single life," says Bacon, "is liberty, especially in certain self-pleasing and humorous minds." But it is reserved for the American woman to remain unmarried because she feels herself too valuable to be entrusted to a husband's keeping. Would it be possible in any country save our own for a lady to write to a periodical, explaining "Why I am an Old Maid," and be paid coin of the realm for the explanation? Would it be possible in any other country to hear such a question as "Should the Gifted Woman Marry?" seriously asked, and seriously answered? Would it be possible for any sane and thoughtful woman who was not an American to consider even the remote possibility of our spinsters becoming a detached class, who shall form "the intellectual and economic *élite* of the sex, leaving marriage and maternity to the less developed woman"? What has become of the belief, as old as civilization, that marriage and maternity are developing processes, forcing into flower a woman's latent faculties; and that the less-developed woman is inevitably the woman who has escaped this keen and powerful stimulus? "Never," said Edmond de Concourt, "has a virgin, young or old, produced a work of art." One makes allowance for the Latin point of view. And it is possible that M. de Goncourt never read "Emma."

There is a formidable lack of humour in the sometimes contemptuous attitude of women, whose capabilities have not yet been tested, toward men who stand responsible for the failures of the world. It denotes, at home and abroad, a density not far removed from dulness. In Mr. St. John Ervine's depressing little drama, "Mixed Marriage," which the Dublin actors played in New York some years ago, an old woman, presumed to be witty and wise, said to her son's betrothed: "Sure, I believe the Lord made Eve when He saw that Adam could not take care of himself"; and the remark reflected painfully upon the absence of that humorous sense which we used to think was the birthright of Irishmen. The too obvious retort, which nobody uttered, but which must have occurred to every-body's mind, was that if Eve had been designed as a care-taker, she had made a shining failure of her job.

That astute Oriental, Sir Rabindranath Tagore, manifested a wisdom beyond all praise in his recognition of American standards, when address-ing American audiences. As the hour for his departure drew nigh, he was asked to write, and did write, a "Parting Wish for the Women of Amer-ica," giving graceful expression to the sentiments he knew he was ex-pected to feel. The skill with which he modified and popularized an alien point of view revealed the seasoned lecturer. He told his readers that "God has sent woman to love the world," and to build up a "spiritual civilization." He condoled with them because they were "passing through great sufferings in this callous age." His heart bled for them, seeing that their hearts "are broken every day, and victims are snatched from their arms to be thrown under the car of material progress." The Occidental sentiment which regards man simply as an offspring, and a fatherless offspring at that (no woman, says Olive Schreiner, could look upon a battle-field without thinking, "So many mothers' sons!") came as naturally to Sir Rabindranath as if he had been to the manner born. He was content to see the passion and pain, the sorrow and heroism of men, as reflections mirrored in a woman's soul. The ingenious gentlemen who dramatize Biblical narratives for the American stage, and who are hampered at every step by the obtrusive masculinity of the East, might find a sympathetic supporter in this accomplished and accommodating Hindu.

The story of Joseph and his Brethren, for example, is perhaps the best tale ever told the world,—a tale of adventure on a heroic scale, with conflicting human emotions to give it poignancy and power. It deals with pastoral simplicities, with the splendours of court, and with the "high finance" which turned a free landholding people into tenantry of the crown. It is a story of men, the only lady being introduced being a disedifying *dea ex machinea,* whose popularity in Italian art has perhaps blinded us to the brevity of her Biblical rôle. But when this most dramatic narrative was cast into dramatic form, Joseph's splendid loyalty to his master, his cold and vigorous chastity, were nullified by giving him an Egyptian sweetheart. Lawful marriage with this young lady being his sole solicitude, the advances of Potiphar's wife were less of a temptation than an intrusion. The keynote of the noble old tale was destroyed to assure to woman her proper place as the guardian of man's integrity.

Still more radical was the treatment accorded to the parable of the "Prodigal Son," which was expanded into a pageant play, and acted with a hardy realism permitted only to the strictly ethical drama. The scriptural setting of the story was preserved, but its patriarchal character was sacrificed to modern sentiment which refuses to be interested in the relation of father and son. Therefore we beheld the prodigal equipped with a mother and a trusting female cousin, who, between them, put the poor old gentleman out of commission, reducing him to his proper level of purveyor-in-ordinary to the household. It was the prodigal's mother who bade her reluctant husband give their wilful son his portion. It was the prodigal's mother who watched for him from the house-top, and silenced the voice of censure. It was the prodigal's mother who welcomed his return, and persuaded father and brother to receive him into favour. The whole duty of man in that Syrian household was to obey the impelling word of woman, and bestow blessings and bags of gold according to her will.

The expansion of the maternal sentiment until it embraces, or seeks to embrace, humanity, is the vision of the emotional, as opposed to the intellectual, feminist. "The Mother State of which we dream" offers no attraction to many plain and practical workers, and is a veritable nightmare to others. "Woman," writes an enthusiast in the "Forum," "means to be, not simply the mother of the individual, but of society, of the State with its man-made institutions, of art and science, of religion and morals. All life, physical and spiritual, personal and social, needs to be mothered."

"Needs to be mothered"! When men proffer this welter of sentiment in the name of women, how is it possible to say convincingly that the girl student standing at the gates of knowledge is as humble-hearted as the boy; that she does not mean to mother medicine, or architecture, or biology, any more than the girl in the banker's office means to mother finance? Her hopes for the future are founded on the belief that fresh opportunities will meet a sure response; but she does not, if she be sane, measure her untried powers by any presumptive scale of valuation. She does not consider the advantages which will accrue to medicine, biology, or architecture by her entrance—as a woman—into any one of these fields. Their need for her maternal ministration concerns her less than her need for the magnificent heritage they present.

It has been said many times that the craving for material profit is not instinctive in women. If it is not instinctive, it will be acquired, because every legitimate incentive has its place in the progress of the world. The demand that women shall be paid men's wages for men's work may represent a desire for justice rather than a desire for gain; but money fairly earned is sweet in the hand, and to the heart. An open field, an even start, no handicap, no favours, and the same goal for all. This is the worker's dream of paradise. Women have long known that lack of citizenship was an obstacle in their path. Self-love has prompted them to overrate their imposed, and underrate their inherent, disabilities. "Whenever you see a woman getting a high salary, make up your mind that she is giving twice the value received," writes an irritable correspondent to the "Survey"; and this pretension paralyzes effort. To be satisfied with ourselves is to be at the end of our usefulness.

M. Émile Faguet, that most radical and least sentimental of French feminists, would have opened wide to women every door of which man holds the key. He would have given them every legal right and burden which they are physically fitted to enjoy and to bear. He was as unvexed by doubts as he was uncheered by illusions. He had no more fear of the downfall of existing institutions that he had hope for the regeneration of the world. The equality of men and women, as he saw it, lay, not in their strength, but in their weakness; not in their intelligence, but in their stupidity; not in their virtues, but in their perversity. Yet there was no taint of pessimism in his rational refusal to be deceived. No man saw more clearly, or recognized more justly, the art with which his countrywomen have cemented and upheld a social state at once flexible and orderly, enjoyable and inspiriting. That they have been the allies, and not the rulers, of men in building this fine fabric of civilization was also plain to his mind. Allies and equals he held them, but nothing more. *"La femme est parfaitement l'égale de l'homme, mais elle n'est que son égale."*

Naturally to such a man the attitude of Americans toward women was as unsympathetic as was the attitude of Dahomeyans. He did not condemn it (possibly he did not condemn the Dahomeyans, seeing that the civic and social ideals of France and Dahomey are in no wise comparable); but he explained with careful emphasis that the French woman, unlike her American sister, is not, and does not desire to be, *"un objet sacro-saint."* The reverence for women in the United States he assumed to be a national trait, a sort of national institution among a proud and patriotic people. *"L'idolâtrie de la femme est une chose américaine par excellence."*

The superlative complacency of American women is due largely to the oratorical adulation of American men,—an adulation that has no more substance than has the foam on beer. I have heard a candidate for office tell his female audience that men are weak and women are strong, that men are foolish and women are wise, that men are shallow and women are deep, that men are submissive tools whom women, the leaders of the race, must instruct to vote for *him*. He did not believe a word that he said, and his hearers did not believe that he believed it; yet the grossness of his flattery kept pace with the hypocrisy of his self-depreciation. The few men present wore an attitude of dejection, not unlike that of the little boy in

"Punch" who has been told that he is made of "Snips and snails, And puppy dogs' tails," and can "hardly believe it."

What Mr. Roosevelt called the "lunatic fringe" of every movement is painfully obtrusive in the great and noble movement which seeks fair play for women. The "full habit of speech" is never more regrettable than when the cause is so good that it needs but temperate championing. "Without the aid of women, England could not carry on this war," said Mr. Asquith in the second year of the great struggle,—an obvious statement, no doubt, but simple, truthful, and worthy to be spoken. Why should the "New Republic," in an article bearing the singularly ill-mannered title, "Thank You For Nothing!" have heaped scorn upon these words? Why should its writer have made the angry assertion that the British Empire had been "deprived of two generations of women's leadership," because only a world's war could drill a new idea into a statesman's head? The war has drilled a great many new ideas into all our heads. Absence of brain matter could alone have prevented this infusion. But "leadership" is a large word. It is not what men are asking, and it is not what women are offering, even at this stage of the game. Partnership is as far as obligation on the one side and ambition on the other are prepared to go; and a clear understanding of this truth has accomplished great results.

Therefore, when we are told that the women of to-day are "giving their vitality to an anaemic world," we wonder if the speaker has read a newspaper for the past half-dozen years. The passionate cruelty and the passionate heroism of men have soaked the earth with blood. Never, since it came from its Maker's hands, has it seen such shame and glory. There may be some who still believe that this blood would not have been spilled had women shared in the citizenship of nations; but the arguments they advance in support of an undemonstrable theory show a soothing ignorance of events.

"War will pass," says Olive Schreiner, "when intellectual culture and activity have made possible to the female an equal share in the control and government of modern national life." And why? Because "Arbitration and compensation will naturally occur to her as cheaper and simpler methods of bridging the gaps in national relationship."

Strange that this idea never "naturally" occurred to man! Strange that no delegate to The Hague should have perceived so straight a path to peace! Strange that when Germany struck her long-planned, well-prepared blow, this cheap and simple measure failed to stay her hand! War will pass when injustice passes. Never before, unless hope leaves the world.

That any civilized people should bar women from the practice of law is to the last degree absurd and unreasonable. There never can be an adequate cause for such an injurious exclusion. There is, in fact, no cause at all, only an arbitrary decision on the part of those who have the authority to decide. Yet nothing is less worth while than to speculate dizzily on the part women are going to play in any field from which they are at present debarred. They may be ready to burnish up "the rusty old social organism," and make it shine like new; but this is not the work which lies immediately at hand. A suffragist who believes that the world needs house-cleaning has made the terrifying statement that when English women enter the law courts they will sweep away all "legal frippery," all the "accumulated dust and rubbish of centuries." Latin terms, flowing gowns and wigs, silly staves and worn-out symbols, all must go, and with them must go the antiquated processes which confuse and retard justice. The women barristers of the future will scorn to have "legal natures like Portia's," basing their claims on quibbles and subterfuges. They will cut all Gordian knots. They will deal with naked simplicities.

References to Portia are a bit disquieting. Her law was stage law, good enough for the drama which has always enjoyed a jurisprudence of its own. We had best leave her out of any serious discussion. But why should the admission of women to the bar result in a volcanic upheaval? Women have practiced medicine for years, and have not revolutionized it. Painstaking service, rather than any brilliant display of originality, has been their contribution to this field. It is reasonable to suppose that their advance will be resolute and beneficial. If they ever condescended to their profession, they do so no longer. If they ever talked about belonging to "the class of real people," they have relinquished such flowers of rhetoric. If they have earnestly desired the franchise, it was because they saw in it justice to themselves, not the torch which would enlighten the world.

It is conceded theoretically that woman's sphere is an elastic term, embracing any work she finds herself able to do,—not necessarily do well, because most of the world's work is done badly, but well enough to save herself from failure. Her advance is unduly heralded and unduly criticized. She is the target for too much comment from friend and foe. On the one hand, a keen (but of course perverted) misogynist like Sir Andrew Macphail, welcomes her entrance into public life because it will tend to disillusionment. If woman can be persuaded to reveal her elemental inconsistencies, man, freed in some measure from her charm—which is the charm of *retenue*—will no longer be subject to her rule. On the other hand, that most feminine of feminists, Miss Jane Addams, predicts that "the dulness which inheres in both domestic and social affairs when they are carried on by men alone, will no longer be a necessary attribute of public life when gracious and grey-haired women become part of it."

If Sir Andrew is as acid as Schopenhauer, Miss Addams is early Victorian. Her point of view presupposes a condition of which we had not been even dimly aware. Granted that domesticity palls on the solitary male. Housekeeping seldom attracts him. The tea-table and the friendly cat fail to arrest his roving tendencies. Granted that some men are polite enough to say that they do not enjoy social events in which women take no part. They showed no disposition to relinquish such pastimes until the arid days of prohibition, and even now they cling forlornly to the ghost of a cheerful past. When they assert, however, that they would have a much better time if women were present, no one is wanton enough to contradict them. But public life! The arena in which whirling ambition sweeps human souls as an autumn wind sweeps leaves; which resounds with the shouts of the conquerors and the groans of the conquered; which is degraded by cupidity and ennobled by achievement; that this field of adventure, this heated race-track needs to be relieved from dulness by the presence and participation of elderly ladies is the crowning vision of sensibility.

"Qui veut faire l'ange fait la bête," said Pascal; and the Michigan angel is a danger signal. The sentimental and chivalrous attitude of American men reacts alarmingly when they are brought face to face with the actual terms and visible consequences of woman's enfranchisement. There exists a world-wide and age-long belief that what women want they get. They must want it hard enough and long enough to make their desire operative. It is the listless and preoccupied unconcern of their own sex which bars their progress. But men will fall into a flutter of admiration because a woman runs a successful dairy-farm, or becomes the mayor of a little town; and they will look aghast upon such such commonplace headlines as those in their morning paper: "Women Confess Selling Votes"; "Chicago Women Arrested for Election Frauds";—as if there had not always been, and would not always be, a percentage of unscrupulous voters in every electorate. No sane woman believes that women, as a body, will vote more honestly than men; but no sane man believes that they will vote less

honestly. They are neither the "gateway to hell," as Tertullian pointed out, nor the builders of Sir Rabindranath Tagore's "spiritual civilization." They are neither the repositories of wisdom, nor the final word of folly.

It was unwise and unfair to turn a searchlight upon the first woman in Congress, and exhibit to a gaping world her perfectly natural limitations. Such limitations are common in our legislative bodies, and excite no particular comment. They are as inherent in the average man as in the average woman. They in no way affect the question of enfranchisement. Give as much and ask no more. Give no more and ask as much. This is the watchword of equality.

"God help women when they have only their rights!" exclaimed a brilliant American lawyer; but it is in the "only" that all savour lies. Rights and privileges are incompatible. Emancipation implies the sacrifice of immunity, the acceptance of obligation. It heralds the reign of sober and disillusioning experience. Women, as M. Faguet reminds us, are only the equals of men; a truth which was simply phrased in the old Cornish adage, "Lads are as good as wenches when they are washed."

Nancy Boyd
Edna St. Vincent Millay (1892–1950)

The sketches that Edna St. Vincent Millay signed with the pseudonym "Nancy Boyd" in the late teens and early 1920s provided her with necessary income while she launched a career as a poet following her graduation from Vassar in 1917. In a 1922 letter, Millay says of Nancy, "Isn't she a blessing? Almost two years now the woman has been well nigh supporting me." The Nancy Boyd pieces appeared chiefly in *Vanity Fair* magazine and were collected in a volume titled *Distressing Dialogues* in 1924. Though the Nancy Boyd sketches have been called "hackwork" by critics more interested in Millay's lyric poetry, they reveal her feminist philosophy and her perception of the absurd posturing that so often characterizes relationships between men and women. Thus they contributed to the "war between the sexes" that was common in American humorous writing in the 1920s—a battle of wits engaged in also by Dorothy Parker, James Thurber, Florence Guy Seabury, and E. B. White. The dialogue form of these sketches—a form that editors Martha Bruere and Mary Beard call the "skit" in *Laughing Their Way* (1934)—also derives from Millay's interest in theater. She was involved for a time with the Provincetown Players in Greenwich Village as both playwright and actress, but her true talent was in poetry, and her fourth book of poems, *Ballad of the Harp-Weaver,* was awarded a Pulitzer Prize in 1923. In the same year she married Eugen Jan Boissevain, a Dutch importer, who was supportive of both her feminism and her literary career. Millay's involvement engaged her in a number of social and political causes, including protests against the convictions of Sacco and Vanzetti and American isolationism in the early years of World War II, turned her writing to propagandistic purposes, as in her radio play *The Murder of Lidice* (1942).

Seldom in good health, Millay died a year after her husband's death, at their home in Austerlitz, New York.

sources   Gould, Jean. *The Poet and Her Book: A Biography of Edna St. Vincent Millay*. New York: Dodd, Mead, 1969; Gurko, Miriam. *Restless Spirit*. New York: Crowell, 1962; Macdougall, Allan Ross. *Letters of Edna St. Vincent Millay*. Camden, ME: Down East Books, 1952.

works   *Distressing Dialogues* (1924)

from *Distressing Dialogues*

The Implacable Aphrodite

scene: *A studied studio, in which nine o'clock tea and things are being served by Miss Black, a graceful sculptress, to Mr. White, a man of parts, but badly assembled. Miss Black is tattooed with batik; Mr. White is as impeccably attired for the evening as a professional violinist.*

He: My dear Miss Black, you are, if you will permit me to say so, the most interesting unmarried woman of my acquaintance.

She *(languidly flicking an ash from a cigarette-holder the approximate length of a fencing-foil)*: Oh, yes?

He: Yes. You are the only unmarried woman I know with whom I find it possible to talk freely on any subject. *(He clears his throat.)*

She *(gazing at him with clear, straightforward eyes)*: You interest me. *(She waits for him to continue.)*

He *(continuing)*: You have such an intrepid mind, I feel, so unblenched a vision. The petty concerns that make up the lives of other people, they are not your life. You see beyond their little disputes, their little aspirations, their little loves, into a world, a cosmos, where men and women can understand each other, can help each other, where the barriers of sex are like a mist in the air, dissipated with the dawn.

She *(cosmically)*: It is true that for me there are no barriers.

He *(almost with excitement)*: I know that! I know that! And that is how I know that you mean what you say—for the very simple reason that you are not afraid to say what you mean—and that at this moment, for example, as you sit there, so beautiful, so more than beautiful, and so all unconscious of your beauty, talking to me like a soul detached, a soul freed of the earth,—you are not all the time considering just how long it will take you to get me to propose to you! *(She starts and blushes a little, but he goes on without noticing.)* Oh, if you only knew what a relief you are, what a rest!—a woman who is not married, who has never been married, and who does not insist that I marry her. Please do not think me boastful. It is not that I am so very attractive. I dare say it is the experience of every eligible man. And doubtless when they have had a good look at me, they decide against me. But unmarried women always give me the uncomfortable feeling that they are looking me over; and I object to being looked over, with matrimony a forethought.

She *(sympathetically)*: I know. But I am sorry for them. They have nothing else with which to occupy their minds. That I am different from these women is through no virtue of my own, but only because I am blessed with a talent which releases my spirit into other channels. Whether the talent be great or small *(she deprecates gracefully toward the clutter of statuary about the studio)* is of no consequence. It is sufficient to ease my need.

He *(following the direction of her gesture, and considering the reclining figure of a nymph on a table beside him)*: What a charming study! Such subtle lines, such exquisite proportions. Who is she?

She: I call her Daphne. She was running, you see,—and has fallen.

He: Oh. But I mean to say, who is your model? You are fortunate to have found a creature at once so delicate and so roundly contoured.

She: Oh.

(There is an appreciable pause.)

She *(frankly)*: Why, you see, I *have* no model. They are so difficult to get, and they are mostly so bad. I—am my own model. You notice the two long mirrors?—I place the stand between them, and work from my reflections.

(There is an appreciable pause.)

He *(pulling down his coat-sleeves over his cuffs, and adjusting his tie)*: What an interesting idea.

She *(laughing gaily)*: Yes—and so economical!

(She rises and lights the alcohol lamp under a small brass tea-kettle. Her heavy, loose robe clings to her supple limbs. The flame sputters. With an impatient exclamation she drops to her knees and considers the lamp

from beneath, with critical attention. The sleeves fall back from her lifted arms; her fine brows scowl a little; her vermilion lips are pouted in concentration.)

He *(with ponderous lightness)*: Miss Black, I dare say that to many of my sex you are a dangerously attractive women.

She *(rising sinuously, and dusting her hands, which seem to caress each other)*: Well,—yes. In fact *(smiling faintly)*, you are the only man in my acquaintance, unmarried or married, who does not importune me with undesirable attentions.

He *(with aesthetic ferocity)*: Of course. I know how it is. They don't see you as I do. They do not desire to leave you free, as I do. They don't know what you are. It is your beauty which attracts them, your extraordinary grace, your voice, so thrillingly quiet, your ravishing gestures. They don't see you as I do. *(He is silent, breathing hard.)*

She *(in a burst of confidence)*: It is true. I don't know what it is about me, but I am besieged by suitors. I have not a moment to myself. All day long, all day long, the bell rings; I open the door; they drop on their knees; I tell them not to be absurd; they insist upon giving me their hearts; I insist that I have no room for anything more in my apartment! they arise, dust their trousers, curse my beauty, gulp, yank open the door,—and the bell rings. You alone, of them all, see me as I am. You know that I am not beautiful, you are undisturbed by my proximity, it is possible for me to talk with you, as—as one star talks to another. *(She leans back wearily and closes her eyes, exposing a long and treacherous throat, full of memories.)*

He *(a little uncertainly)*: Well—I—it is true that I—er—admire you for your true worth, that I really appreciate you, and that your external attributes have nothing to do with that appreciation. But it would be impossible for any man, who could be called a man, to be blind to your incredible charm, your inscrutable, unconscious fascination. For I know it is unconscious,—you are lovely as a flower is lovely, without effort. I am aware of all this, although, as you say, I am unmoved by it.

(She turns her head slowly, and opens upon him a pair of wondering, topaz eyes. He swallows audibly, but meets the look without flinching.)

He *(stoutly)*: What does move me, and to what extent you cannot possibly imagine *(he shifts convulsively in his chair)*, is your unparalleled genius, the poise and vigour of your work. I want you to go on—to grow—to grow—and to be free!

She *(tensely)*: I *must* be free. I must.

He: I know. And if there is anything I can do to make you freer—

She: I know. I know. *(Selecting a cigarette from the lacquer tray at her elbow, she thoughtfully twists it into her cigarette-holder.)* I am sorry that you think me beautiful. But I suppose it cannot be helped. *(She sighs.)* You must forgive me, but I am always a little sorry when a man becomes even conscious of me as a woman. Nothing may come of it, of course,—in this instance, I am sure, nothing will— *(She flashes at him a little candid smile.)* But there is always the danger, for we are, among other things, human beings, and—oh, I am troubled that you said that! *(She twists her long hands; her jade rings click together.)*

He *(sitting forward on his chair and taking her restless fingers firmly in his trembling hands):* Have no fear of me. Believe me, if it came to that, I should go. You should never guess. Rather than hurt you, I should go. I should get up and go, suddenly, without even saying good-bye, and you would never guess.

She *(smiling a little lonely smile):* I know. I know you would. You are like that.

He *(intensely):* I would do anything rather than hurt you in the slightest degree,—so high do I rate your talent.

She: I know. *(She leans back her head and closes her eyes.)* It is good to feel that I have your friendship. I have so little—friendship.

He *(thickly, staring at her pained and perfect mouth):* You will have my friendship always, as long as you want it. And even when you tire of me, and don't want it any more, you will still have it. Remember that. Woman though you are, you stir me more deeply by your genius than ever a man has done. *(He bows his head on her hands.)*

She *(looking thoughtfully down at the top of his head):* You are so kind, so kind to be distressed for my sake. Please don't be distressed. Come let's have our tea. I am really all right, you know. It's just that, at times, I am a little sad.

He *(lifting his head and looking into her sad eyes):* Yes, you are sad. And I am sad, too. How curious that we should both be sad! If only I could do something to comfort you. Please don't look like that.

She *(with a gay smile that is obviously a little forced):* Very well! There now!—I am quite happy again, you see! Come, let's have our tea.

(He sits back in his chair, and looks curiously at the arms of it, feeling that he has been away for a long time. She busies herself with the tea things.)

She *(after a moment, peering into the black and silver Chinese tea-pot):*

Do you know, it's extraordinary, the way I feel about tea: I have to have it. It's the one thing I couldn't possibly get along without. Money, clothes, books, mirrors, friends—all these I could dispense with. But tea,—I have to have it. Fortunately, its connotation, as being the accomplice of spinsterhood, is not so offensive to me as it is to most women. If it will help me to remain a spinster, then it is my staunchest ally! *(She laughs gaily.)*

He *(wincing, but recovering himself):* I'm just that way about my pipe. *(Suddenly remembering his pipe, he gropes for it pitifully, as for the hand of a comrade in the dark. But it occurs to him that she probably objects to pipe-smoke. He withdraws his hand from his pocket, sighing.)*

She *(without looking up):* Why don't you smoke your pipe?

He *(incredulously):* Wouldn't it annoy you?

She: Heavens, no!

(He draws his pipe from his pocket and fills it, gratefully, meanwhile watching her. She is cruelly slicing a lemon, by means of a small dagger with which a Castilian nun has slain three matadors; it strikes him that she looks gentle and domestic. A great peace steals over him.)

He *(contentedly):* What a pleasant room this is.

She *(delicately poising in her hand a sugar-tongs made from the hind claws of a baby gila-monster, and glancing lovingly about the room):* Yes. It breaks my heart that I have to leave it. Two lumps, or three?

He: Have to leave it? Er—no, thanks, I don't like tea—well, three lumps—have to *leave it?* (He grasps his cup and saucer and holds them before him, as if they were an unfamiliar pair of infant twins.)

She: Yes. You see *(conversationally),* I'm sailing for Europe on the fifteenth, and—

He *(hoarsely):* Fifteenth of what? *(His cup and saucer rattle together now like a pair of dice.)*

She *(pleasantly):* Fifteenth of this month. It will be of infinite value to me in my work, I am sure,—and I think only of that. Yet I hate to leave these rooms. I've been here—

He: Don't—don't—don't talk—be quiet—Oh, God—let me think! *(With awful care he deposits his cup and saucer on the table at his elbow. She watches him intently.)*

He *(suddenly sliding from his chair to the floor and kneeling before her):* But what about me? What about me?

She *(coldly):* I don't understand you.

He: You say you're going because it will help your work,—but think of me! What will happen to me?

She: I'm sure I don't know. It hadn't occurred to me to consider.

He *(shouting):* No! Of course not! Oh, you're cold, you are—and cruel, my God! Your work! *(He laughs scornfully.)* All you think about is those damn little putty figures! And here am I, flesh and blood,—and what do you care?

She *(icily):* Less and less.

He *(groaning):* And you can say that—and me loving you the way I do! You don't mean it! Oh, if you'd only marry me, I'd make you care. I'd make you so happy!

She *(with revulsion):* Oh, really,—I must *ask* you—

He: I don't care how much you work—work your head off! A man's wife *ought* to have some little thing to take up her time. But as for—oh, Lord—*(He buries his face in the folds of her gown.) What* am I going to do?

(She has no suggestion to offer.)

He *(abruptly rising and glaring down at her):* Do you know what I think?—I think you're enjoying this! I think it's the breath of life to you!

She *(earnestly):* No, really. I assure you—I am frightfully distressed—I had no idea you felt like this—I—

He *(wildly):* You're a lying woman!

She *(rising, white with the fury of the righteous unjustly accused):* Will you be so good as to go?

He *(laughing boisterously, then in a subdued and hopeless voice):* Very well. Of course I'll go if you want me to. But my heart I leave here.

She *(languidly):* Pray don't. I have room for nothing more in the apartment.

(With a growl he yanks open the door and leaps forth, slamming it behind him. She goes to the table and pours herself a cup of cold tea.)

She *(after a moment of silence, running her jaded fingers through her hair):* Oh, dear, I *wish* I were not so restless!

CURTAIN

Anita Loos

(1893–1981)

Born in California, Loos was a child actor before she began a
successful career as a screenwriter. Her first accepted sce-
nario, *The New York Hat*, was produced by the Biograph
Company in 1912 and directed by D. W. Griffith, who later
hired her on a salary basis. By 1919 she had written scripts
and/or titles for about 200 films that were noted for their wit,
and for such stars as Mary Pickford, Lionel Barrymore,
Lillian and Dorothy Gish, Norma and Constance Talmadge,
and Douglas Fairbanks. Following her marriage to writer-
director John Emerson, she collaborated with him on a series
of films and had two plays produced on Broadway: *The
Whole Town's Talking* (1923) and *The Fall of Eve* (1925).
However, it was the serialization in *Harper's Bazaar* of
Gentlemen Prefer Blondes in 1925 that brought her phenomenal success and an international reputation. Written as
the diary of Lorelei Lee, a female version of H. L. Mencken's
"boobus americanus," the novel had 83 American printings
and was translated into 13 languages. Aldous Huxley and
H. G. Wells were so impressed with the novel that they
declared Loos to be the only American woman either wanted
to meet, and A. E. Hotchner claimed that philosopher
George Santayana called the novel "the most important
philosophical work ever written by an American." Although
considered the original "dumb blonde" in American popular
culture, Lorelei is used by Loos to criticize the values and
manners of American society in the 1920s and is, therefore,
in the tradition of the wise-innocent figure of earlier American humor. We laugh at Lorelei, as we laughed at the rubes
who were her predecessors, but we also laugh with her at
those who attempt to intimidate or take advantage of her: the
wealthy and pompous, the sugar daddies and lotharios.

While Loos continued her writing career with *But Gen-tlemen Marry Brunettes* (1928), numerous screenplays during the 1930s and 1940s, plays, and her two volumes of autobiography—*A Girl Like I* (1966) and *Kiss Hollywood Good-by* (1974)—she also returned again and again to *Gentlemen Prefer Blondes*, collaborating on various stage, film, and musical versions for almost fifty years.

SOURCES   Coe, Richard, "Anita Loos: A Living Dynamo Tapping a Deep Well of Creativity." *The Washington Post.* 27 May 1973: M1+; Hotchner, A. E. "Gentlemen Still Prefer Blondes." *Theater Arts.* July 1953: 26–27+; Loos, Anita. *A Girl Like I.* New York: Viking, 1966 and *Kiss Hollywood Good-by.* New York: Viking, 1974; Miller, Merle. "Did Anita Loos Write the Great American Novel?" *Town and Country.* April 1973: 66.

WORKS   *Gentlemen Prefer Blondes* (1925) and *But Gentlemen Marry Bru-nettes* (1928)

Gentlemen Prefer Blondes

from CHAPTER ONE

March 16th:

A gentleman friend and I were dining at the Ritz last evening and he said that if I took a pencil and a paper and put down all of my thoughts it would make a book. This almost made me smile as what it would really make would be a whole row of encyclopediacs. I mean I seem to be thinking practically all of the time. I mean it is my favorite recreation and sometimes I sit for hours and do not seem to do anything else but think. So this gentleman said a girl with brains ought to do something else with them besides think. And he said he ought to know brains when he sees them, because he is in the senate and he spends quite a great deal of time in Washington, d.c., and when he comes into contract with brains he always notices it. So it might have all blown over but this morning he sent me a book. And so when my maid brought it to me, I said to her, "Well, Lulu, here is another book and we have not read half the ones we have got yet." But when I opened it and saw that it was all a blank I remembered what my gentleman acquaintance said, and so then I realized that it was a diary. So here I am writing a book instead of reading one.

But now it is the 16th of March and of course it is to late to begin with

January, but it does not matter as my gentleman friend, Mr. Eisman, was in town practically all of January and February, and when he is in town one day seems to be practically the same as the next day.

I mean Mr. Eisman is in the wholesale button profession in Chicago and he is the gentleman who is known practically all over Chicago as Gus Eisman the Button King. And he is the gentleman who is interested in educating me, so of course he is always coming down to New York to see how my brains have improved since the last time. But when Mr. Eisman is in New York we always seem to do the same thing and if I wrote down one day in my diary, all I would have to do would be to put quotation marks for all other days. I mean we always seem to have dinner at the Colony and see a show and go to the Tocadero and then Mr. Eisman shows me to my apartment. So of course when a gentleman is interested in educating a girl, he likes to stay and talk about the topics of the day until quite late, so I am quite fatigued the next day and I do not really get up until it is time to dress for dinner at the Colony.

It would be strange if I turn out to be an authoress. I mean at my home near Little Rock, Arkansas, my family all wanted me to do something about my music. Because all of my friends said I had talent and they all kept after me and kept after me about practising. But some way I never seemed to care so much about practising. I mean I simply could not sit for hours and hours at a time practising just for the sake of a career. So one day I got quite tempermental and threw the old mandolin clear across the room and I have really never touched it since. But writing is different because you do not have to learn or practise and it is more tempermental because practising seems to take all the temperment out of me. So now I really almost have to smile because I have just noticed that I have written clear across two pages onto March 18th, so this will do for today and tomorrow. And it just shows how tempermental I am when I get started.

March 19th:

Well last evening Dorothy called up and Dorothy said she has met a gentleman who gave himself an introduction to her in the lobby of the Ritz. So then they went to luncheon and tea and dinner and then they went to a show and then they went to the Trocadero. So Dorothy said his name was Lord Cooksleigh but what she really calls him is Coocoo. So Dorothy said why don't you and I and Coocoo go the Follies tonight and bring Gus along if he is in town? So then Dorothy and I had quite a little quarrel because every time that Dorothy mentions the subject of Mr. Eisman she calls Mr. Eisman by his first name, and she does not seem to realize that when a gentleman who is as important as Mr. Eisman, spends quite a lot of money educating a girl, it really does not show reverence to call a gentleman by his first name. I mean I never even think of calling Mr. Eisman by his first name, but if I want to call him anything at all, I call him "Daddy" and I do not even call him "Daddy" if a place seems to be public. So I told Dorothy that Mr. Eisman would not be in town until day after tomorrow. So then Dorothy and Coocoo came up and we went to the Follies.

So this morning Coocoo called up and he wanted me to luncheon at the Ritz. I mean these foreigners really have quite a nerve. Just because Coocoo is an Englishman and a Lord he thinks a girl can waste hours on him just for a luncheon at the Ritz, when all he does is talk about some exposition he went on to a place called Tibet and after talking for hours I found out that all they were was a lot of Chinamen. So I will be quite glad to see Mr. Eisman when he gets in. Because he always has something quite interesting to talk about, as for instants the last time he was here he presented me with quite a beautiful emerald bracelet. So next week is my birthday and he always has some delightful surprise on holidays.

I did intend to luncheon at the Ritz with Dorothy today and of course Coocoo had to spoil it, as I told him that I could not luncheon with him today, because my brother was in town on business and had the mumps, so I really could not leave him alone. Because of course if I went to the Ritz now I would bump into Coocoo. But I sometimes almost have to smile at my own imagination, because of course I have not got any brother and I have not even thought of the mumps for years. I mean it is no wonder that I can write.

So the reason I thought I would take luncheon at the Ritz was because Mr. Chaplin is at the Ritz and I always like to renew old acquaintances, because I met Mr. Chaplin once when we were both working on the same lot in Hollywood and I am sure he would remember me. Gentleman always seem to remember blondes. I mean the only career I would like to be besides an authoress is a cinema star and I was doing quite well in the cinema when Mr. Eisman made me give it all up. Because of course when a gentleman takes such a friendly interest in educating a girl as Mr. Eisman does, you like to show that you appreciate it, and he is against a girl being in the cinema because his mother is authrodox. . . .

March 22nd:

Well my birthday has come and gone but it was really quite depressing. I mean it seems to me a gentleman who has a friendly interest in educating a girl like Gus Eisman, would want her to have the biggest square cut diamond in New York. I mean I must say I was quite disappointed when he came to the apartment with a little thing you could hardly see. So I told him I thought it was quite cute, but I had quite a headache and I had better stay in a dark room all day and I told him I would see him the next day, perhaps. Because even Lulu thought it was quite small and she said, if she was I, she really would do something definite and she said she always believed in the old addage, "Leave them while you're looking good." But he came in at dinner time with really a very very beautiful bracelet of square cut diamonds so I was quite cheered up. So then we had dinner at the Colony and we went to a show and supper at the Trocadero as usual whenever he is in town. But I will give him credit that he realized how small it was. I mean he kept talking about how bad business was and the button profession was full of bolshevicks who make nothing but trouble. Because Mr. Eisman feels that the country is really on the verge of the bolshevicks and I become quite worried. I mean if the bolshevicks do get in, there is only one gentleman who could handle them and that is Mr. D. W. Griffith. Because I will never forget when Mr. Griffith was directing Intolerance. I mean it was my last cinema just before Mr. Eisman made me give up my career and I was playing one of the girls that fainted at the battle when all of the gentlemen fell off the tower. And when I saw how Mr. Griffith handled all of those mobs in Intolerance I realized that he could do anything, and I really think that the government of America ought to tell Mr. Griffith to get all ready if the bolshevicks start to do it.

Well I forgot to mention that the English gentleman who writes novels seems to have taken quite an interest in me, as soon as he found out that I was literary. I mean he has called up every day and I went to tea twice with him. So he has sent me a whole complete set of books for my birthday by a gentleman called Mr. Conrad. They all seem to be about ocean travel although I have not had time to more than glance through them. I have always liked novels about ocean travel ever since I posed for Mr. Christie for the front of a novel about ocean travel by McGrath because I always say that a girl never really looks as well as she does on board a steamship, or even a yacht.

So the English gentleman's name is Mr. Gerald Lamson as those who have read his novels would know. And he also sent me some of his own novels and they all seem to be about middle age English gentlemen who live in the country over in London and seem to ride bicycles, which seems quite different from America, except at Palm Beach. So I told Mr. Lamson how I write down all of my thoughts and he said he knew I had something to me from the first minute he saw me and when we become better acquainted I am going to let him read my diary. I mean I even told Mr. Eisman about him and he is quite pleased. Because of course Mr. Lamson is quite famous and it seems Mr. Eisman has read all of his novels going to and fro on the trains and Mr. Eisman is always anxious to meet famous people and take them to the Ritz to dinner on Saturday night. But of course I did not tell Mr. Eisman that I am really getting quite a little crush on Mr. Lamson, which I really believe I am, but Mr. Eisman thinks my interest in him is more literary.

Florence Guy Seabury

(1881–1951)

Born in Montclair, New Jersey, Seabury attended Columbia
University and the New York School for Social Work, and
later became a fellow at the Russell Sage Foundation in New
York. Following her marriage (in the 1920s) to David Seabury, a noted psychologist, she became interested in
psychology and taught modern applied psychology at
Briarcliff Junior College. A socialist and settlement house
worker in the early decades of the century, she became an
active suffragist and served for a time as editor of *The
Woman Voter*. During this period she became a member of
Heterodoxy, a club, according to Mabel Dodge Luhan, "for
unorthodox women" that flourished in Greenwich Village
from 1912 to approximately 1940 and that included a
number of radical feminists, artists, and suffragists. In addition to her political writing, Seabury contributed satiric
articles to *Harper's, McCall's,* and *The New Republic,* some
of which were collected in *The Delicatessen Husband and
Other Essays* (1926). Written after the passage of the female
suffrage amendment in 1920, the essays deal with the
changes in relations between the genders brought about by
women's fight for equality, and reflect Seabury's work in
social welfare, psychology, and women's rights, as well as her
wit. Using mock case studies and a parody of the scientific
method to explore changing ideas about sex roles, morals,
and manners, Seabury suggests some of the causes and effects
of confusion and resentment in heterosexual relationships
and some possible solutions. Like Alice Duer Miller, who
was also a member of Heterodoxy, Seabury implies that an
egalitarian society is not something to be feared but welcomed as providing both men and women with greater
opportunities for personal fulfillment.

SOURCES   Schwarz, Judith. *The Radical Feminists of Heterodoxy: Greenwich Village 1912–1940*. Lebanon, NH: New Victoria Publishers, 1982; "Florence Guy Seabury." Obituary. *New York Times*. 8 October 1951: 17.

WORKS   *The Delicatessen Husband and Other Essays* (1926)

from *The Delicatessen Husband and Other Essays*

The Delicatessen Husband

It was six-thirty and Saturday night. Perry Winship was tired. With arms full of bundles he fumbled in the dark for his key, secured the wrong one, and strained at the lock. In his effort to open the door, he dislodged his load: a bag of buns deliberately rolling across the pile and tumbling over the floor. Perry swore, put his stuff on the stairs, and felt over his keys for the one with the oval end. It fitted. Gathering his packages, he made his way into the apartment. It was dark: Ethel had not returned. She was always being kept at the laboratory on Saturday, press of work, she explained. It had been like this for two years now.

Perry switched on the light in the kitchenette and carefully unwrapped his purchases, placing them in a row along the shelf. Confound it, he had forgotten the butter, and only a crumby scrap was left from morning. Grabbing his hat, he descended the stairs, his temper rising. He hated going to the delicatessen. Despite his needs those indispensable institutions distinguished from tailor shops and candy parlors by their windows and showcases with cubist dreams of sausages, curious pastes, highly colored salads and noisome cheeses, were not, to him, convenient places at which to purchase ready-to-eat foods. They were emblems of a declining civilization, the source of all our ills, the promoter of equal suffrage, the permitter of the business and professional woman, the destroyer of the home. They were generations removed from his ideals.

He never entered one of them without a shuddered malediction. As usual, people were waiting in line for the attention of the white-aproned clerk: the inevitable fat woman, crowding broadly against the counter— large and greasy, determined to take her time in the momentous choice between a bit of bologna and a slice of corned beef; a small boy clutching a coin, wrapped in newspaper, to pay for a loaf of rye bread for Pop's supper; a thin, tired young chap with a long list of groceries, sprawled in a feminine hand, and a stylish, bobbed-hair stenographer prepared to purchase two Swiss cheese sandwiches, with French, not German, mustard, please. Perry turned sullenly and made his way to a similar exhibition, two blocks beyond.

He was not in a happy frame of mind. Somehow, he had never successfully adjusted himself to one room, bath, and kitchenette. The home of his childhood was always more or less in his mind, a pleasant frame house in a small up-state city. Not pretentious, not even harmonious in architecture, with dormer windows and gabled roof in perpetual clash with Greek pillars on the porch, it loomed, nevertheless, in Perry's dreams, as vision of the ideal, the perfect, abiding-place. There were his mother's Boston ferns in the bow-window, the shabby old sofa and the comfortable rocking chairs in the sitting room, and the large kitchen, where he could always find his mother the minute he entered the house. She was never out—he remembered no occasion in his life when his "Hello, Ma," at the front door had failed to find an echoing response from the back of the house.

To see Perry reading his paper on his way home in the subway, one would not expect to discover in him a seething, brooding rebellion. He is big and athletic and should be engrossed in news of the Giants and Yanks, Dempsey and Carpentier. But appearances are misleading. Perry scans the headlines and stock transactions, then turns directly to the page labeled "Of Interest to Women." Passing over the fashion notes and chit-chat, he reads greedily:

MENU FOR MAY 10TH
Dinner
Cream of asparagus soup, roast stuffed veal, hashed brown potatoes, fresh string beans and old-fashioned strawberry shortcake with whipped cream.

All his favorites are there. With equal relish he studies the news about leftovers. To Perry a stew, shepherd pie, or even hash, anything reminiscent of a regularly cooked roast, is utterly delectable. No left-overs are in Perry's life. He lives from can to mouth.

Perry always possessed views, but in recent years his condemnations have been increasing almost to the point of a grievance. He is vaguely uncomfortable from early morning, when he tries to crowd his tall frame into a bath-tub designed by cunning apartment architects to fit a Lilliputian, until night, when he takes down the folding-bed disguised as a book-case and desk and tries vainly to discover a comfortable spot on the lumpy mattress. The trouble is that Perry wants a home as nearly like the one of his childhood as it is possible to achieve. But Ethel, his wife, will not live in the suburbs, where such houses could logically be found. She has tried commuting and has discovered that it is too difficult to manage with the type of work she is doing.

Ethel is a modern, self-supporting woman. Like eight million others of her sex, she spends her days in gainful occupation out of the home. Since all government statisticians concede that it isn't gainful to be at work in the home, Ethel is perfectly satisfied, even happy to be out of it. She would never be found on the mourner's bench with those who deplore that economic pressure in these days of exorbitant prices makes it necessary for wives to add to the family budget. In fact, it really isn't true in her case. Perry could support her in a modest sort of way—and he wants to do so. It's a matter of Ethel's temperament. Perry's ideals and her talents are in conflict.

When Perry met Ethel, shortly after her graduation from Vassar, his ideas were but vague preferences. She had achieved honors in mathematics and specialized in chemistry, yet despite this highbrow tendency, she was a radiant creature, with rare feminine charm. Perry saw and worshiped.

She told him frankly that she preferred test-tubes and measuring-glasses to enameled sinks and aluminum cooking-dishes, however bright and new. He didn't believe it; sure that she didn't understand the depths of her own nature. Nor the influence of his. All women, he believed, are domestic at heart and if the desire for cooking and dish washing has been unnaturally suppressed, marriage will miraculously unfold it. Ethel was sufficiently in love to hope for the best. She too wanted a home and all that it means. She too had dreamed dreams. But she wanted also to be herself and to remain so after marriage, as Perry would remain himself.

Three months of housekeeping resulted in such havoc: burned food, broken dishes, general confusion and fatigue beyond the Coué-point that even Perry admitted something must be done. He was frankly mystified by the exhibition of Ethel's incompetence in domestic matters. He had always supposed that any woman could keep house and would regard it as a supreme joy to be mistress of a home of her own. When he returned from work, however, he had neither an edible dinner nor Ethel. She was stretched out on her bed trying to recover, and remained an abstracted companion all the evening. For her part, Ethel announced her intention of resuming the relatively easy life of a wage-earner. Her position in the laboratory of Proudfoote's Perfect Products was still open. There, before her marriage, she had spent her days in blissful analysis of cold creams, scented soaps, tooth pastes and hair tonics.

"And we now we'll have the same jolly evenings together we had during our engagement," she told Perry. "In Civil War days drafted men could hire substitutes. Housework is warfare to me. I shall use my salary for a real cook who will make you more comfortable than I could if I spent ten years more trying to learn how."

The plan was good enough, but the times were relatively cookless. Maids were corralled at high wages, but they did not like a cramped kitchen in a small apartment. With no mistress to take responsibility, troubles developed. The changing procession from the Winship apartment suggested an America-in-the-Making Exhibit of Immigrant Nationalities. Ethel sought advice and tried the experiment of extra-skilled visiting service. She had graduate students in domestic science, who wore immaculate linen dresses and systematized their diet by calories and vitamines. The house was spotless, the kitchen card-catalogued and indexed and they lived so hygienically that Perry rebelled. He said he would rather eat a few germs and have dyspepsia now and then than feel like a specimen in a hospital laboratory.

Unskilled and skilled labor being tried and found wanting, nothing remained but to give up housekeeping. So they moved into smaller, though more expensive, quarters. It is one of the paradoxes of New York City that it costs more to hire a tiny, kitchenette apartment than a large, old-fashioned flat with high ceilings where the effectiveness of the plumbing is in inverse proportion to the number of fireplaces. Cliffdwellers consider size a disadvantage.

So mornings, nowadays, Ethel and Perry make toast and coffee with an electric apparatus concealed behind a screen in the corner of the room. They consume it hurriedly and Ethel rinses the dishes while Perry smoothes the bed and folds it decorously into its camouflage. They emerge, pack themselves into subway trains going in opposite directions, and each hangs to a strap until the destination is reached. They do not meet for lunch. Perry takes his at an arm-chair joint, Ethel goes to a cafeteria. Evenings, once in a while, they try a restaurant, a ready-made table d'hôte, in seven courses, numbered so that diners can tell whether they are eating soup, appetizer, entrée or dessert. Perry leaves with the homeless expression of a stray cat, and after several treats of ptomaine, even Ethel usually prefers their kitchenette meals. So Perry has become a restive, turbulent, rebellious patron of the delicatessen.

Perry keeps a little flower under his mother's picture on the chiffonier. After all, she was his ideal of the true and womanly. Never in her busy life did she permit her husband or any of her four sons to eat food prepared or cooked out of the sacred precincts of the home kitchen. Perry told Ethel recently that he doubts if he can maintain his morale much longer on canned salmon, tuna fish, bologna sausage, frankfurters, cold ham and potato salad.

It is a difficult situation, because there seems to be no compromise. Ethel is an excellent chemist, and an exceedingly poor home-maker. If she had lived a hundred years ago, with no outlet for the forces of her nature, nothing to exist for except a domestic routine, she would probably have been one of those irritable, inefficient wives and tart mothers who make an entire family miserable, seeing their duty and doing it.

It isn't that Ethel has a fretful disposition. She hasn't. Only when she is not following her native bent she is out of key with the universe, and the sense of befuddlement makes her seem crochety. In her likes and dislikes, her caprices and incapabilities, she is like a man—because she has never been forced into the stereotyped feminine groove. As a little girl, she romped and played out-of-doors with her brothers. Games and sports, not dolls and toy dishes, filled her horizon. In school and in college beside study there were athletics and clubs and tramping, and, in the summer, camping.

Actually, because her father was well-to-do, she had had even less contact with household routine than Perry. For he often helped his mother with the dishes and swept and cleaned the house when she was tired. The processes of home-keeping seem normal and easy to him. He cannot help believing, deep down in his heart, that if Ethel loved him as a true wife should, she would find them vastly more interesting and absorbing than mere chemistry. Ethel, for her part, does not see why she must choose between her career and Perry. She wants both. Modern life has set her free, but her liberty, to him, is martyrdom.

If Perry is a victim of the new order, Maurice Elliot is one of its crucified. For what is mere physical discomfort and a lost dream compared with mental anguish and disgrace before your social class? Maurice lives in the East Sixties, near Fifth Avenue. It takes five butlers to pass a guest from the front door to the drawing room. So many men stand about in idleness the place suggests an employment bureau. When Maurice married Beatrice, she seemed exactly like any other high-heeled, flat-chested, pretty débutante, with not an idea in her head beyond clothes and gayety. Maurice, who feared strong women as the pestilence, felt complacently certain she would uphold the traditions of the Elliots. She did, for a season or so. Then came disaster in the shape of her friendship with Marcia Flint—one of those charming and dangerous leaders of her sex—a cross between the Venus de Milo and Jeanne d'Arc.

Marcia taught Beatrice all about women from cave times on. She lent her a whole library of information on the subject of her sex, its submergence and emergence. In particular, the vote being won, Marcia stressed the newer activities. She inoculated Beatrice with the belief that if women do not achieve self-support and refuse to live by the pauperizing hand of man, the struggle of the ages will be lost. Meanwhile, Maurice was absorbed in his own affairs: a golf tournament, a new yacht and a deal in foreign bonds. He saw very little of Beatrice but supposed she was carrying on her social obligations and supervising their offspring, Maurice, Jr.

One morning, contrary to custom, Beatrice came to breakfast. She didn't seem dressed quite as usual. Maurice frowned. He thought she looked like a waitress in her black serge dress, white collar and cuffs. Abruptly and jerkily she explained. She had a job. Hereafter she would earn her own living. It wasn't exactly what she wanted: Miss Ingram's finishing school having dealt so tenderly with the three R's she couldn't qualify for stenography. So she had taken a course in shampooing and facial massage and was beginning work that morning in the Countess de Gandinzi's Beauty Shoppe.

Maurice stared, trying to grasp her words. She recited them like a piece prepared for graduation. Out of respect for the three butlers, Maurice said nothing. He did not try to finish his breakfast, but sat looking at Beatrice as if she were some entirely strange and incomprehensible creature. Courtesy was still with him:

"Shall I take you to Madame de Ganinzi's in the car?"

"No, thanks, I'll use the L—the other girls do."

Maurice staggered over to his mother's, who summoned Beatrice's parents and a family council was held. Dowager Elliot laid down the law: no resistance. They should act as if they didn't know about it. If Beatrice couldn't be a martyr she would soon be weary. It was only a fad. Girls had been upset since the war—too bad peace came so soon to take away their womanly activities. Being with the Countess wasn't so bad as it might have been. Several women of good birth had gone into trade. It was more respectable than it used to be—with names of nobility on the door. Beatrice was naturally indolent. A week of work would satisfy her wild impulse.

Maurice paced up and down the library wringing his hands. He felt like a man in a delirium, called suddenly to play a great tragic part, like Othello or Macbeth.

"It will ruin me. They will laugh at the club. Down town they'll think I'm bankrupt—can't support my wife. A beauty parlor! And what will my boy say when he grows up? And the servants?"

The Dowager's predictions were wrong. Beatrice, as a hairdresser, was gloriously happy. It gave her the first personal expression of her life. At noon she chummed with the girls, eating sandwiches and coffee sent in from Dinsway's Delicatessen and Lunch. When Maurice discovered this last disgrace, he collapsed. Now he cannot pass a delicatessen without a nervous chill. His reactions are so violent that his doctors fear a neurosis and have so informed Beatrice. For some reason, she only smiles and goes on serenely.

Delicatessens, it appears, do not dominate any strict social level. They are omnipresent and omnipotent; contaminating rich and poor. Enrico Brunello, Ivan Borovitch, Isaac Blutstein and Gustaf Ollson succumbed to them from the days of nursing bottles. Because of them, even Timothy Grady has long avoided starvation. Norah Grady is a cleaner in an office building, for Tim's earnings as pick and shovel man in Micky Deneen's gang do not begin to feed their ten hungry children. Norah puts the ever-present baby in a Day Nursery, and by a local system of caretaking, each child, out of school hours, takes charge of the next younger. Wurstberger's, on the corner, does the rest.

Timothy doesn't complain, but he's discontented. In his heart he is a sort of polygamist. He would like to divide Norah into twins: so half of her could go out, cleaning and earning, while the other half stayed home, baby-rearing, and waiting for his return, with a fine large dinner of beef and cabbage, boiled potatoes, soda muffins and pie.

"Sure, it's not like the days of me old home, at all," he delights to announce glumly.

" 'Deed it's not," Norah agrees, picturing, instead of days cleaning and the corner store, a long green field showing through the windows of a rollicking old kitchen, and pans of milk sitting placidly in the pantry.

Norah has not heard of the economic independence of woman; but there never was a time she didn't experience it. Her work supports herself and her half of the Gradys, and with only the brief annual interruptions, for which she is never to blame, it always has. "It's either kids, or the old folks, it is."

In her simple philosophy, a woman's job is to lend a hand, whether it's neighbors or friends or relatives. It doesn't occur to her that the triple rôle of wife, mother and wage-earner is heavy to carry. She sees it mostly from Tim's point of view and she has unbounded sympathy for him. Sure, he'd like to find her in when he comes back from work, and he'd like to have all the Gradys, with clean hands and faces, gathered around the kitchen table for a sit-down supper. She knows, too, how he hates store-cooked things. Doesn't she herself, now? But what is there to do, things being what they are? She only prays that little Tommy won't go to the hospital again, from eating that store stuff, poison he got from a tin, the doctors said. She's troubles enough, already.

After all, however, Timothy and Norah will get along well enough; their sorrows are mainly material: Maurice can make shift, for his are social. The pinch comes at Perry's level. For the middle-class man has always been taken care of in his personal and domestic life. He has been brought up with the idea that household processes go on systematically and automatically with a mother, a sister or a wife in command of her sharply defined sphere. With his heart turned backward and his eyes unable to focus on the future, he has all the immediate discomfort of social change. It seems to him only delicatessens.

There are always a few who accept transitions without weeping and vituperation. They may have no scholastic jargon or statistics to quote, and yet be conscious that today they are somehow playing a game that most of us must play; when half the world is in the Elizabethan age and the rest in 1999 A.D.; when living is a makeshift between the patriarchal plantation and the dim coöperative future in which food, clothing and possibly infants, will come in a sealed package.

Perhaps Perry is no more the victim of circumstance than was the aboriginal hunter. He is cursed with the task of bringing into his walled apartment his share of the canned tongue and chicken wings; but he sits down with the consciousness that he did not have to kill the bird or skin the pig, while the coffee is cooked on a fire no longer dependent on the delicate art of splitting wood. It may even be that he is better off than his grandfather and has a larger share in his home. For the Lord of the Manor was lord in appearance only, being chiefly a necessary adjunct to producing and supporting a family. He was an alien beyond the masculine line of sitting-room, bedroom, and chimney-corner. A delicatessen husband has a greater companionship in marriage than that. At any rate, he is gaining a respect, even for a boiled egg, that no amount of theory could inspire.

Zora Neale Hurston
(1891–1960)

The knowledge of black folk-tales and speech rhythms that were Hurston's birthright as well as the focus of her anthropological studies permeates her fiction and gives it a warmth and rollicking humor that is reminiscent of Sojourner Truth's human rights speeches in the nineteenth century. Hurston was not a crusader in the same sense, but she was one of the earliest black writers to seek and find strength in her Afro-American heritage. Born in the all-black town of Eatonville, Florida, which was later the subject of some of her research in black American folklore, Hurston attended Howard University and Barnard College in the 1920s, and later studied anthropology with Franz Boas at Columbia University. As a member of the Harlem Renaissance during the 1920s, Hurston occupied a position analogous to that of Dorothy Parker in the Algonquin Round Table of the same period: as the resident female wit, she was admired but not always liked by her peers. To some in the Harlem Renaissance, Hurston's immersion in black folklore and folktales represented an "Uncle Tom" attitude of acquiescence to white supremacy, a suspicion enhanced by her financial dependence on a white patron. The recent rediscovery and reevaluation of Hurston's work, however, reveals that she anticipated a number of black women writers, such as Alice Walker, Paule Marshall and Toni Cade Bambara, for whom black cultural history is a source of identity and comfort. Hurston held herself apart from what she termed "the sobbing school of Negrohood" and called bitterness "the underarm odor of wishful weakness." The humor in her work represents pride and joy, and a central theme of her work is individual self-fulfillment. Janie, the heroine of Hurston's best-known novel, *Their Eyes Were Watching God* (1937), ultimately finds happiness with a man with whom she can laugh as an equal; and her autobiogra-

phy, *Dust Tracks on a Road* (1942), takes a wry, witty look
at the life of a woman who, as the title of a collection of her
short fiction reflects, could say, *I Love Myself When I Am
Laughing*. The marriage described in "Turpentine Love" is
based on good humor, and Hurston finds wonderful irony in
Becky Moore's having eleven children and no husband because "she has never stopped any of the fathers of her
children from proposing." The store-front observers in
"Pants and Cal'line" form what John Lowe calls a "communal comic chorus" that witnesses Cal'line's stalking of her
errant husband.

SOURCES   Hemenway, Robert E. *Zora Neale Hurston: A Literary Biography*.
Urbana: University of Illinois Press, 1977; Lowe, John. "Hurston, Humor, and the
Harlem Renaissance." *The Harlem Renaissance Re-examined,* ed. Victor
Kramer. New York: AMS Press, 1987, 283–313; Walker, Alice. "Zora Neal
Hurston: A Cautionary Tale and a Partisan View" and "Looking for Zora." *In
Search of Our Mothers' Gardens*. San Diego: Harcourt, Brace Jovanovitch, 1983.
83–116.

WORKS   *Dust Tracks on a Road* (1942) and *I Love Myself When I am
Laughing* (1979)

from *I Love Myself When I Am Laughing*

Turpentine Love

Jim Merchant is always in good humor—even with his wife. He says he
fell in love with her at first sight. That was some years ago. She has had all
her teeth pulled out, but they still get along splendidly.

He says the first time he called on her he found out that she was subject
to fits. This didn't cool his love, however. She had several in his presence.

One Sunday, while he was there, she had one, and her mother tried to
give her a dose of turpentine to stop it. Accidentally, she spilled it in her
eye and it cured her. She never had another fit, so they got married and
have kept each other in good humor ever since.

Becky Moore

Becky Moore has eleven children of assorted colors and sizes. She has
never been married, but that is not her fault. She has never stopped any of
the fathers of her children from proposing, so if she has no father for her
children it's not her fault. The men round about are entirely to blame.

The other mothers of the town are afraid that it is catching. They won't let their children play with hers.

Pants and Cal'line

Sister Cal'line Potts was a silent woman. Did all of her laughing down inside, but did the thing that kept the town in an uproar of laughter. It was the general opinion of the village that Cal'line would do anything she had a mind to. And she had a mind to do several things.

Mitchell Potts, her husband, had a weakness for women. No one ever believed that she was jealous. She did things to the women, surely. But most any townsman would have said that she did them because she liked the novel situation and the queer things she could bring out of it.

Once he took up with Delphine—called Mis' Pheeny by the town. She lived on the outskirts on the edge of the piney woods. The town winked and talked. People don't make secrets of such things in villages. Cal'line went about her business with her thin black lips pursed tight as ever, and her shiny black eyes unchanged.

"Dat devil of a Cal'line's got somethin' up her sleeve!" The town smiled in anticipation.

"Delphine is too big a cigar for her to smoke. She ain't crazy," said some as the weeks went on and nothing happened. Even Pheeny herself would give an extra flirt to her over-starched petticoats as she rustled into church past her of Sundays.

Mitch Potts said furthermore, that he was tired of Cal'line's foolishness. She had to stay where he put her. His African soup-bone (arm) was too strong to let a woman run over him. 'Nough was 'nough. And he did some fancy cussing, and he was the fanciest cusser in the country.

So the town waited and the longer it waited, the odds changed slowly from the wife to the husband.

One Saturday, Mitch knocked off work at two o'clock and went over to Maitland. He came back with a rectangular box under his arm and kept straight on out to the barn to put it away. He ducked around the corner of the house quickly, but even so, his wife glimpsed the package. Very much like a shoe-box. So!

He put on the kettle and took a bath. She stood in her bare feet at the ironing board and kept on ironing. He dressed. It was about five o'clock but still very light. He fiddled around outside. She kept on with her ironing. As soon as the sun got red, he sauntered out to the barn, got the parcel and walked down the road, past the store and out into the piney woods. As soon as he left the house, Cal'line slipped on her shoes without taking time to don stockings, put on one of her husband's old Stetsons, worn and floppy, slung the axe over her shoulder and followed in his wake. He was hailed cheerily as he passed the sitters on the store porch and answered smiling sheepishly and passed on. Two minutes later passed his wife, silently, unsmilingly, and set the porch to giggling and betting.

An hour passed perhaps. It was dark. Clarke had long ago lighted the swinging kerosene lamp inside.

Jessie Redmon Fauset
(1882–1961)

Jessie Fauset wrote of the characters in her third novel, *The Chinaberry Tree* (1931), that they were "colored people who speak decent English, are self-supporting and have a few ideals." Such would be an accurate description of Fauset's own background. Born in Camdem County, New Jersey, near Philadelphia, as the daughter of an African Methodist Episcopal minister, Fauset was raised with middle-class values but with the slender income of a minister's family and a constant awareness of racial prejudice. A scholarship to Cornell University, from which she graduated in 1905 as a member of Phi Beta Kappa, enabled her to begin a career in teaching, editing, and writing that featured her participation as one of the leading members of the NAACP and the Harlem Renaissance. Her association with W. E. B. DuBois began while she was still in college, and her first essays and stories were published in DuBois' *The Crisis* as early as 1912. In 1919, the same year that she received an M.A. in French from the University of Pennsylvania, she was named literary editor of *The Crisis*, a position she held until 1926 and one in which she played a major role in promoting the careers of such Harlem Renaissance writers as Jean Toomer, Countee Cullen, and Langston Hughes. From 1927 to 1944, Fauset taught high-school French in New York, meanwhile continuing her career as a writer. Between 1924 and 1933, Fauset published four novels—*There is Confusion* (1924), *Plum Bun* (1929), *The Chinaberry Tree* (1931), and *Comedy: American Style* (1933)—as well as continuing to publish essays and poetry in *The Crisis* as a contributing editor. Well-read and well-traveled (she studied in France in 1924 during one of several trips to Europe), Fauset was not typical of blacks and especially black women of her day, yet she was keenly aware of American racism and the need for blacks to have their own literary and artistic models. A sense of irony rather than outrage pervades her writing; her stance is that racial prejudice is self-evidently absurd. The particular dilemmas of mulattoes who are able to "pass" for white, and the resultant possibility of blacks being prejudiced against other blacks, are themes in *Comedy: American Style*. In her poetry, Fauset deals not only with racial issues, but with gender issues such as the sexual double standard and unfaithfulness in a manner similar to that of Dorothy Parker and Edna St. Vincent Millay, her contemporaries. "Touché" combines these concerns as the dark-haired lovers remember not only former lovers, but lovers with "blue eyes" and "gold hair."

SOURCES   Dannett, Sylvia. *Profiles of Negro Womanhood.* Vol. II: 20th Century. New York: Negro Heritage Library, 1966; Johnson, Abby Arthur. "Literary Midwife: Jessie Redmon Fauset and the Harlem Renaissance." *Phylon* (June 1978): 143–53; Sylvander, Carolyn Wedin. *Jessie Redmon Fauset: Black American Writer.* Troy, NY: Whitston Publishing Co., 1981.

WORKS   "Touché," *Caroling Dusk* (1927) and *Comedy: American Style* (1933)

from *Caroling Dusk*

Touché

Dear, when we sit in that high, placid room,
"Loving" and "doving" as all lovers do,
Laughing and leaning so close in the gloom,—

What is the change that creeps sharp over you?
Just as you raise your fine hand to my hair,
Bringing that glance of mixed wonder and rue?

"Black hair," you murmur, "so lustrous and rare,
Beautiful too, like a raven's smooth wing;
Surely no gold locks were ever more fair."

Why do you say every night that same thing?
Turning your mind to some old constant theme,
Half meditating and half murmuring?

Tell me, that girl of your young manhood's dream,
Her you loved first in that dim long ago—
Had *she* blue eyes? Did *her* hair goldly gleam?

Does *she* come back to you softly and slow,
Stepping wraith-wise from the depths of the past?
Quickened and fired by the warmth of our glow?

There I've divined it! My wit holds you fast.
Nay, no excuses; 'tis little I care.
I knew a lad in my own girlhood's past,—
Blue eyes he had and such waving gold hair!

Helen Rowland

(1875–1950)

In 1936, Ishbel Ross wrote of columnist Helen Rowland, "she
has an individual wit and an easy cynicism on men, marriage
and love. Her aphorisms are usually as brilliant as they are
bitter." Rowland was one of a number of early-twentieth-
century columnists and essayists, including Alice Duer Miller
and Florence Guy Seabury, who addressed the foibles of men
and the issue of gender inequality in popular, widely-circu-
lated periodicals. Rowland began her career at the age of
sixteen when she sold a satiric dialogue to the *Washington
Post,* and after the death of her father she left her native
Washington for New York, where she was hired to write for
the Sunday edition of the New York *World.* When her first
marriage (of three) ended, she began a weekly satiric column
in the *World,* syndicating it herself to other papers until it
came to the attention of S. S. McClure, who had established
the first U.S. newspaper syndicate. Rowland's column for
McClure—and later for the Wheeler syndicate and King
Features—had the successive titles "Widow Wordalogues,"
"The Sayings of Mrs. Solomon," "Meditations of a Married
Woman," and "Marry-go-Round," but the theme remained
constant: men are vain and faithless, women are at their
mercy, and marriage is an inherently unequal relationship.
Eight collections of Rowland's columns were published, in-
cluding *The Digressions of Polly* (1905), *The Widow* (1908),
Reflections of a Bachelor Girl (1909), *The Sayings of Mrs.
Solomon* (1913), *A Guide to Men* (1922), and *This Married
Life* (1927). In her use of the column form, Rowland is part
of a tradition that reaches back to Frances Whitcher and
"Fanny Fern" in the nineteenth century and continues today
in the work of Ellen Goodman and Erma Bombeck. Her
concerns in *This Married Life* are likewise widely shared in
women's humor. "It Must Be Thrilling to Be a Man" is

251

reminiscent of Charlotte Perkins Gilman's "If I Were a Man" in its assumption that men's clothes and bodies are more comfortable to live in than women's, and "Why Can't a Woman be 'Middle-Aged'?" takes on the perennial subject of the value our culture places on women's youthful appearance.

SOURCES   Herzberg, Max J. *The Reader's Encyclopedia of American Literature.* New York: Crowell, 1962. 980–981; Ross, Ishbel. *Ladies of the Press: The Story of Women in Journalism by an Insider.* New York: Harper and Brothers, 1936. 379–381.

WORKS   *The Digressions of Polly* (1905): *The Widow* (1908); *Reflections of a Bachelor Girl* (1909); *The Sayings of Mrs. Solomon* (1913); *A Guide to Men* (1922) and *This Married Life* (1927)

from *This Married Life*

If She Could Advertise

Wanted—A Substitute Wife—for my Husband.

Somebody to greet him with a glad, bright smile and a bark of joy when I am kept late at the office, or have a club-committee meeting.

Somebody to tell him how tired he looks, fetch his slippers, find his dressing-gown and rub eau-de-cologne on his forehead, so that I may have time to brush my hair, cream my face, and get my beauty sleep.

Somebody to laugh at his jokes and listen sympathetically while he tells of his latest troubles with the office help, when I have a headache.

Somebody to go to girl shows and cabarets with him, while I go to see a good play or stay at home and read a good novel.

Somebody to put his favorite records on the phonograph, brighten up the house and wear the frilly sort of clothes he secretly admires—backless evening gowns and freezing lace hose—while I get into a woolly dressing-gown and old soft slippers and curl up before the fire.

Somebody to wait up for him when he stays out late, listen to his "explanations" and pretend to believe them, while I get a full night's sleep.

Somebody to remind him to write to his Mother.

Somebody to get splinters out of his fingers, tell him when to take his tonic, and listen raptly when he talks about his golf.

Somebody to watch him at a dinner party and see that he doesn't eat anything that disagrees with him—while I make myself interesting to the man next to me.

Somebody to tell him how wonderful he is and coax him back into a good humor, after he and I have had a spat.

Somebody to coddle him, worry about him, amuse him, jolly him, scold him, restrain him and stimulate him.

Somebody to do all those things, which I *ought* to do, *want* to do, and never find time to do! Everything—except *love* him!

Must be gentle, kind, patient, steady, dull—and not too beautiful. Wanted—oh, *wanted*—A Substitute Wife for my Neglected Husband.

(Signed) Every Tired Business Woman.

It Must Be Thrilling to Be a Man

It must be thrilling to be a man!

It must be wonderful always to get the best food, the best service and all the waiter's attention.

It must be glorious to be able to eat a dozen clams, a portion of filet of sole, half a broiled fowl—and to go to bed and *sleep* afterward just as though nothing had happened!

And to get up next morning with an appetite for waffles and lamb chops!

It must be wonderful to feel as clean, and pure, and almost righteous as a man looks after a shave and a cold shower and a dose of bromide.

It must be delicious never to be expected to write a "duty letter" or to pick up your own clothes; never to have to think about what to have for dinner or to worry about whether the laundry has come home—just to let all life's little responsibilities slip off your shoulders like water off a mackintosh!

It must be wonderful to feel that your morals are not your own responsibility, and that it is up to some woman to "guide you to heaven."

It must be wonderful never to care whether your nose is shiny or not, or to worry about your hair coming out of curl.

It must be thrilling to know that you will always be "as young as you feel," and that you will be fascinating just as long as you have a few strands of hair left to plaster across your forehead.

It must be comforting to face forty without the slightest fear that you will be out of the "vamping" class—and to believe at fifty that a girl of nineteen loves you for yourself alone!

It must be consoling to know that, no matter how poor or plain or passé you may be, you can always find some woman willing to dine with you, flirt with you—and even to marry you!

It must be wonderful to have pretty, cuddly, little women look up at you worshipfully and ask your "advice."

It must be great to feel that when you deliver an opinion, somebody will listen to you!

It must be wonderful to be able to feel "all dressed up," just by sticking a flower in your button-hole and carrying a cane.

It must be delightful to be able to carry all your belongings in your pockets, instead of having to struggle with a hand-bag, a vanity case, a change-purse, and half a dozen other pieces of "junk."

It must be comforting to know that once you have gotten into your evening clothes, nothing is going to drop off your shoulders or rip off the waistband, and that you are not going to catch pneumonia.

It must be wonderful to know that, when you die, if you have managed to keep out of jail and the newspaper, everybody will speak of you as a "good man."

It must be wonderful to have someone believe everything you tell her!

It must be *wonderful* to be a man!

Man's Sweet Dream

To a man, the great mystery of life, is "what a woman does with her time, all day!"

In his blithe philosophy, all she need do, is to press a button—and presto! the house starts running itself, and goes right on running, while she sits around polishing her fingernails and meditating on the future of the soul.

That is why she "worries so much!" That is why she is so restless, and peevish, and introspective. If only she had something to *do!*

But you know how it is! Clothes pick themselves up off the floor and hop gaily into the laundry hamper or back onto the closet hooks.

Shoes whistle to each other, choose their partners and do a fox trot onto the shoerack.

Dishes leave the table at a signal, plunge merrily into the dishpan, and then give themselves a hot shower and a rub-down before filing into place on the shelves.

The clock whisks the dust off its hands and feet, and the piano wipes its own face.

The butcher psycho-analyzes the family and discovers its suppressed desires—and lo, the leg of lamb comes stalking up to the kitchen door, all covered with mint sauce.

Potatoes take a running high-jump into the oven, and the vinegar and paprika, and olive-oil get together and do a pas seul, when they see the salad preparing itself.

Buttons find their places like well-trained chorus girls, and socks run around until they discover the exact shade of darning wool, with which to cover their shame.

Tailors, dressmakers, milkmen and tradesmen tiptoe in and out like fairy sprites, miraculously doing their little "bit"—and then, fade away and never come back again to collect.

Washing machines never break down, fires never go out, cooks never get tired or ill or balky, grocerymen never make mistakes, telephones never interrupt, the laundry counts itself, babies never cry—water runs up hill, the moon is made of green cheese—

And *housekeeping* is one long day of rest!

What *does* a woman do with her time all day?

Why Can't a Woman be "Middle-Aged"?

Some day, I am going to be frankly and jollily middle-aged.

Some day—some halcyon day!—I am going to throw away my powder puff, vanity-case and lipstick, do my hair comfortably, and walk boldly in flat-heeled shoes and clothes to match them.

Why can't a woman be frankly middle-aged?

Why does she feel that she must struggle as though for dear life, to hang on to her slipping youth?

Why does she feel panicky at the sight of the first gray hair or the first wrinkle?

A man has no such tragic sensation.

When he first espies that cluster of snow above his ears, it may give him a slight shock of surprise, but he is not in the least appalled.

He is even a little pleased with himself—he feels that it makes him "interesting." And "distinguished looking!"

Catch *him* moving the mirror hastily back from the window!

Why does a little woman with a few smile-wrinkles around her eyes and a few extra pounds of flesh on her comfy, motherly-looking hips, feel a cold fear clutching at her heart, when she observes her equally fat and wrinkled husband looking speculatively at a flapper?

Why can't a woman sit back and enjoy growing comfortably rotund—as a man does?

Why does she feel apologetic, when she chances to find herself amongst a group of flippant, flighty young things and half-baked youths?

A man, in the same group, feels only stimulated and "pepped up," or bored and "superior," according to his mood.

He never doubts for a moment, that he could be any flapper's "ideal," just as he is!

He thanks Heaven that he is no "cake-eater!"

Why does a woman ruin her hair with dyes, torture her feet with tight, high-heeled shoes, wreck her health with banting and rolling, and shatter her peace of mind with anxiety and heart-aches, the moment she feels that middle-age is about to set its finger upon her?

A man dreads growing *old*. He dreads the day, when he will lose his teeth, and have to give up his business and his games.

That is perfectly natural.

But he accepts, even welcomes, middle-age, as the fruitful time of his life; the time when he can enjoy the fruits of his hard work—can take up golf, let out his waistband, dictate to younger men, and impress the world with his wisdom and importance and success.

Never for an instant does he doubt his personal charm, his fatal fascination—never, so long as he can look in the mirror and see a bright cravat beneath his face and a few strands of hair above it!

Why, oh why, does a woman let middle age put her out of countenance?

Woman may have the ballot, she may wear knickerbockers, she may practice law and earn money and smoke cigarettes (if she wants to)—but never, never will there be any real equality between the sexes, until women have the right to be frankly *middle-aged,* as men are!

Some day I am going to throw away my powder puff and vanity-case!

Some day, I am going to be frankly and jollily middle-aged!

(But, not yet—oh Lord! Not yet!)

Dorothy Parker
(1893–1967)

Dorothy Parker is one of the few female humorists who are
frequently included in anthologies and critical studies of
American humor, a fact that may have more to do with her
participation in the famous Algonquin Round Table during
the 1920s than with an actual critical appreciation of her
work. In fact, in the foreword to his collection *The Best of
Modern Humor* (1983), Mordecai Richler explains that he
has not included Parker's work because he finds it "brittle,
short on substance, and . . . no longer very funny." Yet it is
precisely the substance of Parker's work—its bittersweet,
serio-comic depiction of the sexual double standard and
uneasy relations between men and women—that has made it
relevant to women's experience for the past sixty years. The
story of "Mrs. Parker," as she was known to her friends, has
particular appeal to Americans: the outwardly witty, self-
confident person who is actually despairing enough to attempt suicide more than once. And if it is her legend that has
kept her work in print, readers should be grateful for it.
Some of Parker's stories, such as "The Waltz," are classic
studies of the devastating effects of female socialization, and
however amused we may be by the contrast between the
woman's private thoughts and her public statements, "The
Waltz" is ultimately a study of male brutality and female
helplessness. Like her contemporary Phyllis McGinley, Parker
was a master of the light-verse form, and she invested that
form with profound social commentary. The titles of her
volumes of verse testify to the wit but also the world-
weariness expressed in her work: e.g., *Enough Rope* (1927),
Laments for the Living (1930), *Death and Taxes* (1931).
Parker is said to have named Alexander Woollcott's apartment "Wit's End," an epithet that prefigures the title of Erma
Bombeck's first book, *At Wit's End,* which was published in

1967, the year that Parker died alone in a New York hotel room. Born Dorothy Rothschild, the author married Edwin Pond Parker in 1917 and kept his name professionally despite their divorce and her subsequent remarriage (twice) to Alan Campbell. Parker's turbulent personal life, which is reflected in her fiction and poetry, was at odds with the public image of her successful career as a writer for *Vanity Fair* and *The New Yorker,* and during the last three decades of her life she wrote very little except book reviews for *Esquire* that were similar in tone to "Mrs. Post Enlarges on Etiquette," which appeared in *The New Yorker* in 1927.

SOURCES   Grant, Thomas. "Dorothy Parker." *Dictionary of Literary Biography.* Vol 11: American Humorists 1800–1950, Part 2, 369–382; Keats, John. *You Might As Well Live: The Life and Times of Dorothy Parker.* New York: Simon and Schuster, 1970; Kinney, Arthur F. *Dorothy Parker.* Boston: Twayne, 1978.

WORK   *Enough Rope* (1927), *Sunset Gun* (1928), *Laments for the Living* (1930), *Death and Taxes* (1931), *After Such Pleasures* (1933), *Not So Deep as a Well* (collected poems) (1936), *Here Lies* (collected stories) (1939) and *The Portable Dorothy Parker* (1973)

from *Here Lies*

The Waltz

Why, thank you so much. I'd adore to.

I don't want to dance with him. I don't want to dance with anybody. And even if I did, it wouldn't be him. He'd be well down among the last ten. I've seen the way he dances; it looks like something you do on Saint Walpurgis Night. Just think, not a quarter of an hour ago, here I was sitting, feeling so sorry for the poor girl he was dancing with. And now *I'm* going to be the poor girl. Well, well. Isn't it a small world?

And a peach of a world, too. A true little corker. Its events are so fascinatingly unpredictable, are not they? Here I was, minding my own business, not doing a stitch of harm to any living soul. And then he comes into my life, all smiles and city manners, to sue me for the favor of one memorable mazurka. Why, he scarcely knows my name, let alone what it stands for. It stands for Despair, Bewilderment, Futility, Degradation, and Premeditated Murder, but little does he wot. I don't wot his name, either;

I haven't any idea what it is. Jukes, would be my guess from the look in his eyes. How do you do, Mr. Jukes? And how is that dear little brother of yours, with the two heads?

Ah, now why did he have to come around me, with his low requests? Why can't he let me lead my own life? I ask so little—just to be left alone in my quiet corner of the table, to do my evening brooding over all my sorrows. And he must come, with his bows and his scrapes and his may-I-have-this-ones. And I had to go and tell him that I'd adore to dance with him. I cannot understand why I wasn't struck right down dead. Yes, and being struck dead would look like a day in the country, compared to struggling out a dance with this boy. But what could I do? Everyone else at the table had got up to dance, except him and me. There was I, trapped. Trapped like a trap in a trap.

What can you say, when a man asks you to dance with him? I most certainly will *not* dance with you, I'll see you in hell first. Why, thank you, I'd like to awfully, but I'm having labor pains. Oh, yes, *do* let's dance together—it's so nice to meet a man who isn't a scaredy-cat about catching my beri-beri. No. There was nothing for me to do, but say I'd adore to. Well, we might as well get it over with. All right, Cannonball, let's run out on the field. You won the toss; you can lead.

Why, I think it's more of a waltz, really. Isn't it? We might just listen to the music a second. Shall we? Oh, yes, it's a waltz. Mind? Why, I'm simply thrilled. I'd love to waltz with you.

I'd love to waltz with you. I'd love to waltz with you. I'd love to have my tonsils out, I'd love to be in a midnight fire at sea. Well, it's too late now. We're getting under way. *Oh.* Oh, dear. Oh, dear, dear, dear. Oh, this is even worse than I thought it would be. I suppose that's the one dependable law of life—everything is always worse than you thought it was going to be. Oh, if I had any real grasp of what this dance would be like, I'd have held out for sitting it out. Well, it will probably amount to the same thing in the end. We'll be sitting it out on the floor in a minute, if he keeps this up.

I'm so glad I brought it to his attention that this is a waltz they're playing. Heaven knows what might have happened, if he had thought it was something fast; we'd have blown the sides right out of the building. Why does he always want to be somewhere that he isn't? Why can't we stay in one place just long enough to get acclimated? It's this constant rush, rush, rush, that's the curse of American life. That's the reason that we're all of us so—*Ow!* For God's sake, don't *kick,* you idiot; this is only second down. Oh, my shin. My poor, poor shin, that I've had ever since I was a little girl!

Oh, no, no, no. Goodness, no. It didn't hurt the least little bit. And anyway it was my fault. Really it was. Truly. Well, you're just being sweet, to say that. It really was all my fault.

I wonder what I'd better do—kill him this instant, with my naked hands, or wait and let him drop in his traces. Maybe it's best not to make a scene. I guess I'll just lie low, and watch the pace get him. He can't keep this up indefinitely—he's only flesh and blood. Die he must, and die he shall, for what he did to me. I don't want to be the over-sensitive type, but you can't tell me that kick was unpremeditated. Freud says there are no accidents. I've led no cloistered life, I've known dancing partners who have spoiled my slippers and torn my dress; but when it comes to kicking, I am Outraged Womanhood. When you kick me in the shin, *smile*.

Maybe he didn't do it maliciously. Maybe it's just his way of showing his high spirits. I suppose I ought to be glad that one of us is having such a good time. I suppose I ought to think myself lucky if he brings me back alive. Maybe it's captious to demand of a practically strange man that he leave your shins as he found them. After all, the poor boy's doing the best he can. Probably he grew up in the hill country, and never had no larnin'. I bet they had to throw him on his back to get shoes on him.

Yes, it's lovely, isn't it? It's simply lovely. It's the loveliest waltz, isn't it? Oh, I think it's lovely, too.

Why, I'm getting positively drawn to the Triple Threat here. He's my hero. He has the heart of a lion, and the sinews of a buffalo. Look at him—never a thought of the consequences, never afraid of his face, hurling himself into every scrimmage, eyes shining, cheeks ablaze. And shall it be said that I hung back? No, a thousand times no. What's it to me if I have to spend the next couple of years in a plaster cast? Come on, Butch, right through them! Who wants to live forever?

Oh. Oh, dear. Oh, he's all right, thank goodness. For a while I thought they'd have to carry him off the field. Ah, I couldn't bear to have anything happen to him. I love him. I love him better than anybody in the world. Look at the spirit he gets into a dreary, commonplace waltz; how effete the other dancers seem, beside him. He is youth and vigor and courage, he is strength and gaiety and—Ow! Get off my instep, you hulking peasant! What do you think I am, anyway—a gangplank? Ow!

No, of course it didn't hurt. Why, it didn't a bit. Honestly. And it was all my fault. You see, that little step of yours—well, it's perfectly lovely, but it's just a tiny bit tricky to follow at first. Oh, did you work it up yourself? You really did? Well, aren't you amazing! Oh, now I think I've got it. Oh, I think it's lovely. I was watching you do it when you were dancing before. It's awfully effective when you look at it.

It's awfully effective when you look at it. I bet I'm awfully effective when you look at me. My hair is hanging along my cheeks, my skirt is swaddled about me, I can feel the cold damp of my brow. I must look like something out of the "Fall of the House of Usher." This sort of thing takes a fearful toll of a woman my age. And he worked up his little step himself, he with his degenerate cunning. And it was just a tiny bit tricky at first, but now I think I've got it. Two stumbles, slip, and a twenty-yard dash; yes. I've got it. I've got several other things, too, including a split shin and a bitter heart. I hate this creature I'm chained to. I hated him the moment I saw his leering, bestial face. And here I've been locked in his noxious embrace for the thirty-five years this waltz has lasted. Is that orchestra never going to stop playing? Or must this obscene travesty of a dance go on until hell burns out?

Oh, they're going to play another encore. Oh, goody. Oh, that's lovely. Tired? I should say I'm not tired. I'd like to go on like this forever.

I should say I'm not tired. I'm dead, that's all I am. Dead, and in what a cause! And the music is never going to stop playing, and we're going on like this, Double-Time Charlie and I, throughout eternity. I suppose I won't care any more, after the first hundred thousand years. I suppose nothing will matter then, not heat nor pain nor broken heart nor cruel, aching weariness. Well. It can't come too soon for me.

I wonder why I didn't tell him I was tired. I wonder why I didn't suggest going back to the table. I could have said let's just listen to the music. Yes, and if he would, that would be the first bit of attention he has given it all evening. George Jean Nathan said that the lovely rhythms of the waltz should be listened to in stillness and not be accompanied by strange gyrations of the human body. I think that's what he said. I think it was George Jean Nathan. Anyhow, whatever he said and whoever he was and whatever he's doing now, he's better off than I am. That's safe. Anybody who isn't waltzing with this Mrs. O'Leary's cow I've got here is having a good time.

Still if we were back at the table, I'd probably have to talk to him. Look at him—what could you say to a thing like that! Did you go to the circus this year, what's your favorite kind of ice cream, how do you spell cat? I guess I'm as well off here. As well off as if I were in a cement mixer in full action.

I'm past all feeling now. The only way I can tell when he steps on me is that I can hear the splintering of bones. And all the events of my life are passing before my eyes. There was the time I was in a hurricane in the West Indies, there was the day I got my head cut open in the taxi smash, there was the night the drunken lady threw a bronze ash-tray at her own true love and got me instead, there was that summer that the sailboat kept capsizing. Ah, what an easy, peaceful time was mine, until I fell in with Swifty, here. I didn't know what trouble was, before I got drawn into this *danse macabre*. I think my mind is beginning to wander. It almost seems to me as if the orchestra were stopping. It couldn't be, of course; it could never, never be. And yet in my ears there is a silence like the sound of angel voices. . . .

Oh, they've stopped, the mean things. They're not going to play any more. Oh, darn. Oh, do you think they would? Do you really think so, if you gave them twenty dollars? Oh, that would be lovely. And look, do tell them to play this same thing. I'd simply adore to go on waltzing.

from *The Portable Dorothy Parker*

Mrs. Post Enlarges on Etiquette

Emily Post's *Etiquette* is out again, this time in a new and an enlarged edition, and so the question of what to do with my evenings has been all fixed up for me. There will be an empty chair at the deal table at Tony's, when the youngsters gather to discuss life, sex, literature, the drama, what is a gentleman, and whether or not to go on to Helen Morgan's Club when the place closes; for I shall be at home among my book. I am going in for a course of study at the knee of Mrs. Post. Maybe, some time in the misty future, I shall be Asked Out, and I shall be ready. You won't catch me being intentionally haughty to subordinates or refusing to be a pall-bearer for any reason except serious ill health. I shall live down the old days, and with the help of Mrs. Post and God (always mention a lady's name first) there will come a time when you will be perfectly safe in inviting me to your house, which should never be called a residence except in printing or engraving.

It will not be a grueling study, for the sprightliness of Mrs. Post's style makes the textbook as fascinating as it is instructive. Her characters, introduced for the sake of example, are called by no such unimaginative titles as Mrs. A., or Miss Z., or Mr. X.; they are Mrs. Worldly, Mr. Bachelor, the Gildings, Mrs. Oldname, Mrs. Neighbor, Mrs. Stranger, Mrs. Kindhart, and Mr. and Mrs. Nono Better. This gives the work all the force and the application of a morality play.

It is true that occasionally the author's invention plucks at the coverlet, and she can do no better by her brain-children than to name them Mr. Jones and Mrs. Smith. But it must be said, in fairness, that the Joneses and the Smiths are the horrible examples, the confirmed pullers of social boners. They deserve no more. They go about saying "Shake hands with Mr. Smith" or "I want to make you acquainted with Mrs. Smith" or "Will you permit me to recall myself to you?" or "Pardon *me*!" or "Permit me to assist you" or even "Pleased to meet you!" One pictures them as small people, darting about the outskirts of parties, fetching plates of salad and glasses of punch, applauding a little too enthusiastically at the end of a song, laughing a little too long at the point of an anecdote. If you could allow yourself any sympathy for such white trash, you might find something pathetic in their eagerness to please, their desperate readiness to be friendly. But one must, after all, draw that line somewhere, and Mr. Jones, no matter how expensively he is dressed, always gives the effect of being in his shirt-sleeves, while Mrs. Smith is so unmistakably the daughter of a hundred Elks. Let them be dismissed by somebody's phrase (I wish to heaven it were mine)—"the sort of people who buy their silver."

These people in Mrs. Post's book live and breathe; as Heywood Broun once said of the characters in a play, "they have souls and elbows." Take Mrs. Worldly, for instance, Mrs. Post's heroine. The woman will live in American letters. I know of no character in the literature of the last quarter-century who is such a complete pain in the neck.

See her at that moment when a younger woman seeks to introduce herself. Says the young woman: " 'Aren't you Mrs. Worldly?' Mrs. Worldly, with rather freezing politeness, says 'Yes,' and waits." And the young woman, who is evidently a glutton for punishment, neither lets her wait from then on nor replies, "Well, Mrs. Worldly, and how would you like a good sock in the nose, you old meat-axe?" Instead she flounders along with some cock-and-bull story about being a sister of Millicent

Manners, at which Mrs. Worldly says, "I want very much to hear you sing some time," which marks her peak of enthusiasm throughout the entire book.

See Mrs. Worldly, too, in her intimate moments at home. "Mrs. Worldly seemingly pays no attention, but nothing escapes her. She can walk through a room without appearing to look either to the right or left, yet if the slightest detail is amiss, an ornament out of place, or there is one dull button on a footman's livery, her house telephone is rung at once!" Or watch her on that awful night when she attends the dinner where everything goes wrong. "In removing the plates, Delia, the assistant, takes them up by piling one on top of the other, clashing them together as she does so. You can feel Mrs. Worldly looking with almost hypnotized fascination—as her attention might be drawn to a street accident against her will."

There is also the practical-joker side to Mrs. W. Thus does Mrs. Post tell us about that: "For example, Mrs. Worldly writes:

" 'Dear Mrs. Neighbor:

" 'Will you and your husband dine with us very informally on Tuesday, the tenth, etc.'

"Whereupon, the Neighbors arrive, he in a dinner coat, she in her simplest evening dress, and find a dinner of fourteen people and every detail as formal as it is possible to make it. . . . In certain houses—such as the Worldlys' for instance—formality is inevitable, no matter how informal may be her 'will you dine informally' intention."

One of Mrs. Post's minor characters, a certain young Struthers, also stands sharply out of her pages. She has caught him perfectly in that scene which she entitles "Informal Visiting Often Arranged by Telephone" (and a darn good name for it, too). We find him at the moment when he is calling up Millicent Gilding, and saying, " 'Are you going to be in this afternoon?' She says, 'Yes, but not until a quarter of six.' He says, 'Fine, I'll come then.' Or she says, 'I'm sorry, I'm playing bridge with Pauline—but I'll be in tomorrow!' He says. 'All right, I'll come tomorrow.' " Who, ah, who among us does not know a young Struthers?

As one delves deeper and deeper into *Etiquette,* disquieting thoughts come. That old Is-It-Worth-It Blues starts up again, softly, perhaps, but plainly. Those who have mastered etiquette, who are entirely, impeccably right, would seem to arrive at a point of exquisite dullness. The letters and the conversations of the correct, as quoted by Mrs. Post, seem scarcely worth the striving for. The rules for the finding of topics of conversation fall damply on the spirit. "You talk of something you have been doing or thinking about—planting a garden, planning a journey, contemplating a journey, or similar safe topics. Not at all a bad plan is to ask advice: "We want to motor through the South. Do you know about the roads?' Or, 'I'm thinking of buying a radio. Which make do you think is best?"

I may not dispute Mrs. Post. If she says that is the way you should talk, then, indubitably, that is the way you should talk. But though it be at the cost of that future social success I am counting on, there is no force great enough ever to make me say "I'm thinking of buying a radio."

It is restful, always, in a book of many rules—and *Etiquette* has six hundred and eighty-four pages of things you must and mustn't do—to find something that can never touch you, some law that will never affect your ways. . . .

And in *Etiquette*, too, I had the sweetly restful moment of chancing on a law which I need not bother to memorize, let come no matter what. It is in that section called "The Retort Courteous to One You Have Forgotten," although it took a deal of dragging to get it in under that head. "If," it runs, "after being introduced to you, Mr. Jones" (of course, it would be Mr. Jones that would do it) "calls you by a wrong name, you let it pass, at first, but if he persists you may say: 'If you please, my name is Stimson.' "

No, Mrs. Post; persistent though Mr. Smith be, I may not say, "If you please, my name is Stimson." The most a lady may do is give him the wrong telephone number.

from *Enough Rope*

Unfortunate Coincidence

By the time you swear you're his,
  Shivering and sighing,
And he vows his passion is
  Infinite, undying—
Lady, make a note of this:
  One of you is lying.

Comment

Oh, life is a glorious cycle of song,
A medley of extemporanea;
And love is a thing that can never go wrong;
And I am Marie of Roumania.

General Review of the Sex Situation

Woman wants monogamy;
Man delights in novelty.
Love is woman's moon and sun;
Man has other forms of fun.
Woman lives but in her lord;
Count to ten, and man is bored.
With this the gist and sum of it,
What earthly good can come of it?

from *Sunset Gun*

Harriet Beecher Stowe

The pure and worthy Mrs. Stowe
Is one we all are proud to know
As mother, wife, and authoress—
Thank God, I am content with less!

from *Death and Taxes*

Summary

Every love's the love before
   In a duller dress.
That's the measure of my lore—
   Here's my bitterness:
Would I knew a little more,
   Or very much less!

PART IV
1930–1960:
Behold the Happy Housewife

Cornelia Otis Skinner
(1901–1979)

Cornelia Otis Skinner was equally successful in two careers: as an actress and as a writer. The former was an interest inherited from her parents, especially her father, Otis Skinner, who was a popular actor on the stage and in silent films from the 1870s through the 1920s. Her mother, Maud, ceased her acting career when Cornelia was born but remained active in theatrical circles. Otis Skinner helped to launch his daughter's career by arranging small parts for her, and she reciprocated by writing a play for him in 1925. Soon she was writing monologues for herself that developed into one-woman shows, as well as writing humorous essays and light verse for such magazines as *The New Yorker, Harper's Bazaar,* and *Ladies' Home Journal.* Skinner's humorous writing began after her marriage in 1928 and the birth of her son; she depicts wife- and motherhood in the amusing but self-deprecating way that later became a staple of the domestic humorists such as Shirley Jackson and Jean Kerr. It was Kerr, in fact, who adapted Skinner's best-known book, *Our Hearts Were Young and Gay* (1942), for the stage. Written with Emily Kimbrough, the book recounts the comic mishaps the two experienced on a trip to Europe, and a film version was released in 1944. Skinner also wrote biography, first of her parents (*Family Circle,* 1948—the last half also serves as her autobiography to the age of twenty), and then a more formal biography of Sarah Bernhardt titled *Madame Sarah* (1967). Her humorous essays have been collected in several volumes, including *Tiny Garments* (1932), *Dithers and Jitters* (1938), and *Soap Behind the Ears* (1941), the last of which includes "The Body Beautiful." The form Skinner uses in most of her humorous essays, as in this one, is what *The New Yorker* called a "casual" and what Mary Beard and Martha Bruère, editors of the 1934 anthology *Laughing*

271

Their Way, called a "sketch": while making fun of herself for some ineptitude or flaw, the speaker simultaneously calls into question the very standard she has violated. In "The Body Beautiful," Skinner not only satirizes the lengths to which women will go for their appearance, but also implies that standards of female beauty are arbitrary and absurd.

SOURCES   *American Women Writers,* Vol. 4; Skinner, Cornelia Otis. *Family Circle.* Boston: Houghton Mifflin, 1948.

WORKS   *Tiny Garments* (1932); *Dithers and Jitters* (1938) and *Soap Behind the Ears* (1941).

from *Soap Behind the Ears*

The Body Beautiful

At least three times a year the average woman tries on dresses in a shop. She finds herself standing before one of those fitting-room mirrors with movable side-panels suggestive of a primitive triptych . . . that is, if she has sufficient imagination to turn the triple reflection of herself in a pink slip into a trio of medieval saints. Such mirrors afford one a lot of seldom beheld angles of one's self and the sudden sight of them comes in the nature of a shock. You find you're staring at yourself rather than at the clothes you're buying; at your profile which somehow isn't at all the way you'd remembered it; at that curious three-quarter view when your face appears to be the shape of a Jordan almond, and at that alarming, almost indecent exposure of the back of your neck. When, furthermore, your eye travels earthward from the nape and is suddenly arrested, not without horror, by the reflection of that portion of the anatomy of which you catch a good glimpse only on those sartorial occasions, and which since the last shopping trip appears to have taken on distressing prominence, you reach the grim conclusion that it's almost too late for clothes to matter.

A recently beheld panorama of myself in the clear, cold light of Bloomingdale's most relentless mirror filled me with such panic, I felt I must do something immediately. Recalling the ads of those numerous "slimming salons" which assure you that within a few weeks and for a price unnamed they can change you from a model for Helen Hokinson into a stand-in for

Katherine Hepburn, I decided to take my troubles and my protuberances to one of them. Ever since the days of boarding-school, when I used to send for every free sample from henna rinses to stove-polish, I have always fallen for ads. The sweetheart of J. Walter Thompson, I have a peasant-like belief in whatever miracle they profess to effect.

I made inquiries among my better-shaped acquaintances and was told that an establishment in the East Fifties was among the best. The place, though small, was impressive. The façade was what is known as "moderne." Instead of the usual show window, it had sort of port-holes in which terra-cotta dryads (they might even have been hamadryads) danced amid bottles of perfume. On the ground floor was a sales and reception room where were displayed cosmetics, evening bags and (although a blizzard was raging outside) dark glasses and suntan oil. The place, decorated in Louis something style, had such an air of luxe and "parfum" about it you felt that, instead of streamlining you, they ought to turn you out looking like a Boucher. (Why didn't I live at that time, anyway?) A marquise disguised as a saleswoman was sitting behind the sort of table at which de Sévigné must have written her letters. It now held an enormous appointment book, some atomizer bottles and a very pure white phone. She asked if there were anything she could do for me and I said, "Yes. Reduce my rear," which shocked her very much; but, being of the aristocracy, she managed to smile politely. "Have you made an appointment for a consultation with Mme. Alberta?" "Mme. Alberta?" I echoed. "I'm afraid I haven't heard about her." From the expression of the marquise I might have said I hadn't heard about the Duchess of Windsor.

"I don't think I need any consultation," I said. "I just want to reduce my . . ." Her eyebrows flickered ever so slightly and I ended lamely, "I just want to lose a few inches."

"All our clients have a consultation first with Mme. Alberta," was her reply. "She happens to be disengaged at the moment. If you'll please go upstairs I'll phone her you're coming." I climbed a mauve-carpeted stair, wondering what sort of consultation lay in store for me. Would Mme. Alberta greet me with a stethoscope or would she be discovered gazing into a crystal? A pretty woman, youngish and frighteningly smart was seated at another period table. I gathered she was Mme. Alberta for she said "How do you do?" She had a very strenuous smile and her accent was so determined to be English it broadened every "a" . . . even in the case of such words as *hand* and *ankle*. It was hard to know how to address her. "Mme. Alberta" sounded embarrassing. She didn't look much like an

Alberta and to call her plain *Madam* was unthinkable. She was one of those women who are so well-groomed they are positively "soignée" . . . In their immaculate presence you feel as if you had several runs in your stockings. She motioned me to a chair and listened to the story of my proportions as if it were a case history. She then quoted me prices and after accepting my check took out a card resembling a hospital chart. On it she wrote my name and address and some things that struck me as being singularly irrelevant in the matter of hip reduction . . . when my child was born, what sicknesses I'd ever had, the current lie about my age, and my blood-pressure which, like my Social Security number, is something I can never remember.

"Now, then, we'll see about your weight."

"I know what I weigh," I said, and added recklessly, "and I don't care. All I'm after is to reduce my . . ."

"Weight and measurements must be taken every treatment." Her tone, though polite, implied she didn't think I was quite bright. "There's the dressing room. Will you disrobe kindly?" I went to what seemed to be a daintily furnished sentry box and disrobed kindly. I felt somehow I was up for a woman's branch of the Army. A trim mulatto brought me a sheet and a pair of paper slippers that were the shape and texture of peanut bags. I tried to drape the sheet so I'd look like a Tanagra figure but it wouldn't work, so I arranged it along the more simple lines of a Navajo blanket and emerged with caution. Mme. Alberta, who was waiting, told me to "come this way" and I followed her down a corridor, not without a vague apprehension that at the finish of the trip I might find myself confronted by an anaesthetist. She led me behind a screen, whisked off my sheet in the manner of a mayor unveiling a statue and placed me on a scale, naked as Lot's wife . . . nakeder, because that lady could at least boast of a good coating of salt.

"But I tell you, I *know* what I weigh," I protested weakly and told her. She shed on me the indulgent smile a night nurse might give a psychopathic patient, took my weight which turned out to be exactly what I'd said and then told *me*. "Now for those measurements," she said. "Miss Jones, will you please come here?" Miss Jones proved to be a lovely young thing in a wisp of sky blue tunic. She was of such bodily perfection one had the suspicion that "Miss Jones" was incognito for "Miss America." We were formally introduced . . . Miss Jones in her bright blue suit, I in my bright pink skin. She handed Mme. Alberta a tape measure in exchange for which Mme. Alberta gave her a pencil and my hospital chart.

"Please mark as I call them, Miss Jones," and as if she hadn't already sufficiently humiliated me, Mme. Alberta began calling out my measurements to the world at large. She measured everything. She even measured my neck, my ankle and length of my arm. I began to wonder if a suit of acrobat fleshings were thrown in with the course.

"I hardly think you need go to all that trouble," I interposed. "It's just my . . ."

"We take all measurements," Mme. Alberta said somewhat acidly and continued to encompass me with the tape measure which was a flexible metal affair . . . very cold and with a tendency to tickle. She accompanied her work with a flow of exclamations that might be taken any way. "Well, *well*!" she'd murmur, or "I *thought* so!" and at times shook her pretty head and went "Tsk! Tsk!"

Having completed her survey, she turned me over to Miss Jones, who had me don a baggy little lemon-colored suit . . . the sort of thing that in my girlhood was known as an Annette Kellerman. It contrasted cruelly with her own trim tunic, and I felt more humble than I had in my recent nakedness. She led the way to an exercise room that contained a mat, a gramophone and far too many mirrors, ordered me onto the mat and proceeded to put me through twenty minutes of hard labor. I rolled and thumped. I stretched and kicked. I jumped and pranced. I also puffed and panted. I stood on my shoulders with my feet in the air; that is, Miss Jones hoisted my feet into the air while I rose up onto a fast-breaking neck and screamed. She never paused to allow me to catch a breath which by now was of such weakened quality it hardly seemed worth while trying to catch it. I tried to take time out . . . to divert her with harmless chatter. But Miss Jones is very strict. Now and then when total collapse seemed imminent, using the therapy of the brass band spurring on exhausted troops, she'd play a lively record on the gramophone calling out "one *and* two *and* three *and* four" as if it were a battle cry. She herself was tireless. She'd do awful things such as picking up her ankle with one hand and holding her foot above her head like a semaphore, and expected me to do likewise. I'm one of those rigid types who, since early childhood, has never been able to lean over and touch my toes—not that I've ever wanted to especially. Moreover, I not only can't raise my foot above my head, I can't even bend far enough to get my hand anywhere near my ankle. Miss Jones tells me I'm seriously hamstrung . . . a nasty expression that makes me feel they've been keeping me in the smoke-house all these years.

It's hard to feel cozy with Miss Jones. She is not only strict, she's exceptionally refined. What I call "middle" she calls *diaphragm*, what I call *stomach* with her goes whimsey and becomes *tummy*, and what I call something else she refers to, with averted eyes, as *derrière*.

The time dragged almost as heavily as my limbs. Finally Miss Jones said I was a good girl and had done enough for the day (the dear Lord knows the day had done enough for me!) and I might go have my massage. I staggered out and into the capable arms of a Miss Svenson who looked like Flagstad dressed up as a nurse. She took me into a small room, flung me onto a hard table and for forty-five minutes went to work on me as if I were material for a taffy-pulling contest. She kneaded me, she rolled me with a hot rolling pin, she did to me what she called "cupping" which is just a beauty-parlor term for good old orthodox spanking. After she'd gotten me in shape for the oven she took me into a shower-room and finished me up with that same hose treatment by which they subdue the recalcitrant inmates of penitentiaries. I was then permitted to return to my sentry-box and my clothes. Once I'd recaptured my breath I felt extraordinarily full of radiant health and rugged appetite. It was time for lunch and visions of beefsteak danced in my head. But Mme. Alberta was lying in wait for me outside. "Here is your diet," she said, handing me an ominous little slip of paper which I fully expected to be marked ℞.

"I don't really care about a diet," I stammered. "You see, it isn't my weight, it's just my . . ."

"We'd like you to try it," she said.

It was a tasty little menu with the usual well-done dab of chop-meat, a few fruit juices and some lettuce garnished by a rousing dressing made with mineral oil. I was to dine at the Colony that evening and could just imagine Eugene's expression if I were to ask him to bring me an order of green salad mixed with Nujol. However, I pocketed the darn thing and used the back of it for a shopping list.

Part of the system at Mme. Alberta's consists in doing quite a lot of extra curricula work. Employing the honor system, Miss Jones expects one to go through a daily routine of prescribed gymnastics at home. For this end (that end I've been referring to) she has tried to lure me into purchasing a mat of purple satin but with Jeffersonian simplicity I maintain that I can gyrate just as unsuccessfully on the moth-honored surface of my old college blanket. Exercise in the privacy of one's domicile is a brisk and splendid idea provided one has any amount of domicile and any modicum of privacy. Space in my apartment is by no means magnificent and the only reasonable expanse of it is in the living-room which in lieu of a door has an open archway and is exposed in every portion to the hall. Having no yellow Annette Kellerman at home I generally gird myself for my exertions in nothing more confining that a pair of old pink rayon bloomers. This means that whenever the door-bell rings I am obliged to leap for sanctuary behind the sofa and I don't always hear the bell—which makes it pretty fascinating for whoever comes to the door. Once, in all innocence and semi-nudity, I gave a private performance for the window-cleaner; since when, on the occasions of his monthly visit, if we have the misfortune to meet, we each look the other way.

A problem that confronts me more, perhaps, than most people is that much of my time is spent in travel. The rooms in the newer of what are known as the "leading" hotels are often of dimensions akin to those of a Pullman roomette. To find a sufficient number of square feet in which to spread out one's blanket and one's self becomes a problem in engineering. Often as not I have to lie with head and shoulders under the bed, one arm beneath the bureau and the other half-way across the sill of the bathroom—a pretty picture indeed for the chambermaid or house detective, should they take the notion to enter with their pass-keys. The overshadowing proximity of furniture is a constant menace. During the course of leg-flinging, rolling upside-down, bicycling, and the rest of Miss Jones' required antics, I have cracked shins on the corners of tables, dislocated digits on the rockers of chairs, stunned myself into momentary insensibility against radiators and kicked cuspidors about like medicine balls. An important feature in reducing the—well, you know—is the thump—double thump, single thump and just plain boops-a-daisy. When executed with sufficient enthusiasm, thumping can produce considerable strain on the structure of the room and there is always the fear that the plaster in the ceiling underneath will start falling and prove fatal to some distinguished traveler like Mrs. Roosevelt or Nelson Eddy.

Reducing, if one goes by the doctrines of the Mme. Alberta school, is a twenty-four-hour job. Aside from the list of more or less stereotyped exercises, one is shown any number of everyday contortions that can, supposedly, be indulged in anywhere, any time. You can, for example, improve your posture by straightening out your spine along the edge of the nearest available door even if, to the casual observer, you appear to be scratching an itching back. You can also, while standing, do those thumps against the handiest walls—say those of the elevator, thereby bringing a moment of diversion into the monotonous life of the operator. Then there are a few less inconspicuous numbers such as standing on tiptoe and stretching up the hands ("Reaching for cherries" is Miss Jones' pretty term for it.), leaning over side-ways from the waist, deep-knee bending and a movement dignified by the name of "abdominal control" that curiously resembles the beginnings of the "danse du ventre." These you are expected to burst forth with at odd hours of the day and night even at the risk of starting the grim rumor that you're coming down with St. Vitus. Then one must walk. "Walk like a goddess" is Miss Jones' advice. So I do. I walk like mad if not particularly like a goddess. Walking in New York is a simple pursuit but in strange towns it leads to any number of surprises. Setting out for the residential section, I suddenly find myself in the purlieus of Hell's Kitchen; or, aiming for a public park, discover that, with the unerring instinct of the homing pigeon, I'm back at the railroad yards. At other times I realize I'm striding enthusiastically down one of those streets of a nature that isn't even questionable. There remains nothing to do but hasten back to the hotel and walk round and round the block until the local policeman begins to grow suspicious.

However, all things come to her who weighs and I discover that I'm tipping the scales to a much lesser degree. Thanks to Miss Jones and Miss Svenson and my own shining determination, the last time Mme. Alberta encircled me with that glacial little measuring trape she found signs of considerable shrinkage and told me she was pleased with me—which made me glow with pride. I doubt if anyone viewing me from the neck down would as yet mistake me for Hedy Lamarr but I'm no longer so horrified by the reflection of myself in a triple mirror and what is more satisfying my clothes are beginning to look like the hand-me-downs of an older and fatter sister. And that is dejà quelque chose.

Betty MacDonald

Anne Elizabeth Campbell Bard
(1908–1958)

Based on the author's own experience of life on a chicken farm in a remote area of the Olympic Mountains in Washington, MacDonald's *The Egg and I* (1945) was an immediate best-seller and the basis of a successful film in 1947 starring Claudette Colbert and Fred McMurray. Intended as a satire on "back-to-the-land romancing," MacDonald's book provided not only what she called "a bad sport's account of life in the wilderness," but also a pointed, if quite humorous, attack on the "I'll-go-where-you-go-do-what-you-do-be-what-you-are-and-I'll-be-happy" philosophy inculcated in her and other young women by the culture. Through the use of understatement, overstatement, exaggeration, and irony, MacDonald punctures the illusions and unrealistic expectations that her *persona*, the young Betty, has about marriage and country life. That MacDonald had a painter's eye is evident before she mentions in the book that her character paints, for MacDonald is a keen observer of the places and people around her: the mountain scenery, the country neighbors, the activities and events of a small rural community. Moreover, there is no shying away from physicality in MacDonald's novel or any attempt to gloss over any of the brutality, crudity, or craziness that she discovers around her. As Clifton Fadiman commented in his review of *The Egg and I*, MacDonald calls a spade a spade, "and there were plenty of spades." Her subsequent books—*The Plague and I* (1948), *Anybody Can Do Anything* (1950), and *Onions in the Stew* (1955)—are similarly autobiographical and exhibit some of the same qualities of style as *The Egg and I*, but they are less successful as works of humor and ultimately less engaging.

279

SOURCES   "Betty MacDonald." *Current Biography* (1946): 362–63; Dresner, Zita Z. "Twentieth Century American Women Humorists." Diss. Univ. of Maryland, 1982; MacDonald, Betty. *Who Me?* Philadelphia: Lippincott, 1959.

WORKS   *The Egg and I* (1945); *The Plague and I* (1948); *Anybody Can Do Anything* (1950) and *Onions in the Stew* (1955)

from *The Egg and I*

People

The most important people in a community are usually the richest or the worthiest or the most useful, unless the community, like ours, happens to be scattered thinly over the most rugged mountains and the largest stand of Douglas fir on the North American Continent. Then the most important people are the closest. Your neighbors. Our neighbors were the Hicks and the Kettles.

My first brush with the Kettles came about two weeks after we moved to our ranch and before we had bought our dozen Rhode Island Red hens, when I in my innocence thought I would walk to a neighbor's and arrange to buy milk and eggs. Bob had gone to Docktown after lumber or I probably never would have made that fruitless voyage.

I remember with what care I donned a clean starched housedress and pressed my Burberry coat. How carefully I brushed my hair and fixed my face and composed little speeches of introduction. "So, you're Mrs. Kettle! Bob has told me so much about you!" or "I'm your new neighbor up on the mountain and I thought it about time to come down out of the clouds and make myself known!" (Ha, ha.)

My first disappointment was a little matter of distance. It was possible to keep my spirit of good will and neighborliness whipped to a white heat for about a mile, then it began to cool slightly and by the fourth mile the whole thing had become a damned bore and I wondered why I ever had the idea in the first place. It had rained hard the night before and the road, normally pocked with holes and pits, was dotted with little lakes and pools, which reached clear across the road and oozed into the salal along the edges. In order to traverse these it was necessary to make detours into the soaking wet brush so that by the end of the first mile my neatly pressed coat slapped wetly against my legs and my hair and shoulders were full of twigs and stickers.

The day was clear and blowy with clouds like blobs of thick white lather sailing along on the wind, which was so strong and so playful that incredibly tall, spindly, snags leaned threateningly toward me, particularly when I was trying to edge around an especially large puddle and couldn't have got out of the way if the snag had shouted *"Timbah!"* before it fell. This fear of falling snags wasn't just idle terror on my part either, because every once in a while there would be a big blundering crash to the right or left of me. As the snag was usually just about to hit the ground by the time I had it located, I finally gave up and decided that if God willed it, God willed it, and there was nothing I could do about it.

On either side of the road were dense thickets of second growth, clear green and bursting with health and vigor. Back of these thickets rose the giant virgin forests, black and remote against the sky. Occasionally a small brown rabbit flipped into the brush just ahead of me and little birds made shy rustling noises everywhere. The mountains looked down scornfully at my skip, hop and jump descent and when I saw their unfriendly faces reflected in the puddles I felt the resisting power of that wild country so strongly that I was almost afraid to look back for fear the road would have closed up behind me and there would be nothing but trees, sky and mountain and no evidence that I had ever been there.

Lost in these gloomy thoughts I trudged on until I turned a bend and suddenly came on the Kettle farm. First there was a hillside orchard, alive with chickens as wild as hawks, large dirty white nuzzling pigs and an assortment of calves, cows, horses and steers. Wild roses laced the fences and dandelions glowed along the roadside and over and above the livestock arose the airy fragrance of apple blossoms.

Below the orchard were a large square house which had apparently once been apple green; a barn barely able to peep over the manure heaped against its walls; and a varied assortment of outbuildings, evidently tossed together out of anything at hand. The pig house roof sported an arterial highway sign and the milkhouse had a roof of linoleum and a wooden Two Pants Suit sign. All of the buildings had a stickery appearance, as any boards too long had been left instead of sawed off. The farm was fenced with old wagons, parts of cars, broken farm machinery, bits and scraps of rope and wire, pieces of outbuildings, a parked automobile, old bed springs. The barnyard teemed with jalopies in various stages of disintegration.

I turned into a driveway that led along the side of the house but there arose such a terrific barking and snarling and yapping from a pack of mongrels by the back porch, that I was about to leap over the fence into the orchard when the back door flew open and someone yelled to the dogs to "stop that goddamn noise!" Mrs. Kettle, a mountainously fat woman in a very dirty housedress, waddled to the corner of the porch and called cordially, "Come in, come in, glad to see you!" but as I drew timidly abreast of the porch my nostrils were dealt such a stinging blow by the outhouse lurking doorless and unlovely directly across from it that I almost staggered. Apparently used to the outhouse, Mrs. Kettle kicked me a little path through the dog bones and chicken manure on the back porch and said, "We was wonderin' how long afore you'd git lonesome and come down to see us," then ushered me into the kitchen, which was enormous, cluttered and smelled deliciously of fresh bread and hot coffee. "I'll have a pan of rolls baked by the time the coffee's poured, so set down and make yourself comfortable." She indicated a large black leather rocker by the stove and so I sat down gratefully and immediately a long thin cat leaped into my lap, settled himself carefully and began purring like a buzz saw. As he purred I stroked him until I noticed a dark knot of fleas between his eyes from which single fleas were disentangling themselves and crawling down on to his nose and into the corners of his eyes and then unhurriedly going back into the knot again. I gently lifted him off my lap and put him down by the stove but he jumped back again and I pushed him off and he jumped back and so finally I gave up and let him stay but stopped stroking him and tried to keep track of the fleas to be sure they went back after each sortie.

The Kettles' kitchen was easily forty feet long and thirty feet wide. Along one wall were a sink and drainboards, drawers and cupboards. Along another wall was a giant range and a huge woodbox. Back of the range and woodbox were pegs to hang wet coats to dry but from which hung parts of harness, sweaters, tools, parts of cars, a freshly painted fender, hats, a hot water bottle and some dirty rags. On the floor behind the stove were shoes, boots, more car parts, tools, dogs, bicycles and a stack of newspapers. In the center of the kitchen was a table about nine feet square, covered with a blue and white oilcloth tablecloth, a Rochester lamp, a basket of sewing, the Sears, Roebuck and Montgomery Ward catalogues, a large thick white sugar bowl and cream pitcher, a butter dish with a cover on it, a jam dish with a cover on it, a spoonholder, a fruit jar filled with pencil stubs, an ink bottle and a dip pen. Spaced along other walls were bureaus, bookcases, kitchen queen, worktables and a black leather sofa. Opening from the kitchen were doors to a hall, the parlor, the pantry (an enormous room lined with shelves), and the back porch. The floor was fir and evidently freshly scrubbed, which seemed the height of useless endeavor to me in view of the chicken manure and refuse on the back porch and the muddy dooryard.

While I was getting my bearings and keeping track of the fleas, Mrs. Kettle waddled between the pantry and the table setting out thick white cups and saucers and plates. Mrs. Kettle had pretty light brown hair, only faintly streaked with gray and skinned back into a tight knot, clear blue eyes, a creamy skin which flushed exquisitely with the heat, a straight delicate nose, fine even white teeth, and a small rounded chin. From this dainty pretty head cascaded a series of busts and stomachs which made her look like a cooky jar shaped like a woman. Her whole front was dirty and spotted and she wiped her hands continually on one or the other of her stomachs. She had also a disconcerting habit of reaching up under her dress and adjusting something in the vicinity of her navel and of reaching down the front of her dress and adjusting her large breasts. These adjustments were not, I learned later, confined to either the privacy of the house or a female gathering—they were made anywhere—any time. "I itch—so I scratch—so what!" was Mrs. Kettle's motto.

But never in my life have I tasted anything to compare with the cinnamon rolls which she took out of the oven and served freshly frosted with powdered sugar. They were so tender and delicate I had to bring myself up with a jerk to keep from eating a dozen. The coffee was so strong it snarled as it lurched out of the pot and I girded up my loins for the first swallow and was amazed to find that when mixed with plenty of thick cream it was palatable. True it bore only the faintest resemblance to coffee as I made it but still it had a flavor that was good when I got my throat muscles loosened up again.

As we ate our rolls and drank our coffee Mrs. Kettle told me that she and Paw had fifteen children, the youngest of whom was then ten. Seven of these children lived at home. The other eight were married and scattered in and around the mountains. Mrs. Kettle began most of her sentences with Jeeeeesus Key-rist and had a stock disposal for everything of which she did not approve, or any nicety of life which she did not possess. "Ah she's so high and mighty with her 'lectricity," Mrs. Kettle sneered. "She don't bother me none—I just told her to take her old vacuum cleaner and stuff it." Only Mrs. Kettle described in exact detail how this feat was to be accomplished.

As Mrs. Kettle talked, telling me of her family and children, she referred frequently to someone called "Tits." Tits' baby, Tits' husband, Tits' farm, Tits' fancywork. They were important to Mrs. Kettle and I was glad therefore when a car drove up and Tits herself appeared. She was a full-breasted young woman and, even though Mrs. Kettle had already explained that the name Tits was short for sister, I found it impossible to hear the name without flinching. Tits was a Kettle daughter and she had a six-month-old son whose name I never learned as she referred to him always as "You little bugger." Tits fed this baby pickles, beer, sowbelly and cabbage and the baby ungratefully retaliated with "fits." "He had six fits yesterday," Tits told her mother as she fed the baby hot cinnamon roll dipped in coffee.

Then there were Elwin Kettle, a lank-haired mechanical genius, who never seemed to go to school, although he was only fifteen, but spent all of his time taking apart and putting together terrible old cars; and Paw Kettle whom Bob aptly described as "a lazy, lisping, sonofabith." The other Kettles were shiftless, ignorant and non-progressive but not important.

On that first visit Mrs. Kettle told me that she had been born in Estonia and had lived there on a farm until she was fourteen; then she had accompanied her mother and father and sixteen brothers and sisters to the United States and, somewhere en route to the Pacific Coast, had been unfortunate enough to encounter and marry Paw. Immediately thereafter she began having the fifteen children who were all born from ten to fourteen months apart and all delivered by Paw. Mrs. Kettle was plunging into a detailed recital of the conception and birth of each, when I hurriedly interrupted and asked about the milk and eggs. She was shocked. Sell milk? They had never even considered it. They separated all of their milk and sold the cream to the cheese factory. Nope, selling milk was out of the question. "What about eggs?" I asked. "Well," said Mrs. Kettle, "Paw just hasn't gotten around to fixing any nests in the hen house and so the chickens lay around in the orchard and when we find the eggs some are good and some ain't." I hurriedly said that that was all right, I could get the eggs in town, took my leave and went home, and there learned that Bob the efficient, Bob the intelligent, had already arranged with the Hicks for milk and eggs.

Evidently my call was the opening wedge, for the next morning, just after I had finished the breakfast dishes and Bob and I were at work on the pig house, we suffered our first encounter with Mr. Kettle. He came careening into the yard precariously balanced on the top of a flight of steps which formed the seat of his wagon and driving a team composed of a swaybacked stallion about eighteen hands high and a slight black mare little larger than a Shetland pony. Mr. Kettle drew them to a flourishing halt just as I pictured them charging through the side of the house, and wished us a cheery good morning. Then leaping from the leaning tower of steps to the ground with the air of a Roman charioteer who had just won a race, he stopped and examined his steeds' flanks, did little things to the harness, a masterpiece of ingenuity consisting of baling wire, bits of rope, heavy twine and odd lengths of strap, then straightened up and lit a small piece of cigar. Bob stood transfixed staring at the wagon and team. The small horse staggered under a pair of great brass hames while the stallion wore none; the front wheels of the wagon were easily four feet in diameter and iron, those in back delicate rubber-tired sulky wheels; the wagon itself was the body of a hayrack without the sides and garnished with a flight of steps sloping toward the rear and leading heavenward. I was more fascinated by Mr. Kettle. He had a thick thatch of stiff gray hair quite obviously cut at home with a bowl, perched on top of which he wore a black derby hat. His eyebrows grew together over his large red nose and spurted out threateningly over his deepset bright blue eyes. He had a tremendous flowing mustache generously dotted with crumbs, a neckline featuring several layers of dirty underwear and sweaters, and bib overalls tucked into the black rubber hip boots. Drawing deeply on the cigar butt Mr. Kettle said, "Nithe little plathe you got here. Putty far up in the woodth though. Latht feller to live here went crazy and they put him away." He scrutinized Bob from under his eyebrows. Bob laughed and said, "Well, how do I look?"

Mr. Kettle said, "All right tho far." He turned to me, "The old lady tellth me you wath down yethtiddy. Gueth I mutht have went to town jutht afore you come. Too bad. Too bad." He continued to smoke and we all looked at each other expectantly. Mr. Kettle broke the silence "Thingth ith putty tough thith year. [We learned the hard way that this was his stock approach to borrowing.] Yeth thir. Tough! The boys WON'T HELP MAW AND ME [his voice seemed to break bounds and rose and fell like the crescendos of a siren] and we can't do it all alone and I GOT TWO THICK COWTH AND WE wondered if you folkth would give uth a hand becauth the boyth are working in the campth in the woodth logging and I CAN'T PLOW ALONE AND THE OLD lady wondered if when you come down YOU WOULD BRING a little kerothene and a little pullet masth, ten cupth of FLOUR AND A FEW RAITHINS if you got 'em." Innocently we agreed to everything and Paw leaped to the flight of steps, clucked to the horses and catapulted out of the yard. From that day forward the flour, chicken feed, eggs, bacon, coffee, butter, cheese, sugar, salt, hay, and kerosene which the Kettles borrowed from us, placed end to end, would have reached to Kansas City—the flour, chicken feed, eggs, bacon, coffee, butter, cheese, sugar, salt, hay, and kerosene which they had already borrowed from the rest of the farmers in the mountains would have reached from Kansas City to New York and back to the coast. There was nothing anyone could do about this borrowing, though. With the nearest store seventeen miles away, you could not refuse to lend someone coffee, flour, eggs, bacon, butter, cheese, sugar, salt, hay or kerosene, because you yourself knew what it was like to run out of any or all of them. Paw Kettle banked on this knowledge and the rest of us charged it off to overhead.

The business of lending our services was something else again, and after that first initial mistake, we seldom if ever granted any of Paw's millions of requests for help—help with the plowing, the sowing, the haying, the milking, the barn cleaning, the chicken house building, the gardening, the cess pool, the outhouse moving. He asked and was refused, but he kept right on asking, for that was Paw's business—begging. He didn't care what humiliations, what insults it entailed—it was better than working.

Actually the Kettle farm was the finest, or rather could have been the finest, in that country. They had two hundred acres of rich black soil, of which about twenty, including the acre or so rooted by pigs and scratched by chickens, were under cultivation. Their orchard, which was never pruned or sprayed, bore old-fashioned crunchy dark red apples, green-gage plums, Italian prunes, russet and Bartlett pears, walnuts, filberts, chestnuts, pie cherries, Royal Anne's and Bings. Their loganberry, currant, raspberry and blackberry bushes bore with only the spasmodic cultivation given them by rooting pigs and scratching chickens; their thirty-five Holstein cows were never milked on time, rarely fed and beset by flies and vermin but they gave milk, apparently from force of habit; their Chester White sows were similarly abused but they bore huge litters which Paw sold for $5.00 each piglet as soon as they were weaned. Occasionally the Kettle animals just up and died. Such deaths were immediately attributed to a vengeful providence and never for a second did any Kettle entertain the idea that dirt or malnutrition had anything to do with it.

Of course, we didn't know all of those things that next morning when with charity in our hearts we set out to help with the plowing, which we honestly thought Paw Kettle intended to struggle with by himself unless Bob helped him. As we cautiously drove the car through the conglomeration of old cars, parts of old cars, Kettle boys under old cars and discarded furniture which studded the driveway, Paw hallooed down by the barn, so Bob let me off to walk to the house and he drove in the direction of Paw. When I got to the house I found Mrs. Kettle in the throes of cleaning the bathroom and jubilant over an apronful of tools, the top of a still and an unopened package from Sears, Roebuck which had been missing for a year or so. The bathroom was definitely an afterthought tacked on to one wall of, and accessible only through, the parlor. It was just a bathroom, containing a solitary tub and evidently used only through the warm weather. Knowing that they had a good stream, a ram and a water tower, I asked Mrs. Kettle why they didn't install an inside toilet. She was incensed. "And have every sonofabitch that has to go, traipsin' through my parlor? When we start spendin' money like drunken sailors it won't be for no lah-de-dah toilet." I slunk into the parlor and after pulling up the green-fringed blinds I did a little self-conscious dusting under the cold surveillance of rows of "Stony Eyes," Gammy's name for chromo portraits, which lined the walls and were apparently the forebears of Maw and Paw photographed post-mortem. The parlor was clean and neat. The dark red brick fireplace morbidly sported a fern where the fire should have been and from the edge of the mantel were suspended, by tacks and strings, folding red paper Christmas bells, cardboard Easter eggs and greeting cards from birthdays, Valentine's day, Christmas and Easter. At one end of the mantel stood a very bold-faced Kewpie doll clad only in an orange ostrich feather skirt and with no back; at the other end was a much-gilded figurine of the Madonna. The furniture was all slippery black leather; the floor slippery mustard and rust linoleum, and the golden oak library table in the center of the room wore a dung-colored tapestry over which were laid at angles a pocket book of Shakespeare, a mother of pearl encrusted photograph album, a stereoscope and a box of photographs which said on the lid in gold, VIEWS OF YELLOWSTONE NATIONAL PARK. From the lamp hook in the center of the ceiling hung three long curls of flypaper limp with age and heavy with petrified files. The whole atmosphere was funereal and remote and there wasn't a marred place or a scratch on anything. I was amazed considering the fifteen children and the appearance of the rest of the house. But, when I watched Maw, come out of the bathroom, firmly shut the door, go over and pull down the fringed shades clear to the bottom, test the bolt on the door that led to the front hallway and finally shut and lock the door after us as we went into the kitchen, I knew. The parlor was never used. It was the clean white handkerchief in the breastpocket of the house.

As soon as we finished the bathroom and parlor it was time to get dinner. For dinner we had boiled macaroni—not macaroni and cheese, just plain boiled macaroni without even salt—boiled potatoes, baked beans and pickles, washed down with large white cups of the inky black coffee which had been sulking on the back of the stove since breakfast.

The men gulped their food and hurried back to the plowing. Bob seemed a little grim. Maw and I lingered over the coffee, the lunch dishes and her complaints that her own sisters had been to see her just a few hours before Georgie, Bertha, Elwin, Joe, John or Charles were born and didn't even know that she was "that way." This did not surprise me a great deal as she looked as though she might be going to give birth to an elephant any moment.

About three o'clock Bob appeared and we left rather suddenly. Bob told me through clenched teeth that he had had to stop every five or ten minutes to mend the harness or to scoop Paw out of the shade of a tree, bush, fence post, even the horses, where he was resting. He was further irritated by young Elwin, a strapping hulk, who crawled out from under his car now and again to shout criticisms of the plowing.

Before this wound had time to heal the Kettle cows started crashing through our fences and eating our fruit trees and our gardens. Beset by flies and long-standing hunger they became a constant menace particularly as the Kettles were experimenting with a small scraggly garden and decided that the quick way to protect it was to mend their own barbed-wire border fences and keep their stock entirely off their property and free to plunder and pillage the entire countryside.

After the cows had broken in for about the tenth time, Bob took them home and stormed into the Kettle yard demanding some immediate action. The dignity and force of his entrance were somewhat impaired by the fact that as he came abreast of the back porch he found himself face to face with Mrs. Kettle who was comfortably seated in the doorless out-house reading the Sears, Roebuck catalogue and instead of hurriedly retiring in confusion she remained where she was but took active part in the enusing conversation.

Bob, very embarrassed, turned his back but continued to state his case. "I don't want to quarrel with my neighbors and I know you old people have a hard time keeping up your fences, but by God if your cows don't stay off our place I'll take the car and chase them so damned far into the hills they'll never come home." Maw said, "Why don't you save gas and shoot the bastards?" Paw appeared just then from the cellar where he had no doubt been resting in the shade of the canned fruit, and launched his "The boyth won't HELP ME AND THE OLD LADY and I can't do it all and we fixth the fentheth and THE BUGGERTH GET OUT ANYWAYS but if you'd come down and give uth a day or two on the fentheth maybe we could KEEP THEM IN . . ." plea, but Maw interrupted with "It's the goddamned bull, Paw, he's did this every summer. Bob, he's et every garden in the valley and he's broke out of every fence and he's got to be shut up."

Paw moved up to lean in the outhouse doorway and said, "Now, Maw, it ain't the bull, itth the flieth. Perhapth, Bob, if you could give uth a hand with the manure, thay a day or tho, we could get rid of the flieth. . . ." Bob recognized defeat when he saw it and anyway you can't be either threatening or forceful with your back to the audience, so he came home and grimly added a strand of barbed wire to our rail fences and mended the rustic gate.

The cows continued to come and, as summer progressed and the flies got worse, the cows got so they could leap four rails and a strand of barbed wire with the grace and skill of antelopes. Bob became desperate and on advice of other experienced farmers, he loaded his shotgun with rock salt. I doubted at the time that this would do any good since the bull, a wizened sallow little bookkeeper type without a vestige of the lusty manliness which is ordinarily associated with the word bull, quite evidently tried to make up for his lack of physique by telling the cows, "Say girls, if you'll follow me I'll take you to a keen restaurant up on that mountain," and no peppering of rock salt was likely to make him give up his only lure. And I was right. Bob shot and the bull roared and retreated a short distance down the road only to return within the hour to be shot again and to roar and retreat again.

By the end of the first spring Bob hated the Kettles with a deadly loathing and I couldn't blame him—they practically doubled his work and certainly impeded his progress. By the time we had weathered the first winter his attitude had softened somewhat, and by the end of the second year he accepted them like one does a birthmark. I enjoyed the Kettles. They shocked, amused, irritated and comforted me. They were never dull and they were always there.

With misfortune constantly stalking them and poverty and confusion always at hand, I was amazed at the harmony that existed among the Kettles. There was no bickering or blaming each other for things that happened—there was no need to, for the fault didn't lie with them, they figured. Taking great draughts of coffee, Mrs. Kettle told me again and again where the fault lay. "It's them crooks in Washington," she said vehemently. "All the time being bribed and buyin' theirselves big cars with our money." To Mrs. Kettle there was but one Government and that was in Washington, D.C. She had no knowledge of any county, city or state governments. "The whole damn shebang" was in Washington, and Washington to her was a place where everyone was in full evening dress twenty-four hours a day attending balls and dinners which seethed with spies, crooks, liquor, loose women, Strauss waltzes and bribes. Politics were the Kettles' out. When the manure in the barn was piled so high Paw couldn't get in to milk the cows or Tits' Mervin had given her a black eye, or there was no chicken feed or money to buy any, Mrs. Kettle would say, "Look! Just look what them crooks in Washington has did. They put them fancy new laws on time payments so Paw can't get a manure spreader. They give Mervin his Indian money so he gits drunk and hits Tits. They're payin' the farmers not to raise chicken feed and the price is so high I can't git the money to buy it. If you want to know what I think," she would take another strengthening gulp of the coffee, then glaring at Paw, Elwin, Tits and me, would conclude, "I think them politicians can take their crooked laws and their crooked bribes and stuff 'em." They would all nod wisely. The blame had been put squarely where it belonged and nobody on the Kettle farm had to go sneaking around feeling guilty.

The Hicks, our other neighbors, lived five miles down the road in the opposite direction from the Kettles. They had a neat white house, a neat white barn, a neat white chicken house, pig pen and brooder house, all surrounded by a neat white picket fence. At the side of the house was an orchard with all of the tree trunks painted white but aside from these trees there was not a shrub or tree to interfere with the stern discipline the Hicks maintained over their farm. It made me feel that one pine needle carelessly tracked in by me would create a panic. Mrs. Hicks, stiffly starched and immaculate from the moment she arose until she went to bed, looked like she had been left in the washing machine too long, and wore dippy waves low on her forehead and plenty of "rooje" scrubbed into her cheeks.

Mr. Hicks, a large ruddy dullard, walked gingerly through life, being very careful not to get dirt on anything or in any way to irritate Mrs. Hicks, whom he regarded as a cross between Mary Magdalene and the County Agent.

When we first moved to the ranch we were invited to the Hicks to dinner and to an entertainment at the schoolhouse. For dinner we had a huge standing rib roast boiled, boiled potatoes, boiled string beans, boiled corn, boiled peas and carrots, boiled turnips and spinach. Mrs. Hicks also served at the same time as the meat and vegetables, cheese, pickles, preserves, jam, jelly, homemade bread, head cheese, fried clams, cake, gingerbread, pie and tea. This was supper. Dinner had been at eleven in the morning. Mrs. Hicks, a slender creature, ate more than any ten loggers but as she took her third helping she would remark sadly, "Nothing sets good with me. Nothing. Everything I've et tonight will talk back to me tomorrow."

After Mrs. Hicks and I had washed the supper dishes we retired to the tiny living room to sit in a self-conscious circle on the golden oak chairs around the golden oak table and the Rochester lamp while Mr. Hicks fumbled fruitlessly with the radio and Mrs. Hicks firmly snipped off between her teeth any loose threads of conversation. Occasionally she would glance sharply at Mr. Hicks and I felt that one false move and she would take him by the collar and put him outside. After one silence so long that I could feel the tidies of the chair sticking to my neck and arms, Mrs. Hicks called Mr. Hicks into the kitchen and I don't know whether she twisted his ear or what but he announced that he was not going to the entertainment as one of the cows was expecting a calf. Bob elected to stay and help with the delivery and Mrs. Hicks and I set off for the Crossroads in her car. We also shared the car with Mrs. Hicks' liver and her bile, neither of which functioned properly and though she had been to countless doctors and had several "wonderful goings over" she had to take pills all of the time. She drove, as did all the natives of that country, on the wrong side of the road, very fast and with both hands off the wheel most of the time. During the course of the drive she missed by a hair two other cars, a cow, a drove of horses, a wagon and a road scraper but not a feint in the blow by blow account of the fight between her liver and her bile. Her liver was so sluggish that it had constantly to be primed in order to make it pump her bile, according to Mrs. Hicks. Just before we went into the auditorium of the schoolhouse, she took two of the priming pills and I was very disappointed not to hear liver's motor start and a cheery chug-chug-splash as it pumped Mrs. Hicks' bile into her bilge or wherever bile goes.

During the drive home Mrs. Hicks entertained me with *her* many miscarriages, *her* sisters' many miscarriages, *her* cows' many miscarriages, and *her* chickens' blowouts. The internal structure of Mrs. Hicks and all of *her* connections were evidently so weak that I was relieved when we reached home without the crankcase dropping out of *her* car. When we got in the house, Bob and Mr. Hicks were celebrating the arrival of a heifer calf with a bottle of beer. Mrs. Hicks' disapproval stuck out all over like spines, but when I lit a cigarette she turned pale with horror. "It's not that I mind so much," she told me later, "I know you're from the city but I'd hate to have you smokin' when any of my friends come in because they might think I was the same kind of woman you was."

Mrs. Hicks was good and she worked at it like a profession. Not only by going to church and helping the poor and lonely but by maintaining a careful check on the activities of the entire community. She knew who drank, who smoked and who "laid up" with whom and when and where and she "reported" on people. She told husbands of erring wives and wives of erring husbands and parents of erring children. She collected and distributed her information on her way to and from town, and apparently kept a huge espionage system going full tilt twenty-four hours a day. Having Mrs. Hicks living in the community was akin to having Sherlock Holmes living in the outhouse, and kept everyone watching his step. I was surprised when I learned that Birdie Hicks had a mother—she was so pure I thought perhaps she had come to life out of the housedress section of the Sears, Roebuck catalogue. But one warm evening that spring I left Bob with the egg records and the baby and boldly struck out for Mrs. Hicks' to stitch some curtains on her sewing machine. When I arrived, Mrs. Hicks, her mother and Cousin June were sitting on the front porch slapping at mosquitoes and discussing their miscarriages. After the introductions had been made I sat down for a while before opening my brown paper parcel and exposing the real reason for my visit. This was considered good manners, for in the country where people only call to borrow or return or exchange, and everyone is hungry for companionship, it is considered very impolite to hastily transact your business and leave. You must exchange views of crops and politics if you are a man, gossip if you are a woman, then state your business, then eat no matter what time of day it is, then exchange some more politics or gossip and at last unwillingly tear yourself away. I had sat on Birdie Hicks' front porch for perhaps two minutes when I realized that hungry as I was for companionship this visit was going to be an ordeal, for Birdie's mother, a small sharp-cornered woman with a puff of short gray hair like a gone-to-seed dandelion, tried so hard to be young that conversation with her was out of the question and her ceaseless activity was as nervewracking as watching someone blow up an old balloon. When we were introduced she said, tossing her head about on its little stem, "Bet you thought I was Birdie's sister instead of her mother. Sixty-four years young next Tuesday and everybody guesses me under forty. He, he, he! Everybody does. It's 'cause I'm so active." Whereupon she shot out of her chair and leaped four feet off the ground after a mosquito. Coming down with the astounded mosquito in her little claw, she caught herself deftly on the balls of her feet, bent her knees so that she was almost squatting, then snapped into a standing position, turned and winked at me. I'm not able to wink and nothing else seemed adequate, so I just sat. Cousin June, a plump middle-aged woman, turned to Mrs. Hicks and said, "Honest to gosh, Birdie, she's like a little kid." Mrs. Hicks said rather testily, "For heaven's sake, Ma, set down. You make me nervous." Mother finally perched on the edge of the porch railing but kept her eyes darting, head bobbing and foot tapping and I felt that she had every pore coiled ready for the next spring.

Cousin June laid down her tatting, rolled back her upper lip, exposing enormous red gums sparsely settled with nubbins of teeth, and began an interminable story of a supposedly funny incident that had taken place at the grange meeting. She laughed so much during the telling that it was difficult to understand what she said and either I missed the point or as I suspect there wasn't any because it sounded like "and . . . ha, ha, ha, ha, . . . ho, ho, ho . . . hehehehe . . . owooooooooooo! Well, anyway this fellow say to me . . . ho, ho, ho, ho, ho, hehehehe, hahahahaha, ooooooooooooooowh . . . I thought I'd die . . . heheheheh heh . . . hahahahahahah. It's about time you got here . . . hahahahahahah . . . heheheh . . . hohohoho." Mother and Birdie were wiping their eyes and urging her to go on and I felt as left out as though they had all suddenly begun to speak Portuguese. In desperation I began unwrapping my package but this also proved embarrassing as they stopped dead in the middle of a neigh, thinking I had brought Birdie a present. Mumbling apologies I slunk in to sew my seams, but apparently their disappointment was short-lived for above the whirring of the machine I could hear "heheheheheheh, hahahahahahah, this fellah says . . ." "Go on, Junie, what did he say, hahahaha?" "Well, hahahahahahah, hohohohohohoh . . ." and the thuds of Mother leaping about after mosquitoes and being young.

When I had finished my curtains Mrs. Hicks served coffee and heavenly fresh doughnuts and, out of kindness and to explain my stolid dullness, said to Mother and Cousin June, "She reads." Mother in the act of hurling herself at the stove to get the coffeepot, stopped so quickly she almost went head-first into the oven. "Well," she said, "so you're the one. Birdie's told me all about you and I'm saving my old newspapers for you." I started to say, "Oh, I can't read that well!" but Mr. Hicks came in then and Mother leaped to his shoulders pick-a-back fashion, which evidently delighted him, for his heavy face glowed and he said, "You look younger'n Birdie, Maw. Might be her daughter!" I glanced at Birdie and we felt together that it made no difference how young Mother looked, for our money, she had lived much too long.

I had meant to leave before it got dark and so didn't bring my flashlight, but the moon was high and the pale green moonlight proved adequate if I discounted stepping high over shadows and coming down with a spine jarring thump into chuckholes. At the top of the second hill a large black bear lumbered slowly across the road just in front of me. He seemed such a pleasant change from Mother and Cousin June that I forgot to be frightened.

The next morning Mrs. Kettle, clad for some mysterious reason in a woolen stocking cap and an old mackintosh, although the day was warm and bright, lumbered up to borrow some sugar. I asked if she knew Mother. She said, "Godalmighty yes. Hops around like she was itchy, yellin' 'Don't I look young—took me for Birdie's sister, didn't you?' " Mrs. Kettle's two huge breasts and two huge stomachs plopped and quivered as she imitated the twittering mother. "Always talkin' about how delicate she is. 'Too little to have more'n one kid. Miscarried eight times,' she says. Considerin' the way she jumps around it's a wonder that ain't all she dropped. Acts like a goddamned flea and looks like a goddamned fool!" For that I quickly got the sugar and tossed in a package of raisins.

When it came time to plant the field crops, the potatoes, the mangels, the rutabagas and kale, that second spring, Bob and I decided that rather than work in these plantings between my regular chores we would hire someone and get this work done all at once, and incidentally right. We inquired of the Hicks first about available odd jobbers but they were rather superior about the whole thing and insinuated, and rightly so, that were I more competent Bob wouldn't have to hire help. That Mr. Hicks never had hired anyone in all the twenty years he had had the ranch; that they really wouldn't know whom to suggest. So we tried the Kettles. They, of course, had hired labor. They often took the cream check to pay a man to gather the eggs and haul in feed, which necessitated selling the eggs to buy feed for the cows so they would produce cream to sell, to pay the man to gather the eggs. This left no money for chicken feed so they would borrow from us as much as they dared and when they didn't dare any more they would let the hired man go, lacking two weeks of his full pay, the chickens would go back to roosting on the front porch and laying in the orchard, the cows would be fed egg mash and the pigs would get the rest of the scratch. The Kettles recommended Peter Moses, a little, old, apple-cheeked man who "odd jobbed" and claimed to be the most patriotic man in the "Yewnited States of America." "Look at them god-damned mountains! Look at them goddamned trees! Look at them god-damned birds! Look at that goddamned water! Every sonofabitchin thing in this whole goddamned country is purty," he told me with tears in his eyes.

Just before he came to work for us Peter Moses had a job working on the county road. The men were blasting out some stumps so a curve could be eliminated, and it was Peter's job to stand with a red flag and stop the cars before the blast. The mail truck came along and Peter waved it through. "Go on! Goddammit, go on!" he yelled and the mailman drove on and just missed the blast which sent two rocks through his windshield and laid a slab of bark on top of his car. He got out of the truck and walked back. "Hey, Peter, did you tell me to go through?"

"Sure did," said Peter.

"Why, you damn fool," said the mailman. "A blast went off almost under the truck and the rocks broke my windshield. Why didn't you hold me back?"

"Can't do 'er," said Peter. "The Yew S. Mail must go through!"

Mrs. Kettle told us how Peter had appointed himself the official smoker-out of draft dodgers during World War I. Mrs. Kettle said naively, "There was some Germans lived up here in the mountains and they had two boys that shoulda went to war but they was hidin' in the hayloft and Peter Moses heard about it and he went up there and seen where they was and reported them to the Government men who had come out to get my boys to enlist." Peter Moses swore that the Kettle boys were so anxious to enlist they were down in the basement hiding behind the canned fruit, when the Government men came.

The Maddocks had one of the most prosperous farms in that country. Six hundred acres of peat, drained and under cultivation; a herd of eighty-six Guernsey cows; a prize bull; pigs, rabbits, chickens, bees, ducks, turkeys, lambs, fruit, berries, nuts, a brick house, new modern barns and outbuildings; their own water and light systems, and a wonderful garden had the Maddocks. They had also five sons who had graduated from the State Agricultural College and Mrs. Maddock herself was said to be a college graduate. We drove past their beautiful ranch on our way to and from Town and one day there was a sign on the mailbox "Honey for sale," I persuaded Bob to stop. We drove through the gateway and up a long gravelled drive which swept around the house and circled the barnyard. We stopped by the milkhouse and a large hearty man in clean blue-and-white-striped overalls came out, introduced himself as Mr. Maddock and invited us to go over the farm. The farm was everything we had heard. The epitome of self-sufficiency. The cows gave milk to the chickens, the chickens gave manure to the fruit trees, the fruit trees fed the bees, the bees pollenized the fruit trees, and on and on in a beautiful cycle of everything doing its share. The exact opposite of that awful cycle of the Kettles' where Peter robbed Paul to pay George who borrowed from Ed. The Maddock livestock was sleek and well cared for. The barns were like Carnation Milk advertisements—scrubbed and with the latest equipment for lighting, milking, cleaning and feeding; the bunkhouses were clean, comfortable and airy; the pigpens were cement and immaculate; the chicken houses were electric lighted, many windowed, white and clean; the duck pens, bee-hives, bull pens, calf houses, turkey runs, rabbit hutches, and the milkhouse were new, clean and modern. Then we went to the house. The house had a brick façade and that was all. The rooms were dark—the windows small and few. The kitchen was small and cramped and had a sink the size of a pullman wash basin. In one corner on a plain sawhorse was a wooden washtub. Mrs. Maddock was as dark and dreary as her house, and small wonder. She told me that she hadn't been off the ranch for twenty-seven years; that she had never even been to "Town" or Docktown Bay. When we said good-bye Mr. Maddock shook hands vigorously. "Well," he asked proudly, "what do you think of my ranch?" At last I understood Mrs. Kettle. There was but one suitable answer to give Mr. Maddock and I was too much of a lady.

Mary MacGregor had fiery red, dyed hair, a large dairy ranch and a taste for liquor. Drunker than an owl, she would climb on to her mowing machine, "Tie me on tight, Bill!" she would yell at her hired man. So Bill would tie her on with clothes lines, baling wire and straps, give her the reins and away she'd go, singing at the top of her voice, cutting her oats in semi-circles and happy as a clam. She plowed, disked, harrowed, planted, cultivated and mowed, tied to the seat of the machine and hilariously drunk. A smashing witticism of the farmers was, "You should take a run down the valley and watch Mary sowin' her wild oats."

Birdie Hicks pulled down her mouth and swelled her thin nostrils when she mentioned Mary's name. "She's a bad woman," said Mrs. Hicks, "and we never invite her to our basket socials." I asked Mrs. Kettle about her. She said, "She's kinda hard but she's real good-hearted. There ain't a man in this country but what has borrowed money from Mary and most of 'em never paid it back. The women don't like her though and all because one time her old man was layin' up with the hired girl and she caught 'em and run a pitchfork into her old man's behind so deep they had to have the doctor come out and cut it out. She said that would teach him and it did because he got lockjaw and died from where the pitchfork stuck him. Mary felt real bad but she said she'd do it again if conditions was the same."

Mary sold cream to the cheese factory. One morning she found a skunk drowned in a ten-gallon can of cream. She lifted the skunk out by the tail and with her other hand she carefully squeezed the cream from his fur. "Just between us skunks, cream is cream," she said as she threw the carcass into the barnyard. She sold the cream and vowed she'd never tell a soul but Bill the hired man told everyone, especially people he saw coming out of the cheese factory with a five-pound round of cheese.

Our first spring on the ranch we didn't have any callers because no one knew we were up there and anyway at that time we didn't have anything to borrow or rather lend nor were we experienced enough to be sought out for advice. Those are the reasons for calling—the time for calling is between four in the morning and seven in the evening and the season is springtime. Summer is too hot, too busy, fall is for harvesting, winter is too wet and rainy. Spring is the time for building, planting, plowing, reproducing and the logical time for calling and borrowing. No one told me this; I learned by bitter experience.

I remember well how the night before I had been awakened by that taut stillness which presages mountain rain. I lay there in the thick dark, at once alert and unreasonably teetering on the edge of terror. No sound, no movement anywhere. Curtains poised in the middle of a sway, half in and half out the window. Shades gone limp. A trailer of my climbing rose clutching the window sill to keep from twitching. Breezes on tiptoe. Trees reaching. Trees bent listening. Everything in the mountains playing statue. Then the signal. Tap, tap. Tap, tap, tap. Tap, tap, tap, tap, tap, tap, tap. A great, soft sigh spread through the orchard, across the burn, over the mountains, everywhere. A frog croaked, the curtains bellied, a shade rattled, an owl hooted apologetically and the rain settled down to a steady hum.

I got up the next morning to a dreary world of bone-chilling air, wet kindling, sulky stove and a huddled miserable landscape. It was Spring's way of warning us not to take her for granted.

It took me from four o'clock until seven-thirty to care for my chicks, get Stove awake and breakfast cooking. Each time I went outdoors I was soaked to the skin by the rain, which was soft, feathery and scented but as penetrating as a fire hose. After using up three sets of outside garments, in chilly desperation I put on my flannel pajamas, woolly slippers and bathrobe until after breakfast. What luxury to be shuffling around in my nightclothes getting breakfast after all those months of being in full swing by 4:15 A.M. with breakfast a very much to the point interval at five or five-thirty. When Bob came in he acted a little as if he had surprised me buttering the toast stark naked. I patiently explained the reason for my attire and was defiantly pouring the coffee when a car drove into the yard. "Dear God, not callers at 7:30 and on this of all mornings!" I prayed. But it was.

A West-side dairy rancher and his sharp-eyed wife. Mr. and Mrs. Wiggins. Mr. Wiggins wanted some advice on fattening fryers and she wanted to look me over. It was very natural on her part as she had probably heard from Birdie Hicks that I smoked and read books and was a terrible manager, but she didn't have to sit on a straight chair in the draughtiest corner of the kitchen with her skirts pulled around her as though she were waiting for her husband in the reception room of a bad house.

I implored Bob, with every known signal, not to leave me alone with this one man board of investigation, but Bob went native the minute he saw another rancher and became a big, spitting bossy *man* and I was jerked from my pleasant position of wife and equal and tossed down into that dull group known as *womenfolk*. So, of course, Mrs. Wiggins and I were left alone. I tried to sidle into the bedroom and slip on a housedress and whisk everything to rights before the baby awoke, but the puppy chose that moment to be sick and instead of throwing up in one place he became hysterical and ran around and around the kitchen belching forth at intervals and mostly in the vicinity of sharp-eyed Mrs. Wiggins. She pulled her feet up to the top rung of her chair and said, "I've never liked dogs." I could see her point all right but it didn't improve the situation any, especially as Sport, our large Chesapeake retriever, managed to squeeze past me when I opened the back door to put the mop bucket out, and bounded in to lay first one and then the other large muddy paw on Mrs. Wiggins' starched lap. She screamed as though he had amputated her at the hip, which of course waked the baby. I retrieved Sport and wedged him firmly in behind the stove, we exchanged reproachful looks, I wiped up his many many dirty tracks, sponged off Mrs. Wiggins and picked up small Anne. As I bathed the baby, Mrs. Wiggins handed me flat knife-edged statements, as though she were dealing cards, on how by seven o'clock that morning she had fed and cared for her chickens, milked five cows, strained and separated the milk, cleaned out the milkhouse, cooked the breakfast, set the bread, folded down the ironing and baked a cake. It took all of the self-control I had to keep from screaming, "SO WHAT!"

Mrs. Wiggins, no doubt, had quite a juicy morsel for the next basket social, but I learned my lesson and from that day forward I was ready for Eleanor Roosevelt at four-seven in the morning.

Phyllis McGinley
(1905–1978)

Phyllis McGinley is one of the few female humorists in
America who need not be rescued from obscurity. Though
her humorous writing, like that of most women, has seldom
been considered by scholars as part of the American humorous tradition, the scope and variety of her publications over
the forty-year period from the 1920s to the 1960s made her
work familiar to a wide audience. When she turned, early in
her career, from serious poetry to light verse (at the suggestion of Katharine S. White, an editor at *The New Yorker*),
she became one of a number of humorous writers to publish
regularly in *The New Yorker*. Marriage, children, and a
move to the suburbs near New York City caused two changes
in her work: she began writing children's books, and her
light verse increasingly focused on suburban family life rather
than the urban topics of her *New Yorker* poems. By the
1950s, women's magazines had become the major publishers
of her work, and she became strongly identified with the
"housewife" writers of that period. Although McGinley
sometimes resented this identification, and although there is
evidence in her poetry of women's frustrations that Betty
Friedan would explore in *The Feminine Mystique* in 1963,
McGinley wrote two books of essays, *The Province of the
Heart* (1959) and *Sixpence in Her Shoe* (1964), defending
woman's traditional role. McGinley's mastery of the light-
verse form is evident in her collection *Times Three: Selected
Verse from Three Decades* (1960). The tone of her verse
ranges from biting to wistful, but is always informed by an
incisive wit.

SOURCES   Wagner, Linda Welshimer. *Phyllis McGinley*. New York: Twayne,
1971; Walker, Nancy. "Phyllis McGinley." *Dictionary of Literary Biography:
American Humor,* Vol 11, Part 2: 317–23.

WORKS   *On the Contrary* (1934); *One More Manhattan* (1937); *A Pocketful of Wry* (1940); *Husbands Are Difficult; or, The Book of Oliver Ames* (1941); *Stones from a Glass House* (1946); *A Short Walk from the Station* (1951) and *Times Three: Selected Verse from Three Decades* (1960)

from *A Pocketful of Wry*

Why, Some of My Best Friends Are Women!

I learned in my credulous youth
   That women are shallow as fountains.
Women make lies out of truth
   And out of a molehill their mountains.
Women are giddy and vain,
   Cold-hearted or tiresomely tender;
Yet, nevertheless, I maintain
   I dote on the feminine gender.

For the female of the species may be deadlier than the male
But she can make herself a cup of coffee without reducing
The entire kitchen to a shambles.

Perverse though their taste in cravats
   Is deemed by their lords and their betters,
They know the importance of hats
   And they write you the news in their letters.
Their minds may be lighter than foam,
   Or altered in haste and in hurry,
But they seldom bring company home
   When you're warming up yesterday's curry.

And when lovely woman stoops to folly,
She does not invariably come in at four A.M.
Singing Sweet Adeline.

Oh, women are frail and they weep.

They are recklessly given to scions.
But, wakened unduly from sleep,
   They are milder than tigers or lions.

Women hang clothes on their pegs
   Nor groan at the toil and the trouble.
Women have rather nice legs
   And chins that are guiltless of stubble.
Women are restless, uneasy to handle,
But when they are burning both ends of the scandal,
They do not insist with a vow that is votive,
How high are their minds and how noble the motive.

As shopping companions they're heroes and saints;
They meet you in tearooms nor murmur complaints;
They listen, entranced, to a list of your vapors;
At breakfast they sometimes emerge from the papers;
A Brave Little Widow's not apt to sob-story 'em,
And they keep a cool head in a grocery emporium.
Yes, I rise to defend
   The quite possible She.
For the feminine gend-
   Er is O.K. by me.

Besides everybody admits it's a Man's World.
And just look what they've done to it!

Apology for Husbands

(In answer to a friend's observation that they're
  "more bother than they're worth")

      Although your major premise, dear,
        Is rather sharp than subtle,
      My honest argument, I fear,
        Can offer scant rebuttal.

      I grant the Husband in the Home
        Disrupts its neat machinery.

His shaving brush, his sorry comb,
  Mar tidy bathroom scenery.

When dinner's prompt upon the plate,
He labors at the office late;
Yet stay him while the stew is peppered,
He rages like a famished leopard.
He rages like an angry lion
  When urged to put a formal tie on,
But should festivities grow hearty,
He is the last to leave the party.
He lauds your neighbor's giddy bonnet
But laughs, immoderate, if you don it,
And loathes your childhood friend, and always
Bestrews his garments through the hallways.

But e'er you shun the wedded male,
  Recall his special talents
For driving firm the picture nail
  And coaxing books to balance.
Regard with unalloyed delight
  That skill, which you were scorning,
For opening windows up at night
  And closing them at morning.

Though under protest, to be sure,
He weekly moves the furniture.
He layeth rugs, he fixeth sockets,
He payeth bills from both his pockets.
For invitations you decry
He furnisheth an alibi.
He jousts with taxi-men in tourney,
He guards your luggage when you journey,
And brings you news and quotes you facts
And figures out the income tax
And slaughters spiders when you daren't
And makes a very handy parent.

What gadget's useful as a spouse?
  Considering that a minute,

Confess that every proper house
should have a husband in it.

from *Stones from a Glass House*

Occupation: Housewife

Her health is good. She owns to forty-one,
    Keeps her hair bright by vegetable rinses,
Has two well-nourished children—daughter and son—
    Just now away at school. Her house, with chintzes
Expensively curtained, animates the caller.
    And she is fond of Early American glass
Stacked in an English breakfront somewhat taller
    Than her best friend's. Last year she took a class

In modern drama at the County Center.
    Twice, on Good Friday, she's heard *Parsifal* sung.
She often says she might have been a painter
    Or maybe writer, but she married young.
She diets. And with Contract she delays
The encroaching desolation of her days.

This One's about Two Irishmen, or, Oliver Ames is a Raconteur

When meekly to Judgment I come,
    When marital virtues are passed on,
For comfort I'll cling to a crumb,
    One noble attainment stand fast on.
Though manifold duties remiss in,
    Addicted to phoning my folks,
I think that They'll have to put *this* in:

I giggled at Oliver's jokes.

> *The new ones, the old ones,*
> *The couldn't-be-sillier;*
> *The pure and the bold ones;*
> *The grimly familiar;*
> *The dialect stories*
> *In dubious brogue;*
> *Entire repertories*
> *Some months out of vogue;*
> *The puns; the inventions—*
> *Whatever their worth,*
> *At merest of mentions*
> *Convulsed me with mirth.*

My prowess with thimble and thread,
  Inadequate doubtless They'll judge it.
From kitchen encounters I fled.
  I wasn't much good with a budget.
That vain was my nature and idle,
  I'll likely be forced to admit.
But Oliver, stanch at my side'll
  Recall how I relished his wit.

> *How raptly I harked to*
> *Each lengthy relation*
> *Of what he remarked to*
> *The boys at the station.*
> *Will tell how I nodded*
> *Not once at a jest,*
> *But bravely applauded*
> *The worst with the best,*
> *No one of the crop, sir,*
> *So whiskered and hoar*
> *I ever cried, "Stop, sir,*
> *I've heard that before."*

Let wives who are clever with bills
  Or versed in the pot and the kettle,
Deride me. I scoff at their skills,
  Convinced of superior mettle.

Yes, let them go ruffle a curtain
Or trim their ineffable toques.
This marriage is solid and certain.
I chuckle at Oliver's jokes.

from *A Short Walk from the Station*

One Crowded Hour of Glorious Strife

I love my daughters with a love unfailing,
I love them healthy and I love them ailing.
I love them as sheep are loved by the shepherd,
With a fiery love like a lion or a leopard.
I love them gentle or inclined to mayhem—
But I love them warmest after eighty-thirty A.M.

Oh, the peace like heaven
    That wraps me around,
Say, at eight-thirty-seven,
    When they're schoolroom-bound,
With the last glove mated
    And the last scarf tied,
With the pigtail plaited,
    With the pincurl dried,
And the egg disparaged,
    And the porridge sneered at,
And last night's comics furtively peered at,
The coat apprehended
    On its ultimate hook,
And the cover mended
    On the history book!

How affection swells, how my heart leaps up
As I sip my coffee from a lonely cup!
For placid as the purling of woodland waters
Is a house divested of its morning daughters.

Sweeter than the song of the lark in the sky
Are my darlings' voices as they shriek good-by—

With the last shoe burnished
  And the last pen filled,
And the bus fare furnished
  And the radio stilled;
When I've signed the excuses
  And written the notes,
And poured fresh juices
  Down ritual throats,
And rummaged for umbrellas
  Lest the day grow damper,
And rescued homework from an upstairs hamper,
And stripped my wallet
  In the daily shakedown,
And tottered to my pallet
  For a nervous breakdown.

Oh, I love my daughters with a love that's reckless
As Cornelia's for the jewels in her fabled necklace.
But Cornelia, even, must have raised three cheers
At the front door closing on her school-bent dears.

Recipe for a Happy Marriage

With a Curtsy to Mr. Burns

John Anderson my jo, John,
  When we were first acquaint,
I had a fault or so, John,
  And you were less than saint.
But once we'd said a brave "I do"
  And paid the parson's fee,
I set about reforming you
  And you reforming me.

John Anderson my jo, John,
  Our years have journeyed fair;

I think, as couples go, John,
   We've made a pleasant pair.
For us, contented man and wife,
   The marriage bond endures,
Since you have changed my way of life
   And I have altered yours.

Let captious people say, John,
   There's poison in that cup.
We found a simple way, John,
   To clear each difference up.
We could not swap our virtues, John,
   So this was our design:
All your bad habits I took on,
   While you adopted mine.
Until the final lightnings strike,
   It's comfortable to know
Our faults we share and share alike,
   John Anderson my jo.

Gwendolyn Brooks

(1917–   )

Born in Topeka, Kansas, Brooks grew up in Chicago, where she began writing at an early age and had a poem published in *American Childhood* when she was thirteen. The publication of other poems in the *Chicago Defender* when she was still in her teens led to her involvement in a poetry workshop at the South Side Community Center, where she studied the modernist poets and worked on integrating in her work both the traditional forms and techniques of English poetry and the idioms and rhythms of black language and music. Her first collection of poetry, *A Street in Bronzeville* (1945), was highly praised and earned her two Guggenheim fellowships. Her second volume, *Annie Allen* (1949) was awarded the 1950 Pulitzer Prize for poetry, the first such prize given to a black American. *Maud Martha* (1955), a novel, and *The Bean Eaters* (1960) continued to explore the content of her previous work: the lives of people residing in Chicago's black ghetto. Her attendance in 1967 at the Second Black Writers' Conference at Fisk University introduced her to radical black poets of the civil rights struggle and influenced her own work. *In the Mecca* (1968), *Riot* (1969), and *Reckonings* (1975) reflect a new concern with writing for blacks about black experience, particularly about the overt and covert effects of racism. Although her work, as Barbara Christian writes, "does not sacrifice the harshness of setting to the inner realities of her characters," one experiences in it "both the lyricism, a soul-singing that is found in Zora Neale Hurston's work, and the harsh cutting edges of [Ann] Petry's *The Street*." Paule Marshall cites Brooks' *Maud Martha* as a turning point in Afro-American fiction in presenting a black woman for the first time not as stereotypical mammy or prostitute or tragic mulatto or oppressed servant, but as a unique and complex human being. In characterizing Maud

Martha and other women in her poetry, Brooks often uses both a sardonic tone and ironic contrast to point out the contradictions between the ways in which the women see themselves and the ways in which they are seen, limited, and devalued by their own families, lovers, class, race, and white American society.

SOURCES Brooks, Gwendolyn. *Report from Part One*. Detroit: Broadside, 1972; Christian, Barbara. *Black Feminist Criticism*. New York: Pergamon, 1985; Evans, Mari, ed. *Black Women Writers: A Critical Evaluation 1950–1980*. New York: Doubleday, 1984; Gilbert, Sandra M. and Susan Gubar. *The Norton Anthology of Literature by Women*. New York: Norton, 1985. 1852–1861; Juhasz, Suzanne. *Naked and Fiery Forms: Modern American Poetry by Women—A New Tradition*. New York: Octagon, 1976.

WORKS *A Street in Bronzeville* (1945); *Annie Allen* (1949); *Maud Martha* (1955); *The Bean Eaters* (1960); *In the Mecca* (1968); *Riot* (1969) and *Reckonings* (1975)

from *A Street in Bronzeville*

obituary for a living lady

My friend was decently wild
As a child.
And as a young girl
She was interested in a brooch and pink powder and a
    curl.
As a young woman though
She fell in love with a man who didn't know
That even if she wouldn't let him touch her breasts she
    was still worth his hours,
Stopped calling Sundays with flowers.
Sunday after Sunday she put on her clean, gay (though
    white) dress,
Worried the windows. There was so much silence she
    finally decided that the next time she would say
    "yes."
But the man had found by then a woman who dressed
    in red.

My friend spent a hundred weeks or so wishing she were
     dead.
But crying for yourself, when you give it all of your
     time, gets tedious after a while.
Therefore she terminated her mourning, made for her
     mouth a sad sweet smile.
And discovered the country of God. Now she will not
     dance
And she thinks not the thinnest thought of any type of
     romance
And I can't get her to take a touch of the best cream
     cologne.
However even without lipstick she is lovely and it is no
     wonder that the preacher (at present) is almost a
     synonym for her telephone
And watches the neutral kind bland eyes that moisten
     the first pew center on Sunday—I beg your pardon
     —Sabbath nights
And wonders as his stomach breaks up into fire and
     lights
How long it will be
Before he can, with reasonably slight risk of rebuke,
     put his hand on her knee.

the date

If she don't hurry up and let me out of here.
Keeps pilin' up stuff for me to do.
I ain't goin' to finish that ironin'.
She got another think comin'. Hey, you.
Whatcha mean talkin' about cleanin' silver?
It's eight o'clock now, you fool.
I'm leavin'. Got somethin' interestin' on my mind.
Don't mean night school.

Alice Childress

(1920–   )

Alice Childress' career as a playwright and fiction writer has
been dedicated to exploring and often exploding stereotypes
of blacks—especially of black women, who in Childress'
work are gutsy, funny, strong women who both defy and
deny being characterized as subservient and docile. Mildred,
the black domestic worker who narrates *Like One of the
Family,* responds directly to the racist attitudes of her white
employers, challenging both their assumptions of her inferiority and their contradictory protestations that she is
regarded as "one of the family." Childress' own background
is similar to those of women whose only employment option
has been domestic service. Born in South Carolina, the great-
granddaughter of a slave, she moved with her grandmother to
Harlem when she was five, and did not finish high school.
She became associated with the American Negro Theatre in
Harlem in 1943, first as an actress and later as a playwright.
Her one-act play *Florence* was produced by this group in
1949; the play, which depicts an encounter between a black
and a white woman in a Jim Crow train waiting room,
established direct interaction between the races as a central
theme in her work. While holding a series of jobs—including
apprentice machinist, governess, and insurance agent—Childress continued to write plays. *Trouble in Mind* won an Obie
Award as the best off-Broadway play of the 1955–56 season,
and *Wedding Band,* which deals with a love affair between a
black woman and a white man in South Carolina in 1918,
was eventually produced at the New York Shakespeare Festival in 1972. But Childress is probably best known as the
author of *A Hero Ain't Nothin' but a Sandwich,* a 1973
novel about an adolescent drug addict that was made into a
film in 1977. Childress' insistence on addressing controversial
subjects with candor and without sensationalism has caused

312

her work to be overshadowed by that of other playwrights, but her devotion to her art and her principles has won her a committed if small following. The narratives that comprise *Like One of the Family* were originally published in Paul Robeson's *Freedom* before being collected in 1956, and the book was reissued in 1986 by Beacon Press.

SOURCES Childress, Alice. "Knowing the Human Condition." *Black American Literature and Humanism.* Ed. R. Baxter Miller. Lexington: University of Kentucky Press, 1981; *Dictionary of Literary Biography,* Vol. 38, 66–79; Harris, Trudier. Introduction to *Like One of the Family . . . Conversations from a Domestic's Life.* Boston: Beacon, 1986, xi–xxxiv.

WORKS *Like One of the Family . . . Conversations from a Domestic's Life* (1956)

from *Like One of the Family . . .*
  Conversations from a Domestic's Life

The Pocketbook Game

Marge . . . day's work is an education! Well, I mean workin' in different homes you learn much more than if you was steady in one place. . . . I tell you, it really keeps your mind sharp tryin' to watch for what folks will put over on you.

What? . . . No, Marge, I do not want to help shell no beans, but I'd be more than glad to stay and have supper with you, and I'll wash the dishes after. Is that all right? . . .

Who put anything over on who? . . . Oh yes! It's like this. . . . I been working for Mrs. E . . . one day a week for several months and I notice that she has some peculiar ways. Well, there was only one thing that really bothered me and that was her pocketbook habit. . . . No, not those little novels. . . . I mean her purse—her handbag.

Marge, she's got a big old pocketbook with two long straps on it . . . and whenever I'd go there, she'd be propped up in a chair with her handbag doubled wrapped tight around her wrist, and from room to room she'd roam with that purse hugged to her bosom. . . . Yes, girl! This happens every time! No, there's *nobody* there but me and her. . . . Marge, I couldn't say nothin' to her! It's her purse, ain't it? She can hold onto it if she wants to!

I held my peace for months, tryin' to figure out how I'd make my point. . . . Well, bless Bess! *Today was the day!* . . . Please, Marge, keep shellin' the beans so we can eat! I know you're listenin', but you listen with your ears, not your hands. . . . Well, anyway, I was almost ready to go home when she steps in the room hangin' onto her bag as usual and says, "Mildred will you ask the super to come up and fix the kitchen faucet?" "Yes, Mrs. E . . . ," I says, "as soon as I leave." "Oh, no," she says, "he may be gone by then. Please go now." "All right," I says, and out the door I went, still wearin' my Hoover apron.

I just went down the hall and stood there a few minutes . . . and then I rushed back to the door and knocked on it as hard and frantic as I could. She flung open the door sayin', "What's the matter? Did you see the super?" . . . "No," I says, gaspin' hard for breath, "I was almost downstairs when I remembered . . . *I left my pocketbook!*"

With that I dashed in, grabbed my purse and then went down to get the super! Later, when I was leavin' she says real timid-like, "Mildred, I hope that you don't think I distrust you because . . ." I cut her off real quick. . . . "That's all right, Mrs. E . . . , I understand. 'Cause if I paid anybody as little as you pay me, I'd hold my pocketbook too!"

Marge, you fool . . . lookout! . . . You gonna drop the beans on the floor!

Shirley Jackson
(1919–1965)

Shirley Jackson's autobiographical sketches of the trials and tribulations of child-rearing and homemaking preceded, and possibly influenced, Jean Kerr's domestic humor. Collected in two volumes, *Life Among the Savages* (1953) and *Raising Demons* (1957), Jackson's work describes with humor the daily problems of family life. "Never has the state of domestic chaos been so perfectly illuminated," declared a *New York Times* review of *Life Among the Savages*. Other reviewers praised Jackson for her ability to reproduce faithfully her children's sayings and doings so that each child emerges as a distinct personality, and for the irony with which she depicts her own *persona* of a harried housewife faced with the conflicting activities, needs and concerns of four young children and a demanding husband, literary critic Stanley Edgar Hyman. Assuming the role of a detached and somewhat bemused observer, Jackson uses realistic detail and deadpan description to present as completely average and commonplace the unusual or bizarre aspects of her family's experience. Her humor, therefore, derives from situational irony, as well as from her posture as one vulnerable to and surprised by events within the family circle. Although she was a successful fiction writer whose works include *The Lottery* (1949), *Hangsaman* (1951), *The Bird's Nest* (1954), and her best seller *We Have Always Lived in the Castle* (1962), she presents herself in her domestic humor as inhabiting only one world, the domestic—a world which is depicted as part prison and part haven. The frustration she sometimes expresses at the myriad responsibilities of being a wife and mother exists alongside considerable anxiety about being left alone, and this conflict may have been responsible for the bouts of often paralyzing depression she suffered during the 1950s and 1960s. At the time of her death, however, she seemed to be recovering from depression and was working on what she defined as her first comic novel, *Come Along With Me*.

S O U R C E S   Breit, Harvey. "Talk with Miss Jackson." *New York Times Book Review*. 26 June 1949: 15; Cobb, Jane. Review of *Life Among the Savages*. *New York Times Book Review,* 21 June 1953: 6; Friedman, Lenemaja. *Shirley Jackson*. Boston: Twayne, 1975; Hyman, Stanley Edgar. Introduction to *The Magic of Shirley Jackson*. New York: Farrar, Straus and Giroux, 1966; Jones, Jean Campbell. Review of *Raising Demons*. *Saturday Review*. 19 January 1957: 45.

W O R K S   *Life Among the Savages* (1953) and *Raising Demons* (1957)

from *Life Among the Savages*

The Third Baby

Everyone always says the third baby is the easiest one to have, and now I know why. It's the easiest because it's the funniest, because you've been there twice, and you know. You know, for instance, how you're going to look in a maternity dress about the seventh month, and you know how to release the footbrake on a baby carriage without fumbling amateurishly, and you know how to tie your shoes before and do knee-chests after, and while you're not exactly casual, you're a little bit off-hand about the whole thing. Sentimental people keep insisting that women go on to have a third baby because they love babies, and cynical people seem to maintain that a woman with two healthy, active children around the house will do *any*-thing for ten quiet days in the hospital; my own position is somewhere between the two, but I acknowledge that it leans toward the latter.

Because it *was* my third I was spared a lot of unnecessary discomfort. No one sent us any dainty pink sweaters, for instance. We received only one pair of booties, and those were a pair of rosebud-covered white ones that someone had sent Laurie when he was born and which I had given, still in their original pink tissue paper, to a friend when *her* first child was born; she had subsequently sent them to her cousin in Texas for a second baby and the cousin sent them back East on the occasion of a mutual friend's twins; the mutual friend gave them to me, with a card saying "Love to Baby" and the pink tissue paper hardly ruffled. I set them carefully aside, because I knew someone who was having a baby in June.

I borrowed back my baby carriage from my next-door neighbor, took the crib down out of the attic, washed my way through the chest of baby shirts and woolen shawls, briefed the incumbent children far enough ahead of time, and spent a loving and painstaking month packing my suitcase. This time I knew exactly what I was taking with me to the hospital, but assembling it took time and eventually required an emergency trip to the nearest metropolis. I packed it, though, finally: a yellow nightgown trimmed with lace, a white nightgown that tied at the throat with a blue bow, two of the fanciest bed-jackets I could find—that was what I went to the city for—and then, two pounds of homemade fudge, as many mystery stories as I could cram in, and a bag of apples. Almost at the last minute I added a box of pralines, a bottle of expensive cologne, and my toothbrush. I have heard of people who take their own satin sheets to the hospital, but that has always seemed to me a waste of good suitcase space.

My doctor was very pleasant and my friends were very thoughtful; for the last two weeks before I went to the hospital almost everyone I know called me almost once a day and said "Haven't you gone *yet?*" My mother- and father-in-law settled on a weekend to visit us when, according to the best astronomical figuring, I should have had a two-week-old baby ready to show them; they arrived, were entertained with some restraint on my part, and left, eyeing me with disfavor and some suspicion. My mother sent me a telegram from California saying "Is everything all right? Shall I come? Where is baby?" My children were sullen, my husband was embarrassed.

Everything was, as I say, perfectly normal, up to and including the frightful moment when I leaped out of bed at two in the morning as though there had been a pea under the mattress; when I turned on the light my husband said sleepily, "Having baby?"

"I really don't know," I said nervously. I was looking for the clock, which I hide at night so that in the morning when the alarm rings I will have to wake up looking for it. It was hard to find without the alarm ringing.

"Shall I wake up?" my husband asked without any sign of pleased anticipation.

"I can't find the *clock*," I said.

"Clock?" my husband said. "Clock. Wake me five minutes apart."

I unlocked the suitcase, took out a mystery story, and sat down in the armchair with a blanket over me. After a few minutes, Ninki, who usually sleeps on the foot of Laurie's bed, wandered in and settled down on a corner of the blanket by my feet. She slept as peacefully as my husband did most of the night, except that now and then she raised her head to regard me with a look of silent contempt.

Because the hospital is five miles from our house I had an uneasy feeling that I ought to allow plenty of time, particularly since neither of us had ever learned to drive and consequently I had to call our local taxi to take me to the hospital. At seven-thirty I called my doctor and we chatted agreeably for a few minutes, and I said I would just give the children their breakfast and wash up the dishes and then run over to the hospital, and he said that would be just fine and he'd plan to meet me later, then; the unspoken conviction between us was that I ought to be back in the fields before sundown.

I went into the kitchen and proceeded methodically to work, humming cheerfully and stopping occasionally to grab the back of a chair and hold my breath. My husband told me later that he had found his cup and saucer (the one with "Father" written on it) in the oven, but I am inclined to believe that he was too upset to be a completely reliable informant. My own recollection is of doing everything the way I have a thousand times before—school-morning short cuts so familiar that I am hardly aware, usually, of doing them at all. The frying pan, for instance. My single immediate objective was a cup of coffee, and I decided to heat up the coffee left from the night before, rather than taking the time to make fresh; it seemed brilliantly logical to heat it in the frying pan because anyone knows that a broad shallow container will heat liquid faster than a tall narrow one like the coffeepot. I will not try to deny, however, that it *looked* funny.

By the time the children came down everything seemed to be moving along handsomely; Laurie grimly got two glasses and filled them with fruit juice for Jannie and himself. He offered me one, but I had no desire to eat, or in fact to do anything which might upset my precarious balance between two and three children, or to interrupt my morning's work for more than coffee, which I was still doggedly making in the frying pan. My husband came downstairs, sat in his usual place, said good-morning to the children, accepted the glass of fruit juice Laurie poured for him, and asked me brightly, "How do you feel?"

"Splendid," I said, making an enormous smile for all of them. "I'm doing wonderfully well."

"Good," he said. "How soon do you think we ought to leave?"

"Around noon, probably," I said. "Everything is fine, really."

My husband asked politely, "May I help you with breakfast?"

"No, indeed," I said. I stopped to catch my breath and smiled reassuringly. "I feel *so* well," I said.

"Would you be offended," he said, still very politely, "if I took this egg out of my glass?"

"Certainly not," I said. "I'm sorry; I can't think how it got there."

"It's nothing at all," my husband said. "I was just thirsty."

They were all staring at me oddly, and I kept giving them my reassuring smile; I *did* feel splendid; my months of waiting were nearly over, my careful preparations had finally been brought to a purpose, tomorrow I would be wearing my yellow nightgown. "I'm *so* pleased," I said.

I was slightly dizzy, perhaps. And there *were* pains, but they were authentic ones, not the feeble imitations I had been dreaming up the past few weeks. I patted Laurie on the head. "Well," I said, in the tone I had used perhaps five hundred times in the last months, "Well, do we want a little boy or a little boy?"

"Won't you sit down?" my husband said. He had the air of a man who expects that an explanation will somehow be given him for a series of extraordinary events in which he is unwillingly involved. "I think you ought to sit down," he added urgently.

It was about then that I realized that he was right. I ought to sit down. As a matter of fact, I ought to go to the hospital right now, immediately. I dropped my reassuring smile and the fork I had been carrying around with me.

"I'd better hurry," I said inadequately.

My husband called the taxi and brought down my suitcase. The children were going to stay with friends, and one of the things we had planned to do was drop them off on our way to the hospital; now, however, I felt vitally that I had not the time. I began to talk fast.

"You'll have to take care of the children," I told my husband. "See that . . ." I stopped. I remember thinking with incredible clarity and speed. "See that they finish their breakfast," I said. Pajamas on the line, I thought, school, cats, toothbrushes. Milkman. Overalls to be mended, laundry. "I ought to make a list," I said vaguely. "Leave a note for the milkman tomorrow night. Soap, too. We need soap."

"Yes, dear," my husband kept saying. "Yes dear yes dear."

The taxi arrived and suddenly I was saying goodbye to the children. "See you later," Laurie said casually. "Have a good time."

"Bring me a present," Jannie added.

"Don't worry about a thing," my husband said.

"Now, don't you worry," I told him. "There's nothing to worry about."

"Everything will be *fine*," he said. "Don't worry."

I waited for a good moment and then scrambled into the taxi without grace; I did not dare risk my reassuring smile on the taxi driver but I nodded to him briskly.

"I'll be with you in an hour," my husband said nervously. "And don't worry."

"Everything will be *fine*," I said. "Don't worry."

"Nothing to worry about," the taxi driver said to my husband, and we started off, my husband standing on the lawn wringing his hands and the taxi tacking insanely from side to side of the road to avoid even the slightest bump.

I sat very still in the back seat, trying not to breathe. I had one arm lovingly around my suitcase, which held my yellow nightgown, and I tried to light a cigarette without using any muscles except those in my hands and my neck and still not let go of my suitcase.

"Going to be a beautiful day," I said to the taxi driver at last. We had a twenty-minute trip ahead of us, at least—much longer, if he continued his zig-zag path. "Pretty warm for this time of year."

"Pretty warm yesterday, too," the taxi driver said.

"It *was* warm yesterday," I conceded, and stopped to catch my breath. The driver, who was obviously avoiding looking at me in the mirror, said a little bit hysterically, "Probably be warm tomorrow, too."

I waited for a minute, and then I was able to say, dubiously, "I don't know as it will stay warm *that* long. Might cool off by tomorrow."

"Well," the taxi driver said, "it was sure warm *yesterday*."

"Yesterday?" I said. "Yes, that was a warm day."

"Going to be nice today, too," the driver said. I clutched my suitcase tighter and made some small sound—more like a yelp than anything else—and the taxi veered madly off to the left and then began to pick up speed with enthusiasm.

"Very warm indeed," the driver babbled, leaning forward against the wheel. "Warmest day I ever saw for the time of year. Usually this time of year it's colder. Yesterday it was *terribly*—"

"It was not," I said. "It was freezing. I can see the tower of the hospital."

"I remember thinking how warm it was," the driver said. He turned into the hospital drive. "It was so warm I noticed it right away. 'This is a warm day,' I thought; that's how warm it was."

We pulled up with a magnificent flourish at the hospital entrance, and the driver skittered out of the front seat and came around and opened the door and took my arm.

"My wife had five," he said. "I'll take the suitcase, Miss. Five and never a minute's trouble with any of them."

He rushed me in through the door and up to the desk. "Here," he said to the desk clerk. "Pay me later," he said to me, and fled.

"Name?" the desk clerk said to me politely, her pencil poised.

"Name," I said vaguely. I remembered, and told her.

"Age?" she asked. "Sex? Occupation?"

"Writer," I said.

"Housewife," she said.

"Writer," I said.

"I'll just put down housewife," she said. "Doctor? How many children?"

"Two," I said. "Up to now."

"Normal pregnancy?" she said. "Blood test? X-ray?"

"Look—" I said.

"Husband's name?" she said. "Address? Occupation?"

"Just put down housewife," I said. "I don't remember *his* name, really."

"Legitimate?"

"What?" I said.

"Is your husband the father of this child? Do you *have* a husband?"

"Please," I said plaintively, "can I go on upstairs?"

"Well, *really*," she said, and sniffed. "You're *only* having a baby."

She waved delicately to a nurse, who took me by the same arm everybody else had been using that morning, and in the elevator this nurse was very nice. She asked me twice how I was feeling and said "maternity?" to me inquiringly as we left the elevator; I was carrying my own suitcase by then.

Two more nurses joined us upstairs; we made light conversation while I got into the hospital nightgown. The nurses had all been to some occupational party the night before and one of them had been simply a riot; she was still being a riot while I undressed, because every now and then one of the other two nurses would turn around to me and say, "Isn't she a riot, honestly?"

I made a few remarks, just to show that I too was light-hearted and not at all nervous; I commented laughingly on the hospital nightgown, and asked with amusement tinged with foreboding what the apparatus was that they were wheeling in on the tray.

My doctor arrived about half an hour later; he had obviously had three cups of coffee and a good cigar; he patted me on the shoulder and said, "How do we feel?"

"Pretty well," I said, with an uneasy giggle that ended in a squawk. "How long do you suppose it will be before—"

"We don't need to worry about *that* for a while yet," the doctor said. He laughed pleasantly, and nodded to the nurses. They all bore down on me at once. One of them smoothed my pillow, one of them held my hand, and the third one stroked my forehead and said, "After all, you're *only* having a baby."

"Call me if you want me," the doctor said to the nurses as he left, "I'll be downstairs in the coffee shop."

"*I'll* call you if I need you," I told him ominously, and one of the nurses said in a honeyed voice, "Now, look, we don't want our husband to get all worried."

I opened one eye; my husband was sitting, suddenly, beside the bed. He looked as though he were trying not to scream. "They *told* me to come in here," he said. "I was trying to find the waiting room."

"Other end of the hall," I told him grimly. I pounded on the bell and the nurse came running. "Get him out of here," I said, waving my head at my husband.

"They *told* me—" my husband began, looking miserably at the nurse.

"It's allllll right," the nurse said. She began to stroke my forehead again. "Hubby belongs right here."

"Either he goes or I go," I said.

The door slammed open and the doctor came in. "Heard you were here," he said jovially, shaking my husband's hand. "Look a little pale."

My husband smiled weakly.

"Never lost a father yet," the doctor said, and slapped him on the back. He turned to me. "How do we feel?" he said.

"Terrible," I said, and the doctor laughed again. "Just on my way downstairs," he said to my husband. "Come along?"

No one seemed actually to go or come that morning; I would open my eyes and they were there, open my eyes again and they were gone. This time, when I opened my eyes, a pleasant-faced nurse was standing beside me; she was swabbing my arm with a piece of cotton. Although I am ordinarily timid about hypodermics I welcomed this one with what was almost a genuine echo of my old reassuring smile. "Well, well," I said to the nurse. "Sure glad to see *you*."

"Sissy," she said distinctly, and jabbed me in the arm.

"How soon will this wear off?" I asked her with deep suspicion; I am always afraid with nurses that they feel that the psychological effect of a hypodermic is enough, and that I am actually being innoculated with some useless, although probably harmless, concoction.

"You won't even notice," she said enigmatically, and left.

The hypodermic hit me suddenly, and I began to giggle about five minutes after she left. I was alone in the room, lying there giggling to myself, when I opened my eyes and there was a woman standing beside the bed. She was human, not a nurse; she was wearing a baggy blue bathrobe. "I'm across the hall," she said. "I been hearing you."

"I was laughing," I said, with vast dignity.

"I heard you," she said. "Tomorrow it might be me, maybe."

"You here for a baby?"

"Someday," she said gloomily. "I was here two weeks ago, I was having pains. I come in the morning and that night they said to me, 'Go home, wait a while longer.' So I went home, and I come again three days later, I was having pains. And they said to me, 'Go home, wait a while longer.' And so yesterday I come again, I was having pains. So far they let me stay."

"That's too bad," I said.

"I got my mother there," she said. "She takes care of everything and sees the meals made, but she's beginning to think I got her there with false pretenses."

"That's too bad," I said. I began to pound the wall with my fists.

"Stop that," she said. "Somebody'll hear you. This is my third. The first two—nothing."

"This is *my* third," I said. "I don't care who hears me."

"My kids," she said. "Every time I come home they say to me, 'Where's the baby?' My mother, too. My husband, he keeps driving me over and driving me back."

"They kept telling me the third was the easiest," I said. I began to giggle again.

"There you go," she said. "Laughing your head off. I wish *I* had something to laugh at."

She waved her hand at me and turned and went mournfully through the door. I opened my same weary eye and my husband was sitting comfortably in his chair. "I said," he said saying loudly, "I said, 'Do you mind if I read?' " He had the New York Times on his knee.

"Look," I said, "do I have anything to read? Here I am, with nothing to do and no one to talk to and you sit there and read the New York Times right in front of me and here I am, with nothing—"

"How do we feel?" the doctor asked. He was suddenly much taller than before, and the walls of the room were rocking distinctly.

"Doctor," I said, and I believe that my voice was a little louder than I intended it should be, "you better give me—"

He patted me on the hand and it was my husband instead of the doctor. "Stop yelling," he said.

"I'm *not* yelling," I said. "I don't like this any more. I've changed my mind, I don't want any baby, I want to go home and forget the whole thing."

"I know *just* how you feel," he said.

My only answer was a word which certainly I knew that I *knew*, although I had never honestly expected to hear it spoken in my own ladylike voice.

"Stop yelling," my husband said urgently. "*Please* stop saying that."

I had the idea that I was perfectly conscious, and I looked at him with dignity. "Who is doing this?" I asked. "You or me?"

"It's all right," the doctor said. "We're on our way." The walls were moving along on either side of me and the woman in the blue bathrobe was waving from a doorway.

"She loved me for the dangers I had passed," I said to the doctor, "and I loved her that she did pity them."

"It's all right, I tell you," the doctor said. "Hold your breath."

"Did he finish his New York Times?"

"Hours ago," the doctor said.

"What's he reading now?" I asked.

"The Tribune," the doctor said. "Hold your breath."

It was so unbelievably bright that I closed my eyes. "Such a lovely time," I said to the doctor. "Thank you so much for asking me, I can't tell you how I've enjoyed it. Next time you must come to our—"

"It's a girl," the doctor said.

"Sarah," I said politely, as though I were introducing them. I still thought I was perfectly conscious, and then I was. My husband was sitting beside the bed, smiling cheerfully.

"What happened to *you?*" I asked him. "No Wall Street Journal?"

"It's a girl," he said.

"I know," I said. "I was there."

I was in a pleasant, clean room. There was no doubt that it was all over; I could see my feet under the bedspread.

"It's a girl," I said to my husband.

The door opened and the doctor came in. "Well," he said. "How do we feel?"

"Fine," I said. "It's a girl."

"I know," he said.

The door was still open and a face peered around it. My husband, the doctor, and I, all turned happily to look. It was the woman in the blue bathrobe.

"Had it yet?" I asked her.

"No," she said. "You?"

"Yep," I said. "You going home again?"

"Listen," she said. "I been thinking. Home, the kids all yelling and my mother looking sad like she's disappointed in me. Like I did something. My husband, every time he sees me jump he reaches for the car keys. My sister, she calls me every day and if I answer the phone she hangs up. Here, I get three meals a day I don't cook, I know all the nurses, and I meet a lot of people going in and out. I figure I'd be a *fool* to go home. What was it, girl or boy?"

"Girl," I said.

"Girl," she said. "They say the third's the easiest."

Margaret Halsey
(1910–   )

Margaret Halsey has said that in her writing she is "a humorist and a moral positivist." She believes in the power of humor to engage people in moral issues, and has acted upon the belief in a series of books that confront racism, McCarthyism, cultural conformity, and political immorality—all with the common-sense wisdom and ironic stance of the traditional American *eiron*, or wise innocent. Halsey compares her work to that of Mark Twain, and her first book, *With Malice Toward Some* (1938) was a bestseller about traveling in Europe that has affinities with Twain's *Innocents Abroad*. With the beginning of World War II, Halsey turned her attention to a several-pronged critique of American culture that has been the focus of her career ever since. As a volunteer at the Stage Door Canteen in New York, she observed the racist attitudes to which black and Jewish servicemen were subjected by those who were supposed to provide them with a respite from training and battle, and she responded with two books: *Some of My Best Friends are Soldiers* (1944) and *Color Blind* (1946). One section of the latter, "Memo to Junior Hostesses," was widely reprinted in books on American social problems in the late 1940s, and exemplifies Halsey's use of common-sense humor—reminiscent of Marietta Holley's approach to women's rights in the nineteenth century—to address socio-political issues. "Intelligence," she says for example, "has absolutely nothing to do with the amount of pigment in the skin. If it had, you would all be much stupider when you are sunburned." In 1963, Halsey attacked the ethics of American politicians in *The Pseudo-Ethic*, using the same wry, common sense approach in order to, among other things, predict the downfall of the Nixon administration. In *This Demi-Paradise: A Westchester Diary* (1960), Halsey joined the ranks of the domestic humorists such as Phyllis McGinley and Jean Kerr who wrote about life in the suburbs following World War II, but even here her political concerns form an important thematic thread as McCarthyism extends its influence to the local American Legion post, which refuses to allow a prominent woman with supposed Communist affiliations to speak in town. Halsey's autobiography, *No Laughing Matter: The Autobiography of a WASP* (1977), is a candid, revealing portrait of a woman who was divorced twice, suffered from agoraphobia long before it was well-understood, and came to terms painfully with her rejection of a repressive WASP upbringing and its "Martin Luther-Cotton Mather syndrome" of authority and superiority.

SOURCES   Bevington, Helen. "An Education in Tolerance." *New York Times* 13 November 1977, 7:72; *Contemporary Authors*, Vols. 81–84; Halsey, Margaret. *No Laughing Matter: The Autobiography of a WASP*. Philadelphia: Lippincott, 1977.

WORKS   *With Malice Toward Some* (1938); *Some of My Best Friends are Soldiers* (1944) and *This Demi-Paradise: A Westchester Diary* (1960)

from *This Demi-Paradise: A Westchester Diary*

February 4th: I do not know whether it is cultural conditioning or a basic glandular difference, but a man driving a car fast over old and ill-repaired macadam sits there with flashing eyes and distended nostrils—thinking in terms of Douglas Fairbanks, Sr., and saying exultantly to himself, "I'm holding her on the road!" A woman, on the other hand, driving at the same pace over the same road, merely thinks dismally, "Oh, gosh, it's bumpy!"

How it may be with other married couples, I do not know, but between Harry and me there is a constant and none too delicately expressed rivalry as to who is the better driver. When one of us backs the car into a parking space, and with a single expert twirl places the rear wheels exactly where they have to be, the congratulations of the other have just that note of excess which conveys incredulity and unflattering surprise.

It is Harry's contention when we go on long trips that my mind, while driving, is always on the scenery, on Cézanne, on Mont Saint-Victoire and on cubes in nature, and never on the road. It is my counter-contention that when Harry drives in traffic, he is always slewed completely around talking animatedly to the people in the back seat, while pedestrians go down before him like wheat before the scythe. Harry, indeed, considers an automobile as a sort of weapon—a kind of extra fist with which to menace other motorists whose normal self-respect he finds offensive. Conversely, Harry's complaint about me is that I wait until every last sloth, inchworm and veteran of the War of 1812 has crossed the road before I even begin to think of taking my pretty little landau out of neutral.

The other area in which our personalities clash is on the issue of neatness. I do not so much mind the fact that the top of Harry's dresser always looks like a plate of scrambled eggs, because that is upstairs and no one sees it but the family. But when I backed out of his little study off the living room the other night, I was moved to ask, "What were you doing in here, Planner? Shoeing horses?"

(A retroactive irritation swept over me because a woman I do not know very well had stopped in that afternoon to collect for the hospital, and the casualness and breezy informality of Harry's study—as seen through the open door—was not the kind they photograph for *House & Garden*.)

"Madame Anal-Erotic," he replied suavely. "Tell me about your toilet training."

Oh, there, Philip Wylie!

March 14:

> "Spring rides no horses down the hill,
> But comes on foot, a goose girl still."

Miss Millay was probably not thinking of it at the time, but she could scarcely have found a better way of saying that March is the month of the Girl Scout cookie drive. I warm to the goose-girl simile, for I am cookie chairman of Cora's Brownie troop . . . and the title of the cookie chairman certainly suggests the barefoot herdswoman rather more than Madame Ambassador.

This is my second year as cookie chairman and I have now learned to take it in stride. Last year, however, both the Brownies and I were new at the job, and my efforts to collate the outflows of cookies with the inflow of money bordered on the frantic.

Last year, for some reason—I suppose because the Girl Scouts wear uniforms, and I am the stuff of which conscientious objectors are made— I was haunted by a pervasive nightmare of Prussian militarism. I could see myself being short of the required sum when the cookie drive was over. I could see the drumhead court-martial and the stern-faced women in the field green. I could see the little back room where they left me with a revolver and bottle of brandy. I could see the Girl Scout Council tapping their riding crops on the table and waiting to hear the shot which would heal the wounded honor of Troop 50, Neighborhood 6.

Actually, of course, there was not much about the enterprise to suggest the late Erich von Stroheim. On an appointed day, I waited in until some truckmen brought thirty-five cartons of cookies and left them in the middle of the living-room floor. It was a mountain of cardboard and only a supply sergeant could have thrilled to it. Then I went out to get something for dinner. When I returned, I found Cora and some friends had come in and they were playing a game for which thirty-five cartons of cookies are the well-nigh perfect equipment. The game was called Run-for-your-lives-the-dam-has-broken.

To this day, I flinch at the memory. How many people in this community bought Girl Scout cookies—thinking the wafers would be circular and the sandwich crackers *virgo intacta*—and found they had purchased merely a sort of perishable gravel?

Nevertheless, I have a soft spot in my heart for the Girl Scouts because I was one myself. I can still remember that for some amount which seems utterly paltry now—something like $10 or $7 or $12 a week—my parents sent me to Scout camp and introduced me to an experience whose glory has not wholly faded, even yet. I can still recall the gorgeous novelty of tent life, the Spenserian magic of the woods by moonlight, the coziness when a downpour drummed on the canvas and the flaps were shut. (Who cared if it was a little stuffy?) I can still recollect the triumph, not quite to be believed, of having learned to swim. And the Jack London, *coureur-de-bois* flavor of the overnight pack trip abideth even yet.

Those memories came back vividly on the day last year when Cora first wore her Brownie uniform. She stood in the hall waiting to show herself to Harry—a small, cocoa-colored shape against the white banisters, her hair in pigtails to accommodate the Brownie skullcap and her face so luminous with innocent pride that it was like a candle burning in a windless place. When Harry opened the door and came in, she saluted. He looked down at her.

Parental tenderness occasionally overwhelms.

The great, gruff regional planner with the lean-flanked intellect and the satiric wit had the hackneyed old "suspicion of moisture" in his eyes. And I myself had a lump in my throat like a croquet ball.

Thus do the unwary fall into cookie chairmanships.

July 30th: There is an inconsistency about suburban wives and mothers which haunts me all summer long. In the warm weather, my homemaking colleagues almost invariably—regardless of age, shape or status—wear sleeveless blouses and Bermuda shorts; and when you see them walking toward you, you cannot help but notice that the mammary development is constrained, rigid and unmoving. The wired points of the bosom bear down on the observer like gun turrets, and the "separation" is as unmistakable as Bering Strait.

However, when these gentle ironclads, these female *Monitors* and feminine *Merrimacs*, turn around and walk away, the eye is confronted with such a plunging and such a rythmic jiggling as to suggest the interior of a churn. Is it the sign of schizophrenic culture, I wonder—the woman so mannered and artificial in the front, so extremely earthy in the back?

As a matter of fact, it is a marvel that no sartorial Tom Paine has yet arisen to point out that the Bermuda short itself is a disfiguring garment.

Disfiguring?

It is utterly heartless.

It cuts off from public view the bland, supportive thigh, leaving only the scowling kneecap to carry, artistically speaking, the torso's weight. It does not flirt and twirl like a kilt. It merely cants, like a couple of old stovepipes thrown down in a vacant lot. To the flying buttock, it is merciless; and an opulent roundness of stomach—which drape of trouser or decorum of skirt can sometimes render not unpleasing—becomes a canteloupe supported on lollipop sticks.

The summer is a strenuous time, in the United States, for the aesthetician, what with the indignity of the Bermuda short and the widely prevalent habit of wearing the shirt tails out. The news magazines talk ad infinitum ad nauseam about our high standard of living; but the ironic fact is that in warm weather, this country looks like the examining room of an understaffed Ukrainian clinic.

The thoughts of the housewife are long, long thoughts; and the lonely hours of cutting down bedspreads into café curtains or cooking up things for the freezer against company coming next week are often filled with fantasies and speculations. Some of these fantasies and speculations would cause the males of the society, could they know about them, considerable alarm in behalf of the status quo.

For instance, I have often wondered, during the summer months, whether we would not have a stronger foreign policy, make more progress toward rights for Negroes and secure a better educational system for the children if we forgot about "comfort"—which we have too much of anyway—and insisted on dressing with beauty and dignity. If we wore the toga of Cincinnatus or the chiton of Socrates—or at least something closer to such garments than Bermuda shorts—might we not begin to resemble those dignitaries in our conduct of public affairs?

(I shall never forget Harry's scorn and outrage when the sack dress came into fashion. "That's what women would have looked like," he said, "if Eve hadn't eaten the apple.")

How much do our clothes unconsciously influence the way we behave?

Take the Madonna of the Suburbs as she sets out to do her errands on an August morning. In reality, she is a decent soul, laboring with commendable persistence (if not always with success) to keep her family away from psychiatry, bankruptcy, conformity and possibly barratry and simony.

But does she *look* like a decent soul?

Does anything about her suggest the warm and comforting materfamilias?

Her hair is fluffed out and puffed out in a style which has a piquant name in the pages of *Vogue*, but which is actually just plain burstmattress. Her eyes are blanked out by sunglasses, so that the impersonal black hollows of the meatless skull substitute for the warm, revealing, human glance. Her lips, on the other hand, are strongly accented with brightly colored unguents, so that, if the upper part of the face is cadaver, the lower part is carnivore.

She wears, our suburban Ceres, Bermuda shorts; and dangling from fingertips and banging against her bare legs—which may or may not be shapely—is a purse or handbag so huge as to suggest that what she has got inside is a small Congressman. To complete this bare garishness, this undraped and denuded eccentricity, she wears playshoes or slippers. This footgear is entirely and uncompromisingly heelless and gives the impression that the wearer is not walking on top of the sidewalk, but wading through it about an inch and half below the surface.

Should that mythical invader from Mars ever swoop to the ground in front of this loyal wife and devoted mother, he would not say, "Take me to your leader." He would turn to his fellow Martians and remark, "Name it and you can have it."

Peg Bracken

(1920–   )

After writing her first novel at the age of ten, Peg Bracken never again attempted fiction. She wrote the humor column for her Clayton, Missouri, high school newspaper and served as the editor of *The Antiochan* magazine while a student at Antioch College. After her marriage, Bracken worked as a freelance copywriter in Cleveland, Ohio, and Portland, Oregon, and began contributing light verse and short humorous pieces to magazines, including the *Saturday Evening Post*. The wide reader response to her *Post* articles, such as "If I Were My Husband I'd Fire Me," made her realize the enormous potential of mixing humor and the housewife, and she settled on prose rather than verse as her form. Her first best-seller was *The I Hate to Cook Book* in 1960, followed by the popular *I Hate to Do Housework Book* in 1962. Soon Bracken was a regular contributor to *Ladies' Home Journal, Cosmopolitan,* and *McCall's,* and she published a succession of collections of her prose, including *I Try to Behave Myself* (1964), *I Didn't Come Here to Argue* (1970), *But I Wouldn't Have Missed It for the World* (1970), *A Window Over the Sink* (1981), and *The Compleat I Hate to Cook Book* (1986). Like Jean Kerr and Erma Bombeck, Bracken uses humor in her work to undermine the seriousness with which post-World War II American culture demanded that women take their homemaking responsibilities. Taking her Grandma Em, who "kept house and never let the house keep her, never let it keep her forever at it" as a guide, Bracken endorses the motto that "those whom the Good Lord has enabled to drop things on the floor She also graced with the ability to bend over and pick them up" (*A Window Over the Sink*). Considering herself a realist rather than a romantic, Bracken has defined the humorist's method as looking for the snail underneath the prettiest leaf, and she claims Mark Twain as her favorite author and greatest literary influence.

SOURCES   Cameron, Frank. "Peg Bracken: An exclusive interview." *Writer's Digest*, May 1970: 24–26; *Contemporary Authors*, New Rev. Series, Vol. 6; Frankel, H. "Peach Called Bracken." *Saturday Review*, 5 September 1964: 22–23.

WORKS   *The I Hate to Cook Book* (1960); *The I Hate to Do Housework Book* (1962); *I Try to Behave Myself* (1964); *I Didn't Come Here to Argue* (1970); *But I Wouldn't Have Missed It for the World* (1970); *A Window Over the Sink* (1981) and *The Compleat I Hate to Cook Book* (1986)

from *The I Hate to Cook Book*

Introduction

Some women, it is said, like to cook.

This book is not for them.

This book is for those of us who hate to, who have learned, through hard experience, that some activities become no less painful through repetition: childbearing, paying taxes, cooking. This book is for those of us who want to fold our big dishwater hands around a dry Martini instead of a wet flounder, come the end of a long day.

When you hate to cook, life is full of jolts: for instance, those ubiquitous full-color double-page spreads picturing what to serve on those little evenings when you want to take it easy. Your're flabbergasted. You wouldn't cook that much food for a combination Thanksgiving and Irish wake. (Equally discouraging is the way the china always matches the food. You wonder what you're doing wrong; because whether you're serving fried oysters or baked beans, your plates always have the same old blue rims.)

And you're flattened by articles that begin "Of course you know that basil and tomatoes are soulmates, but *did* you know . . ." They can stop right there, because the fact is you didn't know any such thing. It is a still sadder fact that, having been told, you won't remember. When you hate to cook, your mind doesn't retain items of this nature.

Oh, you keep on buying cookbooks, the way a homely woman buys hat after hat in the vain hope that this one will do it. And, heaven knows, the choice is wide, from the *haute cuisine* cookbook that is so *haute* it requires a pressurized kitchen, through Aunt Em's Down-on-the-Farm Book of Cornmeal Cookery, all the way to the exotic little foreign recipe book, which is the last thing you want when you hate to cook. Not only are there pleasanter ways to shorten your life, but, more important, your husband won't take you out for enchiladas if he knows he can get good enchiladas at home.

Finally, and worst of all, there are the big fat cookbooks that tell you everything about everything. For one thing, they contain too many recipes. Just look at all the things you can do with a chop, and aren't about to! What you want is just one little old dependable thing you can do with a chop besides broil it, that's all.

Also, they're always telling you what any chucklehead would know. "Place dough in pan to rise and cover with a clean cloth," they say. What did they *think* you'd cover it with?

This terrible explicitness also leads them to say, "Pour mixture into 2½ qt. saucepan." Well, when you hate to cook, you've no idea what size your saucepans are, except big, middle-sized, and little. Indeed, the less attention called to your cooking equipment the better. You buy the minimum, grudgingly, and you use it till it falls apart. If anyone gives you a shiny new cooking utensil for Christmas, you're as thrilled as janitor with a new bucket of cleaning solvent.

But perhaps the most depressing thing about those big fat cookbooks is that you have to have one. Maybe your mother-in-law gives you a bushel of peppers or a pumpkin, and you must make piccalilli or a pumpkin pie. Well, there's nothing to do but look it up in your big fat cookbook, that's all. But you certainly can train yourself not to look at anything else.

Now, about this book: its genesis was a luncheon with several good friends, all of whom hate to cook but have to. At that time, we were all unusually bored with what we had been cooking and, therefore, eating. For variety's sake, we decided to pool our ignorance, tell each other our shabby little secrets, and toss into the pot the recipes we swear by instead of at.

This is an extension of the result. It is seasoned with a good sprinkling of Household Hints (the *crème de la crème* of a private collection of 3,744). Mainly, though, it contains around two hundred recipes.

These recipes have not been tested by experts. That is why they are valuable. Experts in their sunny spotless test kitchens can make anything taste good. But even *we* can make these taste good.

Their exact origins are misty. Some of them, to be sure, were off-the-cuff inventions of women who hate to cook and whose motivating idea was to get in and out of that kitchen fast. But most of them were copied from batter-spattered file cards belonging to people who had copied them from other batter-spattered file cards, because a good recipe travels as far, and fast, as a good joke. So, in most cases, it is impossible to credit the prime source, although the prime source was probably a good cook who liked to.

Bless her, and bow low. We who hate to cook have a respect bordering on awe for the Good Cooks Who Like to Cook—those brave, energetic, imaginative people who can, and do, cook a prime rib and a Yorkshire pudding in a one-oven stove, for instance, and who are not frightened by rotisseries. But we've little to say to them, really, except, "Invite us over often, please." And stay away from our husbands.

And, if you hate to cook, expect no actual magic here, no Escoffier creations you can build in five minutes or even ten. But you might well find some recipes you'll like—to use the word loosely—to make now and again. Perhaps you'll even find some you will take to your heart. At the very least, you should find a hands-across-the-pantry feeling, coming right through the ink. It is always nice to know you are not alone.

The Leftover
or Every Family Needs A Dog

Some women can keep a leftover going like an eight-day clock. Their Sunday's roast becomes Monday's hash, which becomes Tuesday's Stuffed Peppers, which eventually turn up as Tamale Pie, and so on, until it disappears or Daddy does. These people will even warm up stale cake and serve it with some sort of a sauce, as some sort of a pudding.

But when you hate to cook, you don't do this. You just go around thinking you ought to. So, much as you dislike that little glass jar half full of Chicken à la King, you don't throw it away, because that would be wasteful. Anyway, you read somewhere that you can put spoonfuls of it into tiny three-cornered pastry affairs and serve them hot, as hors d'oeuvres.

Actually, you know, deep down, that you never will. You also know you won't eat it yourself for lunch tomorrow because you won't feel like it, and you know it won't fit into tomorrow night's dinner, which is going to be liver and bacon, and you know you can't palm it off on Junior (kept piping hot in his little school-going thermos) because he wouldn't even touch it last night when it was new. You know how Junior is about pimentos.

But still you can't quite bring yourself to dispose of it! So you put it in the refrigerator, and there it stays, moving slowly toward the rear as it is displaced by other little glass jars half full of leftover ham loaf and other things. And there it remains until refrigerator-cleaning day, at which time you gather it up along with its little fur-bearing friends, and, with a great lightening of spirit, throw it away.

Do you know the really basic trouble here? It is your guilt complex. This is the thing you have to lick. And it isn't easy. We live in a cooking-happy age. You watch your friends redoing their kitchens and hoarding their pennies for glamorous cooking equipment and new cookbooks called *Eggplant Comes to the Party* or *Let's Waltz into the Kitchen,* and presently you begin to feel un-American.

Indeed, it is the cookbooks you already have that are to blame for your bad conscience and, hence, for your leftover problems. For instance, consider that two thirds of a cupful of leftover creamed corn. They'll tell you to use it as a base for something they call Scrumptious Stuffed Tomatoes. Mix some bread crumbs and chopped celery with the corn and season it well, they'll say, with a fine vague wave of the hand, and then stuff this into your hollowed-out tomatoes and bake them.

Now, ideas like this are all very well for the lady who likes to cook. This is a challenge to her creative imagination. Furthermore, she'll know *how* to season it well (coriander? chervil?) and while the result may not be precisely Scrumptious, it will probably be reasonably okay.

However, if you hate to cook, you'll do better to skip the creamed-corn gambit and simply slice those nice red tomatoes into thick chunks and spread them prettily on some nice green parsley or watercress and sprinkle them with salt and pepper and chopped chives and serve them forth. Because you're not about to use much creative imagination on that stuffing, inasmuch as the whole idea didn't send you very far to begin with; and your Scrumptious Stuffed Tomatoes are going to taste like tomatoes stuffed with leftover corn.

Then there is another thing these cookbooks do. They seem to consider *everything* a leftover, which you must do something with.

For instance, cake. This is like telling you what to do with your leftover whisky. Cake isn't a leftover. Cake is cake, and it is either eaten or it isn't eaten; and if the family didn't go for that Mocha Frosting, you give the rest of the cake to the neighbor or to the lady downstairs before it gets stale. (Maybe *she'll* make something out of it, but you won't have to eat it. Maybe she'll even throw it away, but if so, you won't know about it, so it won't hurt. Like what happened to that twenty-second batch of nameless kittens you finally had to take to the city pound, there are some things you don't exactly want to know.) And certainly you don't want to let the cake get stale so you can make a Stale-Cake Pudding for the family. They're the ones who left so much of it the first time, remember?

Or cheese. Cookbooks will tell you what to do with your leftover cheese. But cheese isn't a leftover; it's a staple. If you'll grate those odd bits and put them in a covered jar in your refrigerator, *toward the front,* you may remember to sprinkle it on things, sometimes, and use it for grilled cheese sandwiches. (Don't believe what they tell you about wrapping cheese in a cloth dipped in wine to keep it fresh, because this doesn't work; it just wastes the wine. Vinegar, used the same way, is somewhat more satisfactory, but it is still an awful nuisance.)

And eggs! Most recipe books show tremendous concern about the egg white, if you didn't use the yolk, or the yolk, if you didn't use the egg white. There are four thousand things you can make and do with an egg white or an egg yolk, all of which call for more cooking and usually result in more leftovers, which is what you were trying to get away from in the first place.

The one thing they don't mention is giving the egg yolk or the egg white to the dog. It's very good for his complexion, and for cats' complexions, too. What did the egg cost? No more than a nickel, probably, and half of that is two and a half cents, which would be cheap for a beauty treatment at twice the price.

Right here we've come to the heart of the matter. Your leftovers were never very expensive to start with. Does the wild rice get left over? Or the choice red out-of-season strawberries? No. It's that dreary little mess of mixed vegetables, worth about six mills in a bull market. You have to think these things through.

Just one more word about the leftover before we get down to where the work is. Home Ec-sperts and other people who made straight A's in Advanced Cream Sauce have gone so far as to rename leftovers "Planovers." They actually want you to cook up a lot more of something than you'll need, and then keep it around to ring exciting changes on, as they put it, through the weeks to come.

It's true that certain people like certain things better the next day. Scalloped potatoes, when they're fried in butter. Or potato salad. Or baked beans. Every family has its little ways. And it's perfectly true that leftover Spanish Rice or Tamale Loaf makes an adequate stuffing for Baked Stuffed Green Peppers, if you get around to doing it before the Spanish Rice or Tamale Loaf starts looking disconsolate.

But when you hate to cook, don't ever fall into the Plan-over Trap. You'll end up hating yourself, too, as you think of that great pile of Something which you'll have to plow through before you can once again face the world clear-eyed and empty-handed.

The word is this: Pare the recipe, if you need to, so that there is only enough for the meal you're faced with. Then buy, as the French do, in small niggling quantities. What is a lady profited if she gains two avocados for nineteen cents instead of one for a dime if she doesn't need the second one and so lets it blacken away?

And the motto to paint on your refrigerator door is this:

WHEN IN DOUBT,
THROW IT OUT.

Just remember: if vegetables have been cooked twice, there aren't enough vitamins left in them to dust a fiddle with. Furthermore, if your refrigerator is jam-packed with little jars, it will have to work too hard to keep things cold. Presently its arteries will harden, and you will have to pay for a service call—the price of which would more than buy a lovely dinner out for you and your husband, with red-coated servitors and soft music.

Finally, and possibly most important, all those leftovers are hard on the family's morale when they open the refrigerator door. Wondering what's for dinner, they begin to get a pretty grim idea, and presently they begin to wonder what's with Mother. The inside of her icebox doesn't look like the insides of the iceboxes they see in the magazine pictures, and Mother loses face.

Actually, the only sort of leftover you need to concern yourself with is meat. It takes more character than most of us have—even those of us who hate to cook—to throw out two or three pounds of cooked beef, lamb, ham, pork, or turkey. So let us consider the meat problem.

Before you do a thing with that great sullen chunk of protein, ask yourself a few questions:

Have you incorporated it into a dish of scalloped potatoes, with plenty of cheese on top?

Have you augmented it with a few slices of Swiss cheese from the delicatessen and served it forth as a Toasted Club Sandwich, in neat triangles surrounding a mound of coleslaw or fruit salad?

Have you re-presented it as an honest cold-cut platter, with deviled eggs in the middle, and ready-mix corn muffins on the side? It's easy to forget the obvious.

And have you ground up a chunk of it with pickles and onions and celery and added some mayonnaise, as a spread for after-school sandwiches?

If you can truthfully answer yes to the foregoing, then, as the British say, you are for it. You are about to start cooking.

Jean Kerr

(1923–   )

Following Betty MacDonald, Cornelia Otis Skinner, and
Shirley Jackson in a line of humorous autobiographical
writers, Jean Kerr's work represented and appealed to the
millions of women who drifted back into the work force,
often part-time, during the 1950s and 1960s or who, after
following the post-World War II dictate to devote themselves
to homemaking, eventually found themselves dreaming about
something else to do. Although Kerr, like MacDonald, ex-
ploits the image of the inadequate, overburdened housewife,
her three autobiographical books—*Please Don't Eat the
Daisies* (1957), *The Snake Has All the Lines* (1960), and
Penny Candy (1970)—are more similar to Skinner's in being
collections of short pieces that appeared in various magazines
and that are related only by the fact that they reveal different
aspects of Kerr's life and personality. In all of her books Kerr
presents sketches of family life that depict her as a harried
housewife, sometimes doubtful of her ability to cope with
four, and then five, young sons. However, the books also
include pieces that reveal Kerr in her roles as wife of drama
critic Walter Kerr, as playwright, as parodist, and as clever
satirist of popular fads and fashions. Consequently, the image
of Kerr that emerges is not of a woman confined to a narrow
domestic existence, but of a woman capable of combining the
demands of homemaking and literature and straddling the
suburbs and Broadway. Because her gripes are minor, her
humor has a good-natured tone that evokes the *persona* not
of a sophisticated career woman but of an insecure individual
who has the same concerns as the average housewife: child
rearing, weight control, physical attractiveness, and housekeeping. At the same time, by poking fun at self-proclaimed
experts who tell women how to look, how to behave, what to
buy, and how to raise children, she encourages women to be

themselves by permitting them to laugh at what is often
promoted as the norm.

SOURCES   Dresner, Zita. "Twentieth Century American Women Humorists."
Diss. University of Maryland, 1982; "Jean Kerr." *Time*. 14 April 1961: 82–85;
Kerr, Jean. Introduction. *Please Don't Eat the Daisies*. New York: Doubleday,
1957.

WORKS   *Please Don't Eat the Daisies* (1957); *The Snake Has All the Lines*
(1960); *Penny Candy* (1970) and *How I Got to Be Perfect* (1978)

from *Please Don't Eat the Daisies*

Introduction

I had the feeling all along that this book should have an Introduction,
because it doesn't have an Index and it ought to have *something*. But I was
getting nowhere until I received this dandy questionnaire from the publicity department at Doubleday.

Now, I'm an old hand at questionnaires, having successfully opened a
charge account at The Tailored Woman. But this was a questionnaire with
a difference. It had heart. Take the item: Why do you write? In less artful
hands this might have been a touchy question, indicating—perhaps—a
last-minute case of nerves at the head office. Instead, one felt that they
cared. They just wanted to know, that's all.

Of course, there were a certain number of routine questions. List your
pen name. (I just call it Ball-Point.) What do you do when you're not
writing? (Buy geraniums.) Husband's name? (Honey.) List your previous
addresses. (Funny, that's what The Tailored Woman was so curious
about.)

But then we began to probe deeper. What is your life's ambition? What
do you hope to accomplish ere dusk sets in? As far as this book is
concerned, who should be notified in case of accident?

It was this next to last question that really yanked me to attention. It
made me realize—and for the very first time—that in my scant twoscore
minus seven years (all right, I'm the same age as Margaret Truman; let
somebody check on *her*) I have already *achieved* my life ambition. That's

something, you know. I feel it sets me apart, rather, like that nice convict who raises canaries in San Quentin.

To go back to the beginning, I was only eight years old, and clearly retarded for my age, when my goal in life dawned on me. I won't say there was a blinding flash, just a poignance, a suspension of time, a sweet recognition of the moment of truth not unlike that memorable instant in which Johnny Weissmuller first noticed that he was Tarzan and *not* Jane.

It was seven-thirty in the morning and my sister, who was six, was pulling my feet out from under the bedclothes and crying, "Oh, get up, get *up*, you mean thing, Mother says I can't go downstairs until you're on the floor!" I withered her with one of my characteristically salty sayings— "Oh, you think you're so smart, Lady Jane Grey!"—but as I stumbled out of bed I realized then and there that all I wanted out of life was to be able to sleep until noon. In fact, I composed a poem right on the spot to celebrate the discovery. I remember the poem (unfortunately reprinted here in its entirety) because it is the only one I ever wrote, unless you want to include a two-line Valentine which said "Thee-whee." The poem:

> Dearer to me than the evening star
> A Packard car
> A Hershey bar
> Or a bride in her rich adorning
> Dearer than any of these by far
> Is to lie in bed in the morning.

Of course I realized even then that you can't sleep until noon with the proper élan unless you have some legitimate reason for staying up until three (parties don't count). But I was in high school before I grasped the fact that *I* was never going to do anything that would keep me up until three. I had been writing short stories which, in the first flush of failure, I sent to *Liberty Magazine* on the innocent but quite mistaken theory that *Liberty* would buy them because everything in the magazine was so terrible. (The only story I can remember now was called "The Pursuit of Happiness" and I wince to report that Happiness was the heroine's name.)

The solution, for me, was obvious: I had to locate a husband who stayed up until three. With this in mind, I ruled out basketball players, who were the natural objects of my affection at the time (I was five feet nine). It had been my observation that all basketball players eventually joined their fathers in the construction business, an activity notorious for its chaste and early uprisings. Besides, I didn't want to marry a basketball player anyway. I really wanted to marry George S. Kaufman and was deterred only by the fact that (a) he had a wife, and (b) I never met him.

It may not seem very romantic, and I don't think Victor Herbert could have done a thing with it, but by the time I was eighteen Walter (my husband) was the only truly eligible man I had ever met. He was an assistant professor who began teaching his classes at three in the afternoon and who directed plays all night. Actually, he got up at *ten* o'clock in the morning, but that was close enough. It was something to build on. And, to be entirely fair, he had certain other endearing qualities. He could play "Ja-Da" on the piano, recite whole sections of *The Waste Land* and make passable penuche. So we were married and I began each day bright and late at the stroke of the noon whistle, a splendid state of affairs which continued for two years or right up to the moment our first son was born.

Now the thing about having a baby—and I can't be the first person to have noticed this—is that thereafter you *have* it, and it's years before you can distract it from any elemental need by saying, "Oh, for heaven's sake, go look at television." At this point I was willing to renounce my master plan—so doth parenthood make cowards of us all—and go to bed at a decent hour like everybody else. Unfortunately, Walter was still staying up until three, busily engaged in making student actors look older by the ingenious device of keeping the stage lights very dim, and I was seeing *him* during the late hours, the children during the early hours, and double all the rest of the time.

It took me quite a while to come to grips with the situation, basically because I was thinking so slowly (from the lack of sleep) and because I had to spend so much time trying to remember to turn off the sterilized nipples before they melted. Eventually, after several years and several children, it came to me that the solution was to hire somebody *else* to get up in the morning.

At the university, we lived basically on a teacher's salary, which is the way you live on a teacher's salary; and this meant that if we were going to have a helpmate, I, Mommy, would have to make some money to pay her. But how? A job was out of the question: getting up in the morning was what I was trying to avoid. It had to be something I could do at home among the cans of Dextri-Maltose. But what? Could I sell little batches of my own special chicken creole soup, which I make by mixing together one can of Campbell's chicken soup with one can of Campbell's creole soup? No.

So I decided to write plays, spurred on by a chance compliment my father had paid me years earlier. "Look," he exploded one evening over the dinner table, "the only damn thing in this world you're good for is *talk*." By talk I assumed he meant dialogue—and I was off.

I won't say that my early efforts were crowned with glory. Oh, I'd say it, all right, but could I make it stick? When my first play was produced in New York, Louis Kronenberger wrote in *Time,* with a felicity it took me only ten years to appreciate, that "Leo G. Carroll brightens up Mrs. Kerr's play in much the same way that flowers brighten a sickroom." (I guess this is what they mean by the nick of *Time*.) I don't know why this and similar compliments for Leo G. Carroll didn't stay my hand forever. As someone pointed out recently, if you can keep your head when all about you are losing theirs, it's just possible you haven't grasped the situation. But what with one thing and another (the advance paid by the doomed producer, and the amateur rights) I was now paying the salary of a very nice girl who had insomnia anyway and who pretended to enjoy distributing pablum and crayons until I emerged, rosy and wrinkled, at eleven.

Thus, as the golden years rolled on, I typed my way through several maids. There was a brief, ghastly period, immediately after we left the university, when it looked as though Walter was going to take a civilian-type job and we might have to live, oh think of it, *normally*. But my fears were groundless and Walter became a drama critic. In many ways, a drama critic leads an ideal existence, or would if he didn't have to see so many plays.

Obviously, it's fun to share the opening-night excitement of a great big hit. And there are, every year, a certain number of plays that must be labeled failures (because they close, for one thing) which are nevertheless fascinating to watch. But then, alas, there are the dogs (the worst of these usually turn up in March or April, which is the origin of the phrase "the hounds of spring"). These are the plays that are so bad you sit there in stunned disbelief, fearing for your sanity while on all sides people are beating their way to the exits. It was after just such an evening that my husband commented, "This is the kind of play that gives failures a bad name."

I don't know what set of standards the critics themselves bring to these occasions. But *I* can sense the presence of a real disaster, where no one will be allowed to enter the area for twenty-four hours, by gauging the amount of incidental information I've picked up about the bit players. We sit so far front that it is possible to read by the light-spill from the stage.

And through the years I have discovered that on a really grueling evening it helps to keep me alert—that is to say, *conscious*—if I study the program notes while the performance is going on. "Biff Nuthall," I read, "here making his debut in New York in the part of the elevator boy, hails from Princeton, New Jersey. He attended the University of Wisconsin, where he achieved notable success as Mosca in a student production of *Volpone*. Mr. Nuthall also plays the oboe."

As you can see, I now have something to chew over; my subconscious is now gainfully occupied. Biff Nuthall as Mosca. I'm sure that boy is loaded with talent, but he'd never be *my* idea of Mosca. Benvolio maybe, or Friar Laurence; but Mosca—with those freckles and that red hair? And if he hails from Princeton, New Jersey, what was he doing going to the University of Wisconsin? What's the matter with Princeton, for heaven's sake? But that's the way some boys are: just because a college is located in their home town, it's not good enough for them. I'm sure you had your reasons, Biff, but it doesn't seem loyal, somehow. And another thing: what do they mean by that curt statement: "Mr. Nuthall also plays the oboe"? Do I imagine it, or is there a rebuke implied there somewhere? Doesn't he play it very well? Or does the press agent, who composed this little biography, not have a very high opinion of the oboe? For his information, the oboe is a noble instrument too much neglected by young people nowadays. What does he want, an entire orchestra composed of violins?

If the cast is long enough, one can while away a whole evening in this manner.

I do have a compulsion to read in out-of-the-way places, and it is often a blessing; on the other hand, it sometimes comes between me and what I tell the children is "*my* work." As a matter of fact, I will read *anything* rather than work. And I don't mean interesting things like the yellow section of the telephone book or the enclosures that come with the Bloomingdale bill about McKettrick classics in sizes 12 to 20, blue, brown, or navy @ 12.95 (by the way, did you know that colored facial tissue is now on sale at the unbelievably low price of 7.85 a carton?). The truth is that, rather than put a word on paper, I will spend a whole half hour reading the label on a milk-of-magnesia bottle. "Philips' Milk of Magnesia," I read with the absolute absorption of someone just stumbling on Congreve, "is prepared only by the Charles H. Philips Co., division of Sterling Drug, Inc. Not to be used when abdominal pain, nausea, vomiting, or other symptoms of appendicitis are present, etc."

For this reason, and because I have four boys, I do about half of my "work" in the family car, parked alongside a sign that says "Littering Is Punishable by a $50 Fine." So far as the boys are concerned, it's not the direct interruptions at home that are hard to adjust to. I don't mind when one of them rushes in to tell me something really important, like the Good Humor man said that banana-rum was going to be the flavor of the week next week. What really drives me frantic and leads to the use of such quantities of Tint-Hair is the business of overhearing a chance remark from another part of the house ("Listen, stupid, the water is supposed to go in the *top*"). Rather than investigate, and interrupt myself, I spend twenty minutes wondering: What water? The top of what? I hope it's just a water gun and not, oh no, not the enema bag again.

Out in the car, where I freeze to death or roast to death depending on the season, all is serene. The few things there are to read in the front-seat area (Chevrolet, E-gasoline-F, 100-temp-200) I have long since committed to memory. So there is nothing to do but write, after I have the glove compartment tidied up.

Once in a while—perhaps every fifteen minutes or so—I ask myself: Why do I struggle, when I could be home painting the kitchen cupboards, *why?* And then I remember. Because I like to sleep in the morning, that's why.

Maybe we'd better have an Index.

from *The Snake Has All the Lines*

The Ten Worst Things about a Man

Actually I feel a bit of a fraud to be picking on men when I always pretend to be so crazy about them. And, deep down inside, I am crazy about them. They are sweet, you know, and so helpful. At parties, men you've barely met will go back to the buffet to get you a muffin and they will leap to their feet to tell you that you've got the wrong end of the cigarette in your mouth. Notice that when you are trying to squeeze into a tight parking place there will always be some nice man driving by who will stick his head out the window and shout, "Lady, you've got a whole *mile* back there!"

But, charming as men are, we can't sit here and pretend they're perfect. It wouldn't be good for them, and it wouldn't be true. Marrying a man is like buying something you've been admiring for a long time in a shop window. You may love it when you get it home, but it doesn't always go with everything else in the house. One reason for this is that most men insist on behaving as though this were an orderly, sensible universe, which naturally makes them hard to live with. The other reason they're hard to live with (and I know this sounds illogical) is that they're so *good*. Perhaps I can clarify that last statement by listing a few of their more intolerable virtues.

1 A Man Will not Meddle in What He Considers His Wife's Affairs

He may interfere at the office, driving secretaries to drink and premature marriage by snooping into file drawers and tinkering with the mimeograph machine. Back home in the nest he is the very model of patience and *laissez-faire*. He will stare at you across the dining-room table (as you simultaneously carve the lamb and feed the baby) and announce, in tones so piteous as to suggest that all his dreams have become ashes, "There's no salt in this shaker."

What a wife objects to in this situation is not just the notion that Daddy has lived in this house for thirteen years without ever discovering where the salt is kept. It's more the implication that only she has the necessary fortitude, stamina, and simple animal cunning necessary to pour the salt into that little hole in the back of the shaker.

2 A Man Remembers Important Things

It really is remarkable the fund of information he keeps at his finger tips: the date of the Battle of Hastings, the name of the man who invented the printing press, the formula for water, the Preamble to the Constitution, and every lyric Larry Hart ever wrote. It is obviously unreasonable to expect one so weighted down with relevant data to remember a simple fact like what size shirt he takes, or what grade Gilbert is in, or even that you told him fifteen times that the Bentleys were coming to dinner. A woman just has to go through life remembering for two. As an example if this, I was recently told about a wife who, from time to time, pinned a tag on her husband's overcoat. The tag read, "Please don't give me a ride home from the station. I have my own car today." However, this technique wouldn't work with my husband because he usually forgets and leaves his overcoat on the train.

3   *A Man Will Try to Improve Your Mind*

Working on the suspicion that women read nothing in the newspapers except bulletins from Macy's and Dorothy Kilgallen, the average man takes considerable pains to keep his scatterbrained wife *au courant* with the contemporary political situation. And we get the following dialogue:

"Did you read Walter Lippmann today on the shake-up in the Defense Department?"

"No, what did he have to say?"

"You should have read it. It was a damn good piece."

"Well, what was the gist of it?"

"Where is that paper? It should be around here someplace."

"It's not around here someplace. It went out with the garbage."

"That's too bad, because it would have clarified the whole situation for you."

"I'm sure. But what was he saying?"

"Oh, he was talking about the shake-up in the *Defense* Department."

"I know that, but what did he *say*?"

"He was against it."

4   *A Man Allows You to Make the Important Decisions*

Because he has such respect for your superior wisdom and technical know-how, he is constantly asking questions like "Does this kid need a sweater?" or "Is that baby wet?" Personally I am willing to go down through life being the court of last appeal on such crucial issues as bedtime (is it?), cookies (can they have another?), rubbers (do they have to wear them?), and baths (tonight? but they took one last night). But, just between us, I have no confidence in a man who wanders out to the kitchen, peers into the icebox, and asks plaintively, "Do I want a sandwich?"

5   *A Man Will Give You an Honest Answer*

If you say, "Honey, do you think this dress is too tight for me to wear?" he'll say, "Yes."

6   *A Man Takes Pride in His Personal Possessions*

A woman will go all her days in the wistful belief that her husband would give her the shirt off his back. Thus she is no way prepared for the cries of outrage that will go up should she ever be rash enough to take the shirt off his back. It doesn't matter that the shirt in question has a torn pocket, a frayed collar, and has, in any case, been at the bottom of the clothes hamper for three years. It's his, and you wear it at your risk.

My husband will say to me, "What are you doing in that shirt, for heaven's sake?" Now he doesn't really want to know what I'm doing. He can see what I'm doing. I'm painting the garage doors. He just wants me to know that that shirt was near and dear to him, and now, as a result of my vandalism, it's totally ruined.

There are two possible solutions to this problem. You can hire a painter to paint the garage doors, or you can dye the shirt purple so he won't be able to recognize it.

7   A Man Believes in Sharing

Men are all advocates of togetherness, up to a point. They will agree that it is "our house," "our mortgage," and, of course, "our song." It is interesting, however, to observe the circumstances under which items that once were "our" joint concern suddenly become your exclusive possession. For instance, a man will return from a stroll through "our back yard" to tell you, "Honey, I think your daffodils are getting clump-bound." Or, on another occasion, "I see that the hinge is off your medicine chest." In my opinion, this policy of dissociating from anything that is temporarily out of order reaches its ultimate confusion with statements like "Hey, your man is here to fix the chimney." My man? I never saw him before in my life.

8   A Man Doesn't Want You to Worry

Since he supposes, and quite correctly, that you worry a great deal about his health, he will go to any lengths to spare you the last alarm about his physical condition. He will say, as though it were the most casual thing in the world, "Well, I almost keeled over in the Grand Central today."

"Good Lord," you will say, "what happened?"

"Nothing, nothing. I leaned against a pillar and I didn't actually fall down."

"But honey, what happened? Did you feel faint? You didn't have a terribly sharp pain in your chest, did you?"

"Oh, no. No, nothing like that".

"Well, what do you mean you almost keeled over?"

"I almost keeled over, that's all."

"But there must have been some *reason*."

"Oh, I guess it's that foot again."

"What foot again? Which foot?"

"Oh, I told you about my foot."

"You most certainly did not tell me anything about your foot."

"The one that's been numb since last summer."

"Your foot has been numb since last summer?"

"Now it's more like the whole leg."

"Good heavens, let's call the doctor. Let's call this minute!"

"Why?"

"Why? Are you out of your mind? Because there's something the matter with your leg, that's why!"

"See, there you go, flying off again. I'm sorry I mentioned it, and there's nothing the matter with my leg, nothing."

9   *A Man Is Reasonable*

Actually there is nothing wrong with a man's being reasonable so long as he doesn't insist on your being reasonable along with him. "Let's be *reasonable*," he keeps saying with about the same frequency that he says, "Go ask your mother," and "What's for dinner?" The occasions on which he thinks you should be reasonable vary, but on the whole it's safe to say that it's any time you're driven past your endurance and out of your mind by shiftless department stores (who promised faithfully to deliver that crib three weeks ago) and irresponsible cleaning women (who simply don't show up on the day you're having sixteen people to dinner). At times like these, a woman wishes only a word of sympathy, like "Yes, yes, they're all a bad lot." And any man who urges his wife to be reasonable and to consider the possibility that Hattie may really *have* "the virus" deserves to wax all the floors himself.

10   *A Man Idealizes His Wife*

This is another way of saying that he hasn't really looked at her in fourteen years. To get me a housecoat for my birthday, my husband will make the unthinkable sacrifice of entering Lord & Taylor's and even penetrating the awesome portals of the lingerie department. There, as I reconstruct the scene later, he selects the slimmest, trimmest little salesgirl on the floor and announces, "She's about your size." Naturally I have to take the thing back and get one four sizes larger.

On second thought, I shouldn't complain about that. If you stop and think, it's really rather charming of him.

PART V
1960–1986: Confronting the Culture

Felicia Lamport

(1916–   )

Felicia Lamport is unusual among female humorists in America for the sheer playfulness of her work. Her light verse turns on word-play similar to that of Ogden Nash; she delights in puns, word inventions, and unlikely rhymes. Yet many of her concerns are similar to those of other women writers: the tyranny of fashion, dieting, women's political power, and the domestic scene. Like other light-verse writers such as Phoebe Cary and Carolyn Wells, she has sometimes turned her hand to literary parody, and one of the most successful results is "The Love Song of R. Milhous Nixon, 1973," in her collection *Light Metres* (1982). Patterned on T. S. Eliot's "The Love Song of J. Alfred Prufrock," the poem is a reflection on the Watergate scandal; whereas Prufrock has measured out his life in coffee spoons, Nixon has measured his in "reels of tape," and the peach that Prufrock does not dare eat is deftly incapsulated in the word "impeach." Lamport's "Majority Problem" echoes Alice Duer Miller's 1915 collection *Are Women People?* as she muses on the arguments about women's use of reason and wonders whether politicians who want women's votes will regard them as human beings. "The Cambridge Lady," like Betty MacDonald's Mrs. Hicks and other righteous women satirized by America's female humorists, is the energetic do-gooder whose rigidity makes her ridiculous. Lamport, who lives in Cambridge, was born in New York and graduated from Vassar in 1937. She began her career as a reporter for the *New York Journal* and then spent several years as a subtitle writer for Metro Goldwyn Mayer. Following her marriage in 1942 to Benjamin Kaplan, she has worked primarily as a free-lance writer, contributing articles and verse to numerous periodicals including *Harper's, The Atlantic, The New Yorker, Life,* and the *Saturday Evening Post.* Her collections of light verse—*Mink on Weekdays* (1950), *Scrap Irony*

(1961), and *Cultural Slag* (1966)—have been illustrated by
Edward Gorey, whose intricate, amusing drawings are an
ideal match for the elegance of Lamport's verse. *Light
Metres*, a selection of Lamport's verse and Gorey's illustra-
tions, was issued in 1982 in a limited slip-case edition signed
by both author and illustrator. An avid chess player, Lamport
has served as director of the American Chess Foundation.

SOURCE   *Contemporary Authors*, Vol. 1 (New Revision Series)

WORKS   *Mink on Weekdays* (1950); *Scrap Irony* (1961); *Cultural Slag* (1966)
and *Light Metres* (1982)

from *Scrap Irony*

Petition for Redress—1956

I'm fed to the teeth
With the sheath.
    It hikes when one sits
    Or it splits,
And if one indulges
It bulges.

From neckline to knees
It's a squeeze.
    It demands an eclipse
    Of the hips,
And frazzles, *sic semper*,
The temper.

I'm fed to the teeth
With the sheath.
    It belongs on a knife,
    Not a wife.
A girl needs a breather.
Unsheathe her!

from *Cultural Slag*

Majority Problem

Women voters now outnumber men in national elections.

Since the cradle-rocking sex is
  Now equipped to swing elections
Every politician's nexus
  Must depend on these reflections:

  Now that Woman has this power
    Will she want to swing it gaily
  With an atavistic glower
    Like her personal shillelagh?
  Does her intellect allow her
    To absorb a rationale
  Or does logic tend to sour
    Her and make her skitter feyly?
  Does she reason like a cow or
    With the wisdom of Disraeli?

Will the candidates who dream of
  Winning women show acumen
That extends to the extreme of
  Postulating that she's human?

The Cambridge Lady

The Cambridge lady's pleasure
  By tradition
Is in work; she looks at leisure
  With suspicion,
Though her arteries may harden
While she keeps her mind and garden
  In condition.

She goes trotting off to lectures
　　By the score,
Voicing questions and conjectures
　　From the floor,
Having made a microscopic
Exploration of the topic
　　Well before.

If she's rich it can't be noticed:
　　She permits
No display of wealth's remotest
　　Perquisites
And she dines in heirloom dresses,
Sure that nothing obsolesces
　　If it fits.

At the heart of each committee
　　That Does Good
For the world or for a city
　　Neighborhood,
She's so keen on group improvement
That she'd join the Brownian movement
　　If she could.

She would rather read Jane Austen
　　Any day
Than the most exciting Boston
　　Exposé
But her mind is open-ended:
She thinks modern art is splendid—
　　In its way.

Though from Portland to Atlanta
　　Now and then
Ladies quail before the Canta-
　　Brigienne,
She looks beautiful and wise
To the presbyotic eyes
　　Of Cambridge men.

Erma Bombeck

(1927–   )

Born in Dayton, Ohio, where she grew up, married, and
raised three children in a suburban community similar to
that described in her books, Bombeck published her humorous columns first in a local weekly in 1963 and then in the
Dayton *Journal Herald*. Addressed to middle-American
women who, like herself, came from working-class families,
married young, had children early, and lived in suburban
tract-house developments with other aspiring middle-class
families, her column achieved enormous success, and by
1985 was syndicated in more than 900 newspapers in the
U.S. and Canada. In addition, she has published eight highly
successful books—*At Wit's End* (1965), *"Just Wait Till You
Have Children of Your Own!"* (1971), *I Lost Everything in
the Post-Natal Depression* (1970), *The Grass Is Always
Greener Over the Septic Tank* (1976), *If Life Is A Bowl of
Cherries, What Am I Doing in the Pits?* (1978), *Aunt Erma's
Cope Book* (1979), *Motherhood: The Second Oldest Profession* (1984), and *Family Ties that Bind . . . and Gag!*
(1987)—all of which express essentially the same message:
the American housewife is the victim of a bad press, greedy
advertisers, and self-proclaimed experts who have never
washed a dish or changed a diaper. By pointing out incongruities between the reality of the housewife's existence
and myths of motherhood promoted by popular culture,
Bombeck's work also pokes fun at many of the trappings of
suburban life and exposes the absurdity of the mass media's
image of the ideal homemaker. Attempting to help free
women from the guilt, depression, and frustration that Betty
Friedan identified as the housewife's syndrome, Bombeck
uses the concrete descriptive details of the local-color realist
as well as the wild exaggeration and parody characteristic of
traditional American humor to burlesque and debunk the

357

images of the superwomen and supermoms offered as role models by television, women's magazines, newspaper columns, and self-help books. Bombeck's concern for women's lives has also been manifested in political action: she has served on the President's Advisory Committee for Women and campaigned for the Equal Rights Amendment. She holds twelve honorary doctorates from American colleges and universities.

SOURCES   Dresner, Zita. "Delineating the Norm: Allies and Enemies in the Humor of Judith Viorst and Erma Bombeck." *Thalia* 7:1 (1984): 28–34; Dunn, Betty. "The Socrates of the Ironing Board." *Life.* 1 October 1971: 66–70; Interview with Nancy Walker. Columbia, MO, May 10, 1981; Skow, John. "Erma in Suburbia." *Time.* 2 July 1984: 56–65; "Up the Wall with Erma Bombeck." *Time.* 13 April 1970: 42.

WORKS   *At Wit's End* (1965); *"Just Wait Till You Have Children of Your Own!"* (1971); *I Lost Everything in the Post-Natal Depression* (1973); *The Grass is Always Greener Over the Septic Tank* (1976); *If Life is a Bowl of Cherries, What Am I Doing in the Pits?* (1978); *Aunt Erma's Cope Book* (1979) and *Motherhood: The Second Oldest Profession* (1984)

from *At Wit's End*

What's a Nice Girl Like Me Doing in a Dump Like This?

It hits on a dull, overcast Monday morning. I awake realizing there is no party in sight for the weekend, I'm out of bread, and I've got a dry skin problem. So I say it aloud to myself, "What's a nice girl like me doing in a dump like this?"

The draperies are dirty (and will disintegrate if laundered), the arms of the sofa are coming through. There is Christmas tinsel growing out of the carpet. And some clown has written in the dust on the coffee table, YANKEE GO HOME.

It's those rotten kids. It's their fault I wake up feeling so depressed. If only they'd let me wake up in my own way. Why do they have to line up along my bed and stare at me like Moby Dick just washed up onto a beach somewhere?

"I think she hears us. Her eyelids fluttered."

"Wait till she turns over, then everybody cough."

"Why don't we just punch her and ask her what we want to know."

"Get him out of here."

"She's pulling the covers over her ears. Start coughing."

I don't know how long it will be before one of them discovers that by taking my pulse they will be able to figure out by its rapid beat if I am faking or not, but it will come. When they were smaller, it was worse. They'd stick their wet fingers into the opening of my face and whisper, "You awake yet?" Or good old Daddy would simply heave a flannel-wrapped bundle at me and say, "Here's Mommy's little boy." (Any mother with half a skull knows that when Daddy's little boy becomes Mommy's little boy, the kid is so wet he's treading water!) Their imagination is straight from the pages of Edgar Allan Poe. Once they put a hamster on my chest and when I bolted upright (my throat muscles paralyzed with fright) they asked, "Do you have any alcohol for the chemistry set?"

I suppose that's better than having them kick the wall until Daddy becomes conscious, then ask, "Do you want the cardboards that the laundry puts in your shirts?" Any wrath beats waking Daddy. There has to be something wrong with a man who keeps resetting his alarm clock in the morning and each time it blasts off smacks it silent and yells, "No one tells me what to do, Buddy."

Personally I couldn't care less what little games my husband plays with his alarm clock, but when I am awakened at 5:30, 6:00, 6:15, and 6:30 every morning, I soon react to bells like a punchy fighter. That's what I get for marrying a nocturnal animal. In the daylight, he's nothing. He has to have help with his shoelaces. In all the years we've been married he only got up once of his own accord before 9:30. And then his mattress was on fire. He can't seem to cope with daytime noises like flies with noisy chest colds, the crash of marshmallows as they hit the hot chocolate, the earsplitting noises milk makes when you pour it over the cereal.

The truth of it is, he's just not geared to function in an eight-to-five society. Once he even fell out of his filing cabinet. Around eleven at night a transformation takes place. He stretches and yawns, then his eyes pop open and he kicks me in the foot and says, "What kind of a day did you have?"

"You mean we're still on the same one?" I yawn.

"You're not going to bed already, are you?"

"Yes."

"Would it bother you if I played the guitar?"

"Yes."

"Well, then maybe I'll read a little before I go to sleep."

"Why not? I have the only eyelids in the neighborhood with a tan."

No doubt about it, if I could arise in a graceful manner, I could cope. It's starting to snow. Thanks a lot up there.

Before moving to the suburbs, I always thought an "Act of God" was a flash of lightning at Mt. Sinai or forty days and forty nights of rain. Out here, they call a snowfall an "Act of God" and they close the schools.

The first time it happened I experienced a warm, maternal glow, a feeling of confidence that I lived in a community which would put its children above inclement weather. The second time, that same week, I experienced a not-so-warm glow, but began to wonder if perhaps the kids could wear tennis rackets on their feet and a tow rope around their waists to guide them. On the third day school was canceled within a two-week period, I was organizing a dog-sled pool.

We racked up fifteen Acts of God that year and it became apparent to the women in our neighborhood that "somebody up there" was out to get us.

It got to be a winter morning ritual. We'd all sit around the radio like an underground movement in touch with the free world. When the announcer read the names of the schools closed, a rousing cheer would go up and the kids would scatter. I'd cry a little in the dishtowel, then announce sullenly, "All right, don't sweat in the school clothes. REPEAT. Don't sweat in the school clothes. Hang them up. Maybe tomorrow you'll visit school. And stay out of those lunch boxes. It's only eight-thirty." My words would fall on deaf ears. Within minutes they were in full snow gear ready to whip over to the school and play on the hill.

Little things began to bother me about these unscheduled closings. For example, we'd drive by the school and our second-grader would point and ask, "What's that building, Daddy?" Also, it was March and they hadn't had their Christmas exchange yet. Our ten-year-old had to be prompted with his alphabet. And the neighborhood "Love and Devotion to Child Study" group had to postpone their meetings three times because they couldn't get the rotten kids from under foot.

"We might as well be living in Fort Apache," said one mother. "If this snow doesn't melt soon, my kid will outgrow his school desk."

We all agreed something had to be done.

This year, a curious thing happened. In the newspaper it was stated that snow was no longer to be considered an Act of God by the state board of education. Their concern was that the children spend a minimum number of hours in school each week and that the buses would roll come yells or high water.

Snow is a beautiful, graceful thing as it floats downward to the earth, and is enhanced greatly by the breathtaking indentation of school bus snow tires. Snow is now considered an Act of Nature in the suburbs. And everyone knows she's a Mother and understands these things.

"Whip it up, group. Everyone to the boots!"

"What do you mean you're a participle in the school play and you need a costume? You be careful in that attic, do you hear? If you fall through and break your neck, you're going to be late for school!"

A drudge. That's all I am. They'll all be sorry when I'm not around to run and fetch.

"So you swallowed the plastic dinosaur out of the cereal box. What do you want me to do, call a vet?"

Lunches. Better pack the lunches. Listen to them bicker. What do they care what I pack? They'd trade their own grandmother for a cough drop and a Holy picture.

Of course, none of these things would bother me if I had an understanding husband. Mother was right. I should have married that little literature major who broke out in a rash every time he read Thoreau. But no, I had to pick the nut standing out in the driveway yelling at the top of his voice, "I am thirty-nine years old. I make fifteen thousand dollars a year. I will not carry a Donald Duck thermos to the office!" Boy, he wouldn't yell at me if my upper arms weren't flabby. He never used to yell at me like that. *He* should worry. He doesn't have to throw himself across the washer during "spin" to keep it from walking out of the utility room. He doesn't have to flirt with a hernia making bunk beds. He doesn't have to shuffle through encyclopedias before the school bus leaves to find out which United States president invented the folding chair.

It's probably the weather. "Everybody out!"

Look at 'em stumbling around the driveway like newborn field mice. It's the weather all right. No leaves on the trees. No flowers. No green grass. Just a big picture window with nothing to look at but . . . *a new bride moving into the cul-de-sac!* Well, there goes the neighborhood. Would you look at her standing at her husband's elbow as he stencils their marvy new name on their marvy new garbage cans? I suppose tomorrow she'll be out waxing her driveway. So give her a few years, and she'll be like the rest of us sifting through the coffee grounds looking for baby's pacifier.

What am I saying? Give her a few years of suburban living and she'll misplace the baby! What was it I was supposed to look for this morning? Maybe I'll think of it. I wonder how much time I waste each day looking for lost things. Let's see, I spent at least two hours yesterday looking for the bananas and enough straight pins to pin up a hem. Lucky the kids came up with the idea of walking across the floor in my bare feet or I'd be looking for pins yet. I suppose I could've uncovered the bananas by smelling breaths, but you have to trust someone sometime when they say no.

The day before that I misplaced the car keys. Of course, that's not my fault. That was the fault of the clown who left them in the ignition. You'd certainly never think to look there for them. Just say I spend about two hours a day looking for stuff. That amounts to 730 hours a year, not counting the entire months of November and December when I look for the Christmas cards I buy half price the preceding January.

I'd have a child growing up on the Pennsylvania Turnpike today if a group of picnickers hadn't noticed her sifting through trash barrels in the roadside park and become curious about how she got there. I wonder if other women piff away all that time looking for nail files and scotch tape.

I knew a woman once who always said, "Have a place for everything and everything in its place." I hated her. I wonder what she would say if she knew I rolled out of bed each morning and walked to the kitchen on my knees hoping to catch sight of a lost coin, a single sock, an overdue library book or a boot that would later inspire total recall.

I remember what I was going to look for . . . my glasses! But that was only if I wanted to see something during the day. So what do I have to see today that I couldn't put off until tomorrow? One of the kids said there was something strange in the oven. Probably a tray of hors d'oeuvres left over from the New Year's party. I'll look for the glasses tomorrow.

In the meantime, maybe I'll call Phyllis and tell her about the new bride. Better not chance it. Phyllis might be feeling great today and then I'd feel twice as crumby as I feel now.

This place will have to be cleaned before they can condemn it. Wouldn't be at all surprised if I ended up like my Aunt Lydia. Funny, I haven't thought about her in years. Grandma always said she ran away with a vanilla salesman. Lay you odds she made her move right after the holidays. Her kids probably hid the Christmas candy in the bedroom closet and the ants were coming out of the woodwork like a Hessian drill team. One child was going through the dirty clothes hamper trying to retrieve her "favorite" underwear to wear to school.

Lydia spotted her nine-year-old dog (with the Christmas puppy plumbing) and ran after it with a piece of newspaper. The dog read a few of the comics, laughed out loud, then wet on the carpet.

Uncle Wally probably pecked her on the cheek with all the affection of a sex-starved cobra and said he wanted to talk about the Christmas bills when he came home.

She passed a mirror and noticed a permanent crease on her face where the brush roller had slipped. Her skirt felt tight. She sucked in her breath. Nothing moved. Her best friend called to tell her the sequin dress she bought for New Year's Eve had been reduced to half price.

Speculating on her future she could see only a long winter in a house with four blaring transistor radios, a spastic washer, and the ultimate desperation of trying to converse with the tropical fish.

You know something. The odds are Aunt Lydia didn't even know the vanilla salesman. When he knocked on the door, smiled and said, "Good morning, madam, I'm traveling through your territory on my way to Forked Tongue, Iowa," Aunt Lydia grabbed her satchel, her birdcage, and her nerve elixir, closed the door softly behind her and said quietly, "You'll do."

Each woman fights the doldrums in her own way. This illustrated guide, *What to Do Until the Therapist Arrives with the Volleyball,* is not unique. Its suggestions may, however, keep you from regressing into a corner in a foetal position with your hands over your ears.

A: KNIT. Learning how to knit was a snap. It was learning how to stop that nearly destroyed me. Everyone in the house agreed I was tense and needed to unwind. So, I enrolled in an informal class in knitting.

The first week I turned out thirty-six pot holders. I was so intent on an afghan you'd have thought I was competing with an assembly line of back-scratcher makers from Hong Kong.

I couldn't seem to stop myself. By the end of the first month of knitting, I was sick from relaxation. There were deep, dark circles under my eyes. My upper lip twitched uncontrollably. There were calluses on both my thumbs and forefingers. I cried a lot from exhaustion. But I was driven by some mad, inner desire to knit fifteen toilet tissue covers shaped like little men's hats by the end of the week.

In the mornings I could hardly wait until the children were out of the house so I could haul out my knitting bag full of yarn and begin clicking away. "All right, group, let's snap it up," I'd yell. "Last one out of the house gets underwear for Christmas."

"It's only six-thirty," they'd yawn sleepily.

"So you're a little early," I snapped impatiently.

"BUT IT'S SATURDAY!" they chorused.

My husband was the first one to suggest I needed professional help. "You've gone beyond the social aspect of knitting," he said. "Let's face it. You have a problem and you're going to have to taper off. From here on in no more yarn." I promised, but I knew I wouldn't keep my word.

My addiction eventually led to dishonesty, lying, cheating, and selling various and sundry items to support my habit. I was always being discovered. The family unearthed a skein of mohair in a cereal box and an argyle kit hidden in the chandelier, and one afternoon I was found feverishly unraveling an old ski cap just to knit it over again. One night when the clicking of the needles in the darkness awakened my husband, he bolted up in bed, snapped on the light, and said quietly, "Tomorrow, I'm enrolling you in 'Knitters Anonymous.' Can't you see what's happening to you? To us? To the children? You can't do this by yourself."

He was right, of course. "Knitters Anonymous" pointed out the foolishness of my compulsion to knit all the time. They eventually weaned me off yarn and interested me in another hobby—painting.

Would you believe it? I did eight watercolors the first week, fifteen charcoal sketches the second and by the end of the month I will have racked up twenty-three oils . . . all on stretched canvases!

B: DRINK. A while back some overzealous girl watcher noted a mass migration of the Red-Beaked Female Lush to split-levels in the suburbs.

That a total of 68 percent of the women today drink, there is no quarrel. But that they've all settled in the suburbs is questionable. Following this announcement, we in the suburbs called an emergency meeting of the "Help Stamp Out Ugly Suburban Rumors" committee. We decided to dispel the stigma once and for all by conducting a sobriety test among women at 8 A.M Monday morning in the town hall.

We uncorked—rather, uncovered—only three sherry breaths, a cognac suspect, and one woman who wasn't sauced at all but who said she always shook that way after getting her four kids onto the school bus in the mornings.

A few of them admitted to nipping away at a bottle of vanilla in the broom closet or getting a little high sniffing laundry bleach, but most of them confessed drinking in the suburbs is not feasible. They cited the following reasons.

Privacy: "You show me a mother who slips into the bathroom to slug down a drink and I'll show you seven children hidden in the bathtub flashing a Popeye home movie on her chest."

Discretion: "To children, drinking means an occasion. When not given a satisfactory occasion to tout, they will spread it all over the neighborhood that Mama is toasting another 'No Baby Month.' "

Guilt: "With the entire block of my friends feeling trapped, bored, neurotic, and unfulfilled, why should I feel good and alienate myself?"

One woman did confess her system of rewarding herself with a drink had gotten a bit out of hand. At first she rewarded herself with a drink for washing down the kitchen walls or defrosting the refrigerator. Now she was treating herself to a drink for bringing in the milk or opening the can of asparagus at the right end.

Undoubtedly the girl watcher was tabulating the many gourmet clubs that have sprouted up in the suburbs. They are the harmless little luncheons where a light wine is served before the luncheon and gourmet foods using brandies and wines are served to stimulate women's interest in cookery.

Some of these are held on a monthly basis to observe some special occasion such as a birthday or an anniversary of a member. In our group, we also observe Mao Tse-tung's backstroke victory, the anniversary of the escape of Winnie Ruth Judd, the January White Sale at Penguin's Department Store, the introduction of soy beans to Latin America, and the arrival and departure dates of the *Queen Mary*. Each month we present an award to the most unique dish served. Last month's prize was copped by my neighbor for a wonderful dessert which consisted of a peach seed floating recklessly in a snifter of brandy.

Frankly I think the girl watchers owe the women of the suburbs an apology for their accusations. Anyone here want to drink to that?

c: READ. One of the occupational hazards of housewifery and motherhood is that you never get the time to sit down and read an entire book from cover to cover.

A spot check of my most erudite friends revealed that the last books they read were: *Guadalcanal Diary, The Cat in the Hat Dictionary, The*

Picture of Dorian Gray, and *First Aid.* (The fifth fell asleep over her "Know Your Steam Iron Warranty and Manual," but we counted it anyway.)

This is a sad commentary on the women who are going to be the mothers of all these scientists and skilled technicians of tomorrow. As I always say, "What doth it profiteth a woman to have a clean house if she thinks anthropologist Margaret Mead is a foot doctor!" (I recommended her to three of my friends.)

First, to find the right book. When you live in a small town you have to be pretty discreet abut the books you check out. I, for one, don't want to be known behind the stalls as "Old Smutty Tongue." On the other hand, I don't want to spend my precious time plowing through *Little Goodie Miss Two Shoes and Her Adventures on Bass Island.*

"You know me pretty well, Miss Hathcock," I said to the librarian. "What book would you suggest for me?"

"*Sex and the Senior Citizen* with a glossary in the front listing all the pages with the dirty parts in boldface type," she answered crisply.

"Now, now, Miss Hathcock. We will have our little humor, won't we? Keep in mind I have very little time for reading and I want a book I can talk about in mixed company."

"If I were you," she said slowly, "I'd check out *Come Speed Read with Me* by M. Fletcher. It guarantees that in three days it will increase your reading speed enormously. You will be literally digesting an entire newspaper in nineteen minutes, novels in thirty minutes, and anthologies in an hour."

I tested myself the minute I got home. It took me forty-five minutes to read one paragraph. Maybe it was possible I had lost my old power of concentration. According to the contents of the first chapter, my diagnosis was a simple one. My eyes jerked and stopped at every word. I read each word, not sentences or images. That would take work.

Whenever I got the chance I picked up my *Come Speed Read with Me* book and spent an hour or two in diligent application.

Yesterday I approached Miss Hathcock at the return desk.

"Well, how did your speed reading go?" she smiled. "Are you ready for the complete works of Churchill? How about *Hawaii?* Or Ted Sorensen's *Kennedy?*"

"Actually," I giggled, "I kept drowsing over chapter two. That's the 'Lack of Attention' chapter. Once I hurdle that, I feel I can whip through the entire thing in no time at all. How about an additional twenty-one days renewal on it?"

"How about *Sex and the Senior Citizen?*" she sighed wearily. "And I'll wrap it in a plain piece of brown paper."

D: TELEPHONE. A noted heart specialist has openly attacked women's use of the extension phone. He has charged these convenient outlets will (a) broaden hips, (b) cause sluggish circulation, and (c) eventually take away her lead over men in life expectancy.

Doctor, you are either naïve on the subject of telephone conditioning or you are pulling our fat, muscular legs.

At the first ring of the telephone, there is an immediate conditioned response that has every kid in the house galloping to the instrument to answer it. You show me a woman who is alert and who wears deep-tread sneakers and I'll show you a woman who gets to answer her own telephone.

Once Mama is settled comfortably on the phone, the children swing into action like a highly organized army on maneuvers, each marching to his favorite. "No, No, Burn Burn" or whatever. Refrigerator doors pop open, cupboards bang back and forth, makeshift ropes carry kids sailing through the air, razor blades appear, strange children come filing through the doors and windows, the aromas of nail polish and gasoline permeate the air, and through it all one child will crawl up on the television set and take off his clothes! There is nothing like it to pep up tired blood.

Some mothers are clickers—that is, rather than interrupt a telephone conversation they will click fingers and point, pound on the table and point, whistle through their fingers and point, or pick up a club and point. So much for circulation.

Other mothers resort to muffled cries as they hold their hands over the receivers. They can't fake it. They've got to administer the whack, clean up the sugar, blow up a balloon, put out the fire, mop up the water *right now!* So much for hip exercises.

A few telephone exponents are a study in pantomime. I used to be mesmerized by a woman who formed the words, "I'm going to give you kids one in a minute," followed shortly by, "I'm going to give you kids two in a minute." She alone knew the magic number whereby she would stop and give them a belt.

Some mothers have even attempted to put a busy box, filled with toys, near their telephones. Of course, kids are too bright to fall for that. You could have Mary Poppins hanging by her umbrella whistling "Dixie" and kids would still roll the onions across the floor and gargle the laundry bleach.

I don't think women outlive men, Doctor. It only seems longer.

Shape Up Before You Ship Out

In the throes of a winter depression cycle, there is nothing that will set you off like a group of fashion authorities who want to know, "Is your figure ready for a bikini this summer?"

I got a flash for you, Charlie. My figure wasn't ready for a bikini last summer. Very frankly, I've hit a few snags.

You see, for years I have built my figure on the premise that "fat people are jolly." I have eaten my way through: pleasant, cheery, sunny, smiling, gay, spirited, chipper, vivacious, sparkling, happy, and sportive and was well on my way to becoming hysterical. Now I find that a group of experts say this is a myth. "Fat people aren't jolly at all. They're just frustrated and fat." You'd have thought they would have said something while I was back on pleasant.

There was a time when I had a twenty-three-inch waist. I was ten years old at the time. As I recall, my measurements were 23-23-23. I'm no fool. Even at ten years, I knew I could never be too jolly with those figures so I started to eat.

In high school I used to reward myself with after-school snacks for (a) not stepping on a crack in the sidewalk, (b) spelling Ohio backwards, (c) remembering my locker combination.

After marriage, I added thirty pounds in nine months, which seemed to indicate I was either pregnant or going a little heavy on the gravy. It was the former. I am listed in the medical records as the only woman who ever gained weight *during* delivery.

My husband, of course, tried to shame me by pasting a picture of Ann-Margaret on the refrigerator door with a terse note, "Count Calories."

He hasn't tried that routine, however, since our trip to the shopping center last spring that coincided with a personal appearance by Mr. Universe.

"I thought we came here to look at a bedroom rug," he snapped. "You see one muscle, you've seen them all," he snorted.

"I've been married eighteen years and I've yet to see my first one," I said standing on my tiptoes. "Just let me see what he looks like."

Mr. Universe worked in a fitted black T-shirt and shorts. If muscles ever go out of style he could always get a job on the beach kicking sand in the faces of ninety-seven-pound weaklings and yelling, "Yea, skinny!" He thumped onto the platform and my jaw dropped.

"For crying out loud, close your mouth," whispered my husband. "You look like someone just dropped a bar bell on your foot."

"Did you ever see so many muscles in your life?" I gasped. "That T-shirt is living on borrowed time. And listen to that. He says it just takes a few mintues a day to build a body like his. Hey, now he's touching his ear to his knees. Can you touch your ear to your knee?"

"What in heaven's name for?" he sighed. "There's nothing to hear down there. Besides, I'd be embarrassed to look like that. My suits wouldn't fit right. And I couldn't bear having all those people staring."

"You're really sensitive about all this, aren't you?"

"I certainly am not," he said emphatically. "It's just that I'm not a beach boy."

"I'll say you're not a beach boy. Remember when that kid wanted to borrow your inner-tube last summer at the pool and you weren't wearing one?"

"Are we going to look at that bedroom rug or aren't we?" he growled.

"Not until you admit that you can't kick seven feet high, throw a football seventy-five yards and jump over an arrow you're holding in both hands."

"Okay, so I'm not Mr. Universe."

"Then you'll take that picture of Ann-Margret off my refrigerator door?"

"Yes. You know, in my day I used to have a set of pretty good arm muscles. Here, look at this. I'm flexing. Hurry up! See it? How's that for muscle?"

Personally I've seen bigger lumps in my cheese sauce, but when you've won a war, why mess around with a small skirmish?

I think the trouble with most women dieters is that they can't get from Monday to Tuesday without becoming discouraged. I am a typical Monday dieter. Motivated by some small incident that happens on a Sunday ("Mama's outgrown her seat belt. We'll have to staple her to the seat covers, won't we?") I start in earnest on a Monday morning to record my era of suffering.

Diary of a Monday Dieter

8:00 A.M.: This is it. Operation twenty pounds. Called Edith and told her what I had for breakfast. Reminded her to read a story in this month's *Mother's Digest*, "How Mrs. M., St. Louis, ate 25 Hungarian Cabbage Rolls a Day and Belched Her Way to a Size 10."

12:30 P.M.: Forced myself to drink a cup of bouillon. Called Edith and told her I noticed a difference already. I don't have that stuffed feeling around my waist. I have more energy and my clothes fit better. Promised her my gray suit. After this week, it will probably hang on me like a sack.

4:00 P.M.: An article in *Calorie* (the magazine for people who devour everything in sight) offers a series of wonderful dinner menus for weight-watchers. As I was telling Edith a few minutes ago, we mothers have an obligation to our families to feed them nutritious, slimming meals. Tonight we are having lean meat, fresh garden peas, Melba thins in a basket, and fresh fruit.

4:30 P.M.: Husband called to say he'd be late for dinner. Fresh garden peas looked a little nude, so added a few sauteed mushrooms and dab of cream sauce. After all, why should the children be sick and suffer because they have a strong-willed mother?

4:45 P.M.: I ate the Melba toast—every dry, tasteless crumb of it! (Come to think of it the basket is missing.) Luckily I had a biscuit mix in the refrigerator and jazzed it up with a little shredded cheese and butter. The magazine said when you begin licking wax from the furniture you should supplement your diet with a snack.

5:00 P.M.: Well, maybe that lousy fruit in the bowl would look pretty good to Robinson Crusoe, but I put it under a pie crust where it belongs. In fifty minutes I'll have a warm cobbler, swimming in rich, thick cream. Who does my husband think he is? Paul Newman?

5:30 P.M.: The kids just asked what I am doing. I'm putting on a few potatoes to go with the gravy, that's what I'm doing. That's the trouble with kids today. Half of the world goes to bed hungry and they expect me to pour good meat drippings down the drain. Kids are rotten. They really are.

6:00 P.M.: Blood pressure has dropped. Stomach is beginning to bloat. Vision is impaired. I've added two more vegetables and a large pizza with everything to the menu. That fink Edith had the nerve to call and ask if she could have the blouse to the gray suit. Edith's a nice girl, but she's a pushy individual who drives you crazy phoning all the time. I told the kids to tell her I couldn't talk. I was listening to my Bonnie Prudden records.

6:30 P.M.: Husband arrived home. I met him at the door and let him have it. If it weren't for his rotten working hours, I could be the slip of the girl he married. He had the gall to act like he didn't know what I was talking about.

No, I don't think I'm ready for a bikini again this year. Heaven knows I try to bend to the dictates of fashion, but let's face it, I'm a loser. When I grew my own bustle, they went out of style. When my hips reached saddlebag proportions, the "long, lean look" came in. When I ultimately discovered a waistline, the straight skirt came into being. I had a few bright moments when they were exploiting the flat chest as denoting women with high I.Q.'s, but then someone revealed a certain clearly unflat movie star's 135 (I.Q. that is) and shot *that* theory down.

Here's my basic equipment, if you fashion moguls care to check it out, but frankly it doesn't look too encouraging.

Shoulders: Two of them. Unfortunately they don't match. One hooks up higher than the other, which they tell me is quite common among housewives who carry fat babies, heavy grocery bags, and car chains.

Midriff: If I can't tighten up the muscles in time for beach exposure perhaps I can use it for a snack tray.

Eyes: Some people with myopic vision look sexy. I look like I have myopic vision. Don't tell me what to do with my eyebrows. I tried several things and either look like Milton Berle or Bela Lugosi with a sick headache.

Waist: It's here somewhere. Probably misfiled.

Hips: Here. They weren't built in a day, friend, so don't expect miracles. Right now, they couldn't get a rise out of a factory whistle.

Knees: Let me put it this way. A poet at a neighborhood cocktail party once described them as "divining rods that could get water out of the Mojave Desert."

Legs: Ever wonder who got what Phyllis Diller discarded?

Guts: Hardly any.

Tell you what. If I don't "shape up" by June, go on to the beach without me. Stop on the way back and I'll serve you a dish of homemade short-cake, topped with fresh strawberries crusted in powdered sugar and wallowing in a soft mound of freshly whipped cream.

Judith Viorst
(1936–   )

If Phyllis McGinley is remembered for adding suburbia to
the list of topics considered appropriate for light verse, Judith
Viorst may well be remembered for contributing the middle-
class housewife's discontent. Raised in a middle-class Jewish
home in suburban New Jersey, Viorst moved to Greenwich
Village soon after college in search of the romanticized
intellectual and artistic experience she had fantasized from
her love of literature and desire to be a writer. Her first
volume of verse, *The Village Square* (1965), based on her life
in Greenwich Village, sets up the *persona* and the issues that
are explored in her subsequent volumes: *It's Hard to Be Hip
over Thirty* (1968), *People and Other Aggravations* (1971),
and *How Did I Get to Be Forty and Other Atrocities* (1976).
Having married and become a housewife and mother, she is
primarily concerned in her work with reconciling different
self-images which are equally real and unreal and which are
mutually dependent upon, as well as limited by, each other:
conventional middle-class housewife and romantic woman of
the world, super mom and reluctant homemaker, social
radical and bourgeois conformist, intellectually responsible
adult and emotionally neurotic adolescent. Viorst's humor
and appeal derive from her ability to express women's
anxieties about who they are and about whether or not who
they are represents the kind of women they want or think
they ought to be. The "I" in Viorst's verses is a woman whose
basic insecurity dooms her to obsessive self-examination and
self-criticism as she attempts to deal with the disappointments and dissatisfactions stemming from her failure to be all
things to all people, including herself. Describing her verse as
"aggravation recollected in tranquillity," Viorst is unique in
expressing with humorous insight the internal, rather than
external, conflicts and problems afflicting contemporary middle-class women.

373

SOURCES   Crawford, Clare. "Author-Mom Judith Viorst Scores as the Tragi-comic Bard of Mid-Life Blahs." *People.* January 1977: 60–61; Dresner, Zita. "Delineating the Norm: Allies and Enemies in the Humor of Judith Viorst and Erma Bombeck." *Thalia* 7:1 (1984): 28–34 and "Twentieth Century American Women Humorists." Diss. University of Maryland, 1982; Lague, Louise. "Judith Viorst: From Suicide to Humor." *The Washington Star* 4 Dec. 1977: D 10–11.

WORKS   *The Village Square* (1965); *It's Hard to Be Hip Over Thirty* (1968); *People and Other Aggravations* (1971); *Yes, Married: A Saga of Love and Complaint* (1972); *How Did I Get to Be Forty and Other Atrocities* (1976) and *Love & Guilt & The Meaning of Life, Etc.* (1979)

from *It's Hard to be Hip Over 30*

The Other Woman

The other woman
Never smells of Ajax or Spaghetti-O,
And was bored with Bob Dylan
A year before we had heard of him,
And is a good sport about things like flat tires and no hot water,
Because it's easier to be a good sport
When you're not married.

The other woman
Never has tired blood,
And can name the best hotels in Acapulco
As readily as we can name detergents,
And wears a chiffon peignoir instead of a corduroy bathrobe,
Because it's easier to try harder
When you're not married.

The other woman
Never has to look at Secret Squirrel,
And spends her money on fun furs
While we are spending ours on obstetricians,
And can make a husband feel that he is wanted,
Because it's easier to want a husband
When you're not married.

Nice Baby

Last year I talked about black humor and the impact
  of the common market on the European
  economy and
Threw clever little cocktail parties in our discerningly
  eclectic living room
With the Spanish rug and the hand-carved Chinese
  chest and the lucite chairs and
Was occasionally hungered after by highly placed men
  in communications, but
This year we have a nice baby
And pablum drying on our Spanish rug,
And I talk about nursing versus sterilization
While the men in communications
Hunger elsewhere.

Last year I studied flamenco and had my ears
  pierced and
Served an authentic fondue on the Belgian marble
  table of our discerningly eclectic dining area, but
This year we have a nice baby
And Spock on the second shelf of our Chinese chest,
And instead of finding myself I am doing my best
To find a sitter
For the nice baby banging the Belgian marble with
  his cup
While I heat the oven up
For the TV dinners.

Last year I had a shampoo and set every week and
Slept an unbroken sleep beneath the Venetian
  chandelier of our discerningly eclectic bedroom,
  but
This year we have a nice baby,
And Gerber's strained bananas in my hair,
And gleaming beneath the Venetian chandelier.
A diaper pail, a portacrib, and him,
A nice baby, drooling on our antique satin spread
While I smile and say how nice. It is often said
That motherhood is very maturing.

from *People and Other Aggravations*

A Women's Liberation Movement Woman

When it's snowing and I put on all the galoshes
While he reads the paper,
Then I want to become a
Women's Liberation Movement woman.
And when it's snowing and he looks for the taxi
While I wait in the lobby,
Then I don't.
And when it's vacation and I'm in charge of
    mosquito bites and poison ivy and car
    sickness
While he's in charge of swimming,
Then I want to become a
Women's Liberation Movement woman.
And when it's vacation and he carries the trunk
    and the overnight bag and the extra blankets
While I carry the wig case,
Then I don't.
And when it's three in the morning and the baby
    definitely needs a glass of water and I have
    to get up and bring it
While he keeps my place warm,
Then I want to become a
Women's Liberation Movement woman.
And when it's three in the morning and there is
    definitely a murderer-rapist in the vestibule
    and he has to get up and catch him
While I keep his place warm,
Then I don't.
And after dinner, when he talks to the company
While I clean the broiler
(because I am a victim of capitalism, imperialism,

male chauvinism, and also Playboy
    magazine),
And afternoons, when he invents the telephone
    and wins the Dreyfus case and writes War
    and Peace
While I sort the socks
(because I am economically oppressed, physically
    exploited, psychologically mutilated, and also
    very insulted),
And after he tells me that it is genetically
    determined that the man makes martinis and
    the lady makes the beds
(because he sees me as a sex object, an earth
    mother, a domestic servant, and also dumber
    than he is),
Then I want to become a
Women's Liberation Movement woman.

And after I contemplate
No marriage, no family, no shaving under my
    arms,
And no one to step on a cockroach whenever I
    need him,
Then I don't.

Anti-Heroine

I'd planned to be Heathcliff's Cathy, Lady Brett,
Nicole or Dominique or Scarlett O'Hara.
I hadn't planned to be folding up the laundry
In uncombed hair and last night's smudged
    mascara,
An expert on buying Fritos, cleaning the cat box,
Finding lost sneakers, playing hide-and-seek,
And other things unknown to Heathcliff's Cathy,
Scarlett, Lady Brett, and Dominique.

Why am I never running through the heather?
Why am I never raped by Howard Roark?
Why am I never going to Pamplona
Instead of Philadelphia and Newark?
How did I ever wind up with an Irving
When what I'd always had in mind was Rhett,
Or someone more appropriate to Cathy,
Dominique, Nicole, or Lady Brett.

I saw myself as heedless, heartless, headstrong,
An untamed woman searching for her mate.
And there he is—with charcoal, fork, and apron,
Prepared to broil some hot dogs on the grate.
I haven't wrecked his life or his digestion
With unrequited love or jealous wrath. He
Doesn't know that secretly I'm Scarlett,
Dominique, Nicole, or Brett, or Cathy.

Why am I never cracking up in Zurich?
Why am I never languishing on moors?
Why am I never spoiled by faithful mammys
Instead of spraying any spray on the floors?
The tricycles are cluttering my foyer.
The Pop Tart crumbs are sprinkled on my soul.
And every year it's harder to be Cathy,
Dominique, Brett, Scarlett, and Nicole.

from *How Did I Get to be 40?*

The Truth

The truth is
If I had it all to do over
I still wouldn't study Swahili,
Learn to fly a plane,
Or take 92 lovers,
Some of them simultaneously.

The truth is
If I lived my life again
I still wouldn't leap before looking,
I still wouldn't count my chickens before they were hatched,
And I'd still, just in case I was hit by a car and had to be
    rushed to the hospital and examined,
Wear clean underwear.

The truth is
If I got a second chance
I still wouldn't know a forward pass from a backward one,
A self-effacing wine from a presumptuous one,
Or a man who, if I let him pick me up, would be rich, sincere,
    and of the same religious persuasion
From a man who, if I let him pick me up, would wind up being
    a homicidal rapist.

The truth is
That I'll always want to be
Pure enough to hate white bread,
Deep enough to admire Patagonian folk art,
Thin enough to go swimming in the nude,
Mature enough to outgrow Erich Fromm,
Nice enough to be nice to my Uncle Bernie,
And secure enough to not need getting married.

But the truth is
That the next time around,
I still wouldn't.

Self-Improvement Program

I've finished six pillows in Needlepoint,
And I'm reading Jane Austen and Kant,
And I'm up to the pork with black beans in Advanced Chinese Cooking.
I don't have to struggle to find myself
For I already know what I want.
I want to be healthy and wise and extremely good-looking.

I'm learning new glazes in Pottery Class,
And I'm playing new chords in Guitar,
And in Yoga I'm starting to master the lotus position.
I don't have to ponder priorities
For I already know what they are:
To be good-looking, healthy, and wise.
And adored in addition.

I'm improving my serve with a tennis pro,
And I'm practicing verb forms in Greek,
And in Primal Scream Therapy all my frustrations are vented.
I don't have to ask what I'm searching for
Since I already know that I seek
To be good-looking, healthy, and wise.
And adored.
And contented.

I've bloomed in Organic Gardening,
And in Dance I have tightened my thighs,
And in Consciousness Raising there's no one around who can top me.
And I'm working all day and I'm working all night
To be good-looking, healthy, and wise.
And adored.
And contented.
And brave.
And well-read.
And a marvelous hostess,
Fantastic in bed,
And bilingual,
Athletic,
Artistic . . .
Won't someone please stop me?

Nora Ephron
(1941–   )

Although perhaps best known now as the author of *Heart-burn,* the 1983 novel that became a 1986 film starring Meryl Streep and Jack Nicholson, Nora Ephron has had a long and active career as a columnist and social critic who uses wit to cut through pretense and expose exploitation—especially of women. Ephron began as a journalist for the *New York Post,* and then became a freelance writer for such magazines as *New York, Cosmopolitan,* and *Esquire.* The first collection of her essays, *Wallflower at the Orgy,* was published in 1970, followed by *Crazy Salad: Some Things About Women* (1975) and *Scribble Scribble: Notes on the Media* (1978). Ephron has also written screenplays, including the 1983 film *Silk-wood.* As a critic of American culture, Ephron is particularly concerned with the ways in which Americans allow themselves to be manipulated by fads and the media, from Minute Rice to *People* magazine. Even before *Heartburn,* which is a thinly fictionalized account of the breakup of her marriage to journalist Carl Bernstein, Ephron's writing was auto-biographical in the sense that she has consistently brought an individual perspective to bear on social issues. The voice in her writing has similarities with the common sense ra-tionality of Marietta Holley's Samantha Allen as she describes the pitfalls of consciousness-raising groups and exposes the conscious exploitation of women by manufac-turers of feminine hygiene products. Ephron is from a family of writers: her parents, Phoebe and Henry Ephron, were screenplay writers who based one of their plays on her letters home from Wellesley; her sister Delia is a well-known author of books for children. The essays in *Crazy Salad* chronicle the change and confusion of the early years of the women's movement, when, to some feminists, participating in the Pillsbury Bake-Off and wearing makeup were both consid-

ered subversive. In "On Never having Been a Prom Queen,"
written in 1972, Ephron deals with both the divisions within
the women's movement itself, which she says "makes the
American Communist Party of the 1930s look like a monolith," and the cultural value placed on women's physical
appearance.

SOURCES   *Contemporary Authors* (New Revision Series), Vol. 12. Gross, A.
"Some Things About Nora Ephron." *Vogue* 173 (May 1983): 287; Walker,
Nancy. "Nora Ephron." *Popular World Fiction*. Washington: Beacham Publish-
ing, 1987. Vol. 2.

WORKS   *Wallflower at the Orgy* (1970); *Crazy Salad: Some Things About
Women* (1975); *Scribble Scribble: Notes on the Media* (1978) and *Heartburn*
(1983)

from *Crazy Salad*

On Never Having Been a Prom Queen

The other night, a friend of mine sat down at the table and informed me
that if I was going to write a column about women, I ought to deal
straight off with the subject most important to women in all the world.
"What is that?" I asked. "Beauty," she said. I must have looked somewhat
puzzled—as indeed I was—because she then went into a long and painful
opening monologue about how she was losing her looks and I had no idea
how terrible it was and that just recently an insensitive gentleman friend
had said to her, "Michelle, you used to be such a beauty." I have no idea if
this woman is really losing her looks—I have known her only a couple of
years, and she looks pretty much the same to me—but she is certainly
right in saying that I have no idea of what it is like. One of the few
advantages to not being beautiful is that one usually gets better-looking as
one gets older; I am, in fact, at this very moment gaining my looks. But
what interested me about my response to my friend was that rather than
feeling empathy for her—and I like to think I am fairly good at feeling
empathy—I felt nothing. I like her very much, respect her, even believe she
believes she is losing her looks, recognize her pain, but I just couldn't get
into it.

Only a few days later, a book called *Memoirs of an Ex-Prom Queen*, by

Alix Kates Shulman (Knopf), arrived in the mail. Shulman, according to the jacket flap, had written a "bitterly funny" book about "being female in America." I would like to read such a book. I would like to write such a book. As it turns out, however, Alix Shulman hasn't. What she has written is a book about the anguish and difficulty of being beautiful. And I realized, midway through the novel, that if there is anything more boring to me than the problems of big-busted women, it is the problems of beautiful women.

"They say it's worse to be ugly," Shulman writes. "I think it must only be different. If you're pretty, you are subject to one set of assaults; if you're plain you are subject to another. Pretty, you may have more men to choose from, but you have more anxiety too, knowing your looks, which really have nothing to do with you, will disappear. Pretty girls have few friends. Kicked out of mankind in elementary school, and then kicked out of womankind in junior high, pretty girls have a lower birthrate and a higher mortality. It is the beauties like Marilyn Monroe who swallow twenty-five Nembutals on a Saturday night and kill themselves in their thirties."

Now I could take that paragraph one sentence at a time and pick nits (What about the pretty girls who *have* friends? What has Marilyn Monroe's death to do with all this? What does it mean to say that pretty girls have a lower birthrate—that they have fewer children or that there are less of them than there are of us?), but I prefer to say simply that it won't wash. There isn't an ugly girl in America who wouldn't exchange her problems for the problems of being beautiful; I don't believe there's a beautiful girl anywhere who would honestly prefer not to be. "They say it's worse to be ugly," Alix Shulman writes. Yes, they do say that. And they're right. It's also worse to be poor, worse to be orphaned, worse to be fat. Not just *different* from rich, familied, and thin—actually worse. (I am a little puzzled as to why Ms. Shulman uses the words "plain" and "ugly" interchangeably; the difference between plain and ugly is as vast as the one between plain and pretty. As William Raspberry pointed out in a recent *Washington Post* column, ugly women are the most overlooked victims of discrimination in America.)

The point of all this is not about beauty—I hope I have made it clear that I don't know enough about beauty to make a point—but about divisions. I am separated from Alix Shulman and am in fact almost unable to judge her work because she is obsessed with being beautiful and I am obsessed with not being beautiful. We might as well be on separate sides altogether. And what makes me sad about the women's movement in general is my own inability, and that of so many other women, to get across such gulfs, to join hands, to unite on anything.

The women's liberation movement at this point in history makes the American Communist Party of the 1930s look like a monolith. I have been to meetings where the animosity between the gay and straight women was so strong and so unpleasant that I could not bear to be in the room. That is the most dramatic division in the movement, and one that has considerably slowed its forward momentum; but there are so many others. There is acrimony between the single and married women, working women and housewives, childless women and mothers. I have even heard a woman defend her affection for cooking to an incredulous group who believed that to cook at all—much less to like it—was to swallow the worst sort of cultural conditioning. Once I tried to explain to a fellow feminist why I liked wearing makeup; she replied by explaining why she does not. Neither of us understood a word the other said.

Every so often, I turn on the television and see one of the movement leaders being asked some idiot question like, "Isn't the women's movement in favor of all women abandoning their children and going off to work?" (I can hear David Susskind asking it now.) The leader usually replies that the movement isn't in favor of all women doing anything; what the movement is about, she says, is options. She is right, of course. At its best, that is exactly what the movement is about. But it just doesn't work out that way. Because the hardest thing for us to accept is the right to those options. I hear myself saying those words: *What this movement is about is options.* I say it to friends who are frustrated, or housebound, or guilty, or child-laden, and what I am really thinking is, If you really got it together, the option you would choose is mine.

I would like to be able to leap across the gulf that divides me from Alix Shulman. After all, her experience is not totally foreign to me: once I had a date with someone who thought I was beautiful. He talked all night, while I—who spent years developing my conversational ability to compensate for my looks (my life has been spent in compensation)—said nothing. At the end of the evening, he made a pass at me, and I was insulted. So I understand. I recognize that people who are beautiful have problems. But so do people who get upset stomachs from raw onions, and men with blue-orange color blindness, and left-handed persons everywhere. I just can't get into it; what interests me these days tends to have more to do with the problems of women who were not prom queens in high school. I'm sorry about this—my point of view is not fair to Alix Shulman, or to my friend who thinks she is losing her looks, or to me, or to the movement. But that's where it is. I'm working on it. Like all things about liberation, sisterhood is difficult.

August 1972

Erica Jong
(1942–   )

Of all the popular feminist novels that were published in the 1970s, Erica Jong's semiautobiographical *Fear of Flying* (1973) was not only the most financially successful but also the most sensational. Reviewed extensively by both male and female critics in popular and academic publications, *Fear of Flying* evoked both praise and damnation for its sexual frankness and raunchy language. Like other "consciousness-raising" novels emerging from the women's movement, *Fear of Flying* deals with female ambivalence about love versus career and the need for security versus the desire for independence, as well as with the conflict between male definitions of women's nature and roles and women's experiences of themselves and the world. However, Jong's work is unique in her use of often rollicking humor to expose the discrepancies between accepted notions of female and male sexuality and between her heroine, Isadora Wing's, sexual fantasies and the reality of her experiences—discrepancies that bring Isadora to a clearer understanding of who she is and what she wants. As Sarah Blacher Cohen asserts, "Isadora is the picaresque heroine satirically commenting on the foibles and pretensions of the educated and affluent in America and Europe. . . . But unlike the conventional rogue who observes more of the world's folly than his own, Isadora wryly scrutinizes herself and candidly reveals her comic eccentricities." Consequently, the reader laughs with Isadora both at others and at her own foolishness, which, as the novel progresses, she gradually sheds. Jong's sequel, *How to Save Your Own Life* (1977), continues the first-person confessions of Isadora, now a famous writer. Later novels include *Fanny* (1980), a parody of eighteenth-century novels, which purports to represent what Fanny Hill might have written if she could have told her own story, and *Parachutes and Kisses* (1984), which con-

386

tinues the story of Isadora Wing. In addition to writing
fiction, Jong is an accomplished poet whose first published
volume, *Fruits and Vegetables* (1971), garnered praise for its
rich, earthy images. Subsequent volumes, such as *Half-Lives*
(1973), *Loveroot* (1975), *At the Edge of the Body* (1979),
and *Ordinary Miracles* (1983), have been cited for their
ironic humor, fresh ideas about male-female relationships,
and the energetic language with which the poet explores and
integrates concepts about the nature of death, love, and the
body.

SOURCES   Cohen, Sarah Blacher. "The Jewish Literary Comediennes." *Comic Relief: Humor in Contemporary American Literature*, ed. Sarah Blacher Cohen. Urbana: University of Illinois Press, 1978, 172–186; Dresner, Zita. "Twentieth Century American Women Humorists." Diss. U of Maryland, 1982; Manfred, Freya. "Blood and Catsup." *Moons and Lions Tailes*. New York: Pergamon Press, 1976, 93–97; Peer, Elizabeth. "Sex and the Woman Writer." *Newsweek* 5 May 1975: 70–77; Reardon, Joan. "*Fear of Flying*: Developing the Feminist Novel." *International Journal of Women's Studies* 1.3 (May/June 1978): 306–320.

WORKS   *Fear of Flying* (1973); *Half-Lives* (1973); *Loveroot* (1975); *How to Save Your Own Life* (1977); *Fanny* (1980) and *Parachutes and Kisses* (1984)

from *Half-Lives*

Seventeen Warnings in Search of a Feminist Poem

For Aaron Asher

1   Beware of the man who denounces ambition;
        his fingers itch under his gloves.

2   Beware of the man who denounces war
        through clenched teeth.

3   Beware of the man who denounces women writers;
        his penis is tiny & cannot spell.

4   Beware of the man who wants to protect you;
        he will protect you from everything but himself.

5   Beware of the man who loves to cook;
        he will fill your kitchen with greasy pots.

6 Beware of the man who loves your soul;
      he is a bullshitter.

7 Beware of the man who denounces his mother;
      he is a son of a bitch.

8 Beware of the man who spells son of a bitch as one word;
      he is a hack.

9 Beware of the man who loves death too well;
      he is taking out insurance.

10 Beware of the man who loves life too well;
       he is a fool.

11 Beware of the man who denounces psychiatrists;
       he is afraid.

12 Beware of the man who trusts psychiatrists;
       he is in hock.

13 Beware of the man who picks your dresses;
       he wants to wear them.

14 Beware of the man you think is harmless;
       he will surprise you.

15 Beware of the man who cares for nothing but books;
       he will run like a trickle of ink.

16 Beware of the man who writes flowery love letters;
       he is preparing for years of silence.

17 Beware of the man who praises liberated women;
       he is planning to quit his job.

from *Loveroot*

Wrinkles

For Naomi Lazard

Sometimes I can't wait until I look
like Nadezhda Mandelstam.
—Naomi Lazard

My friends are tired.
The ones who are married are tired
of being married.
The ones who are single are tired
of being single.

They look at their wrinkles.
The ones who are single attribute their wrinkles
to being single.
The ones who are married attribute their wrinkles
to being married.

They have very few wrinkles.
Even taken together,
they have very few wrinkles.
But I cannot persuade them
to look at their wrinkles
collectively.
& I cannot persuade them that being married
or being single
has nothing to do with wrinkles.

Each one sees a deep & bitter groove,
a San Andreas fault across her forehead.
"It is only a matter of time
before the earthquake."
They trade the names of plastic surgeons
like recipes.

My friends are tired.
The ones who have children are tired
of having children.
The ones who are childless are tired
of being childless.

They love their wrinkles.
If only their wrinkles were deeper
they could hide.

Sometimes I think
(but do not dare to tell them)
that when the face is left alone to dig its grave,
the soul is grateful
& rolls in.

Rita Mae Brown

(1944–   )

Best known for her first novel, *Rubyfruit Jungle* (1973), an
exuberant, picaresque, semiautobiographical depiction of
growing up gay in America, Rita Mae Brown began her
writing career as a poet with the collections *The Hand that
Cradles the Rock* (1971) and *Songs to a Handsome Woman*
(1973). Initially rejected by New York publishing companies
as too limited in appeal, *Rubyfruit Jungle* was first published
by a small feminist press, Daughters, Inc., before being
acquired by Bantam Books in 1977 and eventually selling
over a million copies. Critics have attributed the popularity of
the novel to the book's "classic American success story" plot;
its heroine, Molly Bolt, a kind of lesbian Huck Finn; and its
humor, which can be broad and ribald or subtly ironic.
Neither a feminist tract nor a pathetic gay coming-out story,
the novel depicts a heroine who, like Erica Jong's Isadora
Wing in *Fear of Flying*, published the same year, asserts and
revels in her sexuality. She also, like the male underdog
heroes in traditional fiction and humor, triumphs over adver-
sity through her wit and resilience. At the same time, Molly
was unique in American literature in being a lesbian who is
attractive to men as well as to women, confident, high-
spirited, and eventually professionally successful, rather than
being portrayed as lesbians had been traditionally: as man-
nish, unhappy, and self-destructive. Brown's next book, *Six of
One* (1978), another commercial success, was also praised
for its humor. Drawn from personal sources, the novel
presents a comic history of a Pennsylvania-Maryland border
town from 1909 to 1980 from the point of view of three
generations of colorful, chatty, down home female inhabitants. Three more novels have followed: *Southern Discomfort*
(1982), about an affair between a white woman and a young
black man, set in Alabama in the 1920s; *Sudden Death*

(1983), about the professional women's tennis circuit; and *High Hearts* (1986), about women and their roles during the Civil War. Although resisting the label "lesbian writer," Brown has said that while she tries to offer positive images of gay women to counter traditional distorted notions, she uses humor to demolish offensive stereotypes in general.

SOURCES *Contemporary Authors,* New Rev. Series, Vol. 11; Fox, Terry Curtis. "Up From Cultdom and Down Again." *The Village Voice* 12 September 1977: 41; Harris, Bertha. Rev. of *Rubyfruit Jungle. The Village Voice* 4 April 1974: 36; Henze, Shelly Temchin. "Rita Mae Brown, All-American." *New Boston Review,* April/May 1979: 17–18; Klemesrud, Judy. "Underground Book Brings Fame to Lesbian Author." *New York Times* 26 September 1977: 38; Webb, Marilyn. Rev. of *Rubyfruit Jungle. Ms.,* June 1974: 35.

WORKS *Rubyfruit Jungle* (1973); *Six of One* (1978) and *Southern Discomfort* (1982)

from *Rubyfruit Jungle*

Chapter 4

Cheryl Spiegelglass lived on the other side of the woods. Her daddy was a used car salesman and they had more money than the rest of us in the Hollow. Cheryl wore a dress, even when she didn't have to. I hated her for that, plus she was always sucking up to the adults. Carrie loved her and said she looked exactly like Shirley Temple and why didn't I look like that instead of roaming around the fields in torn pants and dirty teeshirts. Cheryl and I had been friends of a sort since first grade so sometimes we played together. Carrie squirmed like a dog with a new bone every time I'd go off to the Spiegelglass's place, partly because she thought I was moving into polite society and partly because she hoped Cheryl would influence me for the better. Leroy usually tagged along. Neither Leroy nor I could stand it when Cheryl carted out her dolls, so when she had doll days we steered clear.

One time Cheryl decided to play nurse and we put napkins on our heads. Leroy was the patient and we painted him with iodine so he'd look wounded. A nurse, I wasn't gonna be no nurse. If I was gonna be something I was gonna be the doctor and give orders. I tore off my napkin, and told Cheryl I was the new doctor in town. Her face corroded.

"You can't be a doctor. Only boys can be doctors. Leroy's got to be the doctor."

"You're full of shit, Spiegelglass, Leroy's dumber than I am. I got to be the doctor because I'm the smart one and being a girl don't matter."

"You'll see. You think you can do what boys do but you're going to be a nurse, no two ways about it. It doesn't matter about brains, brains don't count. What counts is whether you're a boy or a girl."

I hauled off and belted her one. Shirley Temple Spiegelglass wasn't gonna tell me I couldn't be a doctor, nor nobody else. Course I didn't want to be a doctor. I was going to be president only I kept it a secret. But if I wanted to be a doctor I'd go be one and ain't nobody gonna tell me otherwise. So I got in trouble, of course. Cheryl went snotty-nosed into her mother and showed her the split lip I just gave her. Ethel Spiegelglass, mother hen, came flying out of that house, with the real aluminum awnings on it, and grabbed me by the teeshirt and gave me a piece of her mind, which was very uncomplimentary to me. She told me I couldn't see Cheryl for a week. That was fine with me. I didn't want to see nobody who'd tell me I couldn't be a doctor. Leroy and I started home.

"You really gonna be a doctor, Molly?"

"No, I ain't. I'm gonna be something lots better than a doctor. If you're a doctor you have to look at scabs and blood, besides only people in one place know your name. I got to be something that everybody knows my name. I'm going to be great."

"Great what?"

"That's a secret."

"Tell, come on, you can tell me, I'm your best friend."

"No, but I'll tell you when you're old enough to vote."

"When's that?"

"When you're twenty-one."

"That's ten years from now. I might be dead. I'll be an old man. Tell me now."

"No. Forget it. Anyway, whatever I am, I'll make sure you get some of the goodies so let me do it my own way."

Leroy settled for that, but with rancor.

We got home and Carrie was hopping mad. Somehow, between my splitting Cheryl's lip and us walking home, she gathered the news. "You big-mouthed brat. Can't play nice, can you? Can't act like a lady, no way. You're a heathen, that's what you are. You going up there and hitting that sweet child. How could you do such a thing? How am I gonna show my face around here? And you doing such a thing so soon after Jenna's passed away. You got no sense of respect. God knows, I've tried to bring you up right. You're not my child. You're wild, some wild animal. Your father must have been an ape or something."

Leroy's mouth fell open. He didn't know about me yet. Damn, I could have killed Carrie for shooting her big mouth off right then. Why'd she have to lay me out in front of fat Leroy? She's the one with no respect.

She ran on and she got me for this offense and that offense as well as one hundred trespasses. She's gonna make a lady out of me that summer, a crash program. She was going to keep me in the house to teach me to act right, cook, clean, and sew and that scared me.

"I can learn them things at night, you don't have to keep me in the house during the day."

"You're staying in this house with me, Miss Molly. No more going out with the roughhouse Hollow gang. That's one of the things wrong with you that I can fix. Your blood's another matter."

Leroy sat down quietly at the table and played with the diagonal pattern on the tablecloth. He wasn't liking this no more than I was. "If Molly stays in then I stay in."

Leroy, I love you.

"You ain't staying in here, Leroy Denman. You're a boy and you go out and play like boys are supposed to do. It's not right for you to learn those things."

"I don't care. I'm going where Molly goes. She's my best friend and my cousin and we got to stick together."

Carrie tried to reason with Leroy but he wouldn't budge until she started telling him what would happen to him if he picked up women's ways. Now old Leroy was shaking. Everybody would point at him and laugh. Nobody would play with him if he stayed in with me and soon they'd take him to the hospital and cut his thing off. Leroy sold out.

"Okay, Aunt Carrie, I won't stay in the house." He looked at me with utter defeat and guilt.

Leroy you ain't no friend of mine.

Carrie went down into the root cellar to get jars and rubber rings. Canning was going to be my first lesson. Before she hit the last step I leaped at the door, shut it, and locked it. She didn't notice it until she was ready to come up. Then she called out, "Molly, Leroy, door's shut, let me out."

Leroy was scared shitless. "Molly, let her out or they'll beat both of us good. Ep will get out the strap. You let her out."

"You take one step toward that door Leroy Denman and I'll slit your throat." I picked up the carving knife to make my words true. Leroy was between the devil and the deep blue sea.

"Molly, let me outa this root cellar!"

"I ain't lettin' you outa that root cellar until you promise to let me go free. Till you promise I don't have to stay in this house and learn to sew."

"I'll promise no such thing."

"Then you staying in that root cellar until Jesus comes back." I walked out the door and slammed it so she could hear, dragging Leroy with me every step of the way. No one was home. Florence was down at West York Market. Ted was at the Esso station and Carl and Ep were at work. No one could hear her pounding on that door and screaming her lungs out except Leroy and me. Her screams just scalded Leroy. "She's dying in there. You got to let her out. She'll go blind in the dark. Molly, please let her out."

"She ain't dying in there, she ain't going blind and I ain't lettin' her out."

"What'd she mean about you not being her child? About you being an animal?"

"She don't know what she's talking about. Talking through her hat. Don't pay no attention to her."

"Well, you don't look like her nor Carl neither. You don't look like any of us. Maybe you ain't hers. You're the only one in the Hollow with black hair and brown eyes. Hey, maybe she found you in the bull rushes like Moses."

"Shut up, Leroy." He was on the track. He was bound to find out sooner or later, since Carrie let the cat outa the bag so I guessed I'd have to tell him. "It's true what she says. I ain't hers. I don't belong to nobody. I got no true mother nor father and I ain't your real cousin. And this ain't my home. But it don't matter. It matters to her when she gets mad at me. She says I'm a bastard then. But it don't matter to me. But we're still cousins in our own way. Blood's just something old people talk about to make you feel bad. Hey Leroy, you don't care none, do you?"

Leroy was buckling under the weight of the news. "If we ain't true cousins then what are we? We got to be something."

"We're friends, though we might as well be cousins cause we're together all the time."

"What does it mean, bastard? What's the difference between you and me if you ain't Carrie and Carl's?"

"It means that your mother, Jenna, was married to Ep when she had you and my mother, whoever she is, wasn't married to my dad, whoever he is. That's exactly what it means."

"Well hell, Molly, what's being married?"

"It's a piece of paper, that's all I can figure. Some people don't even have to stand in front of a preacher, so it ain't religion. You can go on down to the courthouse and sign up like Uncle Ep signed up for the Marine Corps. Then you hear words said over you and you both sign this piece of paper and you're married."

"Could we get married?"

"Sure, but we got to be old, fifteen or sixteen, at least."

"That's only four more years, Molly. Let's get married."

"Leroy, we don't need to get married. We're together all the time. It's silly to get married. Besides I'm never gettin' married."

"Everybody gets married. It's something you have to do, like dying."

"I ain't doing it."

"I don't know, Molly, you're headin' for a hard life. You say you're gonna be a doctor or something great. Then you say you ain't gettin' married. You have to do some of the things everybody does or people don't like you."

"I don't care whether they like me or not. Everybody's stupid, that's what I think. I care if I like me, that's what I truly care about."

"Now that's the damndest dumb thing I ever heard. Everybody likes themself. Fact, Florence says you got to learn not to like yourself so much and like other people."

"Since when have you started listening to Florence? I can't like anybody if I don't like myself. Period."

"Molly, you are flat out crazy. Everybody likes themself, I am telling you."

"Oh yeah, smartass? Did you like yourself when you told Carrie you'd go out and play and leave me trapped inside with a sewing basket?"

Leroy's face flashed shame. Bull's eye. He switched the subject to save himself having to think on that one any more. "If you're not gonna get married then I won't either. Why do people get married anyway?"

"So's they can fuck."

"What?" Leroy's voice went into a high-pitched trail.

"Fuck."

"Molly Bolt, that is a dirty word."

"Dirty or not, that's what they do."

"Do you know what it means?"

"Not exactly but it has something to do with taking all your clothes off and messing around. Remember how upset Florence got when those two dogs were stuck together? That's what it is, I think. I don't know why anyone would want to do it, because those dogs didn't look very happy about it. I know that's what it is, besides I seen dirty books Ted hides under his mattress and you should see them. It'd make you sick for sure."

"Dirty books?"

"Yeah, Ted's been reading them ever since his voice started cracking. You ask me, I think his mind is cracking right along with it, myself."

"How'd you find out he was reading them?"

"Spied on him. After you go to sleep he turns the light back on so I knew he was up to something and I snuck out for a peek. There he was reading. Now the only books in this house are the Bible and our school books. I know he ain't reading none of them."

"You are truly smart, Molly," Leroy said with admiration.

"Yeah, I know."

Carrie's screams and poundings had died down by this time. "Let's go back and see if she is ready to make a deal."

A soft whimper came from behind the cellar door when I knocked on it. "Mom, you ready to come out now? You ready to make that deal?"

"I'm ready, just let me outa this dark hole. It's full of bugs."

I unbolted the door and opened it. Carrie was sitting on the root cellar steps like a little girl, holding her arms and crunched over. She looked up at me with pure hate and flew out of the cellar like a jack-in-the-box. She grabbed me by the hair before I could dodge and started hitting me in the face, stomach, and when I doubled over like a porcupine, she hit me on the back with both fists at once. I could feel my eye start to close up already. I was so busy trying to get away from her that I didn't hear what she was calling me. Leroy fled the house in total terror. He didn't once try to gang up on her. If he'd blasted her with a couple good kicks, I might have gotten away. But Leroy never was tactical, plus he had a streak of the coward in him.

That night I was sent to bed without supper. I didn't care because I couldn't eat my supper anyway. My mouth was all swelled up ugly, and it hurt to talk. The whole crew got Carrie's version of my sins and I couldn't open my mouth in self-defense. I guess she thought she'd shame me in front of all of them, but I stared at her with real pride as I marched into the bedroom. She wasn't going to beat me down, no how. Let 'em all get mad at me. I wasn't giving her a goddamned inch, not one. I crawled in bed but I was so sore I couldn't sleep and late that night I heard Carrie and Carl get in a blowout. Only time I ever heard Carl raise his voice, and I bet the rest of the house heard him too. "Carrie, the child's high-spirited and she's smart, you got to remember that. That kid's quicker than all of us put together. She started reading all by herself when she was three with no help from any of us. You got to treat her with some respect for her brains. She's a good girl, just full of life and the devil, that's all."

"I don't give a goddamn how brainy she is, she don't act natural. It ain't right for a girl to be running all around with the boys at all hours. She climbs trees, takes cars apart, and worse, she tells them what to do and they listen to her. She don't want to learn none of the things she has to know to get a husband. Smart as she is, a woman can't get on in this world without a husband. We can't be sending no girl to school as it is. It's the boys we got to worry about. Them's the ones will be earning livings. You make too much of her head."

"Molly is going to college."

"Big talk."

"My daughter is going to college."

"Your daughter, your daughter. That's a laugh. That's the first time I heard you say that. She's Ruby Drollinger's bastard that's who she is. Where do you get off with this daughter crap?"

"She's mine as much as if I'd been her real father and I watch out for her."

"Real father. What right have you got to talk about being a real father? If you'd been a real father I'd have my own daughter and she wouldn't be like that wild hellcat you stick up for. She'd be a real little lady like Cheryl Spiegelglass. Your daughter, you make me sick."

"Honey, you're all upset. You don't know how you're sounding. Molly is yours, just as if she was your own. A child's got to have parents and you're her mother."

"I am not her mother. I am not her mother," Carrie shrieked. "She didn't come from my body. Florence had babies come from her body, and she tells me it's not the same. She knows. She told me I'll never know what it's like to be a real mother. What do you know? Men don't know about these things. Men don't know anything."

"Mother, father, what's the difference, Cat? It's how you feel about the child, it's got nothing to do with your body. Molly is my daughter, and if it's the last thing I do, I'm going to see that girl gets a chance in this world neither one of us had. You want her to spend her life like us, sitting back here in the sticks, can't even make enough money for a new dress or dinner in a restaurant? You want her to live a life like you—dishes, cooking, and never going out except maybe to a movie once a month if we can afford it? The child's got brightness in her, Cat, so let her be! She'll go to big cities and be somebody. I can see it in her. She's got dreams and ambition and she's smart as a whip. Nobody can pull one over on that kid. Be proud for her. You got a daughter to be proud of."

"You turn my guts. She'll be somebody. That's all I need, Molly traipsing off to a big city like Philadelphia and thinking she's better than the rest of us. She's got high ways now. You make her worse. She'll go off to college and a big city and forget you ever lived. That's the thanks you'll get. She don't care for nobody but her own self, that kid. She's a savage animal, locked me in the cellar. You don't live here with her every day and see her like I do. She's wild I tell you. And how far's she gonna get with all her brains considering her background? We ain't people that can do her good in fancy places. She'll be ashamed of us. And she's a bastard to boot. You got pipe dreams for your daughter." She hit on daughter with such bile it made me shudder.

"Cat, my mind is made up. Molly is having her chance whether you like it or not. She's getting an education. Now you learn to live with it, and you're not to lock her in this house with you. Let her run all over the whole goddamn county and let her knock shit out of Cheryl Spiegelglass. I never liked that kid anyway."

"I have one think to say to you, Carl Bolt. We've never had a fight between us until that child came under our roof. And we never would have a fight like this if you could have given me a baby, but you had syphilis, that's what you had. You ain't fit to be nobody's father. If I could have had my own all this would be different. This is all your doing and I'll never forget it."

"My mind's made up." His voice was soft with hurt feelings.

"We'll just see about that," Carrie hedged. She had to get the last word in, whether anyone listened or not.

Toni Cade Bambara

(1939–   )

Born and raised in New York City, Toni Cade Bambara
received a B.A. from Queens College and an M.A. from City
College. In addition to traveling and lecturing in the United
States and abroad, Bambara has held positions as a New
York City welfare investigator, a program director at New
York City community center, an English instructor in the
SEEK program at City College, a member of Black Studies
programs at Rutgers and Duke Universities, a consultant in
Women's Studies at Emory and Atlanta Universities, and
writer-in-residence at Spelman College. Bambara's dual con-
cern for black consciousness and feminism are articulated in
The Black Woman (1970), a collection of essays that she
edited. She next published an anthology, *Tales and Short
Stories for Black Folks*, which was named Outstanding Book
of 1972 in juvenile literature by *The New York Times*.
Collections of her own short stories, *Gorilla, My Love*
(1972) and *The Sea Birds Are Still Alive* (1977), have been
critical and popular successes, and her novel *The Salt Eaters*
won the American Book Award in 1981. Although most of
the stories in *Gorilla, My Love* are concerned with children
or written from the point of view of a young black girl
coming into maturity, "My Man Bovanne" is representative of
Bambara's fiction in its depiction of black life—relationships
at home and in the neighborhoods—its use of street dialect,
its celebration of black pride, and the warmth and wit with
which Bambara draws her characters, especially adolescents,
elderly people, and females of all ages and types. Moreover,
the story deals with a theme that, as Mary Helen Washington
notes, appears in the work of black women writers from Zora
Neale Hurston and Dorothy West to Lorraine Hansberry and
Paule Marshall: the conflict between mothers and daughters,
old-generation traditional values and new-generation militant

400

ideals. However, Bambara's deft use of irony shatters the stereotype of the Black Mother, upsets clichés about roles, and recasts the conflict in a new light.

SOURCES   Chevigny, Bell Gale. "Stories of Solidarity and Selfhood." Rev. of *Gorilla, My love. Village Voice* 12 April 1973: 39–40; Evans, Mari, ed. *Black Women Writers: A Critical Evaluation 1950–1980*. New York: Doubleday, 1984; Macauley, Robie. Rev. of *The Sea Birds Are Still Alive. New York Times Book Review* 27 March 1977: 7; Tate, Claudia, ed. "Toni Cade Bambara." *Black Women Writers At Work*. New York: Continuum, 1983, 12–38; Tyler, Anne. "At the Still Center of a Dream." Rev. of *The Salt Eaters. Washington Post Book World* 30 March 1980: 1–2; Washington, Mary Helen. Introduction. *Black-Eyed Susans*. New York: Anchor Books; 1975.

WORKS   *Gorilla, My Love* (1972)

from *Gorilla My Love*

My Man Bovanne

Blind people got a hummin jones if you notice. Which is understandable completely once you been around one and notice what no eyes will force you into to see people, and you get past the first time, which seems to come out of nowhere, and it's like you in church again with fat-chest ladies and old gents gruntin a hum low in the throat to whatever the preacher be saying. Shakey Bee bottom lip all swole up with Sweet Peach and me explainin how come the sweet-potato bread was a dollar-quarter this time stead of dollar regular and he say uh hunh he understand, then he break into this *thizzin* kind of hum which is quiet, but fiercesome just the same, if you ain't ready for it. Which I wasn't. But I got used to it and the onliest time I had to say somethin bout it was when he was playin checkers on the stoop one time and he commenst to hummin quite churchy seem to me. So I says, "Look here Shakey Bee, I can't beat you and Jesus too." He stop.

So that's how come I asked My Man Bovanne to dance. He ain't my man mind you, just a nice ole gent from the block that we all know cause he fixes things and the kids like him. Or used to fore Black Power got hold their minds and mess em around till they can't be civil to ole folks. So we at this benefit for my niece's cousin who's runnin for somethin with this Black party somethin or other behind her. And I press up close to dance with Bovanne who blind and I'm hummin and he hummin, chest to chest like talkin. Not jammin my breasts into the man. Wasn't bout tits. Was bout vibrations. And he dug it and asked me what color dress I had on and how my hair was fixed and how I was doin without a man, not nosy but nice-like, and who was at this affair and was the canapés dainty-stingy or healthy enough to get hold of proper. Comfy and cheery is what I'm tryin to get across. Touch talkin like the heel of the hand on the tambourine or on a drum.

But right away Joe Lee come up on us and frown for dancin so close to the man. My own son who knows what kind of warm I am about; and don't grown men call me long distance and in the middle of the night for a little Mama comfort? But he frown. Which ain't right since Bovanne can't see and defend himself. Just a nice old man who fixes toasters and busted irons and bicycles and things and changes the lock on my door when my men friends get messy. Nice man. Which is not why they invited him. Grass roots you see. Me and Sister Taylor and the woman who does heads at Mamies and the man from the barber shop, we all there on account of we grass roots. And I ain't never been souther than Brooklyn Battery and no more country than the window box on my fire escape. And just yesterday my kids tellin me to take them countrified rags off my head and be cool. And now can't get Black enough to suit em. So everybody passin sayin My Man Bovanne. Big deal, keep steppin and don't even stop a minute to get the man a drink or one of them cute sandwiches or tell him what's goin on. And him standin there with a smile ready case someone do speak he want to be ready. So that's how come I pull him on the dance floor and we dance squeezin past the tables and chairs and all them coats and people standin round up in each other face talkin bout this and that but got no use for this blind man who mostly fixed skates and skooters for all these folks when they was just kids. So I'm pressed up close and we touch talkin with the hum. And here come my daughter cuttin her eye at me like she do when she tell me about my "apolitical" self like I got hoof and mouf disease and there ain't no hope at all. And I don't pay her no mind and just look up in Bovanne shadow face and tell him his stomach like a drum and he laugh. Laugh real loud. And here come my youngest, Task, with a tap on my elbow like he the third grade monitor and I'm cuttin up on the line to assembly.

"I was just talkin on the drums," I explained when they hauled me into the kitchen. I figured drums was my best defense. They can get ready for drums what with all this heritage business. And Bovanne stomach just like that drum Task give me when he come back from Africa. You just touch it and it hum thizzm, thizzm. So I stuck to the drum story. "Just drummin that's all."

"Mama, what are you talkin about?"

"She had too much to drink," say Elo to Task cause she don't hardly say nuthin to me direct no more since that ugly argument about my wigs.

"Look here Mama," say Task, the gentle one. "We just tryin to pull your coat. You were makin a spectacle of yourself out there dancing like that."

"Dancin like what?"

Task run a hand over his left ear like his father for the world and his father before that.

"Like a bitch in heat," say Elo.

"Well uhh, I was goin to say like one of them sex-starved ladies gettin on in years and not too discriminating. Know what I mean?"

I don't answer cause I'll cry. Terrible thing when your own children talk to you like that. Pullin me out the party and hustlin me into some stranger's kitchen in the back of a bar just like the damn police. And ain't like I'm old old. I can still wear me some sleeveless dresses without the meat hangin off my arm. And I keep up with some thangs through my kids. Who ain't kids no more. To hear them tell it. So I don't say nuthin.

"Dancin with that tom," say Elo to Joe Lee, who leanin on the folks' freezer. "His feet can smell a cracker a mile away and go into their shuffle number post haste. And them eyes. He could be a little considerate and put on some shades. Who wants to look into them blown-out fuses that—"

"Is this what they call the generation gap?" I say.

"Generation gap," spits Elo, like I suggested castor oil and fricassee possum in the milk-shakes or somethin. "That's a white concept for a white phenomenon. There's no generation gap among Black people. We are a col—"

"Yeh, well never mind," says Joe Lee. "The point is Mama . . . well, it's pride. You embarrass yourself and us too dancin like that."

"I wasn't shame." Then nobody say nuthin. Them standin there in they pretty clothes with drinks in they hands and gangin up on me, and me in the third-degree chair and nary a olive to my name. Felt just like the police got hold to me.

"First of all," Task say, holdin up his hand and tickin off the offenses, "the dress. Now that dress is too short, Mama, and too low-cut for a woman your age. And Tamu's going to make a speech tonight to kick off the campaign and will be introducin you and expecting you to organize the council of elders—"

"Me? Didn nobody ask me nuthin. You mean Nisi? She change her name?"

"Well, Norton was supposed to tell you about it. Nisi wants to introduce you and then encourage the older folks to form a Council of Elders to act as an advisory—"

"And you going to be standing there with your boobs out and that wig on your head and that hem up to your ass. And people'll say, 'Ain't that the horny bitch that was grindin with the blind dude?' "

"Elo, be cool a minute," say Task, gettin to the next finger. "And then there's the drinkin. Mama, you know you can't drink cause next thing you know you be laughin loud and carryin on," and he grab another finger for the loudness. "And then there's the dancin. You been tattooed on the man for four records straight and slow draggin even on the fast numbers. How you think that look for a woman your age?"

"What's my age?"

"What?"

"I'm axin you all a simple question. You keep talkin bout what's proper for a woman my age. How old am I anyhow?" And Joe Lee slams his eyes shut and squinches up his face to figure. And Task run a hand over his ear and stare into his glass like the ice cubes goin calculate for him. And Elo just starin at the top of my head like she goin rip the wig off any minute now.

"Is your hair braided up under that thing? If so, why don't you take it off? You always did do a neat cornroll."

"Uh huh," cause I'm thinkin how she couldn't undo her hair fast enough talking bout cornroll so countrified. None of which was the subject. "How old, I say?"

"Sixtee-one or—"

"You a damn lie Joe Lee Peoples."

"And that's another thing," say Task on the fingers.

"You know what you all can kiss," I say, gettin up and brushin the wrinkles out my lap.

"Oh, Mama," Elo say, puttin a hand on my shoulder like she hasn't done since she left home and the hand landin light and not sure it supposed to be there. Which hurt me to my heart. Cause this was the child in our happiness fore Mr. Peoples die. And I carried that child strapped to my chest till she was nearly two. We was close is what I'm tryin to tell you.

Cause it was more me in the child than the others. And even after Task it was the girlchild I covered in the night and wept over for no reason at all less it was she was a chub-chub like me and not very pretty, but a warm child. And how did things get to this, that she can't put a sure hand on me and say Mama we love you and care about you and you entitled to enjoy yourself cause you a good woman?

"And then there's Reverend Trent," say Task, glancin from left to right like they hatchin a plot and just now lettin me in on it. "You were suppose to be talking with him tonight, Mama, about giving us his basement for campaign headquarters and—"

"Didn nobody tell me nuthin. If grass roots mean you kept in the dark I can't use it. I really can't. And Reven Trent a fool anyway the way he tore into the widow man up there on Edgecomb cause he wouldn't take in three of them foster children and the woman not even comfy in the ground yet and the man's mind messed up and—"

"Look here," say Task. "What we need is a family conference so we can get all this stuff cleared up and laid out on the table. In the meantime I think we better get back into the other room and tend to business. And in the meantime, Mama, see if you can't get to Reverend Trent and—"

"You want me to belly rub with the Reven, that it?" "Oh damn," Elo say and go through the swingin door.

"We'll talk about all this at dinner. How's tomorrow night, Joe Lee?" While Joe Lee being self-important I'm wonderin who's doin the cookin and how come no body ax me if I'm free and do I get a corsage and things like that. Then Joe nod that it's O.K. and he go through the swingin door and just a little hubbub come through from the other room. Then Task smile his smile, lookin just like his daddy and he leave. And it just me in this stranger's kitchen, which was a mess I wouldn't never let my kitchen look like. Poison you just to look at the pots. Then the door swing the other way and it's My Man Bovanne standin there sayin Miss Hazel but lookin at the deep fry and then at the steam table, and most surprised when I come up on him from the other direction and take him on out of there. Pass the folks pushin up towards the stage where Nisi and some other people settin and ready to talk, and folks gettin to the last of the sandwiches and the booze fore they settle down in one spot and listen serious. And I'm thinkin bout tellin Bovanne what a lovely long dress Nisi got on and the earrings and her hair piled up in a cone and the people bout to hear how we all gettin screwed and gotta form our own party and everybody there listenin and lookin. But instead I just haul the man on out of there, and Joe Lee and his wife look at me like I'm terrible, but they ain't said boo to the man yet. Cause he blind and old and don't nobody there need him since they grown up and don't need they skates fixed no more.

"Where we goin, Miss Hazel?" Him knowin all the time.

"First we gonna buy you some dark sunglasses. Then you comin with me to the supermarket so I can pick up tomorrow's dinner, which is goin to be a grand thing proper and you invited. Then we goin to my house."

"That be fine. I surely would like to rest my feet." Bein cute, but you got to let men play out they little show, blind or not. So he chat on bout how tired he is and how he appreciate me takin him in hand this way. And I'm thinkin I'll have him change the lock on my door first thing. Then I'll give the man a nice warm bath with jasmine leaves in the water and a little Epsom salt on the sponge to do his back. And then a good rubdown with rose water and olive oil. Then a cup of lemon tea with a taste in it. And a little talcum, some of that fancy stuff Nisi mother sent over last Christmas. And then a massage, a good face massage round the forehead which is the worryin part. Cause you gots to take care of the older folks. And let them know they still needed to run the mimeo machine and keep the spark plugs clean and fix the mailboxes for folks who might help us get the breakfast program goin, and the school for the little kids and the campaign and all. Cause old folks is the nation. That what Nisi was sayin and I mean to do my part.

"I imagine you are a very pretty woman, Miss Hazel."

"I surely am," I say just like the hussy my daughter always say I was.

Nikki Giovanni

(1943–   )

The poetry and prose of Nikki Giovanni is characterized by a tough wit and an irreverence that seem always to have been part of her personal credo. From her days as a student activist at Fisk University in the 1960s to her public appearances and readings, Giovanni has been an outspoken, controversial writer whose pride in being black and female infuses her work. She was born Yolande Cornelia Giovanni, Jr., in Knoxville, Tennessee, and grew up in a middleclass suburb of Cincinnati. Her years at Fisk transformed her from a Goldwater supporter to an advocate of black power during the civil rights movement, and after graduation she organized the first Cincinnati Black Arts Festival before attending graduate school, first at the University of Pennsylvania School of Social Work and then at the School of Fine Arts of Columbia University. By the time she was in her mid-twenties, Giovanni had published two books of poetry—*Black Feeling, Black Talk* (1967) and *Black Judgement* (1968)—and she quickly began to receive recognition as a talented and militant black writer. Some thought it audacious for her to publish an autobiography before she was thirty, but *Gemini* (1971), subtitled *An Extended Autobiographical Statement on My First Twenty-Five Years of Being a Black Poet,* is a series of essays that express her views on not only her own life, but also families, politics, and images of blacks on television and film. Giovanni's own association with the media began in 1971 when she made a recording of some of her poetry read against a background of gospel music; the success of this album, *Truth Is On Its Way,* led to even greater public recognition and a number of awards, including life membership in the National Council of Negro Women and an honorary doctorate from Wilberforce University. Since the early 1970s, Giovanni has published several volumes of poetry, including *The Women and the Men* (1975), which includes the poem "Woman," and *Cotton Candy on a Rainy Day* (1978), from which "Housecleaning" is taken. The poems speak in a self-assured voice of women's problematic relationships with men—an enduring theme in women's humor—and in the ironic inversions of their closings are reminiscent of the method of Dorothy Parker.

SOURCES   *Dictionary of Literary Biography,* Vol. 41, pp. 135–151; Giovanni, Nikki. *Gemini: An Extended Autobiographical Statement on My First Twenty-five Years of Being a Black Poet.* New York: Bobbs-Merrill, 1971.

WORKS   *Gemini* (1971); *The Women and the Men* (1975) and *Cotton Candy on a Rainy Day* (1978)

from *The Women and the Men*

Woman

she wanted to be a blade
of grass amid the fields
but he wouldn't agree
to be the dandelion

she wanted to be a robin singing
through the leaves
but he refused to be
her tree

she spun herself into a web
and   looking for a place to rest
turned to him
but he stood straight
declining to be her corner

she tried to be a book
but he wouldn't read

she turned herself into a bulb
but he wouldn't let her grow

she decided to become
a woman
and though he still refused
to be a man
she decided it was all
right

from *Cotton Candy on a Rainy Day*

Housecleaning

i always liked housecleaning
even as a child
i dug straightening
the cabinets
putting new paper on
the shelves
washing the refrigerator
inside out
and unfortunately this habit has
carried over and i find
i must remove you
from my life

Ntosake Shange
(1948–   )

Born Paulette Williams, in Trenton, New Jersey, Shange
adopted her Zulu name in 1971 as an act of protest against a
racist culture and an assertion of her independence as a black
woman in an oppressive society. After graduating from Barnard College in 1970, Shange moved to California where, in
addition to working on a master's degree at the University of
Southern California, she became involved with the black and
women's movements of the early 1970s. Her associations
with jazz musicians, African dance, third-world women writers and artists, and feminist support groups led to readings in
San Francisco of the performance pieces that eventually were
produced in New York as her "choreopoem" *For Colored
Girls Who Have Considered Suicide . . . When the Rainbow
is Enuf* (1975). An immediate success, praised by New York
critics such as Jack Kroll and Edith Oliver for its dramatic
power, poetic beauty, social irony, and strong passion, *For
Colored Girls . . .* also became a focus of controversy in the
black community for its feminist stance and for what was
perceived by some as a negative portrayal of relationships
between black men and women. However, as Michele Wallace
points out, the real concern of the play is to undercut the
deprecatory stereotypes of black women that have been
promulgated in American culture and to explore honestly the
realities of being black and female in America. Shange's use
of humor, street idiom, poetry, and realistic detail to depict
the joys and horrors that black women experience in growing
up, coming of age, and confronting the dual obstacles of
gender and race is also evident in her subsequent work: the
play *Spell #7* (1979); the novels *Sassafras, Cypress, and
Indigo* (1982) and *Betsey Brown* (1985); and the nonfiction
collection *See No Evil: Prefaces, Essays, and Accounts,
1976–1983* (1984). These varied works are connected by

410

their verbal energy, humor, emphasis on the emotional responses that unite rather than divide human beings, vivid depictions of characters and settings, and the links that Shange establishes between African, Afro-American, and other third-world American women's cultures, styles, and rhythms.

SOURCES   *Contemporary Authors*, Vols. 85–88; Grumbach, Doris. "Ntosake Shange's Trio." *The Washington Post* 22 August 1981: 1–2; Tate, Claudia, ed. "Ntosake Shange." *Black Women Writers At Work*. New York: Continuum, 1983. 149–174; Wallace, Michele. Rev. of *For Colored Girls . . . Who Have Considered Suicide When the Rainbow is Enuf. The Village Voice* 16 August 1976: 108–109; Willard, Nancy. "Life Abounding in St. Louis." *New York Times Book Review* 12 May 1985: 12.

WORKS   *For Colored Girls Who Have Considered Suicide . . . When the Rainbow is Enuf* (1975); *Sassafras, Cypress, and Indigo* (1982) and *Betsey Brown* (1985)

from *For Colored Girls Who Have Considered Suicide . . .*
When the Rainbow is Enuf

Lady in Red

without any assistance or guidance from you
i have loved you assiduously for 8 months 2 wks & a day
i have been stood up four times
i've left 7 packages on yr doorstep
forty poems 2 plants & 3 handmade notecards i left
town so i cd send to you have been no help to me
on my job
you call at 3:00 in the mornin on weekdays
so i cd drive 27½ miles cross the bay before i go to work
charmin charmin
but you are of no assistance
i want you to know
this waz an experiment
to see how selfish i cd be
if i wd really carry on to snare a possible lover
if i waz capable of debasin my self for the love of another

if i cd stand not being wanted
when i wanted to be wanted
& i cannot
so
with no further assistance & no guidance from you
i am endin this affair

this note is attached to a plant
i've been waterin since the day i met you
you may water it
yr damn self

from *Nappy Edges*

wow . . . yr just like a man!

he said hangin out with her waz just like hangin out witta man/ she
cd drink & talk pungently/ even tell a risqué joke or two/ more n
that/ she cd talk abt art/ & that musta made her a man/ cuz she sure
cdnt scratch her balls/ or pee further n him/ or fuck a tiny fella in
the ass/ she didn't have a football letter/ & she cdnt talk abt how
many women she'd had/ but then we dont know that either/ all we
know is he said she waz just like a fella/ & here she waz thinkin she
waz as good as any woman/ which to her meant she waz as good as
any fella/ but that's an idea without a large following in these parts/
any way the way the relationship evolved/ he & this woman he waz
thinkin waz like a fella/ well they worked together alla the time/
had poetry readings/ did exercises/ saw shows/ cut-up everybody
else's work on the phone/ & you must know since/ she hadta be a
fella to understand/ probably you awready guessed/ their shared
craft waz poetry/ cuz words/ are a man's thing/ you know/ the
craftsmen/ the artisan/ the artist/ they are all in men/ why else wd
you haveta put 'ess' on the end of every damn thing/ if it waznt to
signify when/ a woman waz doin something that men do/

so anyway they were poets/ & this guy well he liked this woman's
work/ cuz it waznt 'personal'/ i mean a man can get personal in his

work when he talks politics or bout his dad/ but women start alla
this foolishness bout their bodies & blood & kids & what's really goin
on at home/ well & that aint poetry/ that's goo-ey gaw/ female
stuff/ & she waznt like that/ this woman they callt a poet/ wrote
mostly abt 'the music'/ ya know albert ayler/ david murray/ bobo
shaw/ olu dara/ archie shepp/ oliver lake/ she even had a whole
series for the art ensemble of chicago/ now this waz phenomenal/
cuz these were men who were poets/ were mostly into coltrane or
bebop/ not havin moved ahead with the times/ & they thot this
woman/ musta slept with alla these guys/ cuz everybody knows/
women dont really know how to listen to music/ or even what's a
gift like billie holiday/ why betty carter & vi redd were never treated
weird by musicians who were men/ they just didnt get any work/ so
this woman who waz a poet/ musta changed her ways considerably/
& the other poets liked that/ there waznt any reason/ to hold up a
readin cuz some bitch waz late gettin up from a good dickin down/
tho some poetry readings never started cuz some men who were
poets cd never get it up.

but this woman she waz alone a lot of the time with her books fulla
these crazy poems abt this wild music/ so that waz awright/ somebody asked her one time to tell the truth/ waz she run out on her
husband/ & she laughed/ they tried to make her blood sister/ a lover
she had in the closet/ but when the mother of both the woman who
waz a poet & the sister suspected of bein a lover in the closet
showed up to a readin with the husband of the mother & the father
of the poet who waz a woman & the lover in the closet/ that rumor
cooled out/ still there waz a problem/ the poet who waz a woman
who wrote like a man faced and that waz that she waz a woman &
when the poets who were men/ were feelin fiercely good abt bein
men/ they often forgot that this waz a woman whom they all said
waz more like a man cuz she cd talk/ & she didnt write none of that
personal stuff/ they forgot they had said this/ & started to make the
wet mouth & heavy arms with her/ & she waz stunned cuz she waz
the one who had no gender to speak of cuz here she waz a woman
who waz really more like one of the fellas/ but that waz when the
fellas were bein poets/ when the fellas were bein fellas/ they didnt
care if she cd talk or not/ & they sometimes didnt recognize her &
told her they met her in seattle last year at their mother's/

she waz very nice to the guys & sometimes fed them like their own
mamas wd have/ or lent them some money like a bank wda if banks
weren't apriori scared to death of poets in need of money/ sometimes
when one of their women threw them out/ they stayed at her house/
cuz there waz never a man at her house/ that waz one of the unspoken rules of her bein considered one of the fellas/ or a poet/ cuz if
there waz a man at her house/ like there waz one time/ when she
forgot that in order to be considered a poet she hadta be one of the
guys/ the poets who were men/ got very indignant & walked out cuz
she waz romancin some fella who waznt even a poet & wdnt be able
to feed them that night/ not that they had callt or anything/ see/
among poets who are men & women deigned poets by these men/
there is a strange/ spontaneity/ that says they cd come visit whenever they liked & she mustnt call cuz their ol ladies didn't understand that she waz one of the fellas/ & they made it hard on any
fella who waznt a poet to be a lover of hers/ cuz they wd show up
all the time with these wounds from the police/ an irate poet/ at-
tackin the doorbell/ one had his nose broken for stealin an image &
landed up in her kitchen/ when the woman who waz a poet waz just
abt to get down to business in her bed/ & that kinda thing is hard for
a man who is not a poet to take/ plus/ they wd quiz the man who
waz not a poet abt poetry/ & since he waz not a poet & didn't know
the verses of the whole cadre/ they determined to warn their com-
rade/ against this sorta man who cdnt recite poems/ & so her life as
a man with the men who were poets waz quite confusing & very
hassled.

so one day she decided that it waz probably awright that the men
who were poets thot of her as one of their own kind/ sometimes/ &
sometimes she waz mistaken for their mother/ or a misplaced lover/
but one day when she waz reading to the group/ in a pub somewhere in new york or california/ she said/ as a woman & a poet/
i've decided to wear my ovaries on my sleeve/ raise my poems on
my milk/ & count my days by the flow of my mensis/ the men who
were poets were aghast/ they fled the scene in fear of becoming un-
clean/ they all knew those verses/ & she waz left with an arena of
her own/ where words & notions/ imply 'she'/ where havin lovers is
quite common regardless of sex/ or profession/ where music &
mensis/ are considered very personal/ & language a tool for exploring space/

the moral of the story:

#1: when words & manners leave you no space for yrself/ make a poem/ very personal/ very clear/ & yr obstructions will join you or disappear/

#2: if yr obstructions dont disappear/ repeat over & over again/ the new definitions/ til the ol ones have no more fight in them/ then cover them with syllables you've gathered from other dyin species/

#3: a few soft words have sent many a woman to her back with her thighs flung open & eager/ a few more/ will find us standin up & speakin in our own tongue to whomever we goddam please.

Cyra McFadden

(1937–   )

The daughter of a celebrated rodeo announcer, Cy Taillon, Cyra McFadden spent her early childhood traveling from one western town to another in the back seat of a Packard, an experience that, she says, meant that she learned to read "from the last page to the first, the result of long exposure to Burma Shave signs." McFadden has detailed these early years in her memoir *Rain or Shine* (1986), in which she credits her "silver-tongued" father for her love of language. Following her parents' divorce, she lived with her mother and stepfather, whose combined neuroses made her yearn for her charismatic father, despite his alcoholism and hand-to-mouth existence at that point. One result of McFadden's (the surname is that of her second husband) checkered childhood and adolescence is a keen perception of the games and pretentions by which many people live, a perception that prepared her well for writing her best-selling satiric novel *The Serial*, published in 1977. *The Serial* is a soap opera in written form and, as the subtitle tells us, a tongue-in-cheek documentary of "a year in the life of Marin County [California]" in the mid-1970s, before the terms "yuppie" and "Valley Girl" were in wide currency. Described accurately by McFadden as social satire, *The Serial* exposes the fads, language, and habits of women who, having little else to do, watch each others' waistlines and husbands. The book also documents some of the experiences of women caught up in the women's movement of the 1970s: divorce, communal living, and consciousness-raising groups. For a number of years a resident of San Francisco, McFadden completed both B.A. and M.A. degrees at San Francisco State University after her second marriage. She has taught English at San Francisco State, and has contributed articles to the *New York Times, McCall's, The Nation,* and *Smithsonian.* She has most re-

416

cently written a biweekly column for the San Francisco *Examiner*.

SOURCES   *Contemporary Authors*, vols. 77–80; McFadden, Cyra. *Rain or Shine: A Family Memoir*. New York: Knopf, 1986.

WORKS   *The Serial* (1977)

from *The Serial*

Carol's Empty Closet

Kate flashed on Sylvia Schmidt right away, on the deck of La Veranda, while she was raising her blood sugar level with a plate of gnocchi. But she kept a low profile rather than going over to rap. For one thing, she was pretty sure the guy Sylvia was having lunch with was her ex-husband and she couldn't remember which one. For another, she and Harvey had just spent this weekend on the dinner-party circuit, and Kate, who'd gained four pounds on guacamole alone, had stepped on the scale this morning and got the bad news.

Of course she still wasn't exactly *gross*. It hadn't helped, though, that Harvey had appeared over her shoulder, watched the needle on the scale swing slowly to the right, shaken his head and hit her with "Wow . . . Fat City."

So here she was, wearing her "fat dress," an ancient chemise now unfashionably short that left her piggy little knees hanging out, while Sylvia was wearing this throwaway-chic jumpsuit Kate had seen in Gigi's window on Friday and hadn't been able to zip when she tried it on. What was worse, the jumpsuit, a French import, had this size tag reading "42."

Okay, okay. She knew she shouldn't be munching out on carbos like this; substitute gratification wasn't the answer. Sylvia Schmidt was eating this austere green salad. But Sylvia didn't have a husband who put her down; she didn't have an ongoing husband at all. She had an A-frame on Panoramic with a sauna and a Jacuzzi instead of a Sutton Manor tract house with beer bottles full of rocks in the toilet tanks. She went to The Golden Door twice a year instead of squeezing in a week in a Tahoe motel, with a kitchenette and a black-and-white TV, at the wrong end of the lake. Sylvia had a together life.

Kate thought wistfully how Gloria Vanderbilt was right and you couldn't be too thin or too rich. She also speculated that Gloria Vanderbilt didn't have to practically live on Knudsen's lo-cal cottage cheese to keep from turning into Gargantua.

"I can't *believe* this," Sylvia said, when she saw Kate and came across the deck. "I mean, talk about your ESP. Wow, I was just picking you up on my radar, you know? Loud and clear. You must have a fantastic aura." She pushed her Dior shades down on her nose and looked over them at Kate's gnocchi. "Hey, I wish I could eat stuff like that. I just have to *look* at it, you know? . . . Fat City."

"I love your jumpsuit, Sylvia," Kate said. "Dynamite. Really."

"Oh, this. It's really old, you know? I keep on wearing it because Harry likes it, that's all; I mean, I figure it's the least I can do."

"Are you and Harry still tight?" Kate asked. "After the divorce and all? I mean, I'm kinda surprised."

"Kate," Sylvia said, "Harry and I can still relate to each other. Just because the relationship is over, that doesn't mean we can't have a *relationship*. Listen, why don't you come on over and hang out with us? You can bring that pasta or whatever it is along if you can lift it. Anyway, I've got something really heavy to lay on you. That's why I was picking up these vibes about you, you know? There aren't any accidents."

"Sylvia," Kate said warily, "I don't know if I'm ready for it. Harvey and I are going through this *dynamic* right now, and it's kinda where I'm at. I haven't got a lot of psychic energy left over for social interaction. So whatever it is, maybe you should just run it by me right here. Off the wall."

"I hear you," Sylvia said. She pulled up a chair, lit a Virginia Slim with her Dunhill lighter and flicked ash into Kate's plate. "Dig on this: *Carol's come out.*"

"Come out of what?" Kate asked, after a pause. "Her tube top?"

"Not to joke," Sylvia said. "She's *gay*. She's been seeing this terrific shrink, the one she used to get it on with, and he just, like, confronted her with it. He said she'd never stop sleeping around until she got upfront and came out of the closet. She told me about it at the Saturday Night Movie. In the *lobby*, can you believe it?"

"My God," Kate said. She was stunned. "How does she *feel* about it? I mean, can she get behind it?"

"She feels *incredible*," Sylvia said, blowing smoke. "She says she's finally gotten a handle on herself. It just hit her: she doesn't have to *fake it* anymore. With men."

Kate thought about the way Carol had faked it with Harvey a few months ago. "Too bad," she said pointedly. "She had a class act going there."

Sylvia put her hand urgently on Kate's arm. She was wearing so many gold circle bracelets Kate was afraid their combined weight was going to make the deck collapse. "Kate," Sylvia said, "don't *do* this to yourself. You come on hostile and you're only hurting yourself, you know? You're interfering with your own *personal growth*."

Kate looked at her cold gnocchi. She looked at her round, bare knees. She wished Sylvia hadn't brought up "personal growth." "Okay," she said, "I'll call Carol. But what am I supposed to say to her?"

"You're *supposed* to tell her how you love her," Sylvia said. "How she's done this terrifically gutsy thing, and she's this beautiful human being, and you can really relate to where she's coming from."

"I know, but that's the *problem*," Kate said. "I mean, I hated Carol's guts when she was straight. Now I'm supposed to love her because she's gay? Isn't that, like, reverse discrimination or something?"

"Kate," Sylvia said slowly, "I think you should ask yourself why you feel so *threatened* by this. You know? You're overreacting, *really*." She stared significantly into Kate's eyes behind her shades. "Think about it . . ."

Kate was outraged. She sat back and pried her arm loose. "Who, *me?*" she said. "Listen, some of my best *friends* are lesbians. I mean, I haven't got any hangups about that stuff at all. I'm open to it. I'm easy."

"Kate," Sylvia said, "stop justifying yourself. You don't have to *justify* yourself with me. I mean, you just *are*, you know? Whatever's right."

"I'll call Carol," Kate said. "I said I'd call her and I'll call her, okay? Hey, Harry's waving his arms around. Maybe you ought to go back there."

Sylvia put out her cigarette and got up, shaking her head. "You really have to work on yourself, kid. You've got to stop thinking in terms like that. 'Ought,' for God's sake. Don't you know there aren't any absolutes anymore?"

Kate wished Sylvia would self-destruct. "I'll talk it over with Carol," she said. "Okay? I mean, Carol should have a line on it . . ."

Kate's New Space

Harvey didn't make the scene at home at all the Friday night before Kate moved out, so she left a note propped against the Salton peanut butter maker giving him her new address and reminding him to feed Kat Vonnegut, Jr., who, she said, was "into Meow Mix."

It rather got to her to split without seeing Harvey at all, but maybe it was better this way, because his absence meant they could avoid charges and countercharges, the whole accusation-and-guilt syndrome that had plagued the marriage from the beginning.

Who was responsible for the communications breakdown? Which of them really was off on his own trip and unable to relate? Who was afraid to be open and honest about feelings, and which habitually forgot to line the garbage can with a Glad bag, so that they didn't indulge in elitist exploitation of the garbage men?

Kate didn't have the answers, except for the bit about the garbage, although she did feel that Harvey was practically a casebook study of a depressive personality acting out through anger. As she told her women's group, she really felt sorry for him because he had so little insight into his real motivations. But she couldn't stay in the same space with a manic-depressive, even when Harvey was in one of his "up" cycles, because, as the group had pointed out repeatedly, to do so was equivalent to being a professional victim who went around wearing a psychic "Kick Me" button. Furthermore, she was tired of Harvey's screwing around.

Given the dynamics of their interface, then, she had to make her move. And even as she fought back tears at the prospect of leaving her Stine graphics, her copper sauté pans, her Billie Holiday records and her Design Research modular seating components—all the painstakingly selected elements of the good life she and Harvey had once set out to share—Kate felt liberated. In political terms—and marriage was an exercise in power politics—she was freeing herself from the oppressor, shaking off her chains.

"Chains" reminded her that she hadn't cleaned out her jewelry box; she went back to the bedroom and got the stuff, stuffing it into a Pucci print bag that had come with a ten-dollar cosmetics purchase at Macy's. Finally, she dropped her house keys into the mailbox, piled her boxes and suitcases into the bus, and set off for Blithedale Canyon and her new, fully actualized life.

Kate had found her new pad through an ad on the bulletin board at the Golden Valley Market, offering a room in a communal living situation to "a mature, mellow female vegetarian into meditation, creativity and shared responsibilities, est graduate preferred." The address proved to be a rambling redwood house up several flights of stone stairs, just the Old

San Francisco summer-vacation cottage she and Harvey had wanted to buy when they moved to Mill Valley. Complete with soaring ceilings and sagging decks, the house, as Kate told Martha, was "simply *screaming* with tranquility." Ahd while her own room proved to be a converted closet, Kate felt immediately in tune with its mellow atmosphere and its other residents.

Brian, who'd interviewed her to see whether she was astrologically compatible with the present occupants, was a landscape architect who free-lanced as a handyperson while he waited for the drought to end so that people could get back to the soil again. Gentle, nonaggressive and stoned out of his mind, he'd struck Kate as slightly off balance yin-and-yangwise but definitely benign. "The whole number here," he told her, "is giving each other space." He'd then shown her the closet.

Harold, who had a Ph.D. in sociology but was currently working as a stock clerk at Alpha Beta until something better shook down, struck her as an incredible intellectual heavy; she also sensed this terrific empathy from him right away. "So you're breaking out of the conventional, societally conditioned role models for women," he said approvingly. *"Far out."* Kate noticed that Harold wore a sterling silver biological equality symbol over his tattered T-shirt: as she told him, it gave her positive vibes.

Woman, who'd changed her name legally from Debbie Ann Sulzberger, was a radical feminist who gave demonstrations in gynecological self-examination and collected money for free speculums for sisters at the bottom of the poverty ladder. Having satisfied herself that Kate had read Shulamith Firestone, Woman welcomed her warmly. "I was sort of hoping for a Third World person," she said, "but it hit me, that woulda been tokenism. Listen, you know anybody with a mimeograph machine?"

Gunther spoke very little English, was in his mid-fifties and ran a small appliance-repair service down in town. "He kind of came with the house," Brian explained to Kate, after Gunther had grunted a greeting at her and disappeared. "The woman who owns the place moved to the Sunset, so Gunther collects the rent and fixes stuff. He's an okay dude, but he's sort of *Germanic* about the money. Isn't into barter and won't take food stamps."

"It's cool," Kate said. "I've got the first and last and the cleaning deposit. And I'm planning to really get down and grind out the macramé." She decided to be open and trusting. "I'm also sort of planning to do some writing," she said. Although living with Harvey had stifled her creativity terrifically, Kate had always felt that macramé was only a substitute for her real gifts of expression. She still had a novel in mind, loosely autobiographical though really about the universal female experience, but had so far only mentally designed the book jacket.

Brian was incredibly receptive. "Hey," he said, "you're a writer. So am I. I read my poetry down at the Book Depot on Wednesday nights, and the feedback's been *unbelievable*. You know anybody with a mimeograph machine?"

The fifth member of the household was Millie, who was eighty-five years old, a lifelong Sierra Club member and indefatigable hiker and, Woman told Kate privately, "a little wiggy. Don't leave anything valuable lying around, like your stash. She's one heavy old lady, and we let her move in because we wanted to make a statement about ageism in America, but she's got these sticky fingers. I'm sure she took my copy of *Against Our Will*, but I can't confront her about it without making waves."

Kate pulled up to the foot of the stone stairs this sunny Saturday morning a week later and looked up at the decrepit house in a happy glow of anticipation. Her first commune . . . and this evening the first house meeting with Kate as a member of her new extended family. Not to acquaint her with the rules, of course, because there weren't any. Just to give her some *guidelines*. . . .

Fran Lebowitz

(1951?–   )

As if to provide an antidote to the self-deprecatory stance of so many *personae* of women's humor, Fran Lebowitz locates her targets outside herself in contemporary urban life: apartment-hunting, editors' deadlines, alarm clocks, taxis. The fact that she is a New Yorker invites comparison to Dorothy Parker, but the pathos and compassion that underlie Parker's wit are nowhere evident in Lebowitz' work. Instead, as Cathleen Schine wrote in *Vogue,* "she writes pedagogical satire, tapping her pointer at the blackboard, waiting stoically for her slackjawed students to catch on." Lebowitz' aggressive humor has no awe and no taboos, and owes more to Oscar Wilde—her acknowledged hero—than to Parker or any of her female predecessors. Born Frances Ann Lebowitz in Morristown, New Jersey, she adopted New York when she was a young adult and supported herself with a variety of odd jobs—driving a cab, cleaning apartments, and selling advertising—before launching a career as a columnist. She has written columns for *Interview* and *Mademoiselle,* as well as reviewing books and films for *Changes* magazine. Lebowitz' two collections of irreverent essays, *Metropolitan Life* (1978) and *Social Studies* (1981), were bestsellers that made her a celebrity, a situation that she reports enjoying: "I consider autographing books the ultimate human activity." Although Lebowitz disavows any connection to the feminist cause (asked about the women's movement, she says flatly, "I'm not in it"), the fact that she writes from the perspective of a tough-minded, opinionated, single urbanite reflects dramatic changes in women's lives in recent decades, and when she writes about subjects that have long been staples of women's humor, such as dieting and children, her stance is that of the bemused rather than the beleaguered.

423

SOURCES   *Contemporary Authors,* Vols. 81–84; Lubow, Arthur. "Screw You Humor." *The New Republic* 179:17 (21 October 1978): 18–22; Schine, Cathleen. "The Wit." *Vogue.* January 1982: 162, 219–220.

WORKS   *Metropolitan Life* (1978) and *Social Studies* (1981)

from *Metropolitan Life*

Manners

I am not a callous sort. I believe that all people should have warm clothing, sufficient food, and adequate shelter. I do feel, however, that unless they are willing to behave in an acceptable manner they should bundle up, chow down, and stay home.

I speak here not only of etiquette, for while etiquette is surely a factor, acceptable behavior is comprised of a good deal more. It demands, for instance, that the general public refrain from starting trends, overcoming inhibitions, or developing hidden talents. It further requires acceptance of the fact that the common good is usually not very and that there is indeed such a thing as getting carried away with democracy. Oppression and/or repression are not without their charms nor freedom and/or license their drawbacks. This can clearly be seen in the following chart.

THE BY-PRODUCTS OF OPPRESSION AND/OR REPRESSION	THE BY-PRODUCTS OF FREEDOM AND/OR LICENSE
WOMEN	
1. Well-kept fingernails	1. The word *chairperson*
2. Homemade cookies	2. The acceptance of construction boots as suitable attire for members of the fair sex
3. A guarantee that at least one segment of the population could be relied upon to display a marked distaste for strenuous physical activity	3. Girl ministers

4. The distinct probability that even a small gathering would yield at least one person who knew how to respond properly to a wedding invitation

4. The male centerfold

5. Real coffee

5. Erica Jong

JEWS

1. Highly entertaining stand-up comedians

1. Progressive nursery schools

2. The Stage Delicatessen

2. Frozen bagels

3. A guarantee that at least one segment of the population could be relied upon to display a marked distaste for strenuous physical activity

3. The Upper West Side

4. The development and perfection of theatrical law as a flourishing profession

4. The notion that it is appropriate for a writer to surrender a percentage of his income to an agent

5. Interesting slang expressions, particularly those used to describe Gentiles

5. Erica Jong

BLACKS

1. Jazz

1. Strawberry wine

2. The provision of the southern portion of the United States with a topic of conversation

2. Negro accountants

3. Tap dancing

3. Inventive forms of handshaking

4. The preservation in our culture of a lively interest in revenge

4. Open admissions

5. Amos 'n' Andy

5. Sammy Davis, Jr.

6. Interesting slang expressions, particularly those used to describe white people

6. The Symbionese Liberation Army

TEEN-AGERS

1. The thrill of illicit drinking

1. Strawberry wine

2. Sexual denial and the resultant development of truly exciting sexual fantasies.

2. Easy sexual access and the resultant premature boredom

3. The swank of juvenile delinquency

3. Social commitment

4. The glamour of alienation

4. People who may very well just be discovering symbolist poetry being allowed to vote

HOMOSEXUALS

1. Precision theatrical dancing

1. *A Chorus Line*

2. Sarcasm

2. Amyl nitrate

3. Art

3. Leather underwear

4. Literature

4. Lesbian mothers

5. Real gossip

5. Heterosexual hairdressers

6. The amusing notion that *Who's Afraid of Virginia Woolf* was really about two men

6. The amusing notion that *Who's Afraid of Virginia Woolf* was really about a man and a woman

Two basic steps must be taken in order to reach the eventual goal of acceptable behavior. The first (which I assume you have already accomplished) is a careful perusal of the above chart. The second is ridding oneself of certain popular and harmful misconceptions, as follows:

It is not true that there is dignity in all work. Some jobs are definitely better than others. It is not hard to tell the good jobs from the bad. People who have good jobs are happy, rich, and well dressed. People who have bad jobs are unhappy, poor, and use meat extenders. Those who seek dignity in the type of work that compels them to help hamburgers are certain to be disappointed. Also to be behaving badly.

There is no such thing as inner peace. There is only nervousness or death. Any attempt to prove otherwise constitutes unacceptable behavior.

Very few people possess true artistic ability. It is therefore both unseemly and unproductive to irritate the situation by making an effort. If you have a burning, restless urge to write or paint, simply eat something sweet and the feeling will pass. Your life story would not make a good book. Do not even try.

All God's children are not beautiful. Most of God's children are, in fact, barely presentable. The most common error made in matters of appearance is the belief that one should disdain the superficial and let the true beauty of one's soul shine through. If there are places on your body where this is a possibility, you are not attractive—you are leaking.

Gloria Steinem

(1934–   )

Gloria Steinim has credited black feminist activist Flo Kennedy with teaching her that "a revolution without humor is as hopeless as one without music." The granddaughter of an active suffragist, Pauline Steinem, who was a delegate to the 1908 International Council of Women, she became involved in the women's movement of the late 1960s after attending a feminist meeting to gather information for an article for *New York* magazine, for which she was a contributing editor. Since 1968, Steinem has been active in the feminist cause as writer, speaker, and political organizer. She was a founding editor of *Ms.* magazine in 1972, and has been a frequent contributor to that publication. Following her graduation from Smith College in 1956, Steinem spent two years in India at the University of Delhi and the University of Calcutta. By 1961 she was working as a freelance writer and consultant for magazines that eventually included *The Ladies' Home Journal, Seventeen, Esquire, Vogue* and *Cosmopolitan*, and she founded *Ms.* in large part to counter the sexism she observed in the content and editorial policies of such magazines. Always quick to perceive irony, Steinem notes that it was difficult to persuade advertisers that "women look at ads for shampoo without accompanying articles on how to wash their hair." Humor has long been a part of Steinem's writing: in the mid-1960s she wrote for the satiric television series "That Was the Week that Was," and later contributed satiric photo captions to a successor to *Mad* magazine called *Help!* Long an admirer of Dorothy Parker, she interviewed and befriended Parker toward the end of her life. Steinem's humor is similar to that of Nora Ephron in its commonsense exposure of the absurdity of sexism, and in this respect she is also in the tradition of Marietta Holly, Alice Duer Miller, and other writers who have satirized men's supposed superiority. "If Men Could Menstruate" is typical of contemporary feminist humor in its critique of male hegemony, its use of previously taboo subject matter, and its assertive tone. The essay could have been inspired by the female Irish taxi driver that Steinem quotes as saying, "Honey, if men could get pregnant, abortion would be a sacrament."

SOURCES   *Contemporary Authors*, vols. 52–56; Steinem, Gloria. Introduction. *Outrageous Acts and Everyday Rebellions*. New York: Holt, Reinhart, 1983. 1–26.

WORKS   *Outrageous Acts and Everyday Rebellions* (1983)

from *Ms.*

If Men Could Menstruate

Living in India made me understand that a white minority of the world has spent centuries conning us into thinking a white skin makes people superior, even though the only thing it really does is make them more subject to ultraviolet rays and wrinkles.

Reading Freud made me just as skeptical about penis envy. The power of giving birth makes "womb envy" more logical, and an organ as external and unprotected as the penis makes men very vulnerable indeed.

But listening recently to a woman describe the unexpected arrival of her menstrual period (a red stain had spread on her dress as she argued heatedly on the public stage) still made me cringe with embarrassment. That is, until she explained that, when finally informed in whispers of the obvious event, she had said to the all-male audience, "and you should be *proud* to have a menstruating woman on your stage. It's probably the first real thing that's happened to this group in years!"

Laughter. Relief. She had turned a negative into a positive. Somehow her story merged with India and Freud to make me finally understand the power of positive thinking. Whatever a "superior" group has will be used to justify its superiority, and whatever an "inferior" group has will be used to justify its plight. Black men were given poorly paid jobs because they were said to be "stronger" than white men, while all women were relegated to poorly paid jobs because they were said to be "weaker." As the little boy said when asked if he wanted to be a lawyer like his mother, "Oh no, that's women's work." Logic has nothing to do with oppression.

So what would happen if suddenly, magically, men could menstruate and women could not?

Clearly, menstruation would become an enviable, boast-worthy, masculine event:

Men would brag about how long and how much.

Young boys would talk about it as the envied beginning of manhood. Gifts, religious ceremonies, family dinners, and stag parties would mark the day.

To prevent monthly work loss among the powerful, Congress would fund a National Institute on Dysmenorrhea. Doctors would research little about heart attacks, from which men were hormonally protected, but everything about cramps.

Sanitary supplies would be federally funded and free. Of course, some men would still pay for the prestige of such commercial brands as Paul Newman Tampons, Muhammad Ali's Rope-a-Dope Pads, John Wayne Maxi Pads, and Joe Namath Jock Shields—"For those Light Bachelor Days."

Statistical surveys would show that men did better in sports and won more Olympic medals during their periods.

Generals, right-wing politicians, and religious fundamentalists would cite menstruation ("*men*-struation") as proof that only men could serve God and country in combat ("You have to give blood to take blood"), occupy high political office ("Can women be properly fierce without a monthly cycle governed by the planet Mars?"), be priests, ministers, God Himself ("He gave this blood for our sins"), or rabbis ("Without a monthly purge of impurities, women are unclean").

Male liberals or radicals, however, would insist that women are equal, just different; and that any woman could join their ranks if only she were willing to recognize the primacy of menstrual rights ("Everything else is a single issue") or self-inflict a major wound every month ("You *must* give blood for the revolution").

Street guys would invent slang ("He's a three-pad man") and "give fives" on the corner with some exchange like, "Man, you lookin' *good!*"

"Yeah, man, I'm on the rag!"

TV shows would treat the subject openly. (*Happy Days*: Richie and Potsie try to convince Fonzie that he is still "The Fonz," though he has missed two periods in a row. *Hill Street Blues*: The whole precinct hits the same cycle.) So would newspapers. (SUMMER SHARK SCARE THREATENS MENSTRUATING MEN. JUDGE CITES MONTHLIES IN PARDONING RAPIST.) And so would movies. (Newman and Redford in *Blood Brothers!*)

Men would convince women that sex was *more* pleasurable at "that time of the month." Lesbians would be said to fear blood and therefore life itself, though all they needed was a good menstruating man.

Medical schools would limit women's entry ("they might faint at the sight of blood").

Of course, intellectuals would offer the most moral and logical arguments. Without that biological gift for measuring the cycles of the moon and planets, how could a woman master any discipline that demanded a sense of time, space, mathematics—or the ability to measure anything at all? In philosophy and religion, how could women compensate for being disconnected from the rhythm of the universe? Or for their lack of symbolic death and resurrection every month?

Menopause would be celebrated as a positive event, the symbol that men had accumulated enough years of cyclical wisdom to need no more.

Liberal males in every field would try to be kind. The fact that "these people" have no gift for measuring life, the liberals would explain, should be punishment enough.

And how would women be trained to react? One can imagine right-wing women agreeing to all these arguments with a staunch and smiling masochism. ("The ERA would force housewives to wound themselves every month": Phyllis Schlafly. "Your husband's blood is as sacred as that of Jesus—and so sexy, too!": Marabel Morgan.) Reformers and Queen Bees would adjust their lives to the cycles of the men around them. Feminists would explain endlessly that men, too, needed to be liberated from the false idea of Martian aggressiveness, just as women needed to escape from the bonds of "menses-envy." Radical feminists would add that oppression of the nonmenstrual was the pattern for all other oppressions. ("Vampires were our first freedom fighters!") Cultural feminists would exalt a female bloodless imagery in art and literature. Socialist feminists would insist that, once capitalism and imperialism were overthrown, women would menstruate, too. ("If women aren't yet menstruating in Russia," they would explain, "it's only because true socialism can't exist within a capitalist encirclement.")

In short, we would discover, as we should already guess, that logic is in the eye of the logician. (For instance, here's an idea for theorists and logicians: If women are supposed to be less rational and more emotional at the beginning of our menstrual cycle when the female hormone is at its lowest level, then why isn't it logical to say that, in those few days, women behave the most like the way men behave all month long? I leave further improvisations up to you.)*

The truth is that, if men could menstruate, the power justifications would go on and on.

If we let them.

*With thanks to Stan Pottinger for many of the improvisations already here.

Ellen Goodman

(1941–   )

Born in Newton, Massachusetts, Ellen Goodman graduated
from Radcliffe College in 1964, married, and began work as
a researcher and reporter for *Newsweek* magazine. From
1965 to 1967 she wrote feature stories for the *Detroit Free
Press* before being hired as a feature writer by the *Boston
Globe*. In 1970 she began to write the "At Large" column for
the *Globe*. Its popularity led the Washington Post Writers
Group, in 1976, to syndicate her column for editorial or op-
ed pages of, eventually, more than 250 newspapers across the
country, resulting in Goodman's appearances as a commentator on such shows as CBS-Radio's "Spectrum" and NBC-
TV's "Today." Her first book, *Turning Points* (1979), explores through interviews how men and women assessed the
effects on their lives of the women's movement (Goodman
was divorced in 1971). Her first collection of newspaper
columns, *Close to Home* (1979), led to the Pulitzer Prize for
distinguished commentary in 1980. Her second collection,
At Large, was published in 1981. Although considered by
some critics to be what Katherine Winton Evans called "a
serious writer about soft subjects," Goodman believes that
she writes about "much more important questions than the
average columnist," pointing out that childrearing, changing
values about marriage and divorce, abortion, equal rights for
women, and questions about basic moral and ethical issues
are more significant topics than much of the trivia that men
pass off as "political" subjects. Because of her wit, her ability
to reveal the ironic incongruities in the way people behave in
professional, social, and personal situations, Goodman has
been compared with Erma Bombeck and Nora Ephron.
However, Goodman's range is wider, her tone more serious,
and her point of view less subjective than theirs. She is, as
reviewers have noted, sensible and humorous, as able to

433

comment with insight on children and personal relationships as on political figures and national affairs.

SOURCES   *Contemporary Authors*, Vol. 104; Evans, Katherine Winton. Rev. of *Close to Home*. *Washington Journalism Review* Jan./Feb. 1980: 66–67; Ivins, Molly. "Virtuous Columns." Rev. of *Close to Home*. *New York Times Book Review* 23 December 1979: 6–7; McWhorter, Diane. "Ellen Goodman." *Washington Journalism Review*, Sept. 1980: 53–55.

WORKS   *Close to Home* (1979) and *At Large* (1981)

from *Close to Home*

Information, Please

Not long ago, during one of those internal shuffles that give meaning to the expression "itinerant journalism," the desk of one employee of a metropolitan daily newspaper was moved to the front of the room.

This, I assure you, meant nothing in terms of status. There is no status in a newspaper. But it put this woman's desk among seven or eight others within range of something called The Door.

Now newspapers are the closest thing in the work world to community drop-in centers. People wander in and out of them carrying every sort of notion and promotion from wedding announcements to dancing-bear advertisements to proclamations about National Taxpayer Week.

Sometimes they even arrive offering themselves as objects of national fascination. There was, for example, a man who used to lumber into my old office in Detroit every January wearing nothing more than a wet bathing suit and doing a seal imitation.

Sitting near any door in a newspaper office thus has certain built-in liabilities. Streams of people are constantly asking you where they should deposit their dancing bears and life stories. Not to mention their wet bathing suits.

Most people would reasonably assume that if they were sitting among seven co-workers, these fascinating inquiries would be divided into seven equal parts. But they would be wrong if only one of this up-front group was female.

The cruel fact of life, as this woman (who shall remain nameless) discovered in months of people-watching, is this: The average stranger would walk into a room, past the charming music critic (and disco dancer), barely glancing at the well-groomed highbrow of the movie critic, avoiding three reporters and one columnist until his eyes fastened on the only person in the room trying madly to find a solution for world hunger ten minutes before deadline.

It was clear that this person and no other had to be the receptionist because she was of the Female Persuasion.

In this way, many brilliant ideas were interrupted and forever lost to the world—including the solution to world hunger. But something was gained. The woman won a daily sense of camaraderie with every female executive who is asked to get the coffee, every woman ever arbitrarily handed a dictation pad, and every female doctor ever asked when the doctor would be in.

In an effort to prove to herself that she was not paranoid, she even conducted a brief sociological study. First she made certain improvements on her own public barriers. She put a bookcase in front of her desk and piled it with newspapers, sweaters and phone books. This, however, only seemed to give people a place to put their elbows and their dancing bears, while asking for information.

Next, under the tutelage of her neighbor she tried to perfect a technique of rudeness. She discovered that there were people who would rather spend ten minutes waiting for her to look up than to disturb the man reading the paper with his feet on the desk behind her.

The woman didn't want to be hostile about this. It wasn't fair to get angry at the poor fellow carrying a case of yogurt samples when he asked where the food editor was. It wasn't his fault. It came with blue booties.

Yet she gradually became desperate to finish a sentence with something other than a question mark. She was willing to try anything short of a sex-change operation.

So, one day, in a fit of anxiety, she placed a handwritten warning on top of the massive barrier which read: This Is Not a Reception Desk.

What was the result of this, the ultimate weapon, you ask? Well, the first two souls were intimidated. They walked to the back of the room to find another woman. The third smiled jovially over the top and asked, "Could you please tell me where the reception desk is?"

The woman was, either way, defeated.

Now there is a new rumor floating through the office. They are playing musical desks again and everyone is going to be moved.

This time, she is looking for a back seat with a thoroughly rear view. If she doesn't get it she intends to come to work thoroughly upholstered and doing a nifty imitation of an empty chair.

Veronica Geng

(1941–   )

Born in Atlanta, Georgia, Veronica Geng grew up in Philadelphia and was graduated from the University of
Pennsylvania in 1963. She has been associated with *The New
Yorker* both as a fiction editor (1977–1982) and as a regular
contributor of the "casuals" that have been a feature of that
magazine since its founding. However, her interest in humor
dates back much earlier, as indicated by her first publication,
In a Fit of Laughter: An Anthology of Modern Humor,
which she edited in 1969. In the same year she wrote *Guess
Who? A Cavalcade of Famous Americans,* for young readers.
Geng's career as a humorous writer dates from 1975, when
she contributed a parody of film reviewer Pauline Kael to the
New York Review of Books. Partners (1984) won critical
praise for the cleverness of Geng's satiric essays, many of
which first appeared in *The New Yorker.* Rosalyn Drexler, in
the *New York Times Book Review,* for example, described
Geng as "a devastating witness of present-day mores" and "an
original," while others noted the incisiveness of her parody,
her talent for mimicry, especially of contemporary rhetoric
and jargon, and the loony incongruity of the things that she
pairs in her pieces—e.g., parodying the style of Henry James
to satirize a group of former sixties radicals. Whether her
target is contemporary art, politics, the media, fads, or just
the people who put wedding announcements in newspapers,
Geng has the wit to expose both the absurdity and potential
perniciousness of the seemingly innocuous. Like parodists
before her, from Judith Sargent Murray to Carolyn Wells and
Jean Kerr, Geng possesses a marvelous ear for the idioms and
verbal styles that distinguish the voices of American culture, a
unique sense of the absurd and incongruous, and a wide-
ranging intelligence that enables her to seize on the approach
to any topic that uncovers its soft spot and raps it with a
lethal wit.

SOURCES   *Contemporary Authors*, Vol. 119; Drexler, Rosalyn. "Bethpage Burdette and Jailhouse Mariachi." Rev. of *Partners*. *New York Times Book Review* 15 July 1984: 12; Kendall, Elaine. Rev. of *Partners*. *Los Angeles Times Book Review* 26 August 1984: 6; Lehmann-Haupt, Christopher. Rev. of *Partners*. *New York Times* 6 July 1984: C24; Moseley, Merritt. "Veronica Geng." *Encyclopedia of American Humorists*. Ed. Steven H. Gale. New York: Garland, 1988, 169–71.

WORKS   *Partners* (1984)

from *Partners*

Petticoat Power

"I find it very helpful to attend business meetings under an alias."
—Estelle Crinoline, Vice-President in Charge of Assistants
at a major conglomerate

Nowadays, the fair sex functions in a managerial capacity in U.S. businesses at every level, from the lowly assistant vice-president to the top-flight vice-presidential assistant. The "gal Friday" has long since become a full-fledged deckhand, and the "steno" has made it into the ranks of flunkies to the powers that be. It is even estimated that women constitute a percentage of all egress-level managers. If you are one of them, the Sword of Damocles is beginning to swing your way, and you will soon see the time when women are promoted over better-qualified minorities and minors.

As a result, the ambitious female of the species need no longer turn furtively to the so-called execu-cosmetology schools, which dispense little more than a bow tie and a fountain pen. The following guide, based on information, should amply fill the needs of women and would-be women in business.

WHAT IS BUSINESS?

The field of business is so manifold that no single article can hope to do more than this one. In the main, however, all businesses are basically alike in their approach, and women would do well to remember the generally uniform surface of the masculine brain even as it offers openings for women.

WHAT MAKES AN EXECUTIVE?

A good executive must first be equipped with the tools of the trade. Top male execs know well the necessity for carrying in their possession at all times some form of credentials (the service revolver, tire iron, or Sword of Damocles). Women must not shrink faintheartedly from doing likewise. Moreover, credentials exist to be used. Show the credentials at once when approaching a colleague. This display lends an air of importance to the encounter; the colleague more readily believes that the meeting is a serious matter, not just casual chitchat.

The executive is also versed in the "hidden language" of the biz-ocracy—the fundamentals that touch every swivel chair in every corridor of power. The General Business Code, prescribed for all commercial transactions in the U.S., is transmitted by breast-pocket-handkerchief semaphore (and may in future be modernized to adopt feminine visual apparatus—e.g., the hairnet). The seven basic signals are:

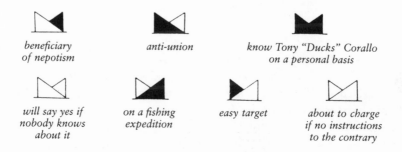

beneficiary   *anti-union*   *know Tony "Ducks" Corallo*
of nepotism   *on a personal basis*

will say yes if   *on a fishing*   *easy target*   *about to charge*
nobody knows   *expedition*   *if no instructions*
about it   *to the contrary*

With the influx of Milady into the executive "sweet," new terms are gradually being added:

afraid of   *could help*   *cream and*   *depressed*
small handbags   *you but won't*   *two sugars*

THE MENTOR

Having mastered these skills, the she-male in business will be served just as well—indeed, better—by attaching herself to a mentor. Every single business, no matter how similar to another, is completely different, and only through a mentor can you learn how mentorship itself works in your chosen field.

A mentor is a man who has reached a ranking position of awesome responsibility at the office; is richly dedicated to home, wife, and children; is actively involved in demanding community and leisure duties; and thus is ideally suited to spend long hours guiding a female co-worker through the intricacies of business.

The mentor is not to be confused with other paternal figures in the company, such as the doctor, proctor, loner, factor, drummer, exterminator, or mortgage shark.

The principal technique involved in finding a mentor is the stakeout. Mentors tend to gravitate toward specific loci of power, such as the shredder room. Keep a diary of their movements. (Entries should be made concurrently or afterward, never before.) Not untypical is the woman who staked out a deserted band shell, tailed the first man who appeared, and eventually followed him to his corporate headquarters, where he taught her how to build a car with her bare hands.

There are four types of mentors. As shown in the following transcriptions of videotaped experiences by distaff mentorees A, B, C, and D, each type of mentor has his characteristic way of showing you the rope:

TYPE 1—INFERENTIAL

A: Good morning, Bob.

MENTOR: What in the *hell* are you wearing?

A: Just a . . . a simple jumpsuit with laminated pongee undercuffs, layered with a . . . a Bavarian vest and a Ralph Lauren cow blanket.

(Mentor laughs contemptuously.)

A *(confidence seeping into her voice)*: I'm grateful for the advice, Bob.

TYPE 2—INSINUATIONAL

B: Have a nice weekend, Jack?

(Mentor stares in a repelled manner at her coiffure.)

B: Is something wrong with my hair?

MENTOR: If you choose to think so.

B: I'll get on it right away. And . . . Jack? *(In a newly assertive tone)* Well . . . thanks.

TYPE 3—MANIFESTATIONAL

C: I have those dioxin reports, Dick.

(Mentor leans across desk, rips the tacky costume jewelry from her

throat and wrists, and tosses it disgustedly into wastebasket.)
    C *(effectively):* Deemed it inappropriate, huh? Say no more.

TYPE 4—VERBAL

D. Morning, Ted.
    MENTOR: You make a better door than a window.
    D: Sorry. Did you see the *Times?*
    MENTOR: Is the Pope Catholic?
    D: Well . . . since it says the bond market has rallied—
    MENTOR: Get off my ear.
    D: —if we take into account the spillover effect from Wednesday's—
    MENTOR: Can the tripe.
    D: —and the new Treasury bonds' gain of—
    MENTOR: Save your wind—you might want to go sailing sometime.
    D: —then the prime rate—
    MENTOR: That *rates* a hee-haw!
    D: —but the Federal Reserve—
    MENTOR: Hang crape on your nose—your brains are dead.
    D: —may indicate that the tax-exempt sector is—
    MENTOR: What are you—foggy in the upper story?
    D: —I mean, now that the pace of new issues—
    MENTOR: Go hire a hall.
    D: Are you—you know—annoyed about something?
    MENTOR: Pull in your head—here comes a termite.
    D *(breaking out in "executive pattern" rash statistically linked to lateral thinking):* Gee, I guess I do need a manicure. 'Preciate the grooming tip!

With the confidence you will gain through this type of interaction with a mentor, you will soon be able to take risks without fear of mistakes. Let's suppose you wish to offer a suggestion about some minor aspect of business practice:

Sample dialogue:

    YOU: I was thinking, why don't we—
    MENTOR: No.
    YOU: But—
    MENTOR: No. Go on, you were doing marvellously.
    YOU: Oh, O.K. Wouldn't it make sense if we have a weekly—

MENTOR: No, absolutely not. Good girl, keep it up.

YOU: I mean, once a week, if each department—

MENTOR: *Jee-zus!* I told you, it's completely out of the question. Here, let's trade places and I'll show you how to do this.

YOU: I think I already know how to do it.

MENTOR: Of course you do. And you were doing beautifully, which is why you need someone to show you an alternative way of doing it.

YOU: Did I make a mistake?

MENTOR: Don't think about your mistakes. Don't ever think about your mistakes. Don't dwell on your mistakes. You'll make plenty of mistakes, but by no means dwell on them.

YOU: Right. Then let me put it this way. I want to restructure this company from the ground up. Just take a moment of your time, if you will, and imagine. In the mail room, raw lean-bodied youngsters, a future chairman of the board perhaps among them, learn the business from the bottom by democratically sodomizing each other in an atmosphere of interracial harmony and union solidarity. Thus prepared for the elevator ascent, to the strains of sense-quickening Muzak they steer from floor to floor their rattling mail carts of communiqués and memos proposing urgent trysts, many with nymphs from a typing pool awakened en masse by affairs with a vice-president whose blazing rise from the Harvard Business School to a position of line command has been short-circuited by a reputation for insatiable erotic appetites. The day begins for the accounting department, too, as hot numbers are speculated upon with mathematical frankness. Everywhere shirtsleeves are rolled up to expose wrists and forearms of unbearably breathtaking virility; panty hose are stripped off so that bare toes may frolic in the nap of the industrial carpeting. Smart pigskin briefcases and brown paper bags alike pop open to reveal black nylon corselets and posing straps, and aesthetically pleasing new birth-control devices, each a product of the newly stirring giant of American technology. By midmorning, as the refreshment wagon tinkles its merry news, quenching fruit juices are sought, caffeine and sugar renounced as redundant stimulants to surging metabolisms. Hands clutch atop reports and blueprints, limbs mingle upon varnished teak conference tables. By noon, sustenance is welcome; home-cooked box-lunch fare is contributed potluck style to the menu of the penthouse executive dining room, where one and all are served by Irish waiters and waitresses, whose rosy-cheeked charms are dispensed as a last course along with the claret. Restored, the staff returns to a worthwhile afternoon of disassembling the structures of power, once again tearing off collar stays and execu-length socks, T-shirts and work boots, with equal-opportunity abandon. The switchboard is as abuzz with interoffice calls for transvestites as a Weimar nightclub, while the computers, engineered for sexy problem-solving by a vanguard élite, are programmed to insert pornographic passages into the briefs of the lawyers, who, thus cast adrift on the uncertain seas of obscenity rulings, fall into confusion and disarray, incapacitated in their campaign to stifle creative urges with their lackey caution. Nepotistic marriages, too, are crumbling under the stress; bourgeois property-owning middle managers and hypocrite artists are selling their exurban retreats and gentrified lofts, reserving motel rooms convenient to the office. As desk lamps are turned this way and that to warm bare flesh, heat melts the grease that has eased the way of sycophants and bootlickers, who, losing their purchase on the success ladder, plunge into the communal endeavor on an equal footing. By late afternoon, all are gathered at the interdepartmental meeting, where brainstorming fully liberates the libido in service of the intellect, culminating in a heady explosion of honest labor. Well exhausted, the satisfied work force contemplates the wreckage of a numbing and exploitative system. Rivalries have been diverted into life-giving channels, oppressive authority has been leveled by the sway of desire, and the stultifying lock-march of corporate sameness has been diversified into a thousand different positions.

MENTOR: You're fired.

Paula Gunn Allen

(1939–   )

Paula Gunn Allen is a scholar of Native American literature
and one of the major contemporary poets in that tradition.
She was born in Cubero, New Mexico, the daughter of a
Laguna-Sioux mother and a Lebanese-American father. She
attended Colorado Women's College and the University of
Oregon, where she received a B.A. in English and an M.F.A.
in creative writing. In 1975 she completed a Ph.D. in
American Studies at the University of New Mexico, and since
that time has taught at several universities, most recently the
University of California-Berkeley. Allen's work as both critic
and writer is infused with her Native American heritage and
with a feminist consciousness. Her first book of poetry, *The
Blind Lion,* was published in 1974 and has been followed by
several others and by a novel, *The Woman Who Owned the
Shadows* (1983). In her scholarship, Allen has worked
tirelessly to bring to Native American writers—especially
women—the attention they deserve, and in her own work she
attempts to mediate between the mythology and heritage of
her Sioux background and the contemporary Anglo culture
that is causing dramatic changes in the lives of all women.
Allen's multiple perspective—as poet and critic, as Sioux
living and working in a white culture—allows her a sense of
irony that permeates her work, accommodating change and
conflict. "Taking a Visitor to See the Ruins" surfaced when
Nancy Walker and Eleanor Bender decided to edit a special
issue of *Open Places* magazine in 1985 devoted to humor,
and issued a call to contemporary authors for examples of
their humorous work. The poem embodies several types of
humor: it describes a practical joke, it rests on a pun, and it
amusingly justaposes traditional pueblo dwellings to high-
rise apartment buildings.

SOURCES   Green, Rayna, ed. *That's What She Said: Contemporary Poetry and Fiction by Native American Women.* Bloomington: Indiana University Press, 1984; Jahner, Elaine. "A Laddered, Rain-bearing Rug: Paula Gunn Allen's Poetry." *Women and Western American Literature,* ed. Helen Winter Stauffer and Susan J. Rosowski. Troy, NY: Whitston, 1984. 311–326.

WORKS   "Taking a Visitor to See the Ruins," *Open Places* 38/39 (Spring 1985)

from *Open Places*

Taking a Visitor to See the Ruins

for Joe Bruchac

He's still telling about the time he came west
and was visiting me. I knew he
wanted to see some of the things

everybody sees when they're in the wilds of New Mexico.
So when we'd had our morning coffee
after he'd arrived, I said,

Would you like to go see some old Indian ruins?
His eyes brightened with excitement,
he was thinking, no doubt,

of places like the ones he'd known where he came from,
sacred caves filled with falseface masks,
ruins long abandoned, built secure

into the sacred lands; or of pueblos
once home to vanished people but peopled still
by their ghosts, connected still with the bone old land.

Sure, he said. I'd like that a lot.
Come on, I said, and we got in my car,
drove a few blocks east toward the towering peaks

of the Sandias. We stopped at a tall
high-security apartment building made of stone,
went up the walk past the pond and pressed the buzzer.

They answered and we went in,
past the empty pool room, past the empty party room
up five flights in the elevator, down the abandoned hall.

Joe, I said when we'd gotten inside the chic apartment
I'd like you to meet the old Indian ruins
I promised.

My mother, Mrs. Francis, and my grandmother, Mrs. Gottlieb.
His eyes grew large, and then he laughed
looking shocked at the two

women he'd just met. Silent for a second, they laughed too.
And he's still telling the tale of the old
Indian ruins he visited in New Mexico,

the two who still live pueblo style in high security dwellings
way up there where the enemy can't reach them
just like in the olden times.

Gail Sausser

(1952–   )

A native of Washington state, Gail Sausser received her B.A. from Fort Wright College in Spokane, where she was involved in theater and studied poetry, and earned an M.A. in psychology at Antioch West, in Vancouver. She selected the pieces that comprise *Lesbian Etiquette* (1986), a collection of humorous essays with cartoons by Alice Muhlback, from three years of humor columns that she had written for three different publications: *Lights, Washington Cascade Voice,* and *Seattle Gay News.* Similar in wit and subject matter to the work of lesbian-feminist stand-up comedian Kate Clinton, Sausser's collection addresses topics ranging from personal to professional and political behavior for gay women. Her use of humor to bring out incongruities between people's expectations and the actualities of their experience enables the reader, whether gay or not, to laugh, and therefore to identify with the situations she describes. An admirer of the humanistic humor of Bill Cosby and Lily Tomlin, as well as a fan of Bette Midler, Sausser expresses in her own writing a wry sense of the absurd and a preference for poking good-natured rather than malicious fun. Consequently, as B. Zahn wrote in a review of the book for *Ours* newspaper, Sausser not only sheds light, in a positive and humorous way, on the life that lesbians lead, pointing out their "clay feet," but also breaks down stereotypes by focusing on the ordinary human qualities, problems, and needs that unite most people.

SOURCES   Grant-Bourne, Katherine. Rev. of *Lesbian Etiquette. Seattle Gay News* 23 May 1986: 2:1; Letter from Gail Sausser, Jan. 30, 1988, including a copy of B. Zahn's review of *Lesbian Etiquette* from *Ours* newspaper.

WORKS   *Lesbian Etiquette* (1986)

from *Lesbian Etiquette*

Lesbian Potlucks Through History

I've gone to so many potlucks since I came out that I once threatened to write a cookbook called "1,001 Things to Make for a Lesbian Potluck." They're such egalitarian events—they enable everyone to prepare according to their abilities and to receive according to their needs. A few years ago there were much stricter rules for the dishes acceptable at potlucks: they had to be vegetarian, made from womyn-grown products, and have redeeming social value. Now we are a much more diverse community. Not only are there vegetarians, there are meat eaters, gourmets and even people who enjoy white sugar (I mention no names).

I'm thankful for the change. I, for one, have eaten enough beans and tofu. But I do feel some nostalgia for those early potlucks which went beyond the above criteria to include intense rituals of chanting, dancing and reciting poetry before food could be consumed. These potlucks were held during the full moons of autumn in the years when I belonged to a small coven and most of my lesbian friends were healers, mystics and hippies. I swallowed gallons of carrot juice, fasted, never touched meat or sugar, and read astrology charts and Tarot cards. (You see, I keep nothing from you about my checkered past.)

Food, I suspect, has played an important role in lesbian history. Many a French lesbian may have been seduced over a seemingly innocent plate of hors d'oeuvres at what was then called a salon but what we now know was a potluck. And perhaps a study should be funded on the role of chocolate in the evolution of lesbianism. Chocolate just happens to contain phenylethylamine, a chemical known to cause a euphoria identical to infatuation. Was it a chocolate croissant that inspired Rene Vivien to write, "I love your carnal lips lingering, still creased by kisses from before . . ."? I think so.

But the history of lesbian potlucks goes much farther back than the French salons. My own favorite part of lesbian history is the age of the great harems of Persia and India. In these harems, a wife rarely saw her husband unless she was a favorite. So what did women do to entertain themselves? Of course, they had lesbian potlucks. They also developed the art of bellydancing, of which I am a devotee. Those present day critics who claim that bellydancing was done only to entice men obviously are unaware that the stages of a woman's life are represented in each part of the dance, and that the cane and sword dances are deliberate parodies of men.

I can see I'm going to have to rewrite history. And why not? The men have.

Going even farther back, I believe there must have been a goddess of lesbian potlucks somewhere amid the Assyrian, Egyptian, or Greco-Roman deities. I mean, they had deities for everything else! The farther back in time you go the stronger the women deities become (see Ishtar, Isis, Kali). Somewhere in there was a lezzie, probably hidden by male misinterpretation or misguided piety on the part of male historians.

It's not easy trying to reclaim the history of lesbian potlucks. My anthropology teacher never told me about Margaret Mead's lesbianism, much less about cults and ancient societies. What do we even know about Lesbos? Not much. Would Elizabeth Taylor play Sappho in a major motion picture? Never—and that's where most of us learn our history.

Well, some things are changing—maybe Meryl Streep will play Sappho one of these days.

Selected Bibliography

Apte, Mahadev L. *Humor and Laughter: An Anthropological Approach.* Ithaca, NY: Cornell University Press, 1985.

Austin, Mary. "The Sense of Humor in Women." *The New Republic* 26 Nov. 1924: 10–13.

Barecca, Regina, ed. *Last Laughs: Perspectives on Women and Comedy.* New York: Gordon and Breach, 1988.

Beatts, Ann. "Can a Woman Get a Laugh and a Man Too? *Mademoiselle* Nov. 1975: 140+.

———. "Why More Women Aren't Funny." *New Woman* Mar./Apr. 1976: 22–28.

Berger, Phil. "The New Comediennes." *The New York Times Magazine* 29 July 1984: 27+.

Bier, Jesse. *The Rise and Fall of American Humor.* Ames: Iowa State University Press, 1968.

Blair, Walter. *Horse Sense in American Humor.* Chicago: University of Chicago Press, 1942.

———. *Native American Humor.* 1937. San Francisco: Chandler, 1960.

———, and Hamlin Hill. *America's Humor: From Poor Richard to Doonesbury.* New York: Oxford University Press, 1978.

———, and Raven I. McDavid, Jr., eds. *The Mirth of a Nation: America's Great Dialect Humor.* Minneapolis: University of Minnesota Press, 1983.

Boskin, Joseph. *Humor and Social Change in Twentieth Century America.* Boston: Trustees of the Public Library of the City of Boston, 1979.

———. "Protest Humor: Fighting Criticism with Laughter." *Bostonia* 54.5 (Dec. 1980): 48–56.

Briggs, Peter M. "English Satire and Connecticut Wit." *American Quarterly* 37.1 (1985): 13–29.

Bruère, Martha Bensley, and Mary Ritter Beard, eds. *Laughing Their Way: Women's Humor in America.* New York: Macmillan, 1934.

Burma, John H. "Humor as a Technique in Race Conflict." *American Sociological Review* 11.6 (Dec. 1946): 710–15.

Cantor, Joanne R. "What Is Funny To Whom?" *Journal of Communication* 26 (Summer 1976): 164–72.

Chapman, Antony J., and Hugh C. Foot, eds. *Humour and Laughter: Basic Issues.* New York: John Wiley, 1976.

————. *Humour and Laughter: Theory, Research, and Applications.* New York: John Wiley, 1976.

————. *It's a Funny Thing, Humour.* New York: Pergamon, 1977.

Chapman, Antony J., and Nicholas J. Gadfield. "Is Sexist Humor Sexist?" *Journal of Communication* 26 (Summer 1976): 141–53.

Cixous, Hélène. "The Laugh of the Medusa." Trans. Keith and Paula Cohen. *Signs* 1.4 (Summer 1976): 875–93.

Cohen, Sandy. "Racial and Ethnic Humor in the United States." *Amerikastudien* 30 (1985): 203–11.

Cohen, Sarah Blacher, ed. *Comic Relief: Humor in Contemporary American Literature.* Urbana: University of Illinois Press, 1978.

————. *Jewish Wry: Essays on Jewish Humor.* Bloomington: Indiana University Press, 1987.

Collier, Denise, and Kathleen Beckett. *Spare Ribs: Women in the Humor Biz.* New York: St. Martin's, 1980.

Conrad, Susan P. *Perish the Thought: Intellectual Women in Romantic America, 1830–1860.* Secaucus, NJ: Citadel, 1978.

Cox, Samuel. *Why We Laugh.* 1876. Boston: Benjamin Blom, 1969.

Cupchik, Gerald C., and Howard Leventhal. "Consistency Between Expressive Behavior and the Evaluation of Humorous Stimuli: The Role of Sex and Self-Orientation." *Journal of Personality and Social Psychology* 30.3 (1974): 429–42.

Curry, Jane. "Women as Subjects and Writers of Nineteenth Century American Humor." Diss. University of Michigan, 1975.

————, ed. *Samantha Rastles the Woman Question.* Urbana: University of Illinois Press, 1983.

Dearborn, Mary V. *Pocahontas's Daughters: Gender and Ethnicity in American Culture.* New York: Oxford University Press, 1986.

Diot, Rolande. "Sexus, Nexus, and Taboos versus Female Humor: The Case of Erica Jong." *Revue Francais D'Etudes Americaines* 30 (Nov. 1986): 491–99.

Donovan, Josephine. *New England Local Color Literature.* New York: Frederick Ungar, 1982.

Douglas, Mary. "Jokes." *Implicit Meanings: Essays in Anthropology.* London: Routledge and Kegan Paul, 1975. 90–114.

Dresner, Zita Zatkin. "Delineating the Norm: Allies and Enemies in the Humor of Bombeck and Viorst." *Thalia: Studies in Literary Humor* 7.1 (1984): 28–34.

————. "The Housewife as Humorist." *Regionalism and the Female Imagination* 3.2/3 (Winter 1977–78): 29–38.

————. "Twentieth Century American Women Humorists." Diss. University of Maryland, 1982.

————. "Women's Humor." *Humor in America: A Research Guide to Genres and Topics.* Ed. Lawrence Mintz. Westport, CT: Greenwood, 1988.

Dudden, Arthur Power, ed. *American Humor.* New York: Oxford University Press, 1987.

Eco, Umberto. "Frames of Comic 'Freedom.'" *Carnival!* Ed. Thomas A. Sebeok. Berlin: Mouton, 1984. 1–9.

Eimerl, Sarel. "Can Women Be Funny? Humor Has Nothing to Do with Sex . . . Or Does It?" *Mademoiselle* Nov. 1962: 151 +.

Ferretti, Fred. " 'Women in Humor' Confer: Is It a Man's World?" *The New York Times* 1 May 1983: "Style" 70.

Fox, Greer Litton. " 'Nice Girl': Social Control of Women through a Value Construct." *Signs* 2.4 (Summer 1977): 805–17.

Freud, Sigmund. "Humor." *The Complete Psychological Works of Sigmund Freud.* Trans. James Strachey. 24 vols. London: Hogarth Press, 1961. Vol. 21. 159–66.

Friedan, Betty. *The Feminine Mystique.* New York: Norton, 1963.

Fury, Kathleen. "Okay, Ladies, What's the Joke?" *Redbook* June 1980; 163–66.

Goldstein, Jeffrey H., and Paul E. McGhee, eds. *The Psychology of Humor.* New York: Academic Press, 1972.

Green, Rayna. "Magnolias Grow in Dirt: The Bawdy Lore of Southern Women." *Southern Exposure* 4 (1977): 29–33.

Grotjahn, Martin. *Beyond Laughter.* New York: McGraw-Hill, 1957.

Habegger, Alfred. *Gender, Fantasy, and Realism in American Literature.* New York: Columbia University Press, 1982.

Hauck, Richard B. *A Cheerful Nihilism: Confidence and "The Absurd" in American Humorous Fiction.* Bloomington: Indiana University Press, 1971.

Haweis, H. R. *American Humorists.* New York: Funk & Wagnalls, 1882.

Heilbrun, Carolyn. "Woman as Outsider." *Reinventing Womanhood.* New York: Norton, 1979. 37–70.

Hertzler, Joyce O. *Laughter: A Socio-Scientific Analysis.* New York: Exposition Press, 1970.

Herzberg, Max J., and Leon Mones. *Humor in America.* New York: D. Appleton-Century, 1945.

Holliday, Carl. *The Wit and Humor of Colonial Days, 1607–1800.* 1912. Williamstown, MA: Corner House, 1975.

Hornstein, Jacqueline. "Comic Vision in the Literature of New England Women Before 1800." *Regionalism and the Female Imagination* 3.2/3 (Winter 1977–78): 11–19.

Hugh-Jones, Siriol. "We Witless Women." *Twentieth Century* July 1961: 16–25.

Hughes, Langston. *The Book of Negro Humor.* New York: Dodd, Mead, 1966.

Jong, Erica. "You Have to be Liberated to Laugh." *Playboy* 27.4 (April 1980): 154 +

Kaufman, Gloria, and Mary Kay Blakely. *Pulling Our Own Strings: Feminist Humor and Satire.* Bloomington: Indiana University Press, 1980.

Kenny, W. Howland. *Laughter in the Wilderness: Early American Humor to 1783.* Kent, OH: Kent State University Press, 1976.

Klein, Julia. "The New Stand-Up Comics." *Ms.* Oct. 1984: 116–26.

La Fave, Lawrence, and Roger Mannell. "Does Ethnic Humor Serve Prejudice?" *Journal of Communication* 26 (Summer 1976): 116–23.

Lakoff, Robin. *Language and Woman's Place.* New York: Harper & Row, 1975.

Levine, Joan B. "The Feminine Routine." *Journal of Communication* 26 (1976): 173–75

Levine, Lawrence W. "Black Laughter." *Black Culture and Black Consciousness: Afro-American Folk Thought from Slavery to Freedom.* New York: Oxford University Press, 1977. 298–366.

Little, Judy. *Comedy and The Woman Writer: Woolf, Spark, and Feminism.* Lincoln: University of Nebraska Press, 1983.

———. "Satirizing the Norm: Comedy in Women's Fiction." *Regionalism and the Female Imagination.* 3.2 (Fall 1977): 39–49.

Losco, Jean, and Seymour Epstein. "Humor Preference as a Subtle Measure of Attitudes Toward the Same and the Opposite Sex." *Journal of Personality* 43 (June 1975): 329–30.

Lowe, John. "Hurston, Humor, and the Harlem Renaissance." *The Harlem Renaissance Re-examined.* Ed. Victor Kramer. New York: AMS Press, 1987. 283–313.

McCullough, Joseph B. "Shades of Red and Black: A Consideration of Modern Humor by Women." *Amerikastudien* 30.2 (1985): 191–201.

McGhee, Paul E. "The Role of Laughter and Humor in Growing Up Female." *Becoming Female: Perspectives on Development.* Ed. Claire B. Kopp. New York: Plenum Press, 1979 183–206.

———. "Sex Differences in Children's Humor." *Journal of Communication* 26 (1976): 176–89.

Masson, Thomas L. *Our American Humorists.* New York: Moffatt, Yard, 1922.

Maurice, Arthur B. "Feminine Humorists." *Good Housekeeping* Jan. 1910: 34–39.

Mindess, Harvey. *Laughter and Liberation.* Los Angeles: Nash 1971.

Mintz, Lawrence E. "Standup Comedy as Social and Cultural Mediation." *American Quarterly* 37.1 (1985): 71–80.

Mitchell, Carol. "Hostility and Aggression Toward Males in Female Joke Telling." *Frontiers* 3.3 (Fall 1978): 19–23.

———. "The Sexual Perspective in the Appreciation and Interpretation of Jokes." *Western Folklore* 36 (1977): 303–29.

———. "Some Differences in Male and Female Joke Telling." *Women's Folklore, Women's Culture.* Ed. Rosen A. Jordan and Susan J. Kalcik. Philadelphia: University of Pennsylvania Press, 1985. 163–86.

Morris, Linda Ann Finton. "Women Vernacular Humorists in Nineteenth-Century America: Ann Stephens, Frances Whitcher, and Marietta Holley." Diss. University of California-Berkeley, 1978.

Newell, Margaretta. "Are Women Humorous?" *Outlook and Independent* 14 Oct. 1931: 206–207+.

Ogden, Annegret S. *The Great American Housewife: From Helpmate to Wage Earner, 1776–1986.* Westport, CT: Greenwood, 1986.

Omwake, Louise. "A Study of the Sense of Humor: Its Relation to Sex, Age, and Personal Characteristics." *Journal of Applied Psychology* 21 (1937): 688–704.

Pavlik, Katherine. "Contemporary Feminist Literature: Satire or Polemic." *American Humor: An Interdisciplinary Newsletter* 7.1 (Spring 1980): 10–16.

Rainer, Peter. "Five Women Comedy Writers Talk About Being Funny for Money." *Mademoiselle* Nov. 1975: 86.

Rather, Lois. "Were Women Funny? Some 19th Century Humorists." *American Book Collector* 21.5 (1971): 5–10.

Rebolledo, Tey Diana. "Walking the Thin Line: Humor in Chicana Literature." *Beyond Stereotypes: The Critical Analysis of Chicana Literature.* Ed. Maria Herrera-Sobek. Binghamton, NY: Bilingual Press, 1985. 91–107.

Repplier, Agnes. *In Pursuit of Laughter.* Boston: Houghton Mifflin, 1936.

Rinder, Irwin D. "A Note on Humor as an Index of Minority Group Morale." *Phylon: The Atlanta University Review of Race and Culture* 26.2 (Summer 1965): 117–21.

Rollins, Alice Wellington. "The Humor of Women." *The Critic and Good Literature* 1.26 (new series) (28 June 1884): 301–02.

———. "Woman's Sense of Humor." *The Critic and Good Literature* 1.13 (new series) (29 March 1884): 145–46.

Rourke, Constance. *American Humor: A Study of the National Character.* New York: Harcourt, Brace, 1931.

Rubin, Louis D., ed. *The Comic Imagination in American Literature.* New Brunswick, NJ: Rutgers University Press, 1973.

Russ, Joanna. *How to Suppress Women's Writing.* Austin: University of Texas Press, 1983.

Sanborn, Kate. *The Wit of Women.* New York: Funk & Wagnalls, 1885.

Schmitz, Neil. *Of Huck and Alice: Humorous Writing in American Literature.* Minneapolis: University of Minnesota Press, 1983.

Sellers, Pat. "Funny Ladies: Stand-up's Newest Standouts." *Cosmopolitan* Sept. 1987: 290–93 +.

Sheppard, Alice. "From Kate Sanborn to Feminist Psychology: The Social Context of Women's Humor, 1885–1985." *Psychology of Women Quarterly* 10 (1986): 155–70.

———. "Funny Women: Social Change and Audience Response to Female Comedians." *Empirical Studies of the Arts* 3.2 (1985): 179–95.

———. "There Were Ladies Present: American Women Cartoonists and Comic Artists in the Early Twentieth Century." *Journal of American Culture* 7 (Fall 1984): 38–48.

Sheppard, R. Z. "She Wits and Funny Persons." *Time* 29 May 1978: 92–96.

Slater, E., and F. H. Freshfield. "The Sense of Humor in Men." *Cornhill* 6 (third series) (1899): 347–52.

Spacks, Patricia Meyer. *The Female Imagination.* New York: Knopf, 1972.

Stillman, Deanne, and Anne Beatts, eds. *Titters: The First Collection of Humor by Women.* New York: Collier, 1976.

Stoddard, Karen M. " 'Women Have No Sense of Humor' and Other Myths: A Consideration of Female Stand-up Comics, 1960–1976." *American Humor: An Interdisciplinary Newsletter* 4.2 (1977): 11–14.

Strasser, Susan. *Never Done: A History of American Housework.* New York: Pantheon, 1982.

Toth, Emily. "Dorothy Parker, Erica Jong, and New Feminist Humor." *Regionalism and the Female Imagination* 2.3 (Winter 1977–78): 70–85.

————. "Female Wits." *Massachusetts Review* 22.4 (Winter 1981): 783–93.

————. "A Laughter of Their Own: Women's Humor in the United States." *Critical Essays on American Humor*. Ed. William Bedford Clark and W. Craig Turner. Boston: G. K. Hall, 1984. 199–215.

Trotter, Elizabeth Stanley. "Humor With a Gender." *The Atlantic Monthly* Dec. 1922: 784–87.

Walker, Nancy. "Do Feminists Ever Laugh? Women's Humor and Women's Rights." *International Journal of Women's Studies* 4.1 (Jan./Feb. 1981): 1–9.

————. "Emily Dickinson and the Self: Humor as Identity." *Tulsa Studies in Women's Literature* 2.1 (Spring 1983): 57–68.

————. " 'Fragile and Dumb': The 'Little Woman' in Women's Humor, 1900–1940." *Thalia: Studies in Literary Humor* 5.2 (Fall/Winter 1982–83): 24–29.

————. "Humor and Gender Roles: The Funny Feminism of the Post-World War Two Suburbs." *American Humor*. Ed. Arthur P. Dudden. New York: Oxford University Press, 1987. 118–37.

————. "Reformers and Young Maidens: Women and Virtue in *Adventures of Huckleberry Finn*." *One Hundred Years of Huckleberry Finn: The Boy, His Book, and American Culture*. Ed. Robert Sattelmeyer and J. Donald Crowley. Columbia: University of Missouri Press, 1985. 171–85.

————. "Susan and Tish: Women's Humor at the Turn of the Century." *Turn-of-the-Century Women* 2.2 (Winter 1985): 50–54.

————. *"A Very Serious Thing": Women's Humor and American Culture*. Minneapolis: University of Minnesota Press, 1988.

————. "Wit, Sentimentality, and the Image of Women in the Nineteenth Century." *American Studies* 22.2 (Fall 1981): 5–22.

Weinstein, Sharon. "Don't Women Have a Sense of Comedy They Can Call Their Own?" *American Humor: An Interdisciplinary Newsletter* 1.2 (Fall 1974): 9–12.

Weisstein, Naomi. "Why We Aren't Laughing . . . Anymore." *Ms.* Nov. 1973: 49–51 +.

Welter, Barbara. "Anti-Intellectualism and the American Woman: 1800–1860." *Mid-America* 48 (Oct. 1966): 258–70.

Winick, Charles. "The Social Contexts of Humor." *Journal of Communication* 26 (Summer 1976): 124–28.

Winterstein, A. "Contributions to the Problem of Humor." *The Psychoanalytic Quarterly* 3 (1934): 303–15.

Yates, Norris. *The American Humorist: Conscience of the Twentieth Century*. Ames: Iowa State University Press, 1964.

Zippin, David. "Sex Differences and the Sense of Humor." *Psychoanalytic Review* 53 (1966): 45–55.